HUMAN GEOGRAPHY READER

Edited by Katherine Nashleanas
University of Nebraska–Lincoln

cognella®
academic publishing

Bassim Hamadeh, CEO and Publisher

Michael Simpson, Vice President of Acquisitions

Jamie Giganti, Managing Editor

Jess Busch, Senior Graphic Designer

Becky Smith, Executive Editor

Monika Dziamka, Project Editor

Stephanie Sandler, Licensing Associate

Sean Adams, Interior Designer

First published in the United States of America in 2014 by Cognella, Inc.

Printed in the United States of America

ISBN: 978-1-62131-888-0 (pbk) / 978-1-62661-331-7 (br)

www.cognella.com   800-200-3908

CONTENTS

This book is dedicated to all of my Human Geography students.

NOTE TO STUDENTS

Each of the following articles was selected with you in mind. The importance of these readings is to help you see as a geographer sees, to practice thinking and observing spatially, and to learn to ask the kinds of questions a geographer would ask. The first readings are designed to ground you in the place of geography as a discipline and explore with you four of the fundamental perspectives of geographers. You will find that *region* is a very important concept in geography, and of the three main types, the development of vernacular regions can sometimes be the most difficult to grasp; therefore I have included an article that concentrates on vernacular regions in North America. Geographers use the terms space and place in very specific ways, so I thought a discussion that differentiates the two would be helpful.

Other readings invite you to consider the world with its complexities intact. The articles can be read in the order presented, which follows most basic human geography texts, but you will find that several of the articles can fit under multiple topics and processes. While reading about the development of tourism in Liverpool, England, for example, you will also be reading about the power of the imagination that imbues places with meaning and identity. You will also explore the importance of location in the brand names of coffee grown in Indonesia and sold exclusively in Tokyo; learn how cell phones are changing the connections between rural, urban, and expatriate communities of Senegal, Africa; or how it is that world cities are now growing networks between them that could rival the economic power of a country. You will read about debates in three separate countries over the place of Islam in the modern world and of the place of women in the Islamic world. I would love to take you on a field trip to England, Indonesia, Nigeria, Senegal or Japan, but since the semester is so short, I'm hoping some of these readings will provide you with a taste of other lands.

Many human geography textbooks spend a good deal of time in their introductory chapters discussing important concepts in geography such as space and place, spatial perspectives, the importance of location, of interaction, mobility, and globalization. These chapters are all very good, but oftentimes attention is not drawn to these concepts in the remaining textbook chapters themselves per se. There is often so much to cover in a human geography course that there isn't time to go back and review the basics, demonstrating how they fit into the current topics under study. That's one of the purposes of these readings: to draw attention to the fundamentals that are critical to a geographic way of seeing the world while also covering some interesting and (hopefully) entertaining subjects that complement the reading you are doing in your textbook.

What are the objectives for this book of readings?
- Provide you with more exposure to and experience with topics in geography that take you out of the confines of your textbook.
- Re-emphasize fundamental concepts in geography and their application to real world events and processes.
- Elevate some of the discussion in class to consider the *metageography* of global city networks and explore the very cutting edge of community networking enabled by the use of cell phones.
- Provide some insights as to how geographers view the world with its complexities intact.
- Provide the means by which you can think more critically about the world around you and thereby become a more well-informed, global citizen.

I have created "snapshots" of each article (except for the first two), that summarize and clarify the main concepts and draw your attention to some of the more important points for us to consider. In some cases I have added maps, diagrams, or pictures to help make the readings more understandable and the narrative more engaging. Ultimately, I hope you will enjoy these readings, that they will enrich your study of human geography, and that you will come away with more of a spatial orientation in your own perspectives of the world.

I would like to thank my team at Cognella for their tireless and proficient work in helping me bring this book together: Monika Dziamka, Chelsey Rogers, Becky Smith, Sarah Wheeler, Jennifer Bowen, Kate Dohe, Jess Busch, and Ivey Preston. Their efforts show quality on every page; any faults or errors in the text are purely my own.

Katherine Nashleanas, Ph.D.
Faculty of Geography and GIScience
University of Nebraska, Lincoln

1. REDISCOVERING THE IMPORTANCE OF GEOGRAPHY

By Alexander B. Murphy

As Americans struggle to understand their place in a world characterized by instant global communications, shifting geopolitical relationships, and growing evidence of environmental change, it is not surprising that the venerable discipline of geography is experiencing a renaissance in the United States. More elementary and secondary schools now require courses in geography, and the College Board is adding the subject to its Advanced Placement program. In higher education, students are enrolling in geography courses in unprecedented numbers. Between 1985–86 and 1994–95, the number of bachelor's degrees awarded in geography increased from 3,056 to 4,295. Not coincidentally, more businesses are looking for employees with expertise in geographical analysis, to help them analyze possible new markets or environmental issues.

In light of these developments, institutions of higher education cannot afford simply to ignore geography, as some of them have, or to assume that existing programs are adequate. College administrators should recognize the academic and practical advantages of enhancing their offerings in geography, particularly if they are going to meet the demand for more and better geography instruction in primary and secondary schools. We cannot afford to know so little about the other countries and peoples with which we now interact with such frequency, or about the dramatic environmental changes unfolding around us.

From the 1960s through the 1980s, most academics in the United States considered geography a marginal discipline, although it remained a core subject in most other countries. The familiar academic divide in the United States between the physical sciences, on one hand, and the social sciences and humanities, on the other, left little room for a discipline concerned with how things are organized and relate to one another on the surface of the earth—a concern that necessarily bridges the physical and cultural spheres. Moreover, beginning in the 1960s, the U.S. social-science agenda came to be dominated by pursuit of more-scientific explanations for human phenomena, based on assumptions about global similarities in human institutions, motivations, and actions. Accordingly, regional differences often were seen as idiosyncrasies of declining significance.

Although academic administrators and scholars in other disciplines might have marginalized geography, they could not kill it, for any attempt to make sense of the world must be based on some understanding of the changing human and physical patterns that shape its evolution—be they shifting vegetation zones or expanding economic contacts across international boundaries. Hence, some U.S. colleges and universities continued to teach geography, and the discipline was often in the background of many policy issues—for example, the need to assess the risks associated with foreign investment in various parts of the world.

By the late 1980s, Americans' general ignorance of geography had become too widespread to ignore. Newspapers regularly published reports of surveys demonstrating that many Americans could not identify major countries or oceans on a map. The real problem, of course, was not the inability to answer simple questions that might be asked on *Jeopardy!*; instead, it was what that inability demonstrated about our collective understanding of the globe.

Geography's renaissance in the United States is due to the growing recognition that physical and human processes such as soil erosion and ethnic unrest are inextricably tied to their geographical context. To understand modern Iraq, it is not enough to know who is in power and how the political system functions. We also need to know something about the country's ethnic groups and their settlement patterns, the different physical environments and resources within the country, and its ties to surrounding countries and trading partners.

Those matters are sometimes addressed by practitioners of other disciplines, of course, but they are rarely central to the analysis. Instead, generalizations are often made at the level of the state, and little attention is given to spatial patterns and practices that play out on local levels or across international boundaries. Such preoccupations help to explain why many scholars were caught off guard by the explosion of ethnic unrest in Eastern Europe following the fall of the Iron Curtain.

Similarly, comprehending the dynamics of El Niño requires more than knowledge of the behavior of ocean and air currents; it is also important to understand how those currents are situated with respect to land masses and how they relate to other climatic patterns, some of which have been altered by the burning of fossil fuels and other human activities. And any attempt to understand the nature and extent of humans' impact on the environment requires consideration of the relationship between human and physical contributions to environmental change. The factories and cars in a city produce smog, but surrounding mountains may trap it, increasing air pollution significantly.

Today, academics in fields including history, economics, and conservation biology are turning to geographers for help with some of their concerns. Paul Krugman, a noted economist at the Massachusetts Institute of Technology, for example, has turned conventional wisdom on its head by pointing out the role of historically rooted regional inequities in how international trade is structured.

Geographers work on issues ranging from climate change to ethnic conflict to urban sprawl. What unites their work is its focus on the shifting organization and character of the earth's surface. Geographers examine changing patterns of vegetation to study global warming; they analyze where ethnic groups live in Bosnia to help understand the pros and cons of competing administrative solutions to the civil war there; they map AIDS cases in Africa to learn how to reduce the spread of the disease.

Geography is reclaiming attention because it addresses such questions in their relevant spatial and environmental contexts. A growing number of scholars in other disciplines are realizing that it is a mistake to treat all places as if they were essentially the same (think of the assumptions in most economic models), or to undertake research on the environment that does not include consideration of the relationships between human and physical processes in particular regions.

Still, the challenges to the discipline are great. Only a small number of primary- and secondary-school teachers have enough training in geography to offer students an exciting introduction to the subject. At the college level, many geography departments are small; they are absent altogether at some high-profile universities.

Perhaps the greatest challenge is to overcome the public's view of geography as a simple exercise in place-name recognition. Much of geography's power lies in the insights it sheds on the nature and meaning of the evolving spatial arrangements and landscapes that make up our world. The importance of those insights should not be underestimated at a time of changing political boundaries, accelerated human alteration of the environment, and rapidly shifting patterns of human interaction.

Alexander B. Murphy is a professor and head of the geography department at the University of Oregon, and a vice-president of the American Geographical Society.

STUDY QUESTIONS

1. What evidence does Alexander B. Murphy provide that the discipline of geography is growing?
2. In the 1960s, what was the social science agenda for many colleges and universities in the U.S., and why was geography overlooked?
3. As institutions of higher learning were focusing on global similarities, what got left out?
4. What value does geography bring to foreign investment?
5. What questions does geography answer that go beyond the game show *Jeopardy!*?
6. Why is geography reclaiming attention today?
7. Where does most of geography's power lie?
8. Why is geography more important today than ever before?

2. THE FOUR TRADITIONS OF GEOGRAPHY

By William D. Pattison

To Readers of the *Journal of Geography*:

I am honored to be introducing, for a return to the pages of the *Journal* after more than 25 years, "The Four Traditions of Geography," an article, which circulated widely, in this country and others, long after its initial appearance—in reprint, in xerographic copy, and in translation. A second round of life at a level of general interest even approaching that of the first may be too much to expect, but I want you to know in any event that I presented the paper in the beginning as my gift to the geographic community, not as a personal property, and that I re-offer it now in the same spirit.

In my judgment, the article continues to deserve serious attention—perhaps especially so, let me add, among persons aware of the specific problem it was intended to resolve. The background for the paper was my experience as first director of the High School Geography Project (1961–63)—not all of that experience but only the part that found me listening, during numerous conference sessions and associated interviews, to academic geographers as they responded to the project's invitation to locate "basic ideas" representative of them all. I came away with the conclusion that I had been witnessing not a search for consensus but rather a blind struggle for supremacy among honest persons of contrary intellectual commitment. In their dialogue, two or more different terms had been used, often unknowingly, with a single reference, and no less disturbingly, a single term had been used, again often unknowingly, with two or more different references. The article was my attempt to stabilize the discourse. I was proposing a basic nomenclature (with explicitly associated ideas) that would, I trusted, permit the development of mutual comprehension and confront all parties concerned with the pluralism inherent in geographic thought.

This intention alone could not have justified my turning to the NCGE (National Council of Geographic Education) as a forum, of course. The fact is that from the onset of my discomfiting realization I had looked forward to larger consequences of a kind consistent with NCGE goals. As finally formulated, my wish was that the article would serve "to greatly expedite the task of maintaining an alliance between professional geography and pedagogical geography and at the same time to promote communication with laymen" (see my fourth paragraph). I must tell you that I have doubts, in 1990, about the acceptability of my word choice, in saying "professional," "pedagogical," and "layman" in this context, but the message otherwise is as expressive of my hope now as it was then.

I can report to you that twice since its appearance in the *Journal*, my interpretation has received more or less official acceptance—both times, as it happens, at the expense of the earth science tradition. The first occasion was Edward Taaffe's delivery of his presidential address at the 1973 meeting of the Association of American Geographers (see *Annals AAG*, March 1974, pp. 1–16). Taaffe's working-through of aspects of and interrelations among the spatial, area studies, and man-land traditions is by far the most thoughtful and thorough of any of which I am aware. Rather than fault him for omission of the fourth tradition, I compliment him on the grace with which he set it aside in conformity to a meta-epistemology of the American university which decrees the integrity of the social sciences as a consortium in their own right. He was sacrificing such wholistic claims as geography might be able to muster for a freedom to argue the case for geography as a social science.

The second occasion was the publication in 1984 of *Guidelines for Geographic Education: Elementary and Secondary Schools*, authored by a committee jointly representing the AAG and the NCGE. Thanks to a recently published letter (see *Journal of Geography*, March–April 1990, pp. 85–86), we know that, of five themes commended to teachers in this source,

> The committee lifted the human environmental interaction theme directly from Pattison. The themes of place and location are based on Pattison's spatial or geometric geography, and the theme of region comes from Pattison's area studies or regional geography.

Having thus drawn on my spatial area studies and man-land traditions for four of the five themes, the committee could have found the remaining theme, movement, there too—in the spatial tradition (see my sixth paragraph). However that may be, they did not avail themselves of the earth science tradition, their reasons being readily surmised. Peculiar to the elementary and secondary schools is a curriculum category framed as much by theory of citizenship as by theory of knowledge: the social studies. With admiration, I see already in the committee members' adoption of the theme idea a strategy for assimilation of their program to the established repertoire of social studies practice. I see in their exclusion of the earth science tradition an intelligent respect for social studies' purpose.

Here's to the future of education in geography: may it prosper as never before.

W. D. P., 1990

I n 1905, one year after professional geography in this country achieved full social identity through the founding of the Association of American Geographers, William Morris Davis responded to a familiar suspicion that geography is simply an undisciplined "omnium-gatherum" by describing an approach that as he saw it imparts a "geographical quality" to some knowledge and accounts for the absence of the quality elsewhere.[1] Davis spoke as president of the AAG. He set an example that was followed by more than one president of that organization. An enduring official concern led the AAG to publish, in 1939 and in 1959, monographs exclusively devoted to a critical review of definitions and their implications.[2]

Every one of the well-known definitions of geography advanced since the founding of the AAG has had its measure of success. Tending to displace one another by turns, each definition has said something true of geography.[3] But from the vantage point of 1964, one can see that each one has also failed. All of them adopted in one way or another a monistic view, a singleness of preference, certain to omit if not to alienate numerous professionals who were in good conscience continuing to participate creatively in the broad geographic enterprise.

The thesis of the present paper is that the work of American geographers, although not conforming to the restrictions implied by any one of these definitions, has exhibited a broad consistency, and that this essential unity has been attributable to a small number of distinct but affiliated traditions, operant as binders in the minds of members of the profession. These traditions are all of great age and have passed into American geography as parts of a general legacy of Western thought. They are shared today by geographers of other nations.

There are four traditions whose identification provides an alternative to the competing monistic definitions that have been the geographer's lot. The resulting pluralistic basis for judgment promises, by full accommodation of what geographers do and by plain-spoken representation thereof, to greatly expedite the task of maintaining an alliance between professional geography and pedagogical geography and at the same time to promote communication with laymen. The following discussion treats the traditions in this order: (1) a spatial tradition, (2) an area studies tradition, (3) a man-land tradition and (4) an earth science tradition.

SPATIAL TRADITION

Entrenched in Western thought is a belief in the importance of spatial analysis, of the act of separating from the happenings of experience such aspects as distance, form, direction and position. It was not until the 17th century that philosophers concentrated attention on these aspects by asking whether or not they were properties of things-in-themselves. Later, when the 18th century writings of Immanuel Kant had become generally circulated, the notion of space as a category including all of these aspects came into widespread use. However, it is evident that particular spatial questions were the subject of highly organized answering attempts long before the time of any of these cogitations. To confirm this point, one need only be reminded of the compilation of elaborate records concerning the location of things in ancient Greece. These were records of sailing distances, of coastlines and of landmarks that grew until they formed the raw material for the great *Geographia* of Claudius Ptolemy in the 2nd century A.D.

A review of American professional geography from the time of its formal organization shows that the spatial tradition of thought had made a deep penetration from the very beginning. For Davis, for Henry

Gannett and for most if not all of the 44 other men of the original AAG, the determination and display of spatial aspects of reality through mapping were of undoubted importance, whether contemporary definitions of geography happened to acknowledge this fact or not. One can go further and, by probing beneath the art of mapping, recognize in the behavior of geographers of that time an active interest in the true essentials of the spatial tradition—*geometry* and *movement*. One can trace a basic favoring of movement as a subject of study from the turn-of-the-century work of Emory R. Johnson, writing as professor of transportation at the University of Pennsylvania, through the highly influential theoretical and substantive work of Edward L. Ullman during the past 20 years and thence to an article by a younger geographer on railroad freight traffic in the U.S. and Canada in the *Annals* of the AAG for September 1963.[4]

One can trace a deep attachment to geometry, or positioning-and-layout, from articles on boundaries and population densities in early 20th century volumes of the *Bulletin of the American Geographical Society,* through a controversial pronouncement by Joseph Schaefer in 1953 that granted geographical legitimacy only to studies of spatial patterns[5] and so onward to a recent *Annals* report on electronic scanning of cropland patterns in Pennsylvania.[6]

One might inquire, is discussion of the spatial tradition, after the manner of the remarks just made, likely to bring people within geography closer to an understanding of one another and people outside geography closer to an understanding of geographers? There seem to be at least two reasons for being hopeful. First, an appreciation of this tradition allows one to see a bond of fellowship uniting the elementary school teacher, who attempts the most rudimentary instruction in directions and mapping, with the contemporary research geographer, who dedicates himself to an exploration of central-place theory. One cannot only open the eyes of many teachers to the potentialities of their own instruction, through proper exposition of the spatial tradition, but one can also "hang a bell" on research quantifiers in geography, who are often thought to have wandered so far in their intellectual adventures as to have become lost from the rest. Looking outside geography, one may anticipate benefits from the readiness of countless persons to associate the name "geography" with maps. Latent within this readiness is a willingness to recognize as geography, too, what maps are about—and that is the geometry of and the movement of what is mapped.

AREA STUDIES TRADITION

The area studies tradition, like the spatial tradition, is quite strikingly represented in classical antiquity by a practitioner to whose surviving work we can point. He is Strabo, celebrated for his *Geography* which is a massive production addressed to the statesmen of Augustan Rome and intended to sum up and regularize knowledge not of the location of places and associated cartographic facts, as in the somewhat later case of Ptolemy, but of the nature of places, their character and their differentiation. Strabo exhibits interesting attributes of the area-studies tradition that can hardly be overemphasized. They are a pronounced tendency toward subscription primarily to literary standards, an almost omnivorous appetite for information and a self-conscious companionship with history.

It is an extreme good fortune to have in the ranks of modern American geography the scholar Richard Hartshorne, who has pondered the meaning of the area-studies tradition with a legal acuteness that few persons would challenge. In his *Nature of Geography*, his 1939 monograph already cited,[7] he scrutinizes exhaustively the implications of the "interesting attributes" identified in connection with Strabo, even though his concern is with quite other and much later authors, largely German. The major literary problem of unities or wholes he considers from every angle. The Gargantuan appetite for miscellaneous information he accepts and rationalizes. The companionship between area studies and history he clarifies by appraising the so-called idiographic content of both and by affirming the tie of both to what he and Sauer have called "naively given reality."

The area-studies tradition (otherwise known as the chorographic tradition) tended to be excluded from early American professional geography. Today it is beset by certain champions of the spatial tradition who would have one believe that somehow the area-studies way of organizing knowledge is only a subdepartment of spatialism. Still, area-studies as a method of presentation lives and prospers in its own right. One can turn today for reassurance on this score to practically any issue of the *Geographical Review,* just as earlier readers could turn at the opening of the century to that magazine's forerunner.

What is gained by singling out this tradition? It helps toward restoring the faith of many teachers who, being accustomed to administering learning in the area-studies style, have begun to wonder if by doing so they really were keeping in touch with professional geography. (Their doubts are owed all too much to the obscuring effect of technical words attributable to the very professionals who have been intent, ironically, upon protecting that tradition.) Among persons outside the classroom the geographer stands to gain greatly in intelligibility. The title "area-studies" itself carries an understood message in the United States today wherever there is contact with the usages of the academic community. The purpose of characterizing a place, be it neighborhood or nation-state, is readily grasped. Furthermore, recognition of the right of a geographer to be unspecialized may be expected to be forthcoming from people generally, if application for such recognition is made on the merits of this tradition, explicitly.

MAN-LAND TRADITION

That geographers are much given to exploring man-land questions is especially evident to anyone who examines geographic output, not only in this country but also abroad. O. H. K. Spate, taking an international view, has felt justified by his observations in nominating as the most significant ancient precursor of today's geography neither Ptolemy nor Strabo nor writers typified in their outlook by the geographies of either of these two men, but rather Hippocrates, Greek physician of the 5th century B.C. who left to posterity an extended essay, *On Airs, Waters and Places.*[8] In this work, made up of reflections on human health and conditions of external nature, the questions asked are such as to confine thought almost altogether to presumed influence passing from the latter to the former, questions largely about the effects of winds, drinking water and seasonal changes upon man. Understandable though this uni-directional concern may have been for Hippocrates as medical commentator, and defensible as may be the attraction that this same approach held for students of the condition of man for many, many centuries thereafter, one can only regret that this narrowed version of the man-land tradition, combining all too easily with social Darwinism of the late 19th century, practically overpowered American professional geography in the first generation of its history.[9] The premises of this version governed scores of studies by American geographers in interpreting the rise and fall of nations, the strategy of battles and the construction of public improvements. Eventually this special bias, known as environmentalism, came to be confused with the whole of the man-land tradition in the minds of many people. One can see now, looking back to the years after the ascendancy of environmentalism, that although the spatial tradition was asserting itself with varying degrees of forwardness, and that although the area-studies tradition was also making itself felt, perhaps the most interesting chapters in the story of American professional geography were being written by academicians who were reacting against environmentalism while deliberately remaining within the broad man-land tradition. The rise of culture historians during the last 30 years has meant the dropping of a curtain of culture between land and man, through which it is asserted all influence must pass. Furthermore work of both culture historians and other geographers has exhibited a reversal of the direction of the effects in Hippocrates, man appearing as an independent agent, and the land as a sufferer from action. This trend as presented in published research has reached a high point in the collection of papers titled *Man's Role in Changing the Face of the Earth*. Finally, books and articles can be called to mind that have addressed themselves to the most difficult task of all, a balanced tracing out of interaction between man and environment. Some chapters in the book mentioned above undertake just this. In fact the separateness of this approach is discerned only with difficulty in many places; however, its significance as a general research design that rises above environmentalism, while refusing to abandon the man-land tradition, cannot be mistaken.

The NCGE seems to have associated itself with the man-land tradition, from the time of founding to the present day, more than with any other tradition, although all four of the traditions are amply represented in its official magazine, *The Journal of Geography* and in the proceedings of its annual meetings. This apparent preference on the part of the NCGE members *for defining geography in terms of the man-land tradition* is strong evidence of the appeal that man-land ideas, separately stated, have for persons whose main job is teaching. It should be noted, too, that this inclination reflects a proven acceptance by the general public of learning that centers on resource use and conservation.

EARTH SCIENCE TRADITION

The earth science tradition, embracing study of the earth, the waters of the earth, the atmosphere surrounding the earth and the association between earth and sun, confronts one with a paradox. On the one hand one is assured by professional geographers that their participation in this tradition has declined precipitously in the course of the past few decades, while on the other one knows that college departments of geography across the nation rely substantially, for justification of their role in general education, upon curricular content springing directly from this tradition. From all the reasons that combine to account for this state of affairs, one may, by selecting only two, go far toward achieving an understanding of this tradition. First, there is the fact that American college geography, growing out of departments of geology in many crucial instances, was at one time greatly overweighted in favor of earth science, thus rendering the field unusually liable to a sense of loss as better balance came into being. (This one-time disproportion found reciprocate support for many years in the narrowed, environmentalistic interpretation of the man-land tradition.) Second, here alone in earth science does one encounter subject matter in the normal sense of the term as one reviews geographic traditions. The spatial tradition abstracts certain aspects of reality; area studies is distinguished by a point of view; the man-land tradition dwells upon relationships; but earth science is identifiable through concrete objects. Historians, sociologists and other academicians tend not only to accept but also to ask for help from this part of geography. They readily appreciate earth science as something physically associated with their subjects of study, yet generally beyond their competence to treat. From this appreciation comes strength for geography-as-earth-science in the curriculum.

Only by granting full stature to the earth science tradition can one make sense out of the oft-repeated addage, "Geography is the mother of sciences." This is the tradition that emerged in ancient Greece, most clearly in the work of Aristotle, as a wide-ranging study of natural processes in and near the surface of the earth. This is the tradition that was rejuvenated by Varenius in the 17th century as "Geographia Generalis." This is the tradition that has been subjected to subdivision as the development of science has approached the present day, yielding mineralogy, paleontology, glaciology, meteorology and other specialized fields of learning.

Readers who are acquainted with American junior high schools may want to make a challenge at this point, being aware that a current revival of earth sciences is being sponsored in those schools by the field of geology. Belatedly, geography has joined in support of this revival. It may be said that in this connection and in others, American professional geography may have faltered in its adherence to the earth science tradition but not given it up.

In describing geography, there would appear to be some advantages attached to isolating this final tradition. Separation improves the geographer's chances of successfully explaining to educators why geography has extreme difficulty in accommodating itself to social studies programs. Again, separate attention allows one to make understanding contact with members of the American public for whom surrounding nature is known as the geographic environment. And finally, specific reference to the geographer's earth science tradition brings into the open the basis of what is, almost without a doubt, morally the most significant concept in the entire geographic heritage, that of the earth as a unity, the single common habitat of man.

An Overview

The four traditions though distinct in logic are joined in action. One can say of geography that it pursues concurrently all four of them. Taking the traditions in varying combinations, the geographer can explain the conventional divisions of the field. Human or cultural geography turns out to consist of the first three traditions applied to human societies; physical geography, it becomes evident, is the fourth tradition prosecuted under constraints from the first and second traditions. Going further, one can uncover the meanings of "systematic geography," "regional geography," "urban geography," "industrial geography," etc.

It is to be hoped that through a widened willingness to conceive of and discuss the field in terms of these traditions, geography will be better able to secure the inner unity and outer intelligibility to which reference was made at the opening of this paper, and that thereby the effectiveness of geography's contribution to American education and to the general American welfare will be appreciably increased.

Notes

1. William Morris Davis, "An Inductive Study of the Content of Geography," *Bulletin of the American Geographical Society*, Vol. 38, No. 1 (1906), 71.

2. Richard Hartshorne, *The Nature of Geography*, Association of American Geographers (1939), and idem., *Perspective on the Nature of Geography*, Association of American Geographers (1959).

3. The essentials of several of these definitions appear in Barry N. Floyd, "Putting Geography in Its Place," *The Journal of Geography*, Vol. 62, No. 3 (March, 1963), 117–120.

4. William H. Wallace, "Freight Traffic Functions of Anglo-American Railroads," *Annals of the Association of American Geographers*, Vol. 53, No. 3 (September, 1963), 312–331.

5. Fred K. Schaefer, "Exceptionalism in Geography: A Methodological Examination," *Annals of the Association of American Geographers*, Vol. 43, No. 3 (September, 1953), 226–249.

6. James P. Latham, "Methodology for an Instrumented Geographic Analysts," *Annals of the Association of American Geographers*, Vol. 53, No. 2 (June, 1963). 194–209.

7. Hartshorne's 1959 monograph, *Perspective on the Nature of Geography*, was also cited earlier. In this later work, he responds to dissents from geographers whose preferred primary commitment lies outside the area studies tradition.

8. O. H. K. Spate, "Quantity and Quality in Geography," *Annals of the Association of American Geographers*, Vol. 50, No. 4 (December, 1960), 379.

9. Evidence of this dominance may be found in Davis's 1905 declaration; "Any statement is of geographical quality if it contains … some relation between an element of inorganic control and one of organic response" (Davis, *loc. cit.).*

10. Geography is represented on both the Steering Committee and Advisory Board of the Earth Science Curriculum Project, potentially the most influential organization acting an behalf of earth science in the schools.

STUDY QUESTIONS

1. What is a monastic view of geography and why doesn't it fit? What has replaced it?
2. How far back in history does the Spatial Tradition in geography go? What is the evidence for this?
3. What is the most common tool of the Spatial Tradition?
4. On what two essentials is the Spatial Tradition based? Provide examples of geographic studies emphasizing each.
5. How far back in history can we trace the Area Studies Tradition?
6. How would you contrast the Spatial Tradition with the Area Studies Tradition?
7. What are the special tools of the Area Studies Tradition?
8. With what other discipline is the Area Studies Tradition aligned?
9. Why is Hippocrates, Greek physician of 5th century B.C., associated with the Man-Land Tradition?
10. Why are social Darwinism and environmental determinism associated with the Man-Land Tradition?
11. *Man's Role in Changing the Face of the Earth* is an indicator of what shift in the Man-Land Tradition?
12. Today the Man-Land Tradition emphasizes what relationship between human beings and the land?
13. With what other disciplines is the Earth Science Tradition affiliated?
14. With whom is the Earth Science Tradition linked in ancient Greece and what was his study?
15. Explain how these four traditions can be pursued concurrently in geography.

Chapter 3 Snapshot
North America's Vernacular Regions

I chose this article for your consideration because one of the most basic concepts in geography is region.

First of all, a region is a conceptual tool geographers use to order space. Fundamentally we can say that those who are within a region (people, activities, phenomena, characteristics) have more in common with each other than those who are outside of the region. Of the three types of region, formal, functional, and vernacular, the vernacular region is often one of the most challenging to conceptualize. A formal region occurs when most people share the same phenomenon, like a specific climate or soil type; a cultural characteristic like ethnicity, language, religion; or even economic activity like wheat-growing or milk production. A functional region exists where people are heterocultural, engage in different occupations, but share a type of membership in common such as subscribing to the same newspaper or using the same pizza parlor. A vernacular region, however, according to our author Wilbur Zelinsky, "is the product of the spatial perception of average people" (20). So what does this mean? Vernacular regions are closely tied to identification with place and with folk culture. This usually means identification with the land over time, by a culture that is rooted in place. Zelinsky compares the work of scholars who study the vernacular regions of Europe, "where folk culture is a potent social and psychological force frequently reflected in the ways boundaries are drawn and areas administered" to those in a "younger, more volatile North America" (20). He asks, "Why bother with phenomena so closely coupled with those relatively old, 'folksy' aspects of North American culture surely scheduled for demolition within a society widely described as increasingly standardized, rootless, and even spaceless?" (20). We will be reading later in the course about popular cultural landscapes that seem to mirror each other no matter where they are located. Gas stations, shopping malls, fast food chains, even some aspects of urban settlements themselves lend a sense of sameness to the landscape and the more globalization seems to spread, the more this sameness seems to spread as well. Are we heading for a placeless society? As much as we see such elements of sameness, there are still forces in the human spirit that struggle to be recognized as unique. Zelinsky observes that "… a grass-roots form of regionalism has been asserting itself throughout much of the world during recent years (a 'regional backlash?'), and may well persist for some decades to come" (20). With this persistence in mind, Zelinsky concludes that the "realization is dawning upon us that popular regions are here to stay, that they are non-trivial in a social-psychological sense, and are allied with other potentially momentous developments" (20).

In the United States, some of the regional differences are connected to history, aspects of the environment, or with certain cultural characteristics of the population. There are "unavoidable regional correlates in the Chicano, Puerto Rican, Cajun, Hawaiian, Cuban, and Native American movements, even if they are muted in the case of the Afro-Americans and various ethnic revivals among 3rd or nth generation immigrant stock of European and Asian derivation" (20). Since about the 1970s, along with the Black Pride movement, we have seen a growth in ethnic pride, a resurgence and interest in ethnic heritage and traditions that also have left their marks on the cultural landscape. Zelinsky observes, "As I have argued elsewhere, new, perhaps qualitatively distinctive regions, large and small, and actually or potentially self-aware, have been sprouting of late within this country, chiefly through the spatial sorting out of special-interest, voluntary migrants in quest of compatible physical and social habitats" (21). He continues,

> We can also find much food for thought in the recent proliferation of regional (and ethnic) periodicals catering to mass markets, the many new regional museums and festivals, and the steady growth of academic, governmental, and popular concern with folklore, a study that is indelibly regional to the core. Linked to all of the foregoing is the burgeoning nostalgia industry … in both the commercial and scholarly realms and a vigorous preservationist movement deeply imbued with a sense of place (21).

He concludes that it is important to identify and understand our own vernacular regions; that as much as we might be seeing a creeping sameness of globalization stealing over the landscape, there is also a strong identification with culture and place and a regional differentiation that makes itself known on the landscape as well.

The question is, how do we get at this regional differentiation if we want to look at the scale of the nation, which would show in the most meaningful way major culturally-based differences as they are attached to place? Are the United States and Canada monolithic in their cultural expressions, or can we see cultural, vernacular regions? In this snapshot, I will be clarifying some of the fundamental ideas Zelinsky is building his research on, and going over his approach to the methodology he is using. It is important to understand where his information is coming from in order to more fully appreciate the value of the maps he has compiled. The maps and the discussion of them are self-explanatory, and you should study each map as Zelinsky describes it.

Zelinsky looks at three past attempts to address this question of methodology in order to select his approach. First is the "prolonged emersion in the area in question" (21). This means going to the location, observing, sending out questionnaires, doing historical research, and doing interviews to gain the most information and deepest insights about a place. This is a superior method for doing such research, but unfortunately, it "cannot be applied to more than one or two states or a few cities during the working lifetime of a single student" (21). A second method would be to use "mail or telephone questionnaires" (21), but these are methodologically flawed for several reasons. The third approach is to use the names of enterprises (business, services, and so on) as they appear in regional telephone directories. Zelinsky chose this method because:

> ... the frequency with which people attach certain names to their enterprises—and the degree to which such names survive—is a relatively sensitive measure of group perceptions of the locus within sociocultural space, and probably along other social and cultural dimensions as well, of the places in question. In other words, the namers, consciously or otherwise, select names with which their clientele can empathize and which should help assure the success of the enterprise in so far as they reflect the inner feelings or aspirations of the local population" (26).

He admits there are several technical difficulties with this approach as well, but with these in mind he still was able to create a series of fourteen maps based on the information he gathered from 276 directories. "The enterprises whose names were tallied comprise all manner of organized, nongovernmental activity, whether for profit or otherwise, and include retail, wholesale, service and manufacturing firms, associations, schools, churches, hospitals, places of entertainment, apartment buildings, cemeteries, parks, and miscellany of other places and activities that happen to be listed in a city directory" (23). With this information in mind, you should be able to appropriately evaluate the maps in Zelinsky's article.

3. NORTH AMERICA'S VERNACULAR REGIONS

By Wilbur Zelinsky

ABSTRACT: The vernacular, or popular, region, "the product of the spatial perception of average people," is a phenomenon that remains too poorly known in North America. It promises to gain importance as the general level of public and scholarly interest in regional, ethnic, and historical questions continues to rise. The larger, subnational North American vernacular regions are studied through an analysis of the frequency of selected regional and locational terms in the names of enterprises (both profit and nonprofit) listed in recent telephone directories for 276 metropolitan areas in the United States and Canada. Despite several technical problems in study design and data procurement, the results are encouraging. A total of fourteen regions can be discerned, some not previously described, while several correspond nicely with culture areas previously mapped from other evidence. Inclusion in the checklist of terms with cultural, but not specifically regional, overtones enables us to compute and map variations in the strength of regional feeling from place to place. This study suggests further dimensions of North America's social and cultural geography that might be derived from a deeper probing of the names applied to our highly varied organized activities.

H OW seriously should the serious geographer take the vernacular, or popular, regions of his country? This breed of areal entities is quite distinct from the more familiar creatures we customarily study. A vernacular region is neither something created by governmental, corporate, or journalistic fiat, nor the scientist's artifact, however sophisticated or otherwise, contrived to serve some specific scholarly or pedagogic purpose.[1] On the contrary, "the vernacular region is the product of the spatial perception of average people," the shared, spontaneous image of territorial reality, local or not so local, hovering in the minds of the untutored.[2]

Until recently, the answer to my initial query, at least in North America, has been: "Not very." While popular regions are granted more than a modicum of respect by scholars in those anciently, persistently settled portions of the Old World where folk culture is a potent social and psychological force frequently reflected in the ways boundaries are drawn and areas administered, we have known and cared about them much less in a younger, more volatile North America. More than likely some students tempted to explore the topic have been deflected by potential allegations of frivolity or cultural slumming. In any event, why bother with phenomena so closely coupled with those relatively old, "folksy" aspects of North American culture surely scheduled for demolition within a society widely described as increasingly standardized, rootless, and even spaceless?[3]

We begin to see reasons for a reversal of this attitude. Quite apart from the sheer thrill of geographic puzzle-solving—and the amusement of the scholarly dilettante—in learning "what is out there," the realization is dawning upon us that popular regions are here to stay, that they are nontrivial in a social-psychological sense, and are allied with other potentially momentous developments.

For reasons we are far from fully grasping, a grass-roots form of regionalism has been asserting itself throughout much of the world during recent years (a "regional backlash?"), and may well persist for some decades to come.[4] Frequently, but not invariably, and with or without political prompting, there are connections with a resurrected or synthetic ethnicity. To take only the most boisterous examples, recall recent events in Canada, Great Britain, France, Yugoslavia, Belgium, or Spain. Within the United States, there are unavoidable regional correlates in the Chicano, Puerto Rican, Cajun, Hawaiian, Cuban, and Native American movements, even if they are muted in the case of the Afro-Americans and various ethnic revivals among 3rd or nth generation immigrant stock of European and Asian derivation. As I have argued elsewhere, new, perhaps qualitatively distinctive regions, large and small, and actually or potentially self-aware,

---

1 This three-fold classification of geographic regions in terms of origin is suggested by Joseph E. Schwartzberg, "Prolegomena to the Study of South Asian Regions and Regionalism," in Robert I. Crane, ed., *Regions and Regionalism in South Asian Studies: an Exploratory Study*, Comparative Studies on Southern Asia, Monograph No. 5 (Durham, N.C.: Duke University Press, 1967), pp. 8991.

2 The entire definition merits repetition: "Perceptual or vernacular regions are those perceived to exist by their inhabitants and other members of the population at large. They exist as part of popular or folk culture. Rather than being the intellectual creation of the professional geographer, the vernacular region is the product of the spatial perception of average people. Rather than being based on carefully chosen, quantifiable criteria, such regions are composites of the mental maps of the population," Terry G. Jordan, "Perceptual Regions in Texas," *Geographical Review*, Vol. 68 (1978), p. 293. The origins of most vernacular regions are obscure or unexplored. It is entirely possible some are the brain children of scholars or other talented individuals that have somehow infiltrated the masses, entering not just the popular culture, but becoming part of folk culture, i.e., materials handed down by oral tradition. We find many instances of this in the realm of folk tales and folk music, e.g., the work of Hans Christian Andersen, Sholom Aleichem, Franz Schubert, Stephen Foster, or W. C. Handy. The same phenomenon seems to have happened with the Corn Belt and the geographically amorphous Bible Belt a generation or two ago, and has just afflicted us with those two deplorable terms the Sun Belt and the Snow Belt.

3 As suggested, for example, in two widely quoted publications, Melvin M. Webber, "Culture, Territoriality, and the Elastic Mile," *Papers*, Regional Science Association, Vol. 13 (1964), pp. 59–69; and Alvin Toffler, *Future Shock* (New York: Random House, 1970), pp. 9194.

4 Perhaps the most useful introduction to recent trends in ethnicity and associated questions concerning social and territorial identity is Harold R. Isaacs, *Idols of the Tribe: Group Identity and Political Change* (New York: Harper & Row, 1975).

have been sprouting of late within this country, chiefly through the spatial sorting out of special-interest, voluntary migrants in quest of compatible physical and social habitats.[5]

We can also find much food for thought in the recent proliferation of regional (and ethnic) periodicals catering to mass markets, the many new regional museums and festivals, and the steady growth of academic, governmental, and popular concern with folklore, a study that is indelibly regional to the core. Linked to all of the foregoing is the burgeoning nostalgia industry (I choose the term with care) in both the commercial and scholarly realms and a vigorous preservationist movement deeply imbued with a sense of place. Furthermore, I suspect that when we have fully decoded whatever it is that has been occurring in North American religion of late, we may find that it too is a component within this interlocking neo-ethnic-regional-nostalgia-preservationist (and environmentalist?) syndrome. Finally, can we ignore the possibility that the recent popularity of perceptual and psychological studies in academic geography may be responding, however obliquely, to these broader currents of change in the popular mind? My contention, then, is that identifying and understanding our vernacular regions is a justifiable, even necessary, pursuit if we wish to apprehend the major social and geographical realities of late Twentieth-Century America, in addition to whatever intrinsic technical appeal we find in such activity. The question remains, however, as to how best to corner our quarry. Of the two largest hurdles to be surmounted—specifying the particular levels of operational interest within the hierarchy of vernacular regions, and devising the means to collect meaningful, reliable information—the former is much the less troublesome.

In this exploratory study, I have chosen to look at the largest subnational vernacular regions. (I believe we can safely assume that the two national territories, the United States and Canada, lead a dual existence as both political and popular entities with reasonably unequivocal boundaries.) Nested within such higher-order regions are at least three lower strata of areas, with the most atomistic being the little urban neighborhood or, possibly, even the block and the rural valley, cove, or other intimate tract, whether named or not. These smaller items, most of which remain to be mapped and studied, are best examined at the local scale rather than from the continental perspective adopted here.

PREVIOUS EFFORTS

The difficulties of data procurement can be illustrated by considering the handful of published approaches to America's popular regions. The ideal modus operandi is prolonged immersion in the areas in question and supplementing personal observation and interviews with whatever documents are pertinent. This is the procedure successfully followed by Gary Dunbar in delimiting the popular regions of Virginia and by Robert Crisler in his studies of the Little Dixie region of central Missouri.[6] Rather analogous is the work of E. Joan Wilson Miller in defining the Ozark Culture Region by means of traditional folk materials, although it is not altogether clear to what degree that area is perceived as such by its inhabitants.[7]

---

5   Wilbur Zelinsky, "Personality and Self-Discovery: the Future Social Geography of the United States," in Ronald Abler, Donald Janelle, Allen Philbrick, and John Sommer, eds., *Human Geography in a Shrinking World* (North Scituate, Mass.: Duxbury, 1975), pp. 108–21.

6   Gary S. Dunbar, "The Popular Regions of Virginia," *University of Virginia Newsletter*, Vol. 38, No. 3 (1961), pp. 10–12; Robert M. Crisler, "An Experiment in Regional Delimitation: the Little Dixie Region of Missouri," unpublished doctoral dissertation, Northwestern University, 1949; and idem, "Missouri's 'Little Dixie,'" *Missouri Historical Review*, Vol. 42 (1948), pp. 130–39.

7   E. Joan Wilson Miller, "The Ozark Culture Region as Revealed by Traditional Materials," *Annals*, Association of American Geographers, Vol. 58 (1968), pp. 51–77.

Unfortunately, this superior method of firsthand survey cannot be applied to more than one or two states or a few cities during the working lifetime of a single student.[8] The obvious alternative is simply to quiz a sample of the population concerning their awareness of their own or other vernacular regions, using a mail or telephone questionnaire when direct physical access is inconvenient. This technique was adopted in Joseph Brownell's pioneering effort to map the extent of the Middle West by eliciting the opinions of postmasters via a postcard survey.[9] In similar postal fashion, regional consciousness within the various sections of West Virginia has been measured and mapped by Charles Lieble.[10] Much the same sort of exercise has also been performed for Southern Indiana, this time by means of questionnaires administered in college classrooms.[11] Terry Jordan has supplemented a truly encyclopedic acquaintance with his native state in the same manner by extracting responses from students in thirty colleges and universities throughout the Lone Star State to produce a most interesting series of Texas regionalizations as they seem to materialize in the collective popular mind.[12] Clearly the most spatially ambitious of the attempts to recognize vernacular regions through methodical, long-distance interrogation is to be found in Ruth Hale's doctoral dissertation.[13] Postcards posing the question "What name is commonly used to refer to the region(s) of your state in which your county is located?" were dispatched to great numbers of agricultural agents, newspaper editors, and postmasters. Replies were received from no less than 6,800 individuals representing virtually all 3,066 counties in the United States. Exploiting these data, she was able to distinguish some 288 regional entities, many of them quite minute and nearly all below the territorial level aimed for in the present study.

Welcome though the results of such questionnaire-based studies may be, they are, nonetheless, methodologically flawed. In every instance cited above, the persons being questioned were members of an occupational or educational elite, and large segments of the public went unrepresented. Of course, it is feasible, though expensive, to draw an acceptable stratified sample of the general population and to generate a high percentage of responses. Such a procedure (as yet untried) still leaves unsolved an even thornier, probably insuperable, difficulty: the virtual impossibility of devising a bias-free questionnaire. And even given the correct wording of questions and proper selection of informants, the very fact of structured confrontation

---

8   I cannot leave this style of apprehending regions by way of personal osmosis without noting that a number of geographers, sociologists, and folklorists do approximate the charting and characterization of popular regions, as an incidental byproduct or otherwise, in regional investigations based upon a combination of sensitive field work and a thorough digestion of all manner of literature. Among many possible examples, see Donald W. Meinig, *Imperial Texas: an Interpretive Essay in Cultural Geography* (Austin: University of Texas Press, 1969); and idem, "Three American 'Northwests': Some Perspectives in Historical Geography," paper presented at Annual Meeting of Association of American Geographers, Cincinnati, 1957. Similarly, multidimensional exploration of the latter region is available in Raymond D. Gastil, "The Pacific Northwest as a Cultural Region," *Pacific Northwest Quarterly*, Vol. 64 (1973), pp. 147–62. At the micro scale, there is that classic study of a Chicago neighborhood, Gerald D. Suttles, *The Social Order of the Slum: Ethnicity and Territory in the Inner City* (Chicago: University of Chicago Press, 1968).

9   Joseph W. Brownell, "The Cultural Midwest," *Journal of Geography*, Vol. 59 (1960), pp. 43–61.

10   Charles L. Lieble, "Regional Consciousness in West Virginia," unpublished doctoral dissertation, University of Tennessee, 1974.

11   James K. Good, "A Perceptual Delimitation of Southern Indiana," *Professional Paper No. 8*, Indiana State University, Department of Geography and Geology (1976), pp. 3–10. A similar, but statistically more sophisticated, method was used to produce a map of the larger, popularly perceived regions of the nation in Kevin R. Cox and Georgia Zannaras, "Designative Perceptions of Macro-Spaces: Concepts, a Methodology, and Applications," in: Roger M. Downs and David Stea, eds., *Image and Environment* (London: Edward Arnold, 1973), p. 171.

12   Jordan, op. cit., footnote 2.

13   Ruth F. Hale, "A Map of Vernacular Regions in America," unpublished doctoral dissertation, University of Minnesota, 1971.

between inquisitor and respondent would almost certainly contribute a significant error to the results of any such social inquiry.

Perhaps the neatest solution to the problems of economizing time and effort and evading the technical boobytraps of questionnaires is to exploit unobtrusive measures of cultural and territorial identity. In a trail-blazing effort of this type, the sociologist John Shelton Reed has recently mapped both the limits and identity of two vernacular regional concepts—the South and Dixie—by calculating the ratio between the incidence of these terms and the term *National* as they appear in telephone directories for selected cities.[14] Inspired by his example, I have shamelessly plagiarized Professor Reed's methodology in the present study, one in which he has barely escaped becoming a coinvestigator.

RESEARCH METHODOLOGY

My procedure is simple in principle, but rather complicated in practice: to ascertain the relative frequency of certain terms appearing in the names of enterprises listed in recent directories for the major cities of the United States and Canada, and to suggest the territorial extent and psychological intensity of the larger, subnational vernacular regions on the basis of these frequencies.

The universe of places studied consists of the central cities of the Standard Metropolitan Statistical Areas of the United States as of 1975 and the Canadian cities of comparable size, i.e., 50,000 or more, 276 localities in all, for which recent (almost entirely 1972 to 1977) telephone directories—or, in four cases (Fitchburg-Leominster, Modesto, Peoria, and Saginaw) only Polk city directories—were accessible.[15] Four nonmetropolitan places were included so that no state or province would go unrepresented, namely: Anchorage, Alaska; Burlington, Vermont; Charlottetown, Prince Edward Island; and Cheyenne, Wyoming.[16] I consulted the directories in various college and municipal libraries, hotels, airports, private homes, and other targets of opportunity, but, above all, in the magnificent Library of Congress collection.

The enterprises whose names were tallied comprise all manner of organized, nongovernmental activity, whether for profit or otherwise, and include retail, wholesale, service, and manufacturing firms, associations, schools, churches, hospitals, places of entertainment, apartment buildings, cemeteries, parks, and a miscellany of other places and activities that happen to be listed in a city directory.

Perhaps the most crucial, and certainly the most difficult, phase of the project was compiling an acceptable checklist of terms. My selection of words with strong locational and cultural content or overtones was based upon: 1) a determination that they occurred often enough in enough different places to merit

---

14   John S. Reed, "The Heart of Dixie: An Essay in Folk Geography," *Social Forces*, Vol. 54(1976), pp. 925–39.

15   For many of our larger metropolitan areas, the practice has been to publish two or more telephone directories, usually one for the central city (and perhaps including the inner suburbs) and one or more for suburban and other outlying areas. In such cases the invariable procedure was to limit my attention to the central city directory, or to the directories for the two central cities in SMS As such as Minneapolis-St. Paul, San Francisco-Oakland, or Tampa-St. Petersburg, because the central city listings are much richer in names of enterprises and the effort to cull duplicated names, a common occurrence, would have been prohibitively time-consuming. I did not consult directories for smaller cities and rural areas because of the enormous effort involved and the relatively meager crop of names to be harvested. Enterprises are relatively infrequent, on a per-capita basis, outside the metropolitan areas, and those that do exist are subjected to weak "onomastic pressure," the necessity to adopt a locally unique name. Such pressure is obviously stronger in larger communities and leads to greater inventiveness and range of choices, as well as some remarkable coinages that can make metropolitan name-watching such a joy, as, for example, in the names of restaurants and drinking places.

16   A directory was unavailable for only a single candidate city, Winston-Salem, N.C. The increment of information from a 277th place did not seem great enough to justify an additional journey or waiting for the arrival of a mail order. Mea culpa.

Table 3.1   Terms Counted and Analyzed in the Study of Cultural Significance of Names of Metropolitan Enterprises

ACADIA (N)[a]	GLOBAL, GLOBE	SOUTHERN, SOUTHLAND[a]
AMERICAN[b]	GULF[a]	SOUTHWEST(ERN)[a]
APACHE	HOLIDAY	STAR
APOLLO	INTERNATIONAL	SUN(BEAM) (LIGHT) (SHINE)
ARGO, ARGONAUT, ARGOSY	MAPLE LEAF	SUNSET
ATLANTIC[a]	MAYFAIR	TOWN & COUNTRY
ATLAS	METRO(POLITAN) MID-AMERICA(N)[a]	UNITED STATES, U.S.[b]
AZTEC(A)	MID-ATLANTIC, MIDDLE ATLANTIC[a]	UNIVERSAL
CANADA, CANADIAN[c]	MIDLAND	VICTORIA
CENTENNIAL	MIDWAY	VIKING
CENTRAL	MIDDLE WEST, MIDWEST(ERN)[a]	VILLAGE
CENTURY	MISSION	WESTERN[a]
CITY(WIDE)	MODERN(E)	
CLASSIC	MONARCH	
COAST(AL)	NATIONAL, NATION WIDE[b,c]	
COLONIAL, COLONY	NEW ENGLAND[a]	
COLUMBIA[b]	NORTH AMERICAN	
COMMUNITY	NORTHEAST(ERN)	
CONTINENTAL	NORTHERN[a]	
COUNTRY(SIDE)	NORTHLAND[a]	
CROWN	NORTH STAR	
DELTA	NORTHWEST(ERN)[a]	
DIXIE[a]	OLYMPIA(IC) (US)	
DOMINION[c]	PACIFIC[a]	
DOWNTOWN(ER)	PHOENIX	
EAGLE	PILGRIM	
EASTERN[a]	PIONEER	
EMPIRE, IMPERIAL	REGAL, ROYAL(E)	
FEDERAL[b]	REGENCY, REGENT	
FRONTIER	SOUTHEAST(ERN)[a]	

[a] Regional term.

[b] National term within U.S.

[c] National term within Canada.

inclusion, and 2) the judgment that they conveyed interesting information about the conceptual worlds of North Americans at the relatively macroscopic scale of this investigation (Table 3.1). Although my prime objective was to identify and delimit the grosser vernacular regions—and thus the listing of the more obvious regional and territorial-locational terms—I could not resist the opportunity to include a number of items that are not specifically geographical but which might convey clues to other dimensions of the cultural personality of the two nations and their constituent regions.

I began with the most comprehensive checklist possible of potentially useful terms after browsing through directories for some of our larger cities, consulting the standard compendium of American nicknames, and generally straining my imagination.[17] The result was a roster of well over 400 terms. A series of

---

17   George E. Shankle, *American Nicknames: Their Origins and Significance,* 2nd edition (New York: Wilson, 1955).

test trials followed, using directories for widely separated places, a process which eliminated most nominees, but also yielded a few items previously overlooked. After several repetitions of this winnowing action, a point of no return was reached, and a final residuum of 73 terms and their close variants, beyond which additional refinement of the list would have cost too much in time and effort.[18] Nevertheless the experience subsequently gained in tallying terms in the 276 directories did indicate needed improvements in the list if this research is ever to be replicated or updated. I cannot help registering my mild astonishment that such terms as *Appalachian, Caribbean, Creole, Desert, Freedom, Great Lakes, Independence, Liberty, Lone Star, Mayflower, Minute Man, Paradise, Patriot, People's, Plains, Prairie, Progressive, Puritan, Rebel,* and *Yankee* fell by the wayside or recalling my poignant farewells to the likes of *Aloha, Bonanza, Camelot, Eldorado, Eureka, Flamingo, Gopher, Mustang, Quaker, Swanee, Thunderbird, Tivoli, Xanadu,* and other exotica.

In scanning the likely alphabetical loci in a directory and recording the number of occurrences of the given terms, a set of exclusionary rules was observed, all in the interest of ascertaining how many truly local naming decisions—with nonlocal significance!—were in evidence. They are as follows:

1. The names of governmental agencies were not considered since the affixing of a national, regional, state, or other jurisdictional name is a political decision, not a cultural choice freely arrived at.
2. Personal surnames, such as Atlas, Crown, Holiday, Royal, Sun, or West, were not considered.
3. Duplicated names were counted only once.
4. Branch or local offices of firms or organizations with multiple locations were not counted, only the central office when it could be identified as such. This rule eliminated virtually all citations of transportation and insurance companies, union locals, chain stores, regional and national franchises of all varieties, and greatly reduced the number of times telephone companies, banks, and many national associations were counted.
5. Names that refer to local streets, neighborhoods, or landmarks or to state or local political jurisdictions were omitted. Thus no note was taken of establishments named after a Western Avenue, Northern Boulevard, Eagle Mountain, or the like, or the cities of Atlantic City, Columbia, Midland, Phoenix, or Victoria.[19]

---

18 This final group is patently and deliberately a mixed bag containing terms classifiable into some nine categories: 1) the largest and most important consisting of items referring to regions, physical features, or to compass directions with a variable load of regional meaning; 2) national terms—*American, Canada, Columbia, Dominion, Federal, National, United States*; 3) international terms—*Continental, Global, International, North American, Universal*; 4) temporal and historical terms—*Centennial, Century, Colonial, Frontier, Mission, Pilgrim, Pioneer*; 5) residential terms and those referring to location with respect to the city: *Central, City, Country, Downtown, Metropolitan, Midway, Town & Country, Village*; 6) references to the Classical World—*Apollo, Argo, Atlas, Classic, Olympia, Phoenix*; 7) environmental terms—*Coastal, Star, Sun, Sunset*; 8) two national totems—*Eagle, Maple Leaf*; and 9) miscellaneous abstractions—*Aztec, Crown, Empire, Holiday, May fair, Regal, Regency, Victoria, Viking*. This may be as appropriate a point as any to note, with regret, the nonexistence of any useful typologies for the name of enterprises. When and if they are produced, they are likely to resemble the set suggested for place-names in George R. Stewart, *American Place-Names* (New York: Oxford University Press,

19 This rule was extremely difficult to apply to occurrences of *Columbia* and *Olympia* in the Pacific Northwest, *Dominion* in Virginia, *Empire* in New York, and similar cases where a term bears both a local and a more general import. I simply used my best judgment. Also quite troublesome were the numerous *Deltas* referring to a deltaic district other than that in the lower Mississippi Valley or to some other implication of the word *Delta*.

Before proceeding to describe and discuss our findings, it may be wise to review the validity of both the premises and the data upon which the analysis depends. As the reader must have surmised several paragraphs ago, the crucial axiom upon which this inquiry rests is that the frequency with which people attach certain names to their enterprises—and the degree to which such names survive—is a relatively sensitive measure of group perceptions of the locus within sociocultural space, and probably along other social and cultural dimensions as well, of the places in question. In other words, the namers, consciously or otherwise, select names with which their clientele can empathize and which should help assure the success of the enterprise in so far as they reflect the inner feelings or aspirations of the local population. There is no direct method to test the validity of this notion, but it is inherently reasonable, and, as we shall see, our empirical results do coincide snugly with the results of other independent investigations in those cases where comparisons are possible.

North American telephone directories constitute a superb source for the names we seek since they list virtually all organized, legal enterprises within a given service territory. But there are several technical difficulties in their use. First, unless the entire directory is searched, we miss those terms that fail to appear at the beginning of a name. Thus, for example, the Canadian Association of Poodle Fanciers would be tallied, but not the Poodle Fanciers of Canada. How much, if any, bias is thereby introduced is unclear; probably very little. Second, the fact that some of the directories encompass most or all of a metropolitan area, while others are limited to a central city, undoubtedly has resulted in uneven coverage from place to place. I can only hope that the bias thus produced is not systematic in character. Third, the set of directories used for this study are not all of the same vintage; but I believe that any temporal bias is minor and, in any case, is randomly distributed over space.[20] Lastly, most of the entries for the metropolises of Quebec are in the French language, so that relatively few English-language or bilingual terms were collected for those places, and they may be less diagnostic of regional or cultural identity than one would like.

The selected terms themselves also pose a few problems. Some are ambiguous or polysemous in nature, e.g., *Classic, Community, Delta,* or *Dominion,* and perhaps all carry multiple levels of meaning, so that the interpretation of their popularity must be cautious. Some terms, originally localized in distribution, have transcended their hearth areas, becoming nationalized, so to speak. Thus one may encounter a Dixie Diner, a New England Seafood Restaurant, or a Western Tack Shop just about anywhere in the land. But this fact should be more of a challenge than an annoyance to the student of North American culture. The most serious of the probable flaws in research design, however, has already been mentioned: a rather arbitrary inclusion of some terms and rejection of other, perhaps equally worthy, candidates. Undoubtedly the most serious source of error in this study is the fallibility of the investigator; there is no telling how many legitimate occurrences of terms have been missed or overcounted or how often the exclusionary rules have been improperly applied. Having confessed these various frailties, what can we learn from the data, shortcomings and all?

---

20   Unfortunately, it would be extremely difficult, perhaps impossible, to retroject this study to a much earlier date because of the spottiness of archival collections of telephone directories; but an updating twenty or thirty years hence might reveal some useful facts about the nature and pace of sociocultural evolution on this continent.

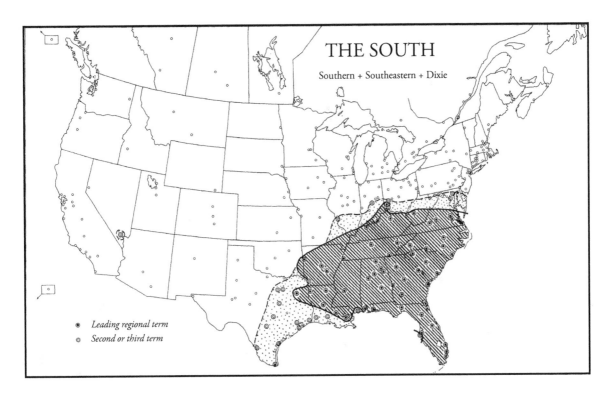

Figure 3.1.   The South.

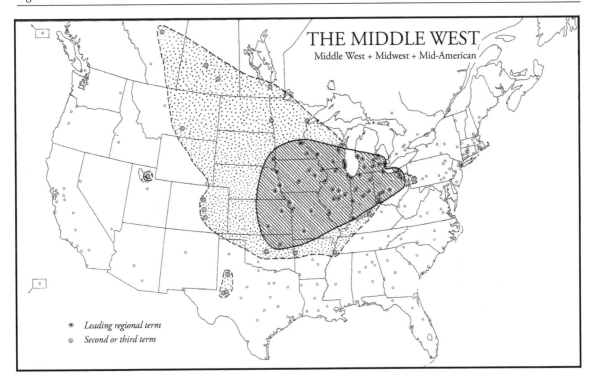

Figure 3.2.   The Middle West: Middle West + Midwest + Mid-American.

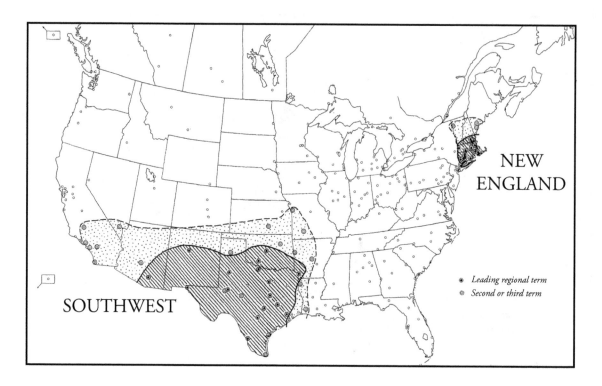

Figure 3.3.   New England: the Southwest.

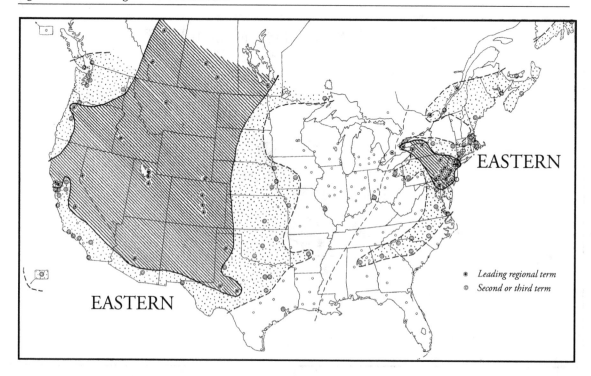

Figure 3.4.   The East; the West.

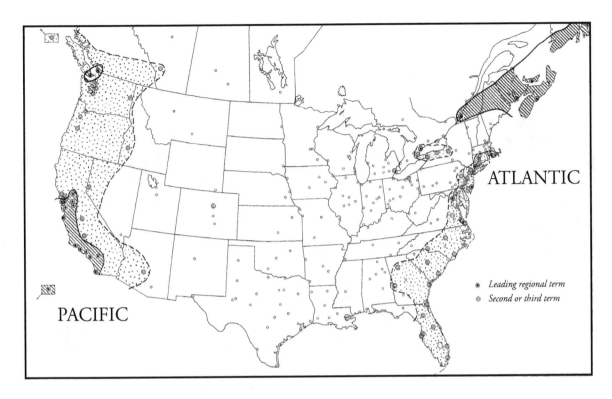

Figure 3.5. The Atlantic Region; the Pacific Region.

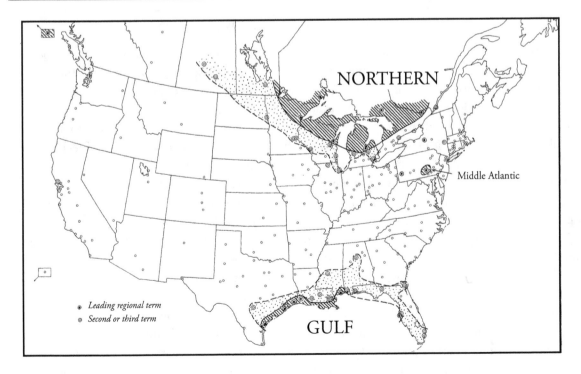

Figure 3.6. The North; the Middle Atlantic Region; the Gulf Region.

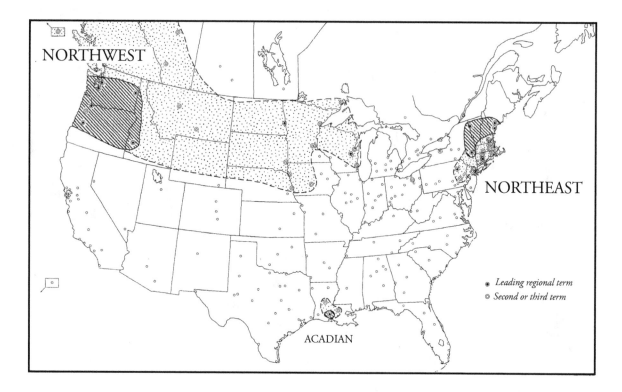

Figure 3.7. The Northeast; the Northwest; Acadia.

THE VERNACULAR REGIONS MAPPED

In a series of seven maps, I have attempted to delimit some fourteen vernacular regions or locational concepts as they are implied by the names of metropolitan enterprises (Figs. 3.1 to 3.7). The territories in question are defined as those in which a given term, or a cluster of closely related terms, outnumbers all other regional or locational terms in all, or nearly all, the included metropolitan areas. In addition to the zone in which the specified entity is dominant, in most instances I have also designated a secondary peripheral zone in which it ranks second or third in frequency within the constellation of regional terms. Obviously, I have indulged in a polite cartographic fiction by extrapolating into a two-dimensional space the generalizations drawn from essentially punctiform data. We cannot safely infer from the mind-set of the metropolitan denizens what the regional notions or affiliations of their rural and small-town neighbors might be; we can only speculate.

The South is probably the most populous and sturdiest of our vernacular regions (Fig. 3.1). Metropolises are shown as popularly perceived to be within the South when the combined count of the terms *Southern, Southeastern*), and *Dixie,* along with closely related, alphabetically proximal items such as *Southland, Southerner, Southernaire, Dixieland,* and the like account for a plurality of the place's regional terms. It is safe to assume, I believe, that this cluster of terms is convergent in cultural meaning. It is important to note that *Southern* and its terminological ilk are only incidentally locational or latitudinal. The metropolises of the southwestern quadrant of the United States are no further from the equator than the South, essentially a sociocultural rather than a geodetic entity. In fact, Southern terms are totally absent in Honolulu, the southernmost of our metropolises! The foregoing observation also applies to the terms *Western, Eastern,* and, with much less force, to *Northern* (except in Canada, where, in sharp contrast, *Northern* is saturated with sociocultural connotations, and *Southern* is little more than a direction). We also find that the terms *Northeastern, Northwestern,* and *Southwestern,* as well as *Southeastern,* can carry strong cultural-historical overtones.

The general shape of the South is reassuringly familiar, and the location of its northern and most of its western edge recalls boundaries staked out in earlier studies (Fig. 3.1).[21] There are two rather unexpected details, however. All of Florida, except St. Petersburg, belongs to the South, albeit rather less staunchly than the states to its north; and southern Louisiana and southeastern Texas are only marginally Southern.

We find even less novelty in the bounding of the vernacular Middle West (Fig. 3.2). When the various terms connoting Middle Western-ness (*Middle West(ern)*; *MidWest(ern)*; *MidAmerican*) are combined, the area of dominance closely simulates earlier regionalizations.[22] It is rather startling, however, to discover that the secondary zone penetrates deeply into Canada's Prairie Provinces and into Colorado and Utah and as far south as Memphis and Fort Smith. The suggestion that Lubbock, Midland, and Odessa, Texas comprise a diluted outlier of the Middle West would be erroneous. The prevalence of the term *Midwest* in west-central Texas appears to reflect a peculiarly Texan, i.e., state-level, rather than national, framework of spatial orientation.[23]

Of the remaining dozen regions, only three have been depicted on earlier maps: New England, Acadia, and the Middle Atlantic region. The placement of both the primary and secondary zones of New England conforms precisely to a prior regionalization based on other evidence (Fig. 3.3).[24] The location of the Southwest in the same drawing fulfills one's expectations, including as it does large portions of Texas, Oklahoma, New Mexico, and Arizona, with a broad secondary fringe stretching into adjacent states. Once again, note that the most literally southwestern of our metropolises, those in southern California and Hawaii, are far removed from the Southwest's heartland.

I have ventured to assign specific territory to the North American East and West, at least as they may be pinned down by the popular mind (Fig. 3.4). The East (for which there are no prior hints in the literature, as far as I am aware) emerges as a surprisingly small, tight cluster of metropolises, mostly within the southwestern half of Megalopolis, but extending northwest to include Hamilton, Ontario. A large irregular secondary zone reaches all the way from Newfoundland to Alabama. Locationally, the West behaves as one would anticipate. This is the most extensive of our popular regions, embracing as it does a good third of the North American ecumene in its primary phase; and when the peripheral zone is added, it includes more than half of our study area. Perhaps the most striking discovery is the deep eastward invasion—as far as London, Ontario and Cincinnati—of frequent occurrences of the term *Western* (Fig. 3.4).

Two concepts that are, in a strict sense, perhaps more locational than regional overlap or parallel the East and West—the Atlantic and Pacific regions (Fig. 3.5). For reasons that are far from clear, *Atlantic* usages outnumber other regional terms in only five metropolises in the far northeast of the study area. Spatially detached from the primary zone are two tracts where *Atlantic* is subordinate but significant: virtually the

---

21 Wilbur Zelinsky, *The Cultural Geography of the United States* (Englewood Cliffs: Prentice-Hall, 1973), pp. 118–19; Raymond D. Gastil, *Cultural Regions of the United States* (Seattle: University of Washington Press, 1975), p. 174; and Reed, op. cit., footnote 14.

22 Brownell, op. cit., footnote 9; Zelinsky, op. cit., footnote 21, pp. 118–19.

23 Terry G. Jordan, personal communication, May 10, 1977.

24 Zelinsky, op. cit., footnote 21, pp. 118–19.

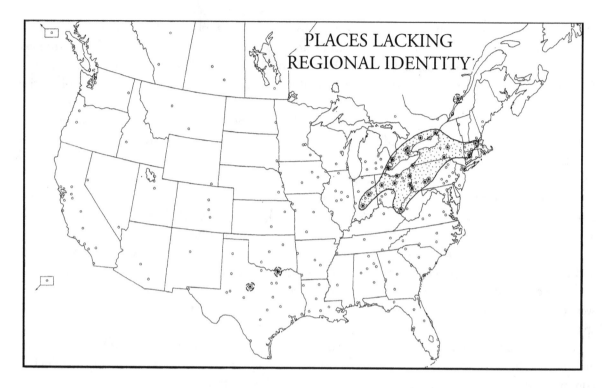

Figure 3.8.   Places lacking regional identity.

---

entirety of the Atlantic Coastal Plain from southern New England to Florida; and a curious exclave along the shores of Lake Ontario. The range of *Pacific* occurrences is predictably restricted to the five states and the Canadian province bordering the ocean. Let me suggest that the two isolated patches of primacy—central and southern California; and Vancouver and Victoria, B.C.—may be synonymous with "The Coast" as it is known in colloquial parlance.

Two of the next three items have never previously seen the cartographic light of day (Fig. 3.6). The regionalization of *Gulf* makes eminently good sense geographically as well as psychologically; but there is reason to wonder about the wedging of the primary North American North into so few places within Ontario, plus the Upper Great Lakes country of the United States—and Anchorage. Latitudinally, many other places qualify as well as, or better than, Green Bay or Saginaw.

By far the weakest and loneliest of our vernacular regions is the Middle Atlantic (Fig. 3.6). The present data add further proof to the contention that, consequential though the Midland region may have been historically and culturally, the regional self-awareness, or articulateness, of its inhabitants has remained quite subdued. Harrisburg, the only metropolis willing to admit a Middle Atlantic allegiance, does indeed lie close to the core of the Midland Culture Area, but at least four other metropolises covered in this study also fall within its boundaries despite the muteness of our onomastic evidence.[25]

---

25   Joseph W. Glass, "The Pennsylvania Culture Region: A Geographical Interpretation of Barns and Farmhouses," unpublished doctoral dissertation, The Pennsylvania State University, 1971; and Wilbur Zelinsky, "The Pennsylvania Town: an Overdue Geographical Account," *Geographical Review,* Vol. 67 (1977), pp. 127–47.

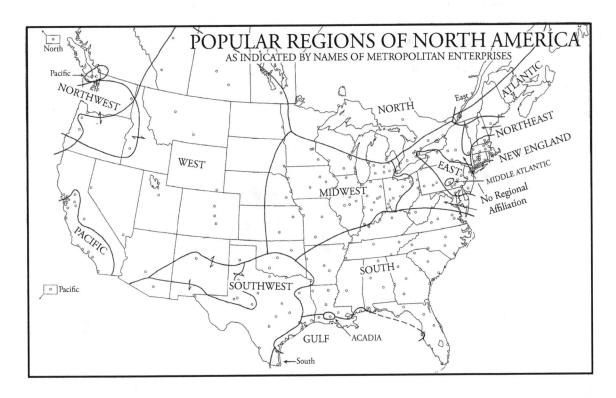

Figure 3.9. The popular regions of North America as indicated by names of metropolitan enterprises.

Our final three regions offer strong contrasts in territorial extent (Fig. 3.7). Although the core section of the Northwest is limited to portions of Washington, Oregon, and Idaho, its secondary zone embraces an enormous tract from Anchorage to the shores of Lake Michigan. Evidently, the idea of the Northwest, originating in the days of the Old Northwest, has remained alive and strongly competitive with other regional concepts within a broader territory than can be claimed by any of the other three compass diagonals. Thus the popular conception of the Northeast dominates the nomenclature of enterprises in only a half dozen places in the New England and Middle Atlantic states, and is a secondary or tertiary motif in the northeastern sector of Megalopolis. Given the limited range of Acadia as a culture area, the small expanse devoted to *Acadian* is scarcely surprising (Fig. 7).[26]

One further regional, or rather a-regional, category imparts an interesting message for which no explanation is at hand (Fig. 8). If we arbitrarily define as lacking in regional identity those metropolises in which no single regional term or cluster of closely related terms occurs five or more times, then we can discern a large contiguous tract of regional anonymity extending from central New England across large portions of New York, Pennsylvania, and Ontario into the eastern Middle West. (Only three other places so qualify: Quebec; Abilene; and Sherman-Denison.) This no-man's-land is merely the trough of a wider zone in which regional sentiments smolder weakly. Why this apathy toward any regional attachments in this particular area? I can advance no plausible hypothesis for the phenomenon, one which does not disappear even after controlling

26   Eric Waddell, *French Louisiana: an Outpost of VAmerique Frangaise, or Another County and Another Culture?* Working Paper No. 4, Departement de Geographic, Universite Laval (Quebec, 1979), p. viii.

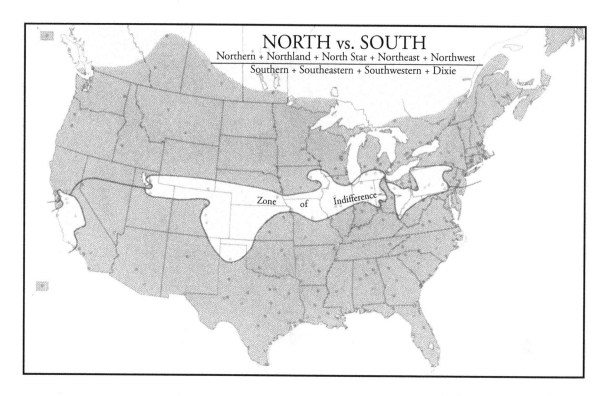

Figure 3.10. North vs. South: Northern + Northland + North Star + Northeast + Northwest. Southern + Southeastern + Southwestern + Dixie.

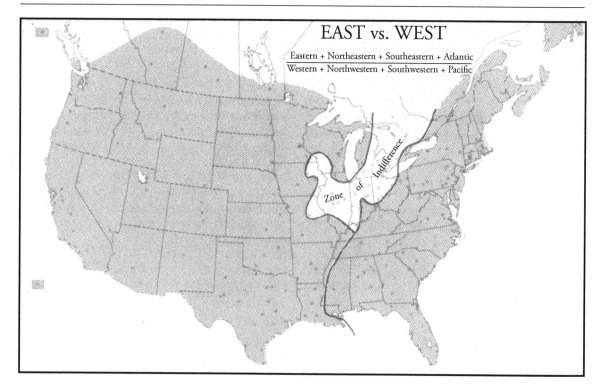

Figure 3.11. East vs. West: Eastern + Northeastern + Southeastern + Atlantic/Western + Northwestern + Southwestern + Pacific.

for size of place. My initial guess, admittedly a desperate one, is that these may be places which happen, for some obscure reason, to be so secure in their social-geographic identity, so self-contained or else so permeated with a sense of "middleness" with respect to other parts of their nations, that they find it pointless to attach regional labels to their activities. Arguing by analogy, why is it that the British, alone among all the nations of the world, do not bother to announce their identity on postage stamps?

All the foregoing maps have been generalized into a single drawing, a summary statement of the vernacular regions of North America (Fig. 3.9). It is necessary to point out that two tracts have been accorded dual memberships, one to both the West and Northwest, the other to the West and Southwest. The data for the six metropolises in question do not admit of any less inelegant solution.

The vernacular region and the culture area are closely related concepts. Both share some common genetic factors, and, by definition, the existence of both is recognized by their inhabitants, even though self-awareness sometimes barely creeps past the threshold of consciousness. Thus the finding that the South, Middle West, and New England as vernacular regions correspond so closely to their delimitation as culture areas by the academic scholar is not unanticipated. Similarly, we have discovered that Acadia and the Midland (or Middle Atlantic area) materialize as cultural entities as well as popular regions, even though less robustly in the latter role. Moreover, it is likely that if the Western, Southwestern, and Northwestern culture areas are ever mapped realistically, their boundaries will not depart too drastically from those set forth here. On the other hand, six of our vernacular regions—the Atlantic, Gulf, North, Northeast, Pacific, and, probably, East—are locational rather than cultural in character, and are unlikely to be duplicated as manifestations of any purely cultural phenomenon. Thus, if required to identify themselves with a culture area, the citizens of Biloxi, Mississippi, for example, would probably respond, "The South," but, if simply asked, "*Where* do you live?" the answer might well be "The Gulf Coast" or some similar locution.

FURTHER INTERPRETATIONS OF THE REGIONAL DATA

In an effort to extract further insights concerning the structuring of popular regions in the North American mind, the data concerning regional terms were subjected to additional arithmetic and cartographic manipulation. The results of comparing the total occurrences of all terms denoting Northernness in each metropolis with those suggesting Southernness fail to startle (Fig. 3.10). The North Extended and the South Extended, each occupying roughly half the study area, and separated by three zones of indifference within which references to either North or South are so few as to be trivial, adjoin each other at or near a median parallel of latitude. The one noteworthy feature on this map is that peninsular tentacle of the Greater South pushing northward all the way across Ohio to Lake Erie scooping up Columbus and Toledo en route. This corridor may well be associated with a heavily traveled commercial and migrational route connecting the Upper South with Toledo and southeastern Michigan.

When this exercise was repeated with terms indicating Westernness and Easternness, our previous suspicions were amply confirmed (Fig. 3.11). The territory claimed by the Greater West is several times larger than that falling within the Greater East. Moreover, if we were to include *Middle West* and associated terms within the Western set, as one is tempted to do, then that NE-SW-sloping line bounding the two areas would probably be rotated clockwise an appreciable interval, while the single blister of indifference in the eastern Middle West might vanish totally. We have here further evidence, if any is still needed, of the extraordinary grip of the idea of the West on the North American popular mind. One might also recall

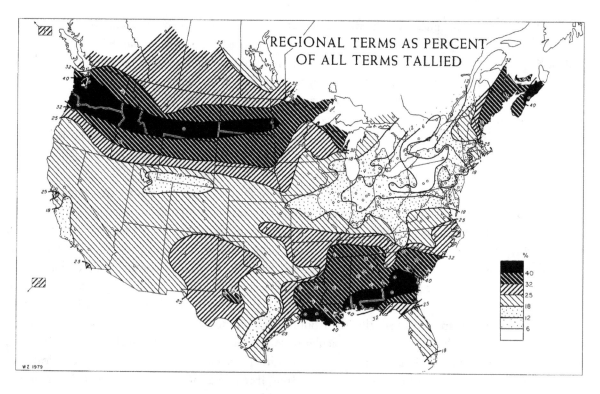

Figure 3.12.   East vs. West: Eastern + Northeastern + Southeastern + Atlantic/Western + Northwestern + Southwestern + Pacific.

that if there is one single term that serves, in both journalistic and popular usage, to label the entire Greater European cultural community, of which North America is, of course, a part, that term is simply, "The West."

Finally, I have attempted to chart variations in the intensity of expressed regional feeling (Fig. 3.12). For each metropolis the total number of occurrences of all twenty-five regional terms was summed; the same was done for the remaining forty-eight presumed cultural terms lacking in direct regional significance, including national and international items; and the regional terms were calculated as a percentage of the total.[27] Although one might challenge the appropriateness of this operation, given the rather arbitrary selection of terms, especially the nonregional variety, I am persuaded that the isolines give us at least a rough first approximation of a genuine psychological surface. As previously suggested, regional sentiment is feeblest in a large part of the northeastern United States and adjacent portions of Canada; but low to moderate values extend all the way across the central latitudes of the United States (Fig. 3.8). In expectable contrast, the currents of regional feeling run strongest within the Deep South, where we have the largest grouping of cities with high readings. The only comparable values occur in the Maritimes and neighboring Maine and in the Northwest Extended, tracts containing far fewer metropolises. Perhaps we can draw some inferences from the fact that those corners of the nation are relatively isolated physically and socially and are also most keenly self-conscious about their regional identity.

---

27   Copies of the results of a factor analysis performed on a 276 by 73 matrix, one that includes the frequency of all terms observed in this study in each of the metropolises, are obtainable from the author upon request.

CONCLUSION

This exploration of the significance of the frequency of selected terms in the names of North American metropolitan enterprises has yielded encouraging results. It has enabled us to identify a plausible set of fourteen relatively large, subnational vernacular, or popular, regions which mesh reasonably well with a related set of regions—the culture areas of our continent. We have also arrived at a tentative mapping of the geographical variation in the strength of regional feeling. In addition, our data suggest the probability that other valuable clues to the geography of North American society and culture can be distilled from the practices we follow in naming organized activities. But perhaps more than anything else this essay has demonstrated how provisional is our knowledge, and how great our ignorance, concerning a topic almost certain to grow in theoretical and practical importance: the nature and meaning of the vernacular regions of late Twentieth-Century North America.

STUDY QUESTIONS

1. What was Wilbur Zelinsky's main source of information for his study?
2. What sort of information was he looking for?
3. How many directories did he use?
4. At what scale was this survey and what was Zelinsky's prime objective?
5. What is the "crucial axiom" of Zelinsky's study?
6. Briefly, what are the four technical difficulties with Zelinsky's method?
7. What were some of the weaknesses with the terms themselves?
8. How did Zelinsky define his territories?
9. What cannot be inferred from this study?
10. Which is the most populous and sturdiest of the 14 vernacular regions Zelinsky identified? What does "sturdiest" mean in this context?
11. What did Zelinsky mean when he said that "Southern and its terminological ilk are only incidentally locational or latitudinal?
12. What was surprising about the evidence obtained about the South?
13. Looking at the map of the Middle West, what accounts for the regional outlier in Texas?
14. Which three maps of vernacular regions have been drawn on other regional maps?
15. Looking at the maps, how are California and Hawaii categorized as both primary and secondary regions?
16. Which is the largest (most extensive) popular region?
17. Which two regions had never been formally documented before this article in 1980?
18. Which is the weakest vernacular region?
19. What accounts for the extensive area of the Northwest secondary region?
20. Are there any places in North America that lack a regional vernacular identity? Where are they?
21. Looking at the map in Fig. 3.11, which three regions have the strongest regional identities? Where is the weakest regional identity?

Chapter 4 Snapshot
Place or Space?

INTRODUCTION

This article investigates the emotional relationship people can have with place in contrast to a sense of alienation that can arise from increasingly globalized spaces (45). Go into a local mall and many of the shops are the same as in other malls, the food courts are the same, the music is the same, the plants and the benches down the middle of the walkways are very similar, if not the same. You could be in a shopping mall in almost any place in the United States. Fast food restaurants or restaurant chains tend to be the same, too. These are some examples of the increasingly globalized spaces Mike Crang is referring to. What do the terms place and space mean as geographers use them? From this very brief introduction we can guess that *place* is a more local and emotional term while *space* is a more global and unemotional term. Crang begins his discussion by associating the concepts of place and space with two schools of thought within geography and provides a historical context for the thinking behind these two schools.

In the 1960s, the vision of geography was that of a spatial science (review *The Four Traditions of Geography*). Geographers were developing spatial models and developing quantitative studies (studies based on statistics and scientific techniques). They were looking for spatial regularities and patterns in things or objects (phenomena) on the surface of the earth that might reveal general rules or models for distributing activities over space—or lead to discovering spatial laws (46). This was considered a *nomothetic* approach to geography. It was a more globalized perception of space as a phenomenon and of human interaction with it. On the other hand, there also were geographers at the time who were interested in the "uniqueness of place, or areal differentiation," and the development of *region*. Instead of looking for general laws that linked phenomena across many places, this approach, called the *ideographic* approach in geography, was looking for what makes places and regions individual and unique. Here already you can begin to see what leads to the different approaches between space and place.

By the 1970s, geography went through a quantitative revolution which drove the nomothetic approach into a dominant position. Geography became defined as a study of distributions in space rather than a study of particular places. This nomothetic approach was based in rational science and was reducing diversity and restricting individuality in attempts to produce a more orderly and efficient way of looking at the world. Yet, there still were geographers who were trying to provide a balance for this scientistic approach that had divided humans into a series of quantifiable attributes. This was a more place-based orientation, reaching for a more holistic, and "human" approach.

ON THE ROAD TO NOWHERE: THE EROSION OF PLACE

Mike Crang observes that people tend to <u>define</u> themselves through a sense of <u>place</u>, not by the points and lines on a map that symbolizes a more spatial perspective. Spaces become places as they become "time-thickened," that is, it is a lived connection over time that binds people and places together; and this is the sort of thing that leads to community. Local community stands in contrast to the impersonality of globalized spaces, and Crang uses the urban landscape as an example; he and others claim that the constructed landscapes of the city and its suburbs lack personality. For many it is difficult to feel emotionally attached or to feel a personal identification with an urban environment and the increasingly impersonal modern spaces being built around us.

So, where did this more impersonal sense of space come from? Crang answers this question by again providing a historical context, and we see it is not a new concern. Going all the way back to the Dark Ages (Medieval period), it was a time when all knowledge came under religious control. Science, as it had been practiced by the Greeks, Romans, and others in the western world (see *The Four Traditions of Geography*) ceased. It was a period of religious learning to the exclusion of other knowledge. The eventual fall of the Roman Empire gave rise to the era of the Enlightenment. Religion no longer controlled or filtered all knowledge. Science was back, making observations and predictions regarding the natural world. Furthermore, there was a sense that, with scientific knowledge, humans could find the key to controlling their environment. As an example of this scientistic approach as it extended into the 19th century, Crang references Thomas Jefferson subdividing territories of the Midwest into proportions and rational divisions of space that, even today, reveal its checkerboard pattern from the air. Jefferson devised this pattern from the nation's capital, "mapping abstract space onto territory." It provided order and rationality over what seemed to Europeans to be a great wilderness of open spaces. There is no emotional attachment to place here in contrast to the indigenous peoples who had inhabited these places, many of which were sacred. The spatial approach "separates the observer from the landscape and imposes an intellectual order upon it" (18). We still see this approach today in the fields of spatial science, spatial analysis, and the development of Geographic Information Systems as we read in *The Four Traditions of Geography*. The Romantic Movement, however, was a reaction to this perception of rational, impersonal space. The Romantics saw beauty and a sense of spirituality in the landscape. Following this tradition, the Romantic movement gave rise to the eventual establishment of the national parks system, preserving landscapes for posterity because these landscapes were unique and "transcended the ordinary" (49).

But there were still bigger changes coming. At the end of the 19th and beginning of the 20th century we see the rise of the railroad. Travel became much faster; the landscapes began to pass by as a blur. Distance was increasingly measured by time, and time was being broken down into homogenized units and uniform time zones. These time zones were essential in keeping trains on schedule across transcontinental space and in keeping trains from running into each other. Efficiency was the key theme of the period—which gave rise to mass production and assembly-line manufacturing. Buildings began to take on a spare, efficient form with clean lines. The human element increasingly gave way to a mass society and the further homogenization of space. However, some "writers began to look on [such] technical advance as bearing too high a price tag. The human landscapes of places to which people are attached are sacrificed to placeless, soulless new spaces which are functionally more efficient but reduce the quality of experience" (49). Based on the work of planners and architects, human landscapes became increasingly uniform, dehumanized, impersonal, and supposedly value-free.

PHENOMENOLOGY/EXISTENTIALISM

So, we now have a sense of the underlying concepts behind space, but what about place? To understand the foundation behind the concept of place, we need to start with the concept of phenomenon. Phenomenon is a term that means object, thing, or event and we begin our conversation with a discussion of what constitutes an object or thing. There are several levels to objects. Take a rock, for example. We could pick out a nice piece of salt-and-pepper granite. A geologist might know it by its chemical composition and the processes by which it was formed. An architect might look at it as a building material; how hard it is and how well it can take a polish. A landscape architect or sculptor might look at it for its aesthetic appeal, while a protester might weigh its heft as a projectile. So, according to phenomenology (the study of phenomena) an "object only really becomes something when it is seen in light of its intended use" (51). That is, "there is an <u>intended object</u> as well as a material thing" (51). The material thing in our example is granite, but the intended object could be geologic sample, finishing material (maybe for a kitchen countertop), a piece of artwork, or a weapon. How does this concept of intended object relate to places? Places, too, are phenomena and they, too have layers of meaning based on their intended use. Crang states that "places were not just a set of accumulated data but involved human intentions as well" (51). How do we get to the intended uses of place? First, we need to look at its essence.

Essence refers to the characteristics of a place. What is it that first draws us to a place, what attracts us? What is it about a place that makes us feel at home? There are the material elements of a place, the people, the weather, the history of a place, perhaps, or at least our history with a place. That is, there is more to a place than just a unique collection of phenomena. The concept of "essence" is used to suggest that people experience something beyond the material properties of places; they can feel an attachment to the spirit of a place. All you have to do is think of a beautiful sunset or a night sky full of stars and your thought may not even be cognizant of the material elements that make up what you are viewing; you are more focused on what these scenes mean, and how they make you *feel*. In fact, some might say that not only do places have essences, but one of "the essential characteristics of humanity is this relationship to meaningful places" (51). Essence is about the unique spirit of a place, an essence that extends beyond material elements of a place—there is some essence that pulls at our emotions and feelings—and we see this in photographs, paintings, poetry, and other literature about place.

People live in the world; they are fundamentally attached to it. We don't think of people free of the condition of being in the world. This is embeddedness, and embeddedness in the world has two important consequences. First, people experience place differently, so "place is a product of how we interact with it" (52) as we saw with our discussion of the layers of meaning of phenomena. In addition, the same place may have different meanings for different people. Think of the City of Omaha—people will experience the city differently depending on whether they live there, commute to work there, or go there to attend the College World Series. All of us are immersed in a geographical world, but this embeddedness is something most of us are not aware of because it is so much a part of who we are and what we take for granted about our <u>place</u> in the world. What we are more conscious of is what we care about and we "have different types and levels of care for different things at different times" (52). For example, many of us didn't have much awareness of a place called Iraq until the United States started sending troops there. Those who have had loved ones there know it in more detail than those of us who have not, but still not as well as those who have served tours there themselves. "Thus, our knowledge of the world is always em-placed, it is always starting from and based around places as centres of our 'care' about the world" (52).

TERRITORIALITY AND BOUNDING PLACES

We also use our sense of place to define ourselves and others. We identify territory and create boundaries around it, distinguishing between insiders and outsiders. It is this territorialization that is connected to familiarity, identity, and care. There is a very famous example of a grouping of low-income high rise units where the common spaces had no boundaries around them indicating they were for the exclusive use of the tenants. There was no sense of boundedness for the people who lived there and this eroded a sense of care about their surroundings and also eroded any sense of community or local pride. There was no one to take responsibility for upkeep or maintenance. The high rise complex quickly became a run-down area full of overgrown weeds and a place for drug dealers and gang members. Because of the way these public housing units were built, there was little identification with place for the inhabitants. Such a "deterritorialised landscape promotes an existential outsidedness—people do not feel like they belong and thus do not care for their environment" (53). How buildings are built and the way space is planned and used matters. New housing units today are often identified with a group name such as "Cedar Creek" or "Pheasant Run" one can see clearly on a wall or sign when entering the complex. In older communities, neighborhood associations are also building a sense of identity and a uniqueness of place. Without this sense of identity, it is easier for one to feel more alienated, detached, and lonely. Place "helps us forget our separateness and the world's indifference" (54).

GLOBAL SPACE—ERODING PLACE?

However, there are other ways than by lack of boundedness that we can lose a sense of local community as well. For example, the more mobile a society becomes, the less attached it becomes to a specific sense of place. Americans are some of the most mobile people on the planet, moving on an average of once every six years. As a result of digital communications and social networking, today we are sometimes closer to people who are at greater distances from us than those who are physically closer to us. Social networks have both stretched our sense of intimate space as well as created more communities stretched over distance (distanciated communities).

More and more globalized products seem to be replacing locally produced goods and landscapes take on a commercialized sameness. In Europe, there is a concern that mass culture (often associated with American culture) is eroding more local, "authentic" forms of culture. In fact, there are some companies that artificially create culture areas as a financial enterprise; or small towns may capitalize on an ethnic identity and ethnic festivals to provide themselves with a distinguishing identity. Other towns may create an artists' community or find some other way to stand out such as creating historical villages (e.g. Colonial Williamsburg) amidst landscapes that seem more and more mass produced. These practices bring up the question of authenticity of place. "Indeed, locals may find themselves dealing with tourists to such an extent that they end up trying to look more 'authentic' than otherwise. They act so as to confirm touristic impressions of what a local should look like" (57). Is there an authentic and *inauthentic* identification with place and is one real and one is not real? How much do all of our experiences contribute to the whole of our identity with place?

SUMMARY

Today, there is an even stronger tug between space and place, between more globalized placelessness and the personal identity that comes with an appreciation of local diversity. However, instead of thinking that loss of local community is the loss of community altogether, perhaps we need to think of community and community membership in new ways. We will still find identity in place, we will still view our lives from being *in-the-world,* and our world will still be either expanded or limited by what we care about however we come to define this through our intention and being embedded in the world.

4. PLACE OR SPACE?

By Mike Crang

- Sense of place and belonging
- Placelessness, alienation and globalisation
- Humanistic geography
- Planning, instrumental rationality and place

Geographers make much use of the words "space" and "place". School books through to research monographs are littered with these terms. But rarely below degree level are readers made to ask what these terms mean and whether they are synonymous with each other. A large debate opened up in geography towards the end of the 1970s picking up on precisely these issues, and it is the related approaches that this chapter will outline. First, there has to be a little context for the discussion, providing an idea of why the debate opened up in particular ways. The majority of this chapter will be spent exploring arguments that the modern world involves the erosion of place specificity through global forces and a consequent impoverishment of human variety and experience. This chapter will look at how some writers have attempted to distinguish the affective, or emotional, relationship people can have with places in contrast to alienation from increasingly globalised spaces.

Schools of Thought

Much of the impetus for this debate in geography came from two competing versions of what geography is basically about, versions that in different forms can be traced back to at least the late nineteenth century

> As soon as we agree that the purpose of every science is accomplished when the laws which govern its phenomena are discovered, we must admit that the subject of geography is distributed among a great number of sciences; if however, we would maintain its independence, we must prove that there exists another object for science besides the deduction of laws from phenomena. And it is our opinion that there *is* another object—the thorough understanding of phenomena. Thus we find that the contest between geographers and their adversaries is identical with the old controversy between historical and physical methods. One party claims that the ideal aim of science ought to be the discovery of general laws; the other maintains that it is the investigation of phenomena themselves.
>
> (Franz Boas, 1887, cited in Stocking 1974:9)

The version of geography that had gained prominence in the 1960s regarded the essence of the discipline to be *spatial science*. This version worked on spatial models, quantitative studies and so forth, looking for regularities and patterns in spatial phenomena that might reveal general processes for distributing activities over space or even lead to discovering spatial "laws". The contrasting vision of geography, one championed by Carl Sauer (Chapter 2) and probably the more traditional version, saw geography as the study of the "uniqueness of place" or "areal differentiation"—that is, what makes places individual. The two approaches have been contrasted as *nomothetic*—about predicting regular patterns over space—and *idiographic*—describing the specifics of places. By the end of the 1960s people were speaking of a "quantitative revolution" having driven the nomothetic version into a dominant position. This defined geography as the study of distribution in space rather than particular places. In the late 1970s two trends helped reignite this debate: one inside the discipline, one outside. First, inside the discipline the growth of humanistic geography led to a re-evaluation of what studying places might mean. Previously it had tended to degenerate into regional monographs looking at the way physical, economic, social and cultural factors (normally in that order) interacted in a particular region. Now humanistic geography shifted the focus to ask more incisive questions about how people related to places (see also Chapter 4). The second trend was a critique coming from both humanism and some forms of Marxism about the sort of thinking that dominated nomothetic geography. Marxists such as Herbert Marcuse (1964), Max Horkheimer and Theodor Adorno (1947) were deeply concerned that the idea of "social laws" and a science of society was being used as, or unintentionally becoming, an instrument of social control and domination. Within geography this could be seen in the rethinking by a once prominent "quantifier" Gunnar Olsson who in his 1975 book, *Birds in Egg*, criticised nomothetic geography for using "a simplified and dehumanising conception of man [sic]" (1975:500) and further worrying that "scientific methodology can be made the handmaiden of authoritarian ideology", until "at the end is a society of puppets with no dreams to dream and nothing to be sorry for" (1975:496). Humanistic writers were often critical of Marxism but shared a concern that the world was becoming more alienating. The calculus of rationality was reducing diversity and restricting individuality in attempts to produce a more orderly and efficient system. Nomothetic science was seen as symptomatic of this process. In one of the first works to explicitly label itself humanistic, Ley and Samuels (1979:2–3) saw one of the tasks to act as a corrective for scientistic approaches. These, they argued, had divided humans into a series of quantifiable attributes and what was needed was a more holistic, actually "human", approach to put Humpty Dumpty together again. As Edward Relph (1981:17) put it, such moves expressed "the desire to develop an alternative to what can be called the 'scientistic geography'—that is the unthinking and uncritical use of scientific method to study all human and social matters of interest to geographers".

This chapter explores the connections between different ideas of geography and the ideas of space and place. It starts by examining how we might think about people relating to places. The first take on this will be a look at the affective links of people and places followed by a look at the philosophical traditions that have been used to help think about this—phenomenology and existentialism. The following section considers whether globalisation erodes senses of place. Taking this a little deeper, the chapter will suggest how capitalist economies may be creating pseudo-places. Finally the chapter poses some questions to this narrative, first in terms of works on modernity that do not see it as some story of declining individuality and finally by situating humanist critiques in terms of their relationship to mass culture.

ON A ROAD TO NOWHERE: THE EROSION OF PLACE

Approaches to "place" have suggested the vital importance of a sense of "belonging" to human beings. The basic geography of life is not encapsulated in a series of map grid references. It extends beyond the idea of location, and thus beyond the ken of locational science. Crucially people do not simply locate themselves, they define themselves through a sense of place. When asked who we are, many of us start with "I'm a Geordie", "I'm a Bristolian", "a Londoner", "a New Yorker" or whatever.

These places are more than simply spots on the globe. The place is standing for a set of cultural characteristics; the place says something not only about where you live or come from but who you are. This can be simply a matter of stereotypes but it has more to it than that. As we go about our daily lives, we learn patterns of interaction, patterns of behaviour, that become taken for granted. We have only to move, go on holiday, undertake fieldwork to see how such patterns are very often place-specific. The continued repetition of particular sorts of behaviour comes to be associated with particular places, and newcomers are socialised into the sorts of behaviour found at those places. The result is places provide an anchor of shared experiences between people and continuity over time. Spaces become places as they become "time-thickened". They have a past and a future that binds people together round them.

This lived connection binds people and places together. It enables people to define themselves and to share experiences with others and form themselves into communities. One of the impetuses to study such relationships was the widespread feeling that they were in some sense under threat. And if relationships to places were undermined then so were communities and people's identities.

> We are told in countless books by architects and historians that cities have become formless malignant growths, and that the pretentious towers of glass and steel within them demonstrate all the design qualities of cardboard boxes covered in graph paper. These office blocks are apparently reoccupied daily by armies of clone-like organisation men and women, issuing from the suburban blandscape wherein lives a race of uniformly bland suburbanites, striving to indulge their materialist tendencies in the latest model of a video-recorder, a package tour to Spain or, at the very least, in the ineffable sameness of the umpteen-billionth hamburger.
>
> (Relph 1981:13)

If it is true that specificities of place are being eroded and if, Relph continues, "the critics are correct, our lives should somehow be diminished" (1981:14). The paradox is that if we were to ask the suburbanites they would scarcely say their life is diminished by the affluent lifestyle described above. Relph suggests modern landscapes are ambivalent "manifestations of technical accomplishment and widespread material prosperity" and yet at the same time of "aesthetic confusion, ethical poverty and a disturbing degree of dependence on technical expertise" (1981:14–15). In this sense, while modern technology creates material affluence it endangers the affective aspects of places. The form of planning encouraged by a narrowly "scientistic" understanding of places may improve living standards but produce dehumanising landscapes (1981:64) where the "current pressure for efficiency and control" and "fast-food and suburban development which establish that modern landscape-making with its relentless rationalism, denies feelings, ignores ethics and minimises the responsibility of individuals for the environments in which they live."

Humanism, Science and Spirituality

Such ideas of the erosion of community and place may need to be set in some historic context. They certainly can be traced back to the ideas of the Romantic poets in the nineteenth century. Chapter 4 suggested how we could see the relationship of poetry, industry and ideas of landscape in the work of the Romantic poet Blake. It is possible to argue the Romantic movement was a reaction to the rise of a rationalised space. At the end of the eighteenth century, the *Enlightenment* gave rise both to humanism in its modern form and rationalistic science, expressed in the belief humans could shape, control and master the earth through free inquiry and science. An example of how this impacted on ideas of space and place was Thomas Jefferson's plans for the North American continent. Jefferson set out a geometrical division of the then known United States, subdividing the space according to proportions and rational divisions, laying out the acreage of plots for townships in carefully planned proportions, taking up the gridiron pioneered by the Spanish in Latin America and defining what plots should go to public buildings (schools, town halls), what to parks and what for residences. Here, then, is a prime example of mapping *abstract space* on to territory, dividing the land up according to an elegant principle and rational logic hundreds of miles removed from the actual scene. Such is a *Cartesian* vision of the world (named after the Enlightenment philosopher René Descartes) which separates the observer from the landscape and imposes an intellectual order upon it. "Clearly the notion of landscape which prevailed in the eighteenth century was closely tied to a humanism which stressed the authority of human reason over nature. This attitude has been preserved in scientific, technical and some academic approaches to landscape up to the present day" (Relph 1981:58). In contrast, the Romantic poets looked for the sublime in the landscape, something that would speak to them of divine beauty and purpose, of awe of the majesty of nature. As Wordsworth put it in a 1798 poem to his sister:

It is in the hour of feeling.

One moment now may give us more

Than years of toiling reason.

(Cited in Relph 1981:36)

This stressed spiritual experience of place rather than rational understanding. It spoke to the unique experience of place which transcended the ordinary. Such transcending moments were suggested to express the divine order. The context for the rise of Romantic ideas can be exemplified by Ruskin's sympathetic comments on the development of Romantic painting:

> Spirituality had been cast out of the world and a mechanical and materialist universe substituted; the aridity of this universe had effectively driven the Romantics to natural scenery both as a source of beauty in contrast to the ugly and false modern world of men, and for its intimations of divine order.

> (Cited in Relph 1981:38)

Technology and the Experience of Space

If such was the feeling in the nineteenth century, then developments at its end and the beginning of the twentieth century strengthened the trend for abstract ideas of space to dominate. The advent of railroads meant that the sensation of travel was one of a uniform movement—separated from the world in a way coaches toiling over winter roads were not. Space could be homogenised into units of time (Schivelbusch 1977). Meanwhile railroads required more accurate time-keeping. At Bristol Temple Meads station a three-handed clock had to be installed with two minute hands, one for London and a second, eight minutes behind, for Bristol. Up to that period noon meant the time when the sun reached its zenith, which is eight minutes later in Bristol than in London. It is easy to imagine the time-tabling difficulties these local times caused railways; difficulties compounded over the vast scale of countries like the USA. So at this period we find uniform time zones imposed, and local timings begin to give way. The telegraph brought near instant transmission of information, the radio brought such transmission to thousands.

The confluence of all these trends meant that the Italian Futurists, such as Martinetti in 1908, would proclaim a manifesto dedicated to functional buildings and with a motif for a new age of speed and light (Thrift 1995). The period saw the end of ornate styles, with floral and baroque touches, and the rise of architects such as Le Corbusier, declaring the house should be seen as a "machine for living in". In the midst of this came the First World War, the first total war, where the technical abilities not just to create weapons but the organisational ability to support armies on a mass scale was shown to its inhuman potential. The machine age had its first machine war (Relph 1981) where people became numbers in a dehumanising slaughter, where casualties became part of an obscene balance-sheet in a war of attrition. At the same period came the rise of Taylorism, time and motion studies that broke down the workers' jobs into tiny discrete tasks, allowing jobs to be subdivided into tasks of mind-numbing repetition, and following that the Fordist assembly line heralding the mass consumer age (see Chapter 9).

It is in response to this that writers began to look on technical advance as bearing too high a price tag. The human landscapes of places to which people are attached are sacrificed to placeless, soulless new spaces which are functionally more efficient but reduce the quality of experience. Relph argues that "further attempts to develop and apply rationalistic techniques of design and planning will result at best in incremental improvements. Indeed, with the continuing arrogation of responsibility to specialists, coupled with all sorts of remote and unanticipated consequences stemming from new technologies, they will probably do far more harm than good" (1981:18). Scientism and the endless pursuit of technological improvement do not speak to issues of ethics or values. Indeed they have declared themselves value-free or neutral. This lack of connection by technical experts is seen as both disempowering and dangerous. W.G. Hoskins (see Chapter 2) in his most famous book, *The Making of the English Landscape* (1955), can barely bring himself to comment on anything "made" in the twentieth century. He stops only long enough to decry the rows of mass-built Victorian houses as "barracks" and to deplore the ugliness of the "slug-like trails" of "atom bombers" in the sky. The technical and rational planning of the landscape is alien to his vision of an organically growing landscape.

North American suburbs with relentless series of plots, carved out and divided up on a geometrical pattern, or the production of thousands of identical houses each sold as "a dream of a home of your own" provide fertile grounds for arguing that these spaces may well destroy a sense of place just as much as tower blocks built according Corbusier's maxim. The important point humanistic geographers have made is not to blame the inhabitants, but to criticise the culture of planners—that is, a faith in scientific, technical logic to the exclusion of ideas of place values. Crucially we have already seen that inhabiting a place over time leads to its incorporation into local people's identities lending a feeling of endurance and persistence. This theme of bounding and controlling places will be explored in a later section. For now the focus may instead be on how people make spaces into "homes" (Relph 1976:17). The philosopher Martin Heidegger argued *dwelling* is one of the essential properties of human existence. Contrary to Cartesian ideas, humans cannot exist as free-floating minds, but rather have to exist in relationship to the world around them—what Heidegger describes as "*being-in-the-world*"(Collier 1991). The next section looks to explore these philosophical underpinnings behind these ideas of relationships to place.

PHENOMENOLOGY/EXISTENTIALISM

One of the major philosophies drawn on in thinking about what a "sense of place" might mean was derived from the work of Martin Heidegger and his reworking of phenomenology. Initially this was a doctrine developed by the German philosopher Edmund Husserl at the beginning of the twentieth century. The way its insights were taken up by Heidegger and later in French Existentialism provides the starting point for a theorisation that gives more purchase on experiential life. From the multiplicity of ideas associated with these philosophical theories geographers picked out three themes that seemed to speak directly about relationships to places. The first came directly from Husserl and dealt with "intentionality," the second deals with the idea of essences, and the third comes from Heidegger and Existentialists, such as Sartre, which dealt with the situated nature of life and knowledge.

Intended Objects and Making Meaning

Husserl was intrigued by what goes to make up an object, what constitutes intelligible phenomena—hence the name of the theory. Husserl produced what is known as an *ontology*—that is, a theory of what exists. His theory saw things not simply as existing, but existing at different levels. While there was an observable world, he argued, there was more to objects than that. One of the ways he suggested this was so was through *intentionality*. For instance, take a football. It is obviously a real object but what is it? The amalgam of leather, plastic and stitching only becomes a "football" when someone intends to kick it or use it for that game. The object only really becomes something when it is seen in light of its intended use. Thus his ontology suggests the phenomenon we call a football resides not only in the thing itself but in how we approach it. There is an *intended object* as well as a material thing. In order to work out the "intentions" that went to form objects, Husserl suggested bracketing out preconceptions and thinking afresh about the taken-for-granted assumptions in everyday life. Such an idea opened up new possibilities in geography. Places were not just a set of accumulated data but involved human intentions as well. We should not just count how many shops there are on a high street, but what the high street means to it users. This idea that there is more to objects and things than their surface appearance—that there is a depth of meaning—has also been developed to think about the essence of things.

Essences and Authenticity

The essence of a thing might be described as the characteristic that defines the object, in that sense its "essential quality". In terms of places this takes the idea a little further than Sauer's (1962:321) definition of geography as dealing with facts that are "place facts" and places that are unique combinations of these things. It suggests the idea of a depth beyond these simple facts; that there is more to place than a unique collection of things. Thinking back to Chapter 4, this has often been used to think about what is called the "*genius loci*"—the unique spirit of place. It is used to suggest that people experience something beyond the physical or sensory properties of places and can feel an attachment to a spirit of place. If the meaning of place extends beyond the visible, beyond the evident into the realms of emotion and feeling then one answer may be turning to literature or the arts as being ways people can express these meanings. Sometimes the claim has been taken further to suggest that not only do places have essences but also that one of the essential features of humanity is this relationship to meaningful places. Thus, returning to Relph's (1976:1) work, he suggests that "[t]o be human is to live in a world that is filled with significant places: to be human is to have and know your place". One of the questions this work raises is whether people can experience places differently or whether the essence, and meaning of a place are universal. Sometimes the phenomenological approach suggests that there is only one true, or "authentic", relationship to a place, and other relationships are either imperfect or "inauthentic". The concern for authenticity comes through the ideas of Martin Heidegger. In his terminology these are ostensibly not value judgements, but generally they are heavily overlain with values, no matter how strongly denied. Thus Heidegger associates inauthentic relationships with *das man*, meaning "the mob" or "the crowd", a term which negatively contrasts urban life with the figure of the rustic peasant in his work (Bourdieu 1991). It is worth being careful, then, that certain political stances—valorising an idea of a rural folk—do not creep unnoted into accounts.

Embedded Knowledge

Heidegger can be useful since he emphasises that the human condition is not that of a rational, free-floating subject. It is very much not the subject of Descartes's "*cognito, ergo sum*" (I think, therefore I am). The human subject only becomes able to think and act, argued Heidegger, through *being-in-the-world*; or, in Sartre's terms, existence comes before essence. Think of a clearing in a wood:can we say the clearing exists independently of the wood? Just so, argued Heidegger, we can't think of humans without thinking of them as embedded in the world. This has two important consequences for the argument here. First, people tend to think and act through material objects. Thus a place is a product of how we interact with it—we have different intentions towards a place if we live there, work there or are passing through on a journey. These all produce different "places" for us. Thus Relph (1976:5) develops from ideas of intentionality to say that consciousness is always consciousness of *something*, not free-floating, and it starts from our position in the world. This is as true of how geographers study places as about people living there. It depends how we approach a place, how we study it, what "results" we will get. To coin a phrase, you have only to pick up a hammer to notice a lot of things that need thumping. Our knowledge about places is not independent of how we go about getting it. Heidegger thus provides one way of rethinking the different meanings places can have. Taking up this point Seamon (1980:148) argues for a focus on the "inescapable immersion in a geographical world" and goes on to suggest how attention must be focused on how people relate to the world at hand, so geography should "unbury and describe this given-ness, of which people usually lose sight because of the mundaneness and taken-for-grantedness of their everyday situation" (1980:149).

Perhaps more importantly is a second implication of this work. Heidegger does not talk about intentions so much as *care*. Since we are always engaged with the world, we must focus our attention on particular aspects at any given time. We thus have different types and levels of care for different things at different times. The world might then be seen as comprising different fields of care, where distant events may be less threatening, and distant places less essential to ourselves than those closely involved (Relph 1976:38). Thus our knowledge of the world is always em-placed, it is always starting from and based around places as centres of our "care" about the world. This approach suggests we always make sense of the world through the materials at hand, not from abstract schema. Nor are objects studied independently of their contexts—rather experience is seen as unified or holistic. Such provides a clear critique of "scientific" studies of place. Relph (1976:5) argues that geography is stretched between knowledge and existence—with the continual danger of abandoning itself to science and losing contact with its sources of meaning. Heidegger thus locates geographical knowledge more closely with existence than abstraction.

Geographers have used this idea of care to look at *inside* and *outside* relationships to places. This is not simply in terms of physical perspective, but experiential relationships and types of knowledge. Scientific studies tend to concentrate on the outside stance, looking at a place as an object rather than experiencing life within it. Indeed, Relph (1976:51) argued that "[t]his attitude of objective outsideness has a long tradition in academic geography and is implicitly apparent in beliefs that geography is some kind of integrating super-science or that there is a real objective geography of places that can be described once and for all." The cataloguing of information about places is looking at them through lens of "instrumental rationality" (ibid.:52) rather than seeing them as organising experience. To this end Relph defines four different sorts of space, or knowledges about space, produced by different relationships to places. At the first step "pragmatic" spaces are organised by our bodily situation (left or right, up or down). Second is perceptual space, organised through our intentions and centred on us—what we focus upon, what we look at, thus tending to be centred on the observer. Existential space is informed by cultural structures as much as our perceptions—it is a space full of social meaning (see Chapter 3). This space is defined in relationship to some human experience or task.

Finally, cognitive space is how we abstractly model spatial relationships. It would be a mistake to use only this last idea of space, as geographers too often tend to.

Box 4.1 Territorial control and urban policy

The desire to control territory has formed a central part in arguments over crime and community in the city. Some commentators have looked at the current urban environment and interpreted crime and vandalism as signs of community breakdown and alienation. One of the proposed solutions for this is the reassertion of community control. This vision sees the city as a dense mosaic of interlocking communities, a patchwork of local groups policing themselves. One part of this is seen in the physical control over space. Commentators such as Alice Coleman (1985) looked at the rise of crime in cities and saw it as a breakdown of a moral order. This they identified with the rebuilding of cities and the rise of public housing projects and tower blocks. One of their arguments was that the communal land around such buildings became a no-man's-land, it was not owned by either the individual or community. One of the proposals for reducing crime was thus the introduction of "defensible space," space to which access rights were controlled—which would give inhabitants more control over their local environment. Such devices include partitioning open spaces, controlling access and exit points to communal areas and so forth.

TERRITORIALITY AND BOUNDING PLACES

Connected to these studies of how people have a place-centred knowledge came a concern with whether people always sought to define themselves and defend themselves (not just physically but also psychologically) through control of territory by creating a bounded (and often exclusive) domain. Taking up ideas of insider and outsider relationships to place, this work suggests people actively structure groups and define each other through creating insiders and outsiders. Peoples from around the world can be found forming groups that both control, define and are defined by territory. It is certainly not something confined to remote peoples. In the 1980s in the USA there was a trend for adolescents to assert their identity through "tagging," marking public spaces with personal or group names. In Los Angeles, it is possible to map out whole ranges of territories controlled by different gangs—demarcated by the graffiti around the city (Davis 1990).

It is not only public housing that has become de-territorialised by nationalised planning. So too has much commercial property, in the interests of standardised products and economic rationality. Instead of a landscape such a homogeneous collection of buildings has been termed a "flatscape" (Gurevitch, cited in Relph 1976:57). In the terms of phenomenology such a "flatscape" or deterritorialised landscape promotes an existential outsideness—people do not feel like they belong and thus do not care for their environment. The planning of space through abstract ideas actually militates against establishing effective communities according to this argument. To exemplify this Relph (1976:51) cites Henry Miller:

> America is full of places. Empty places. And all these empty places are crowded. Just jammed with empty souls. All at loose ends, all seeking diversion. As though their chief object of existence was to forget.

The contrast drawn is with a sense of unique places to which people can feel they belong. The loss of bounded, controlled territory further undermines people's senses of identity, where normally people control this through relationships of "I", "We" and "Other". If "I" is the personal sense of identity, then "we" is the shared identity often sustained through shared relationships to places, and "other" can be defined as outsiders (see Chapter 6). If the mediation of this process through places breaks down, then people's identities may become less stable (for a different account, see Chapter 10). The loss of a sense of belonging would make the world more alienating, since it would increase the feeling of loneliness. Tuan (1992:36) observes there has been a steady trend of reducing the communal belonging since the Middle Ages, an increasing individuation of people producing the "threatening awareness of being alone in a world that is ultimately unresponsive". Unresponsive because we have fewer people bound together, linked to us by more than their interest and goodwill. Tuan (1992:44) goes on to cite the novelist Albert Camus to explain this chilling knowledge that "it is only our will that keeps these people attached to us (not that they wish us ill but simply because they don't care) and that the others are *always* able to be interested in something else". Place, Tuan argues, "helps us forget our separateness and the world's indifference. More generally speaking, culture makes this amnesia possible. Culture integrates us into the world through shared language and custom, behaviour and habits of thought" (ibid.).

GLOBAL SPACE—ERODING PLACE?

Many of the trends towards the homogenisation of places relate to the creation of a global space through improved communications, both physical and electronic. To continue focusing on Relph's work (1976:92), he suggests that the spread of markets bringing distant produce, the increase of highways and mass transport have undermined the idea of a locality. Instead there are all too often only moments in the spread of standardised tastes and fashions. These it is argued are not "public" trends but "mass" trends, not common standards developed in a locality by a community—as assumed by Sauer's idea of the cultural landscape (Chapter 2)—but developed by designers and professional taste engineers elsewhere. Ritzer (1993) argues that the McDonald's fast-food chain typifies this process. Indeed he suggests naming the process McDonaldisation of the world. The chain prides itself on producing exactly standardised products—even if in France the Big Mac becomes La Royale, the product is the same. Staff are trained to greet customers with the same phrases, the same manufactured enthusiasm and courtesy (see Chapter 9). There is a standard range of designs for the restaurant itself and a set of façades for its exterior. The characters and labels used to "brand" a standardised product are often seen as superficial. Relph (1981) commented that the playground outside a McDonald's, "McDonaldland", was precisely a combination of bright shiny exteriors, labelled with exciting TV characters to entice children in before leaving them disappointed at the banality of the product:

> McDonaldland epitomised everything to do with commercial strip development. In its brightness and its suggestion of fantasy that is not realised, in its superficial gloss to disguise a very ordinary product, in its intimations of adventure and freedom that barely obscure a precise and rigid organisation, and especially in its obvious and seductive appeal for commercial ends.
>
> (1981:73)

The relationship to territory, and indeed to nature through the mass production of animals for fast food, is suggested to be the extreme of the technical relationship criticised at the start of this chapter. However, we can be more sophisticated in thinking through the spread on a "placeless" society.

Meyrowitz (1985) noted the shift from cultures inhabiting specific areas to a more mobile society, so whereas people used to interact in a cultural area, relationships are now increasingly distantiated. Thus many interactions occur at meeting points, or "liminal" border spaces between cultures. He suggests that in terms of executives and corporate elites we might study the non-local cultures of airports as these people fly from meeting to meeting. In a modern world it may be that there are fewer cultures that are "place-bound." Perhaps they were so closely linked to places in the past only by the limitations of communication rather than in some essential way, in which case the "loss of place" does not really matter. Auge (1995:34) suggests using the word place to refer to a "culture localised in time and space" but suggests that we might see the current situation as one of "spatial overabundance", where elements of cultures often associated with different places are coming together in the same space at the same time (see Chapter 10). It is tempting in this situation to look back with nostalgia towards some imagined past stability, but this is not a useful research tactic. Nor is examining all cultures as though they are, or should, be localised and bounded. Instead we need to look at how in some cases cultures are localised while in others there are "non-places". So we might look at the distinctiveness of the two, accepting that both forms exist. In this case we might look at Meyrowitz's airport lounge and say the difference between this "non-place" and a "place" is that the form is dominated by "contractual solitariness", individuals or small groups only relating to wider society through limited and specific interactions, compared to "places" where there is an "organic sociality", where people have long term relationships, and interactions do not solely serve an immediate functional purpose (Auge 1995:94). In these non-places our understandings are thus governed by texts, be they instructions to show your passport, timetables, or adverts suggesting products we should buy. Such situations can be found on roads, in supermarkets, at airports, and in increasing numbers. In each case the relationship to the environment is distanced and often dominated by images—thus on motorways travel is punctuated by signposts to places the motorway now bypasses and as we look out of the car window, we are set apart and distanced from the landscape—in phenomenological terms, we are existential outsiders.

Americanisation and a Geography of Taste

The temptation to look for some ideal point in the past to contrast these trends to is very strong—and indeed is reinforced in the philosophy of Heidegger. However, such change also has a geography in itself. For instance much of the worry over placelessness in Europe can be seen as a worry over mass culture or the "commodification of culture". That is a fear that local, "authentic" forms of culture are being displaced by mass-produced commercial forms. We can see these worries when Euro Disney near Paris was compared in the popular press to taking a blow torch to a Rembrandt—as an act of cultural violence. Mass culture has a particular symbolic geography here, where mass often means American (Brantlinger and Naremore 1991). Many of the European arguments over loss of uniqueness have to be read in the context of United States cultural and economic dominance in the latter half of this century. The European relationship to US culture industries is thus very often one of threat and loss (Morley and Robins 1993:19).

Chapter 5 outlined how the encounter with the "New World" helped shape ideas of what was European. But we can also find a strong romance for America in contemporary Europe. Earlier, road movies were mentioned as one way film and landscape are linked together (Chapter 6). In some cases the romance of the road movie in Europe is that it represents America as freedom from a claustrophobia felt in Europe; it offers an escape from being tied to places. Thus the film director Wim Wenders portrays America as a place and an idea, a country that privileges mobility—that invented the term and thing called a mobile home. Such an idea of mobility and being at home contrasts with the sorts of visions of belonging in a place seen above and associated with ideas of "homeland", *Heimat* or *hembygd*. This is the characteristic Wenders finds attractive and uses so that "[t]he idea is that, not being at home [my heroes] are nevertheless at home with themselves … Identity means not having to have a home" (in Morley and Robins 1993:25). Instead of thinking about the loss of community in places, we might follow ideas about the "communion of the freeway" and look at this experience of mobility as being about a different sense of belonging (see Chapter 6). Equally the spread of the "strip", the commercial landscape of neon and cars is not necessarily seen as a bad thing. Thus architect Robert Venturi (1973) suggested that planners needed to learn from the strip rather than despise it. In its unplanned, gaudy, commercialism running down the side of major roads it spoke to what people wanted and enjoyed. By comparison architects and planners often spoke for people, in a paternalistic manner, telling them what they *should* want. Venturi argued that the truly popular American architecture was Las Vegas, not the sort that won academic prizes. What was needed was an appreciation of the drama of the strip at night.

We must be cautious not to impose our own ideas about "placeless" landscapes on others. Thus Campbell (1992) argues that on many urban estates with serious crime problems, the male youths often involved have an extremely strong sense of belonging, of occupying and controlling the territory. They are anything but placeless. Or in terms of landscapes that seem alienating we might do well to think of Rowles's work with the elderly. He found they had senses of place about imagined places as well—both those of memory and distant places associated with where children now lived. Thus he writes of one of his informants:

> She was reluctant to talk about physical restriction, reduced access to services, spending more time at home, problems of social abandonment, or fears for the future. Instead, as we sat in her parlor poring over treasured scrapbooks in which she kept a record of her life, she would animatedly describe trips to Florida … the current activities of her grand-daughter in Detroit, a thousand miles distant. She would describe incidents in her neighborhood during the early years of her residence. Blinded by preconceptions I could not comprehend at first the richness of the taken-for-granted world she was unveiling.

(1978:55)

The landscape for his informants was more than a picture or a collage—it was a "reservoir of feeling"(ibid.:59). It is crucial then that when thinking through senses of place, these ideas are seen in a social context about what appeals to whom, about how different people may feel they belong in different ways and value landscapes very differently.

Manufacturing Difference

There is an industry that sets out to "imagineer" places, to create "uniqueness" in order to attract attention, visitors and, in the end, money. Landscapes can be engineered, their culture commodified for financial gain. If places are becoming increasingly alike, the rewards for standing out are increasing. Such manufactured difference often takes the form of façades placed over standardised substructures—designed to tone in with an area or to distinguish an otherwise ordinary building. This tendency, in part, gives rise to criticisms of a superficial or depthless culture—where apparently historic façades are actually modern fabrications. This would seem to contradict Relph's assertion that "there has been a relative desacralising and desymbolising of the environment … particularly for everyday life" (1976:65). Instead we might argue that increasing attention is being given to the symbolism of the built environment. These may not be the symbols of allegedly organic community or the religious symbolism of Gothic cathedrals, but symbols they are. Western cosmologies still take material form—but are now expressed through commodities (see Chapter 8). The fear of a homogeneous, rationalised world has haunted the twentieth century—the fear of what Max Weber called the "iron cage of bureaucratic rationality". As Chapter 6 showed, films such as Fritz Lang's *Metropolis* worried about the effects of "instrumental rationality" giving rise to totalitarian systems, where people became simply numbers or functions. However, the increasing use of façades, the overt concentration on symbolism, suggests a different vision of society. Fritz Lang's vision hardly fits in with say the Tonga Rooms in the Fairmount Hotel in San Francisco, where the bar has been themed as a Pacific Island—complete with thatched "hut" roofs for tables, waterfall behind the counter, artificial lake, with an island hut for the band and simulated tropical thunderstorms. To characterise this we might prefer Ernest Gellner's adaptation that this is the "rubber cage of fictitious re-enchantment" (cited in Anderson 1990:71). It is this shift that has led some to characterise the world as moving from modern rationalism to postmodern style.

Such simulation (discussed further in Chapter 8) can be argued to create "pseudo-places" that only exist through the active creation of mythical spaces. Phenomenologically they are suggested to be "inauthentic", being outside inventions rather than expressions of the culture of the locale. Their symbolism tends to be created by and directed at outsiders, so they might be called "other-directed" (Relph 1976:92). A prime example is Disneyland or what Relph lampoons as Vacationlands:

> The products of "Disneyfication" are absurd, synthetic places made up of a surrealistic combination of history, myth, reality and fantasy that have little relationship with a particular geographical setting.
>
> (Ibid.:95)

Examples of the process would obviously include such places as "Bibleland" in the USA (Lowenthal 1984), the Pare d'Asterix in France and could also be extended to include the rise of themed pubs (say "Irish pubs" run by a UK chain). One of the industries most associated with this trend is the tourist industry. Commentators such as MacCannell (1976, 1992) have argued that many tourist sites sell visitors an image of an "authentic" place. That is, they "stage" authentic places—in recreating local customs. So the Basque town of Fuentarrabia had a civic celebration of its history of independence in which all the locals took parts, but since the 1960s this has been marketed not as a festival for the locals but as one put on for the tourists (Greenwood 1977:136). The diversity of cultures celebrated by Sauer becomes the provider of local colour to a mass tourist industry. Indeed locals may find themselves dealing with tourists to such an extent that they end up trying to look more "authentic" than otherwise. They act so as to confirm tourists impressions of what a local should look like.

SUMMARY

These accounts of the dilemmas over a sense of place open up many problematics that geographers are still exploring. It is a geography of modern life, or even postmodern life, that has trends of homogenisation and differentiation across the globe:

> Modern environments and experiences cut across all boundaries of geography and ethnicity, of class and nationality, of religion and ideology; in this sense modernity can be said to unite all mankind. But it is

a paradoxical unity, a unity of disunity; it pours us all into a maelstrom of perpetual disintegration and renewal, of struggle and contradiction, of ambiguity and anguish.

(Berman 1983:15)

It is possible to see the challenge of current societies to "make oneself somehow at home in the maelstrom"(Berman 1983:345). Rather than pine for some past community, it is important to recognise that along with the loss of organic communities come new freedoms, new opportunities and excitements—the chance to escape the claustrophobia sometimes produced in closed societies, the possibilities of chance encounters and new experiences. The agenda for geography might then be to find new ways of feeling at "[h]ome in a world of expanding horizons and dissolving boundaries" (Morley and Robins 1993:5). Chapter 10 takes these issues up by looking at spaces not as containers of cultures but as being formed from routes and from crossings of people and cultures. These will suggest that the idea of place and a single culture coinciding may be inappropriate and indeed may rely on inappropriate ideas of human experience (Augé 1995).

FURTHER READING

Augé, M. (1995) *Non-Places: Introduction to an Anthropology of Supermodernity.* Verso, London.

Ley, D. and Samuels, M. (1978) *Humanistic Geography: Prospects and Problems.* Croom Helm, London.

Meyrowitz, J. (1985) *No Sense of Place.* Oxford University Press, Oxford.

Relph, E. (1976) *Place and Placelessness.* Pion, London.

———(1981) *Rational Landscape and Humanistic Geography.* Croom Helm, London.

———(1987) The Modern Urban Landscape. Croom Helm, London.

Ritzer, G. (1993) *The McDonaldization of Society: An Investigation into the Changing Character of Contemporary Social Life.* Pine Forge Press, Thousand Oaks.

Rowles, G. (1978) *Prisoners of Space? Exploring the Geographical Experience of Older People.* Westview, Boulder.

Sack, R. (1986) *Human Territoriality: Its Theory and History.* Cambridge University Press, Cambridge.

STUDY QUESTIONS

1. What is the main argument presented in this chapter?
2. Space and place are founded on which two traditions in geography? Give examples.
3. How is "place" connected to a sense of belonging?
4. What is it that makes "place" unique?
5. Explain "Spaces become places as they become 'time-thickened.'"
6. How is it that the specificities of place are being eroded?
7. Contrast the Age of Enlightenment with the Romantic Movement in relationship to space and place.
8. How did the advent of the railroad at the end of the 19th century change our perception of space?
9. How did technical advances that appeared in WWI, apparent in Taylorism and Fordism, mark their presence regarding the tension between space and place?
10. In what way or ways did phenomenology open up new possibilities in geography regarding places?

11. How is existentialism applied to a geographic sense of place?
12. What is the significance of embedded knowledge and care to our sense of place?
13. What are some of the factors that account for a greater homogenization of places?
14. How does Relph characterize the viewpoint of some critics of city and suburban landscapes and the landscapes of material affluence?
15. In what way are suburbanized places linked to rationalized space?
16. Do people always seek to define themselves and defend themselves through control of territory by creating a bounded (and often exclusive) domain? What happens when this process breaks down?
17. According to Meyrowitz, what does a more mobilized society do to our sense of place and of relationships? Provide an example.
18. How does our author suggest we look at this dichotomy of localized place and "non-place?"
19. What is meant by a "commodification of culture?" Provide an example.
20. What does it mean to "imagineer" a place and why is it done? Provide an example.
21. What is your author's view of such modern fabrications?
22. What is the drawback to selling visitors an image of an "authentic" place?

Chapter 5 Snapshot
Sacred Spaces and Tourist Places

Sacred spaces and tourist places often go hand-in-hand. Although religious adherents and tourists may be looking at the same physical place, their meanings and experiences may be very different. As we read in the previous article, *Place or Space?*, places can have different layers of meaning. We call this "a simultaneity of places emerg[ing] in parallel geographies of both the sacred and the touristic" (65). For Thomas S. Bremer, what distinguishes place from space is meaningfulness and value. "What begins as undifferentiated space becomes place as we get to know it better and endow it with value" (65). This is similar to Crang's "time-thickened" places. Bremer, however, makes a distinction between two kinds of places, what he calls the *locative* and the *itinerant*. The locative represents the permanence of a landscape, something that does not change over time. You can think of the Empire State Building in New York or San Francisco's Golden Gate Bridge. But in contrast, the itinerant represents that which does shift and change over time. In a fast-moving urban environment, for example, a store that was a women's accessory shop one week could turn around and become a local ethnic food mart or shoe store the next. The truth is, all landscapes are in some way itinerant over time; it's just that some changes take longer than others. Any sense of place as locative, that it is stable and unchanging, is just a perception. Take, for example, the Twin Towers in New York City. For so long they were the dominant profile on the New York skyline, built to last, emphasizing an "enduring stability that makes a place distinctly recognisable" (66). Yet, as we saw with the tragedy on September 11, 2001, the permanence of the Twin Towers was really an illusion. "Today, their absence reminds us that the permanency of place is always a contingent stability; the itinerant nature of place inevitably brings change to otherwise enduring landscapes" (66). Places are contingent (dependent) on both circumstance and time.

FEATURES OF PLACE

So, there is a tension of sorts between the locative and itinerant in all places and this brings up two additional features of place. The first one is that "all places are social" (66). Places are provided with meaning by those that live in or experience them; and, in turn, places can affect the relationships of the people who are there. For example, we provide different meanings for restaurants and churches and, at the same time, those places will also limit the way we act in them. "Priests, ritual specialists, and others who inhabit and control sacred sites command the respect of religious adherents who recognize their importance in part because of their association with the auspicious nature of the site. At the same time, the prestige of the place itself gains recognition due to the presence and activities of religious leaders and specialists who practice there" (66). But meanings can also change over time as social relations change. If these meanings do not change for everyone at the same time, however, conflict can result. We will come back to this point a little later.

The second major feature of place actually has to do with time. Locations have pasts, presents, and futures. "The history of the place and its commemorative value help to maintain personal and collective memories that in turn contribute to contemporary perceptions of self and other" (67). So place has both spatial and temporal characteristics and this relates back to the locative and itinerant characteristics of place as well. The locative has more of a characteristic of timelessness that lies outside of historical time. This enables communities to claim historical precedence and control. The itinerant "derives in part from social contention over the control and significance of the site" (68). One can easily think of the contested territory between the Israelis and the Palestinians. Both claim locative control over the same territory, and both are contesting itinerant changes made by the other. The stability of a place, then, ultimately relies on the tension between ownership and interpretation. "Ownership and interpretation of a particular site involves control over narratives of place. Places are made in human spatial experience, and the stories that people tell of those experiences give places their meanings and sustain them as distinct locales in the landscape. In other words, place gains its meaningfulness and retains its importance in narratives …"(68).

TRAVEL PRACTICES IN DISCOURSES OF PLACE

Space also transforms into places as we travel through them. So we can say that "places … emerge in human practices of travel" (68). There are many types of travel including migration, pilgrimage, and tourism and these include communication networks as well as various institutions (such as banks, travel agencies, and hotels) that facilitate this travel. These junctures, from types of travel to the institutions we depend to help us travel, can, in some ways, define the experience we have of place and become part of the travel stories we tell. There are also barriers against travel. Some people view the new, more stringent security measures at airports to be a barrier to travel or at least would cause some pause of dread. In other cases, there are some places that are open to religious adherents that are not open to tourists. One example of this is the city of Mekkah in Saudi Arabia. Only Moslems can enter the city; tourists are diverted around the city. On the other hand, both religious adherents and tourists can experience the majesty of the Ganges River; for tourists it is one of the most famous rivers in the world while for Hindus, it is their holiest site. Religious sites that are also touristic destinations are dependent on the travel practices mentioned above; however, tourists' and pilgrims' "respective practices and resulting interpretations of [their] significance make distinct places of it" (69). This is Bremer's simultaneity of places, "they remain both religious and touristic" (69), and there are clear distinctions between the two.

The locative and itinerant plays a role here, too. Religious places tend to be more locative. There is a sense of permanence that "transcends the contingencies of human mortality" (69). Sacred sites are expected to survive longer than any one individual and, in fact, they serve as an "enduring symbol of, and orientation for, the continuance of the religious community itself" (69). Such religious sites become the center of the world for their communities, what Eliade calls the *axis mundi*. "These *axes mundi* decree a locative stability that allows the community to endure in a changing world" (70). Bremer uses as an example of the clash between different interpretations of locative place, the attempt of the Church of Jesus Christ of Latter-day Saints in the 19th century to establish a New Jerusalem in North America. The locative claims of the Mormons were at odds with the locative claims of more established Christian sects in the same place who saw the Mormons' attempts as an "itinerant force of an alternative voice" on the already established religious landscape.

PLACES OF TOURISM

Touristic places face other issues. Often tourists want to visit other places without leaving behind the comforts of home; they want to visit new places yet they also want to take something of their places with them. In this way, "tourists can be regarded as exemplary modern subjects" (70). Consumer demand requires that places be commodified (be considered a commodity being presented on the marketplace) to respond to touristic needs; hotels, restaurants, easy access places, language translations, souvenir shops, and so on. That is, tourists "serve as consumers in a marketplace of aesthetically pleasing experiences" (71). However, tourists also want authentic experiences; they will look for places off the beaten path that will distinguish them as "insiders" as opposed to other tourists. Here we can see that "both pleasure tourists and religious adherents have a keen interest in the authentic experience of place" (71); that is, touristic and religious interests tend to reinforce each other. "On the one hand, the authentically sacred character of a religious place makes it an appealing attraction for traditional tourists. At the same time, tourist attention helps to sustain the locative claims of the place as a meaningful site in the religious tradition" (71). Hence, tourists and religious adherents engage in a "symbiotic reciprocity" that makes places both sacred spaces and tourist places.

IDENTITY AND PLACE

There is a close relationship between identity and place; that is, there is a *simultaneity* between identity and place. Our identity is linked to social relationships and social relations create place while place influences social relations. In regards to sacred spaces and tourist places, religious people endow place with the meaning that stems from their core religious beliefs, which also reconfirms and strengthens their identity. Tourists, on the other hand, look for "aesthetic pleasure [that creates] an authentic place of beauty and power" (72) that reconfirms or nurtures their sense of identity.

CONCLUSION

Tourists and religious adherents create different sets of places layered onto the same physical setting. For the religious, sites are sacred and for the tourist sites are aestheticized and commodified.

There isn't just one interpretation of authenticity and other interpretations are wrong, "individuals can imagine the appeal of the site in terms of their own sense of self" (72). These different meanings do not have to be mutually exclusive either, but can serve to reinforce each other in locative ways.

5. SACRED SPACES AND TOURIST PLACES

By Thomas S. Bremer

Tourists encounter places of religion in nearly every corner of the world. Wherever religious people have made places of interaction with sacred powers, touristic practices are able to establish a site worthy of visitation. At religious sites that host significant numbers of tourists, a simultaneity of places emerges in parallel geographies of both the sacred and the touristic. Moreover, the meaningful content of these overlapping places relies upon narratives of identity that consolidate the bonds that religious adherents and tourist visitors feel toward the place. In short, religious tourist sites tell stories that articulate coherent identities.

The stories that make these sites meaningful relate first of all to a heuristic distinction between space and place. Space refers to an undifferentiated expanse lacking in meaningful content. On the other hand, place distinguishes particular locales by punctuating the meaningless expanse of space with meaningfulness. As the cultural geographer Yi-Fu Tuan notes, "'Space' is more abstract than 'place.' What begins as undifferentiated space becomes place as we get to know it better and endow it with value" (Tuan 1977:6). Indeed, the value that distinctive communities or particular individuals attribute to a site differentiates it from other places and from the monotonous expanse of space in general. This in turn emphasizes the particularity of place in contrast to the homogeneity of space. This can be visualized in terms of maps. A map is not so much a representation of space as it is a guide to the meaningful content that differentiates space into particular places. Michel de Certeau (1984:116–132) discusses a "bipolar distinction between 'map' and 'itinerary'"; he demonstrates how historically "the map has slowly disengaged itself from the itineraries that were the condition of its possibility." Thus, we do not see space on a map; a map of space would be nothing more than a blank sheet of paper. Instead, we see the configuration of particular places in relation to each other in a given segment of space. Map is not territory, as Jonathan Z. Smith (1993:309) correctly points out, but as artifacts of past itineraries, maps do provide a visual image of the places that make a territory meaningful and therefore recognizable to particular communities and individuals.

Meaningful places, however, do not remain static. In acknowledging the contingencies and dynamics apparent in all places, the author has discussed elsewhere what he calls the itinerant dimensions of place in contrast to the locative (Bremer 2004:12). A locative view of place emphasizes the power, stability, and permanence of location. Material markers of a particular place, whether they be naturally occurring topographic features such as mountains, rivers, lakes, and caves, or built environments of human interactions such as buildings, shrines, enclosures, and fortifications, announce an air of enduring stability that makes the place distinctly recognizable. Try imagining, for instance, the island of Manhattan without visualizing its stunning skyline highlighted with the towering presence of the Empire State building, the Chrysler building, and other distinctive landmarks that make its breathtaking materiality so memorable and lasting.

But the locative stability of the Manhattan skyline disguises its itinerant reality. In contrast to the apparent permanency of the locative, the itinerant dimensions of place are the ephemeral and unstable realities that belie the illusion of permanence. The itinerant draws attention to the contingencies of place that inevitably erode whatever enduring qualities a particular place may possess. Not too long ago it would have been difficult to imagine the Manhattan skyline without the imposing presence of the Twin Towers at the World Trade Center. Today their absence reminds us that the permanency of place is always a contingent stability; the itinerant nature of place inevitably brings change to otherwise enduring landscapes.

FEATURES OF PLACE

The tension between the enduring stability of the locative and the forces of change that characterize the itinerant draw attention to two features that every place displays. First, all places are social. In other words, places involve relationships between various individuals and groups of people. It is impossible to think of a particular place without inferring a social dimension. The meaningfulness of a given place derives to a large extent from its status in the relations that people have with each other. Even sites of solitude or social estrangement contain a social dimension, perhaps more so than those that thrive on contact and interaction with others. Indeed, the absence of society can be a powerful social force.

The importance of place in social relationships goes beyond its role as the site where people interact. In fact, place serves as an integral element in all social relations, both as a determinant of those relations and as a product of them as well. This is especially evident in places of religion. The special character of a holy site endows its occupants with a degree of social prestige. Priests, ritual specialists, and others who inhabit and control sacred sites command the respect of religious adherents who recognize their importance in part because of their association with the auspicious nature of the site. At the same time, the prestige of the place itself gains recognition due to the presence and activities of religious leaders and specialists who practice there. Hence, the social and spatial dimensions reinforce each other and sustain their special character in an inextricable relationship of reciprocal meaningfulness.

Because places are social, they are never unchanging. The meaningfulness of a particular place derives from practices that establish them and maintain them, and from the discursive force of those practices in the communities that regard them as special or peculiar. These practices and the rhetorical powers they deploy change over time in the ongoing ebb and flow of the social relations where they occur. As a result, the place itself changes as its meanings shift for the individuals and communities who find it distinctive.

Because places continually reflect the dynamic processes of shifting meanings, they are vulnerable to contestation by various interested parties, a point aptly demonstrated in regard to sacred sites in particular (Chidester and Linenthal 1995:1–42). Various groups have strongly vested interests in particular places. These interests may be economic, political, religious, moral, aesthetic, nostalgic, or some combination of these. When the interests of different groups are at odds, places can become the focus of intense conflicts. These struggles can involve questions of actual ownership or control of a particular site, or they may involve nothing more than a rhetorical battle over the specific meanings of the place. The social aspect of place thus plays itself out in the discursive outcome of these never-ending attempts to define and control the site.

Besides their inherently social nature, the second feature that all places display is a temporal dimension. Places occur at the intersection of the spatial and the temporal domains. Or, to put it another way, the meaningfulness of a particular place relies on cultural assumptions about time. Spatial location has little significance without temporal location; places include pasts, presents, and futures. The history of the place and its commemorative value help to maintain personal and collective memories that in turn contribute to contemporary perceptions of self and other. Current practices that sustain the place's meanings rely on the calendrics of "social time," a term that Emile Durkheim (1965:23) coined in reference to a category of time that expresses "a time common to the group." This contrasts with the personal experience of time that he describes as "sensations and images which serve to locate us in time." Finally, the perceptions of place also coincide with assumptions about how time will operate in (or on) the future.

Of course, not all groups regard time as a continuity of past, present, and future. But other cultural perceptions of time likewise impact understandings of place. For instance, a cyclical notion of time coincides with a view of place as cyclically significant. In ancient Mesoamerica, for instance, the unification of the double count calendar system relied on a cosmological union of time and space; consequently, the ritual "binding of the years" practiced in Mesoamerican religions involved an elaborate linking of significant places into a cosmological whole. These places would reemerge periodically as auspicious sites in the recurring rounds of the calendar cycles (Aveni 1980:154–158; Carrasco 1999:88–114; Greenhouse 1996:144–174).

But whether a particular culture perceives time as a linear continuity, a cyclical repetition, or some other configuration, its temporal assumptions figure into its understandings of place. Moreover, as Carol Greenhouse (1996:4) demonstrates, the primary significance of time relates to cultural formulations of agency that give legitimacy to the dominant political order within a particular society. These formulations of agency likewise create the meaningful significance that defines particular places.

The formulation of subjective agency through cultural assumptions about time suggests that time is in fact part of the social character of place. Thus, the two fundamental features of place—the social and the temporal—are closely related. And both in turn relate to the locative and itinerant dimensions of place. Locative claims tend to regard place as timeless; the perception of permanence implies that a particular site escapes the forces of historical change. These sorts of claims also serve as rhetorical strategies in the politics of place; they operate discursively in the relations of power between and among communities that find the site meaningful in some way. Indeed, a declaration of permanence imposes a particular group's interpretation of the site and helps to consolidate its control by foreclosing any competing claims on the place. In contrast, the itinerant dimensions of place are embedded in the dynamic forces of time; the contingencies of place rely on cultural assumptions about how time operates. Moreover, the itinerant quality of places derives in part from social contention over the control and significance of the site. The unstable and changing nature of a place reflects social differences and consequent struggles over actual ownership and ultimate interpretation of the place.

Ownership and interpretation of a particular site involves control over narratives of place. Places are made in human spatial experience, and the stories that people tell of those experiences give places their meanings and sustain them as distinct locales in the landscape. In other words, place gains its meaningfulness and retains its importance in narratives, a fact that Michel de Certeau (1984:115) draws attention to when he notes regarding stories that "every day, they traverse and organize places; they select and link them together; they make sentences and itineraries out of them. They are spatial trajectories." These spatial trajectories are evident, for example, in the images of Manhattan's skyline. Certainly, the narration of the human experiences of the place reveals Manhattan's most profound significance. The stories of human drama, triumph, tragedy, or simply of the mundane unfolding of daily lives invest the places of the city with a myriad of meanings that pervade its character. Among the most powerful of those stories relate to the absence of the Twin Towers at the World Trade Center. The downtown site evokes the horror that struck the island and its occupants on September 11, 2001. The narration of those events and their aftermath are profound elements in the meaning of Manhattan as a place.

TRAVEL PRACTICES IN DISCOURSES OF PLACE

The stories that articulate the meaningful value of a particular locale are a dimension of the travel practices that make places. An important element in the itinerant nature of all places is the travel practices that make places possible to begin with. The undifferentiated expanse of space undergoes its transformation into distinct places in the human itineraries that experience the landscapes they traverse and then narrate those experiences to themselves and to others. Places thus emerge in human practices of travel.

Travel practices encompass all sorts of human translocal movements, as the author has discussed elsewhere (Bremer 2004:12–13; 2005:9262). These include migration, pilgrimage, business and trade, tourism, military deployments, research excursions, family visitations, and many other manners of travel. The practices that constitute these movements go beyond actual travel itself. Certainly travel practices involve various modes of transportation, most commonly airlines, trains, buses, and automobiles. But they also include communication networks that facilitate travel, including telecommunications and the Internet, as well as media that make travel desirable and feasible such as radio and television broadcasts, newspapers and magazines, and other forms of mass communication. Modern travel practices also include banking facilities that allow convenient and trustworthy currency exchange; accommodations for lodging and food services; and any other services or products that meet the needs and desires of modern travelers.

Yet travel practices go beyond modern infrastructures and services that make global travel possible, convenient, and comfortable. They include any practice, discourse, or circumstance that either necessitates translocal movements or that generates desires for and encourages people to travel. In the context of market capitalism, the construction and promotion of travel destinations constitutes important travel practices. Making a locale desirable for travelers to visit or settle there, and participating in discourses of place that travelers pay heed to, all are part of travel practices in the modern world. Likewise, the exclusion of populations deemed undesirable, both resident and transient, must be counted among modern travel practices. Thus, border controls and the policing of sites qualify as well.

Like other places, religious sites that host tourist visitors are sustained with travel practices. But although religious adherents and non-adherent tourists both occupy the same site at the same times, their respective practices and resulting interpretations of its significance make distinct places of it. Thus, religious sites of tourism maintain what Bremer (2004:4) has called a simultaneity of places. Neither their religious quality nor their touristic character can make a total claim on these places—they remain both religious and touristic, occupied by both religious adherents and other tourists whose respective experiences of the site are quite different from each other. True, the experiences of particular individuals may cross between the religious and the touristic, as when tourists participate in religious activities or when religious followers indulge in the touristic attractions of their sacred precinct (pilgrims, for instance, often indulge in touristic practices in the course of their religious journeys). Yet the hybridity of these sites does not allow a seamless blending of the two; careful observations reveal clear distinctions between the places of religion and the places of tourism, despite the very real overlaps that inevitably constitute religious sites of tourism.

The narratives of sacred places occur within the discourses of particular religious traditions. This is not to say that all sacred places must be associated with a recognized religious body. It simply means that the meaningful experience articulated in the narrative of the place must have some larger discursive framework that orients an understanding of sacrality. To deem a place sacred, there must be an understanding of what the sacred entails. This understanding, I contend, relies on discourses of particular religious traditions. Such reliance usually takes a positive form. Christians who regard a site as sacred because it is a place of God participate positively in a Christian theological discourse; they reinforce what they regard as the accepted Christian tradition. On the other hand, the narrative of a sacred place may pose a negative counter-discourse to the religious tradition. An auspicious gathering place for a band of Satanists, for instance, poses a threatening alternative to normative Christian discourse. As Elaine Pagels (1995) demonstrates, the discursive origins of Satan in Jewish apocalyptic sources became part of normative Christian traditions that vilify anyone who pays respect to the demonic figure. Yet, the Satanists' claims of sacrality nevertheless rely on normative Christian traditions to suggest their own criteria and parameters of sacred experience.

The experience of the sacred in particular places tends to reinforce locative claims, especially in monotheistic traditions. Thus, places regarded as sacred often have an air of permanency that transcends the contingencies of human mortality; the sacred places of a religious tradition will survive long after individual religious adherents have passed away. In fact, sacred sites serve as an enduring symbol of, and orientation for, the continuance of the religious community itself. Their importance also makes them geographical centers that orient the spatial worlds of religious communities. In many cases they become literal centers of the world. As an example, Mircea Eliade (1959:23), a great advocate of locative claims of sacred places, argues: "Revelation of a sacred space makes it possible to obtain a fixed point and hence to acquire orientation in the chaos of homogeneity, to 'found the world' and to live in a real sense." He consistently emphasizes the role of sacred places in orienting religious communities, as when he describes "techniques of *orientation*" as "techniques for the *construction* of sacred space" (Eliade 1959:29). To Eliade, a sacred space represents the center of the world; it is, in his famous term, an *axis mundi*. Even moveable objects can operate in this locative, orienting manner. Eliade's example of the *kauwa-auwa,* or sacred pole, of the Achilpa people of Australia (an example that Jonathan Z. Smith (1992:1–23) critiques), demonstrates how an itinerant object can serve locative ends. According to Eliade:

> This pole represents a cosmic axis, for it is around the sacred pole that territory becomes habitable, hence is transformed into a world. … During their wanderings the Achilpa always carry it with them and choose the direction they are to take by the direction toward which it bends. This allows them, while being continually on the move, to be always "in their world" and, at the same time, in communication with the sky into which Numbakuyla [their creator god] vanished.

> (Eliade 1959:33)

Sacred space, in Eliade's estimation, organizes around particular sites, or even particular objects, that become orientational centers in the religious community's world. These *axes mundi* decree a locative stability that allows the community to endure in a changing world.

The rhetorical force of these locative claims seeks to squelch the contested, itinerant nature of these places. The assertion of an enduring, unchanging place that serves as the center of a community's world attempts to foreclose counterclaims that would undermine the authority of those who control the *axis mundi* and the normative tale of its significance. Individuals and groups vested in maintaining the status quo will resist the itinerant aims of a counter-discourse that seeks to transform the sacred geography according to alternative mythic and social realities. To give one example, this resistance was apparent in the persecution of the Church of Jesus Christ of Latter-day Saints in nineteenth-century America. Part of the Mormon revision of Christianity involved a reconfiguration of the sacred geography; fundamental to the Church's efforts was the establishment of a New Jerusalem on the American continent. The tenth article of faith of the Latter-day Saints states in part: "We believe … that Zion will be built upon this [the American] continent" (Talmage 1949:2, 345–355). This New Jerusalem, according to the words of Jesus in *The Book of Mormon,* will be a place where "the powers of heaven shall be in the midst of this people; yea, even I will be in the midst of you" (3 Nephi 20:22). Their struggle to build the place of Zion in the American west posed a discursive threat to more established Christian sects who responded with a vicious campaign of persecution against the Mormons. The conflict resulted in the execution of their founder and the removal of the Saints to a new homeland in Utah. Indeed, the itinerant force of an alternative voice usually elicits a strong response from those with a vested interest in the locative claims of established sacred geographies.

PLACES OF TOURISM

In contrast to the struggles that establish and sustain religious sites, places of touristic appeal demonstrate other discursive concerns. The conventional practices of tourism participate most acutely in discourses on modernity (Adler 1998). In fact, tourists can be regarded as exemplary modern subjects. They seek out the experience of unfamiliar places by leaving the familiarity of home, but the conventions of tourism tend to domesticate these novel places by commodifying the experiences that visitors have of them. Thus, touristic experience conforms to the forces of modern capitalism, especially in its globalizing capacity to encompass all places in the marketplace of consumer demand. Tourists, then, as they participate in this marketplace, serve as practitioners of modernity (Bremer 2005:9262).

The specific practices that typically constitute modern tourism include specialized forms of travel practices, including activities such as sightseeing, picture taking, and souvenir shopping. But tourists partake in far more than what the stereotypes of touristic behavior suggest. Tourism, as Franklin and Crang (2001:15) point out, involves "material practices that serve to organize and support specific ways of experiencing the world." Besides the commodification of places and experiences brought about by modern capitalism, the touristic way of experiencing the world also relies on a modern aesthetic sense. Consequently, tourists serve as consumers in a marketplace of aesthetically pleasing experiences.

Fundamental to tourists' experiences is an aesthetic obsession with authenticity (Redfoot 1984; Olsen 2002). Tourist discourses attribute significant value to authenticity; the most authentic experiences are the most aesthetically pleasing. This explains tourists' desire for destinations "off the beaten path." The glee expressed in finding that out-of-the-way place where there are no tourists employs a touristic discourse on authenticity that bolsters one's own esteem as a traveler by ironically disparaging others as tourists. By denying one's own status as a tourist, one gains esteem at the expense of others less adept in the practice of authentic travel. In a fundamental paradox of touristic practice, contrasting oneself with lowly "tourists" makes one a better tourist (Culler 1981:130–131; MacCannell 1999:91–107).

In places of religion, the touristic discourse on authenticity coincides with religious discourses of place. Indeed, both pleasure tourists and religious adherents have a keen interest in the authentic experience of place. To some extent, touristic concerns and religious interests respond to and reinforce each other to produce a meaningful sacred site. On the one hand, the authentically sacred character of a religious place makes it an appealing attraction for traditional tourists. At the same time, tourist attention helps to sustain the locative claims of the place as a meaningful site in the religious tradition. Together, the touristic and religious perspectives engage in a symbiotic reciprocity that makes certain sites both sacred religious places and appealing travel destinations. They are both sacred spaces and tourist places.

IDENTITY AND PLACE

The narratives produced in the discourses of these places also articulate particular identities. There persists a close relationship between place and identity. As I have argued elsewhere:

> The making of place, sacred or otherwise, always involves the making of identities; conversely, the construction of identity always involves the construction of places. On the one hand, the meaningful content of a particular place relies on the production of both subjects who inhabit the place and subjects who observe, comment on, and interpret the place, including both insiders and outsiders. On the other hand, all subjects are situated; to attain subjective agency means at the most fundamental level to occupy a particular place, both in the physical and social senses. Thus, place and identity emerge together in a relationship of simultaneity.

(Bremer 2003:73–74)

This simultaneous relationship between place and identity relies on a reciprocal meaningfulness that binds people and places together. If one's identity involves a "meaningful self-image of affiliation with an imagined community" (Bremer 2004:144), or, as Moya (2000:8) puts it, "our conceptions of who we are as social beings," then identity, like place, is foremost a matter of social relationships. The meaningful content of an individual's being depends on her or his association with various social groups as imagined in her or his own cultural and historical contexts. At the same time, an affinity of meanings provides a basis for imagining a distinct community to identify with.

At religious places of tourism, visitors attribute meanings according to their own social affiliations. Religious people understand such places as sacred in accord with their own affiliation with a particular religious community. The meaningfulness of the place for such visitors derives from their community's understanding of the religious tradition. In contrast, tourists who do not regard themselves as members of the religious community ascribe different meanings to the place. The touristic propensity for aesthetic pleasures creates an authentic place of beauty and power in conformity with modern aesthetic tastes. This in turn offers an aesthetic dimension to tourists' modern identities.

CONCLUSION

The religious understandings of a site create one set of places, while touristic interpretations produce a different set of places. Certainly, this simultaneity of places offers an abundant opportunity for overlap and convergence. But the social realities of identity require a certain distinctiveness that allows individuals to imagine the appeal of the site in terms of their own sense of self. The stories that visitors hear at religious sites of touristic appeal, and the tales they recite to themselves and others, make distinctive places in a landscape of coherent identities. Sacred for the religious, aestheticized and commodified for the tourists, these places contribute decisively to the social affiliations and personal identities of those who enter their precincts.

REFERENCES

Adler, J. (1998) "Origins of sightseeing," in C.T. Williams (ed.) *Travel Culture: Essays on What Makes Us Go*, Westport, CT: Praeger.

Aveni, A.F. (1980) *Skywatchers of Ancient Mexico*, Austin: University of Texas Press.

The Book of Mormon: An Account Written by the Hand of Mormon, upon Plates Taken from the Plates of Nephi (1987) (J. Smith, Trans.), Salt Lake City: Church of Jesus Christ of Latter-day Saints.

Bremer, T.S. (2003) "Il Genius Loci Ignotus di Eranos e la Creazione di un Luogo Sacro," in E. Barone, M. Riedl, and A. Tischel (eds) *Eranos, Monte Verita, Ascona*, Pisa, Italy: Edizioni ETS.

Bremer, T.S. (2004) *Blessed with Tourists: The Borderlands of Religion and Tourism in San Antonio*, Chapel Hill: University of North Carolina Press.

Bremer, T.S. (2005) "Tourism and religion," in L. Jones (ed.) *The Encyclopedia of Religion*, New York: Macmillan.

Carrasco, D. (1999) "The New Fire Ceremony and the binding of the years," in D. Carraso (ed.) *City of Sacrifice: The Aztec Empire and the Role of Violence in Civilization*, Boston: Beacon Press.

Certeau, M. de (1984) *The Practice of Everyday Life* (S. Rendall, Trans.), Berkeley: University of California Press.

Chidester, D. and Linenthal, E.T. (eds.) (1995) *American Sacred Space,* Bloomington: Indiana University Press.

Culler, J. (1981) "Semiotics of tourism," *American Journal of Semiotics* 1(1–2): 127–140.

Durkheim, E. (1965) *The Elementary Forms of the Religious Life* (J.W. Swain, Trans.), New York: The Free Press.

Eliade, M. (1959) *The Sacred and the Profane: The Nature of Religion* (W.R. Trask, Trans.), New York: Harvest/HBJ.

Franklin, A. and Crang, M. (2001) "The trouble with tourism and travel theory?," *Tourist Studies* 1: 5–22.

Greenhouse, C.J. (1996) *A Moment's Notice: Time Politics Across Cultures,* Ithaca: Cornell University Press.

MacCannell, D. (1999) *The Tourist: A New Theory of the Leisure Class* (3rd edn), Berkeley: University of California Press.

Moya, P.M.L. (2000) "Introduction: reclaiming identity," in P.M.L. Moya and M.R. Hames-Garcia (eds) *Reclaiming Identity: Realist Theory and the Predicament of Postmodernism,* Berkeley: University of California Press.

Olsen, K. (2002) "Authenticity as a concept in tourism research: the social organization of the experience of authenticity," *Tourist Studies* 2(2): 159–182.

Pagels, E.H. (1995) *The Origin of Satan,* New York: Random House.

Redfoot, D.L. (1984) "Touristic authenticity, touristic angst, and modern reality," *Qualitative Sociology* 7(4): 291–309.

Smith, J.Z. (1992) *To Take Place: Toward Theory in Ritual,* Chicago: University of Chicago Press.

Smith, J.Z. (1993) *Map Is Not Territory: Studies in the History of Religions,* Chicago: University of Chicago Press.

Talmage, J.E. (1949) *A Study of the Articles of Faith; Being a Consideration of the Principal Doctrines of the Church of Jesus Christ of Latter-day Saints* (28th edn), Salt Lake City: The Church of Jesus Christ of Latter-day Saints.

Tuan, Y.-F. (1977) *Space and Place: The Perspective of Experience,* Minneapolis: University of Minnesota Press.

STUDY QUESTIONS

1. How does author Thomas S. Bremer distinguish between space and place?
2. Explain the locative and itinerate dimensions of place.
3. Explain in what ways places are social, and how is this feature of place related to religion?
4. In what ways do places also occur at the intersection of the spatial and the temporal domains?
5. What does Bremer mean when he refers to the simultaneity of places especially in relation to tourist and religious places?
6. What is the relationship between the sacred and the locative?
7. A sacred space represents the center of the world, the axis mundi. This axis mundi decrees a locative stability that allows the community to endure a changing world. Individuals and groups vested in maintaining the status quo will resist the itinerant aims of a counter-discourse that seeks to transform the sacred geography according to alternative mythic and social realities. How does this statement reflect the experience of the Church of Jesus Christ of Latter Day Saints in 19th century America?
8. How do tourists serve as practitioners of modernity?
9. Describe the modern aesthetic sense that tourists seek in their specific way of experiencing the world; how does this relate to religious sites?
10. How do place and identity emerge together in a relationship of simultaneity?
11. Explain how a religious understanding of a site creates one set of places while touristic interpretations produce a different set of places.

Chapter 6 Snapshot
Displaced Livelihoods: Introduction

As part of our unit on population and migration, we also consider the movement of refugees. We see the maps of refugee movements and we recognize that this is a huge movement of people who are not moving voluntarily. What is it like to be a refugee? What kinds of choices do they have to make? What kinds of opportunities are available to them, and can they actually hope for a brighter future upon having made this move? What happens to these people that we cannot see from the spatial perspective of a map?

According to Karen Jacobsen, over 30 million people in just the beginning of the 21st century have been forced to move—two-thirds have moved within their own countries seeking a safer place to be, while one-third have fled across their country's national borders. We often think of images of thousands of refugees walking wearily along dusty roads or clustered in camps that seem to go on forever, but this kind of mass migration of misery is the exception rather than the rule. Most refugees come a few at a time, trying to find a safe haven somewhere or at least seek to join some community of refugees already at a defined place. Usually refugees make one of two choices once they cross borders; either they can go to a camp site set up by international agencies or they instead will choose to blend into a local community in the host country; that is, they become self-settled. More of the self-settled refugees choose to live in rural areas than urban ones, and most refugee camps are also placed in rural areas or the distant outskirts of urban areas. Under most circumstances refugees will wait until the last minute to flee and they use up most of their finances and other assets just to make the move. They arrive destitute but with a strong desire to establish some sort of stable livelihood.

Besides facing a dangerous journey into another country with no resources to speak of, these refugees also do not know how long they will need to be "out-of-country" and away from home. First of all, if they go to an established international humanitarian camp, they do not know how long the aid will last, and if they are just trying to blend into the local population, they do not know how they will be received. They do not know how long their country's unstable conditions will last, and they do not know how long it will be until they can return. They do know it would be highly unlikely that they would be invited to become citizens in their host country (country of asylum) and it would be even less likely they would be able to settle in a third country such as the United States or England, France, or Germany. They are sort of stuck in limbo, what is called a *protracted situation*. Jacobson has reported that as of 2003, there were 38 different protracted situations in the world, accounting for 6.2 million refugees in total. So, whether refugees are living in camps or living in local communities (self-settled), they will be in protracted situations, not knowing when they will be able to return. If they are living in camps, they will not know how long emergency aid will last, if they are self-settled, they will not likely have access to any emergency aid unless provided by a local group or religious institution. They do not feel stable or safe, they will not know if there will be school for their children, and they will likely have to start over in some kind of new livelihood, if they are lucky enough to find any work opportunities at all.

What makes refugees different from other migrants? Refugees and migrants may share a number of conditions in common, but refugees have been a protected group ever since the establishment of the 1951 Convention by the United Nations High Commissioner for Refugees (UNHCR). All UN member

Country or Region	# of Protracted Situations	Millions of Refugees
Africa (not including North Africa)	22	2.3
Central Asia, Southwest Asia, North Africa, Middle East	8	2.7
Rest of Asia	5	.670
Europe	3	.530

states that have signed this agreement have promised to provide refugees with protection and assistance, something not offered to other migrants ... or nationals. In fact, for those refugees receiving humanitarian aid, their camps usually set them apart from nationals. When it comes to meeting basic needs, the programs set up to support the refugees are usually superior; however, when it comes to economic opportunities like trade or employment or working the land, the refugees are usually at a disadvantage (84).

WHO ARE REFUGEES AND ASYLUM-SEEKERS?

Most commonly, a refugee is someone who is displaced by persecution, war, or conflict, who has fled across an international border, and is in need of international humanitarian assistance (84). In addition, however, "refugees enjoy a specific legal status associated with a complex and longstanding set of legal requirements and based on a definition set out in international agreements and refugee law" (84). Just crossing an international border is not enough for someone to gain legal status as a refugee. These people are considered *asylum-seekers*. They can only become refugees if and when this status has been assigned by the state.

There are two ways an asylum-seeker can become a refugee. The first is when this status is granted on an individual basis. This "requires that [his or her] experience of persecution warrants refugee status according to the definition set out in the 1951 Convention. Those who undergo this lengthy determination procedure are referred to as <u>Convention refugees</u> (84). However, there are times when so many people from one country cross the borders of their neighbor; it would be too cumbersome to grant individual status to each one. In this case, refugee status is granted on a *prima facie* basis for an entire group. The purpose of this group mechanism "is to ensure admission to safety, protection from refoulement [forced repatriation], and basic humanitarian treatment to those patently in need of it" (84). Most of the world's refugees have *prima facie* status, and in 2003, some 64 percent of the world's 9.7 million refugees were granted *prima facie* status. *Prima facie* status is what is called a presumptive status; that is, it is presumed that all of these individuals would qualify as Convention refugees should they apply individually. This presumptive status solves several administrative problems, but it cannot sort out those who should *not* be accorded this status such as criminals and combatants that do not deserve this status (84).

SOME CHARACTERISTICS OF PROTRACTED REFUGEE SITUATIONS

1. <u>Cross-Border Movements</u>. As stated earlier, most refugees travel as individuals or in small groups, traveling in secrecy and seeking aid where they can find it. Refugee populations accumulate over time, but people are constantly moving back and forth across the border. This pattern has important implications for refugees' economic activities (85).

2. <u>Patterns of Settlement</u>. Earlier it was mentioned that refugees usually either settle in official refugee camps or choose to settle themselves in local, indigenous communities. "A significant proportion of refugees stay away from camps or official settlement sites, and settle themselves among the local population—in rural hamlets and small towns, in 'refugee villages,' near towns, or in the shanty towns of megacities"(85). Known as a pattern of self-settlement or dispersed settlement, these individuals often do not register with the authorities and therefore do not have official status as refugees. They do not receive any official assistance from the government, "relying instead on the hospitality of the host community" (85). "Of the 14.6 million persons of concern to the United Nations High Commissioner for Refugees in 2001, 60 percent were self-settled. Thirteen percent were settled in urban areas, while 47 percent lived in rural areas (or their type of settlement was unknown). Forty percent resided in camps" (86). These patterns of settlement will affect the economic experience and livelihoods of refugees. For example, "many refugee households use camps as part of a broad strategy of survival, in which the workers live outside in order to farm or find employment, and the non-workers (elderly, mothers, and children) live in the camp where they have access to assistance" (87). Refugees "might return to the camps during the hungry season, or when there are security threats outside, or to use the camp schools" (87). People who live in the camps, might also "go into towns to engage in various economic activities or to go to school" while "local people frequent the camps, too—making use of schools and health clinics set up by aid agencies, buying and selling in camp markets, or sometimes posing as refugees in order to get food aid" (87).

3. <u>Why Refugees Do Not Go Home</u>. Refugees usually live in their host countries for at least 3 years and often much longer. They cannot go home because of war, persecution, and ethnic strife and it is unsafe for them to return. In addition, there are two linked reasons why long-term refugees do not return in these situations.

   A. Peace seldom spreads across a country at the same time. There often are pockets of resistance or new local conflicts break out, so many refugees adopt a "wait and see" attitude that can sometimes last for several years. "As part of their repatriation programs, UNHCR sets up 'go and see' visits, in which refugees are taken on visits to their home areas, to see and appraise the situation for themselves, then come back and report to others in the camp (87). Relief agencies are usually as concerned as the refugees themselves regarding a safe return.

B. A second reason why refugees do not return, even where peace agreements have held and security is not a major concern, is because economic conditions in home countries devastated by years of conflict make the reconstruction of livelihoods very difficult. Roads can be torn up, fields may be laced with mines or unexploded ordinance, social networks have been disrupted or obliterated, and financial capital is gone. There are other problems as well. Refugees could have obligations to help family members still living in the home country, and they could have developed livelihoods better than they would be able to achieve should they return home. Some refugees want to use their status to move on to a third country such as the United States, and for other refugees, memories of home and loss of family members are just too traumatic for them to ever consider returning home. *Prima facie* refugees sometimes face an additional problem once conflict in their home countries is over. "In some countries, the government decides that refugees should return, and requires that those wishing to remain in the host country regularise their immigration papers and either qualify as Convention refugees (prove their eligibility as individual refugees rather than *prima facie* ones) or risk being deported" (88).

REFUGEE LIVELIHOODS

Karen Jacobsen uses an assets framework to understand the economic impact of conflict and displacement on a refugee household. "Each household has a portfolio of assets, or types of capital, which are the things it needs, uses, and has access to, in order to pursue livelihoods" (see p. 89 for examples). As mentioned earlier, however, most refugees have used up all of their assets and capital just getting out of the country. In other cases, "assets are stolen or destroyed (stripped) and access to them is blocked or endangered" (89). Refugees also have limited contact with markets and vendors along with decreased circulation of goods, services, and money. Social services are quite limited. In Jacobsen's research, "almost all of the economically active refugees ... were engaged in informal, sector-based, small enterprises of some kind—often supplemented with wage work, such as part-time employment with aid agencies (as teachers or translators or program staff). Refugees in camps often sell food ration cards or they engage in "piecework" on local farms or households when they can. In addition, "... where cultivatable land was available or could be negotiated from the local community (usually by UNHCR), refugees engaged in agriculture on a small scale, sometimes harvesting enough to sell in local markets" (48). For other refugees, it is not a matter of continuing a livelihood they participated in at home, but creating a whole new livelihood based on the opportunities at hand.

THE NEED FOR CASH AND CREDIT

Refugees get cash from some sort of economic activity, but usually they have to have some sort of start-up cash or credit to start their economic enterprise to begin with. In addition, camps provide for many basic needs, but not all of them. For example, "firewood for cooking is not provided as part of the ration, and refugees must either buy it from local vendors (for which they need cash) or leave the camp to find it in the bush, often quite a risky venture" (90). Unfortunately, in most host countries, there are few sources of cash or credit for refugees. Even if they have money, refugees face insecure environments with a lack of safe facilities for saving cash. In some refugee camps, community-based rotating credit associations can be established but refugees usually have to be solvent or have a source of income before they have access to credit. The most fortunate refugees are those who have relatives who live in developed countries and can send them remittances (90).

THE INSTITUTIONAL CONTEXT OF DISPLACED LIVELIHOODS

At the global level it is clear that refugees have rights guaranteed under the 1951 Convention, especially social and economic rights. There is also a global expectation that refugees will receive humanitarian aid, protection, and advocacy. At the national level, it is the host government's policy toward refugees which may or may not be in line with the government's international obligations" (91). At the local level, it is the host community, including the response of local authorities, economic problems, and attitudes of the local population, that affect refugee livelihoods.

What is the host government's policy regarding refugees' economic activities? The 1951 Convention stipulates that lawful refugees should be "granted most favourable treatment accorded to nationals of a foreign country in the same circumstances as regards the right to engage in wage-earning employment" (50). This means that refugees have the right to engage in agriculture, industry, handicrafts, and commerce and to be able to establish commercial and industrial companies (92). Refugees cannot be taxed higher or be required to pay duties or other charges *other or higher than those which are or may be levied on their nationals in similar situations"* (Article 28 emphasis added). Refugees should be allowed to transfer assets from one location to another, for the purposes of resettlement, and the 1951 Convention requires that the Contracting State "shall as far as possible facilitate the assimilation and naturalization of refugees" (92). Unfortunately, "the economic rights assigned refugees by the 1951 Convention are clear, but to be effective they need to be implemented by host governments and this implementation often fails to take place" (93). In order to discourage permanence and to encourage repatriation, it has become increasingly common for host governments to restrict all kinds of refugee activities outside of designated camp areas (93).

What about the local response? What is the relationship between the local population and the refugees? A majority of refugees settle in rural areas, far from a national capital. The ability of refugees to work and move around freely outside of camps is contingent upon the good will and cooperation of most of the local population, their leaders, and the local authorities" (93). Local chiefs and villagers can enable refugees to settle in the community. In fact, there may be several groups with vested interests in the success or failure of refugees in their communities. "One of the key issues mediating the relationship between the host community and refugees is access to land. If refugees want or need access to land, they usually negotiate this with either the government or UNHCR. They also need "access to the commons to obtain basic necessities like firewood or construction timber, or grass for grazing if they want to keep livestock" (93). If land is scarce, then tensions can run high; but if land is plentiful, the situation can be much calmer and more amicable (see, for example the experience of the Angolan refugees in Zambia, p. 93).

Besides access to land, there are other concerns as refugees attempt to develop livelihoods within local communities. Security can be a big problem for the refugees if their working lands lie outside of the camp, and once refugees start to become successful, what had been a willingness to help can turn to resentment from the local community. Then, as refugee numbers continue to grow, resentment grows as well. "In this context, refugees often become scapegoats and are more vulnerable and more likely to lack protection of their rights, including the right to work" (94). In other instances, "local people believe that the presence of refugees is linked to the rise in criminal activity, delinquency, street prostitution, and drug proliferation" even if these conditions existed before the refugees' arrival. According to Jacobsen, a shift in policies regarding the economic and social systems for nationals and refugees could go a long way toward providing a better balance between these two groups.

6. DISPLACED LIVELIHOODS

Introduction

By Karen Jacobsen

At the beginning of the twenty-first century, well over 30 million people have been displaced by conflict and violence in their home countries. A significant proportion of these—perhaps 20 million worldwide—remain internally displaced within their home country, some moving to safer villages nearby, others to urban areas.[1] Relatively few people have the resources to move far beyond their place of origin; in conflict zones, as in natural disasters, many people do not leave their homes at all, risking great danger and deprivation. Perhaps a third of those forcibly displaced by conflict and violence cross the border of their countries to seek safety and asylum in other countries, mostly in the developing world. By the end of 2003, according to the Office of the UN High Commissioner for Refugees (UNHCR), these refugees numbered some 9.7 million people, a decrease of about nine percent from the year before. Most did not travel much beyond the border zone of neighboring countries, staying close enough to monitor the situation at home, and preferring to be in a place somewhat familiar to them. Others traveled further, to the urban areas of host countries or, if they had the resources, onward to more distant destinations.

The popular image of refugees is that of a mass influx during an emergency: thousands of traumatized people pouring across a border and congregating in camps, where relief agencies try to meet their health and food needs. At this writing, December 2004, it is the emergency in Darfur, Sudan, that is in the news, but for every year of the past decade there were other sites: Liberians in 2003, Afghans in 2001, Kosovars in 1999, Rwandese in 1994. However powerful, these familiar images do not capture the reality of refugee life. For one thing, mass influxes of tens of thousands that occur over a short time are quite rare. Most forcibly displaced people move in small groups or as individuals, stopping to seek assistance en route and slipping across borders when they can, to join fellow refugee communities. Many refugees take up residence in camps under the care of various authorities, but a much greater number live among the local community, in rural or urban areas, and never register or seek international assistance. Common to almost all refugees, however, is the destitution that results from their flight experience, paired with a strong desire to support themselves by pursuing livelihoods. The ways in which they do this, the obstacles they face, and the assistance that comes to them from many sources, is the subject of this book.

A second reality of refugee situations, not captured by TV images, is the protracted nature of displacement. Once the emergency phase with its rush of aid and media attention has passed, many relief agencies depart—along with most of the humanitarian assistance, which was aimed at meeting emergency needs. In most cases, however, the conflict in the refugees' home countries does not end with the emergency phase, and for thousands of refugees, return is not an imminent possibility. The mass repatriation of Albanian Kosovars from Macedonia and Albania that took place a scant six weeks or so after they were displaced from Kosovo in 1999 was an exception. In most cases—for Afghans, Congolese, Somalis, Liberians, Burmese, Sudanese, and many other nationalities—some repatriation occurs, but new outbreaks of violence and conflict arise, and refugees traverse the border, unable to return to live securely in their homelands. If mass repatriation does occur, there are always many who remain behind, unable or unwilling to return. Perhaps their homes have been destroyed or occupied by others; some are too traumatized by the events they have witnessed or experienced in their home countries; others continue to fear persecution if they return.

Most refugees remain in their country of first asylum for years as the civil strife and insecurity in their home countries plays out. For most there is little likelihood either of their being invited to become citizens of the asylum country or being resettled in a third country. Stuck in this limbo, refugees are in what is known as *protracted situations.* According to UNHCR:

> Using a crude measure of refugee populations of 25,000 persons or more who have been in exile for five or more years in developing countries, and excluding Palestinian refugees who fall under the mandate of UNRWA, it is estimated that, at the end of 2003, there were 38 different protracted situations in the world, accounting for some 6.2 million refugees in total. The great majority of such situations were to be found in Africa (not including North Africa), which comprised 22 major protracted refugee situations including 2.3 million refugees. However, in terms of numbers, the majority of refugees in protracted situations were located in the region covering Central Asia, Southwest Asia, North Africa and the Middle East …, where eight major protracted situations accounted for 2.7 million refugees. [The rest of] Asia comprised five major protracted refugee situations including 670,000 refugees, whereas the three major protracted situations in Europe accounted for 530,000 refugees.[2]

Whether in camps or self-settled among the local population, the living circumstances of refugees in protracted situations are economically challenging and unsafe, with few means to support or educate themselves and their children. They face security problems ranging from harassment by the authorities to crime and forced military recruitment. Refugees living in the border zones of host countries frequently suffer from the spillover of conflict from the home country and must pursue livelihoods in undeveloped and isolated areas, where both displaced and local people struggle to support themselves with few resources and many challenges.

One of the most daunting problems facing refugees in protracted situations is the decline in the level and quality of humanitarian assistance that occurs once the emergency phase has passed. In camps, this decline can be gradual and intermittent or quite sudden. For self-settled refugees not living in camps, there are almost no official sources of assistance, and they must rely on the good will of their hosts. In these circumstances, the resilience and creativity of the refugees are revealed in a wide range of survival strategies. Though faced with economic deprivation and marginalization, many refugees maintain their cultural practices and values, join and form communities, and meet all manner of livelihood challenges in new and familiar ways. How refugees do this—how they adapt their survival strategies and develop new ones to maximize all available resources and opportunities, and the obstacles they face in doing so—is explored in this book.

In exploring refugees' survival strategies and the obstacles they face, we are drawn into the political economy of war and displacement, and the global politics of asylum in the twenty-first century. Refugees are a subset of all international migrants, who numbered some 200 million in 2004.[3] While migrants share many similar livelihood experiences, the difference for refugees is the existence of a well-established international refugee regime led by the United Nations High Commissioner for Refugees (UNHCR), whose office, since 1950, has been mandated by UN member states to provide refugees with protection and assistance. Refugees offer us an opportunity to see how this humanitarian system acts as a direct source of livelihood support, and creates—albeit inadvertently—a set of obstacles arising from poorly designed programs and policies. The book ends with a discussion of ways in which international refugee assistance could better support livelihoods, and proposes a model for refugee policy that takes into account the political factors influencing host countries' responses to refugees in the twenty-first century. This book moves between a local and a global perspective. We examine the day-to-day activities of refugees as they pursue livelihoods in their communities, and we consider the role of the international organizations and states that assist or obstruct those same livelihoods.

The remainder of this chapter sets out some definitions used in this book and the economic rights of refugees prescribed in international refugee law. Chapters Two and Three explore the main sites—refugee camps and urban areas—where long-term refugees live and pursue livelihoods in host countries. These chapters describe how markets emerge, and the economic impact of refugees' activities both on the host community and the wider region. In Chapter Four, our perspective widens to explore the economic activities of refugees who leave their first countries of asylum and travel to third countries, either through resettlement or as asylum-seekers. This chapter explores the economic experience of refugees in third countries, and particularly how their links with their home countries affect their ability to pursue livelihoods and emerge from poverty. Chapter Five explores the role of the international refugee regime—international humanitarian organizations, nongovernmental relief agencies, donor countries and host governments—in supporting or obstructing the livelihood strategies of refugees. Can humanitarian assistance go beyond food aid and emergency services to support refugee livelihoods? We explore whether microfinance services and income generating programs offer realistic alternatives to traditional forms of humanitarian assistance, which usually come in the form of relief grants. Chapter Six concludes by considering alternative approaches to supporting the livelihoods of refugees in protracted situations. We consider how refugee assistance programs can be designed so as also to help host populations who are often as poorly off as the refugees, and who face their own economic and security problems. In many host countries, humanitarian services for refugees exist in parallel to a separate, underfunded set of services for the surrounding population. Refugees and nationals live apart, with separate systems for food and nutrition, education, health, and water and sanitation. As in all cases where such separation exists, the systems are far from equal, and often the balance tilts in favor of the refugees when it comes to meeting basic needs. On the other hand, when it comes to economic activities like trade or employment or working the land, it is the refugees who are at the disadvantage. Parallel and unequal systems represent a waste of resources, and an unfair and politically untenable distribution of supplies. This closing chapter proposes a model of refugee assistance that could improve the lot of both refugees and host populations. The model takes into account the current political climate of growing restrictions on refugees. The feasibility of the model is discussed, in light of refugee assistance policies in host countries that come closest to the model's approach. We end with a look at the kinds of advocacy strategies that could move institutions in these desirable directions. Ending this book with such a proposed model is intended to offer a challenge and stimulate debate on how to take the problem of refugee assistance forward.

WHO ARE REFUGEES AND ASYLUM-SEEKERS?

In common parlance, refugees are people displaced by persecution, war, or conflict, who have fled across an international border and are in need of international humanitarian assistance. However, underlying this common usage of the word, is specific legal status associated with a complex and longstanding set of legal requirements and based on a definition set out in international agreements and refugee law.[4] Once states have ratified these international agreements—which most have by 2004—the act of conferring formal refugee status on a person includes assigning to him or her a set of rights and protocols, including protection and access to international humanitarian assistance. This gives those with formal refugee status a privileged position *vis à vis* other immigrants, and it is a status that is not quickly and easily conferred by states. Crossing a border in flight from danger is not sufficient to acquire it. People who have just fled across a border are technically *asylum-seekers;* in order to acquire refugee status they must first be assigned the status by the state. There are two ways in which this assignment is made: on an individual basis and as part of a group determination. The individual determination procedure requires that a person prove to the state that [his or her] experience of persecution warrants refugee status according to the definition set out in the 1951 Convention. Those who undergo this lengthy determination procedure and receive formal refugee status are referred to as "Convention refugees."[5] However, when a host country is confronted with many thousands of refugees from the same country, the procedures for conferring refugee status on an individual basis are too cumbersome, and an alternative mechanism has been devised which is known as group determination of status on a *prima facie* basis.[6] According to Bonaventure Rutinwa, group determination means the state recognizes those in a mass influx as refugees based on "the readily apparent, objective circumstances in the country of origin giving rise to exodus." The purpose of this group mechanism is "to ensure admission to safety, protection from refoulement [forced repatriation], and basic humanitarian treatment to those patently in need of it."[7] Most of the world's refugees have *prima facie* status. In 2003, some 64% of the world's 9.7 million refugees were granted refugee status on a group or *prima facie* basis, and less that a quarter (24%) were granted refugee status following individual determination.[8]

Prima facie refugee status is a presumptive status, that is, it presumes that the people granted refugee status would be defined as refugees if they underwent individual determination; and therefore, that they should be treated as refugees and entitled to all the rights of refugees, as stipulated by the 1951 Convention and other applicable instruments. However, while this mechanism is convenient in mass influx situations, it leads to several problems, which will be revisited later in this book. One is the difficulty of excluding criminals and combatants or other elements that are not deserving of international protection.[9] When these elements create problems for the host country, all the refugees suffer the consequences. In this book, for the sake of convenience, all people crossing the border from conflict-affected countries are referred to as refugees, regardless of their assigned legal status in the host country.

SOME CHARACTERISTICS OF PROTRACTED REFUGEE SITUATIONS

Cross-Border Movements

The picture of an acute mass influx, in which thousands of refugees cross the border in a short space of time, describes relatively few refugee situations. Most refugees travel as individuals or in small groups, leaving when they are able and often in secrecy; their movements constituting many trickles back and forth across borders over extended periods of time—depending on the ebb and flow of conflict in their home country. There are periods of increased refugee movement, but many countries never experience a mass influx; instead, refugee populations accumulate over prolonged periods, with return movements frequently interspersed. The situation of Liberian refugees in Côte d'Ivoire, described by Tom Kuhlman is illustrative:

> By the end of 1990, the Liberian refugee caseload in Côte d'Ivoire had increased to 272,000. In succeeding years, the numbers rose and fell as the civil war worsened or abated. The maximum may have been as high as 400,000 in the mid-1990s From 1996 onwards, many refugees returned home, well before UNHCR began its organized repatriation programme in 1997; by the end of 2000, 70,500 refugees had been repatriated with UNHCR assistance, but more had left of their own accord. Even as the repatriation was underway, the violence in Monrovia in 1998 provoked a new wave of 23,000 refugees towards Côte d'Ivoire.[10]

This movement back and forth across the border is characteristic of protracted refugee situations, and as we shall see, has important implications for refugees' economic activities.

Patterns of Settlement

Once across a border, refugees are in the country of first asylum, or the host country, and their first task is to find accommodation. An important decision is where and how to live. A significant proportion of refugees stay away from camps or official settlement sites, and settle themselves among the local population—in rural hamlets and small towns, in "refugee villages," near towns, or in the shanty towns of megacities. This pattern is known as self-settlement or dispersed settlement. Many do not register with the authorities, and thus are without legal status. Generally, self-settled refugees do not receive official government or international assistance, relying instead on the hospitality of the host community. They share local households or set up temporary accommodation, and are helped with shelter and food by their own networks or by community or religious organizations. According to Sarah Dryden Peterson and Lucy Hovil,

While "official" refugees fall under the control of the national government structures … self-settled refugees tend to operate within the local government structures, both rural and urban. They are integrated into their host community, pay graduated tax, contribute to the local economy, and even run in local council elections. However, their legal status remains insecure and ambiguous: they fall within the category of *prima facie* refugees, but are in danger of being seen as illegal immigrants.[11]

In some host countries, self-settled refugees are left undisturbed, but when there are very large numbers—or mass influxes—host governments often restrict refugees to areas near the border, usually in camps or settlements of some kind. This policy is based on various concerns, including security, manageability of large numbers, and the desire to prevent refugees from moving to the urban areas. In some cases, refugees themselves prefer to live in camps, since there they have access to humanitarian resources, including the possibility of resettlement. We will return to these issues in later chapters.

As shown in Table 6.1, of the 14.6 million persons of concern to UNHCR in 2001, some 60 percent were self-settled—13 percent (1.9m) in urban areas, and 47 percent (6.9m) dispersed in rural areas (or their type of settlement was unknown)—the other 40 percent (5.8m) resided in camps. In Africa and Asia, more than 50 percent of refugees live in camps and ten percent live in urban areas.[12] However, we should be cautious about these statistics. Refugees often desire to remain flexible about their living arrangement, and this means they can be unwilling to be counted and reluctant to reveal their exact locations to authorities. The numbers and proportions of refugees in different types of settlements are notoriously difficult to determine, although it is generally accepted that the number of self-settled refugees is much higher than that of refugees living in camps.[13]

Whether refugees choose to self-settle in urban or rural areas, or to live with humanitarian assistance in camps and official settlements, will affect their economic experience in the host country. However, as we discuss in Chapter Two, settlement is a fluid process, depending on when refugees arrived, their survival strategies, the local socioeconomic and security conditions, and the actions of local and national authorities. Earlier arrivals may settle in different situations than later ones. Self-settled refugees can be forcibly relocated into camps by local authorities, and sometimes refugees move out of camps and become self-settled, or back into them. Many refugee households use camps as part of a broad strategy of survival, in which the workers live outside in order to farm or find employment, and the non-workers (elderly, mothers, and children) live

Table 6.1   Location of Officially Reconized Refugees.

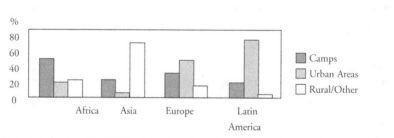

Source: Figures from UNHCR Statistics Unit. Chart adapted from *Alchemy Project Annual Report, 2003* (famine.tufts.edu/work/refugees.html).

in the camp where they have access to assistance. Refugees move in and out of the camps to find work, to trade, to explore repatriation options, to join the rebels, to visit, or to move to the city. They might return to the camps during the hungry season, or when there are security threats outside, or to use the camp schools. If camps are near towns, refugees living in the town pay social visits or come to the camp when resettlement interviews are being conducted. In turn, camp refugees go into towns to engage in various economic activities or to go to school. Local people frequent the camps too—making use of schools and health clinics set up by aid agencies, buying and selling in camp markets, or sometimes posing as refugees in order to get food aid. Refugees living in camps are never fully separated from the local community because of the difficulty of preventing movement in and out by both refugees and local people. Many host areas have a history of migration and mingling with the people who are now refugees. For example, in north-western Tanzania, the town of Kigoma on the shore of Lake Tanganyika has long been a migration target for Congolese on the other side of the lake, and Congolese and Tanzanians have historically mixed together for purposes of trade, marriage, entertainment, and seasonal work. This fluidity has strong implications for the constraints and opportunities for refugees' economic activities and their impact on the host community.

Why Refugees Do Not Go Home

In most protracted situations—where refugees have lived in host countries for at least three years (and often many more)—refugees cannot go home because the war, conflict, or persecution of ethnic groups in their home countries is not over, and it is unsafe for them to return. This is presently the case for refugees from Liberia, the Democratic Republic of the Congo (DRC), Burundi, Mauritania, Algeria, Sudan, Burma, Colombia, and others. What about situations where the war is over, where peace accords have been signed, and perhaps even where the government calls for refugees to return? This is currently the case in Rwanda, Angola, Sierra Leone, and—to some extent—in Afghanistan (although the conflict is not over), Bosnia, and Eritrea, among others. There are two linked reasons why long-term refugees do not return in these situations. One is that individuals still do not consider it safe, either for their particular ethnic group, or for the region of the country to which they would return. Peace is seldom spread homogenously across post-conflict countries,[14] and there are often pockets of resistance or ongoing conflict, which pose dangers to returnees. It is not uncommon for conflict to break out in parts of the country, as the peace is consolidated. This has occurred in Liberia repeatedly, and in Angola, Sierra Leone, eastern Congo, southern Sudan and Afghanistan. Many refugees adopt a "wait and see" attitude, and remain in their host countries—sometimes for several years—after peace accords are signed. As part of their repatriation programs, UNHCR sets up "go and see" visits, in which refugees are taken on visits to their home areas, to see and appraise the situation for themselves, then come back and report to others in the camp. If their judgment of the situation is negative, this will be communicated to others, quickly dampening prospects for return. Shelly Dick quotes a Liberian refugee living in Ghana in 2000:

> I would like to go back [to Liberia] some day, but not while Taylor is in power. I have friends who went back in 1995. Then the war came again in 1996 and things were much worse for them than the first time they ran. They had to run back to Ghana for a second time. They said going back to Liberia was the worst mistake they ever made. How can you go back to that kind of insecurity?[15]

Refugees' concerns about safe return are usually shared by relief agencies. In recent years, repatriation programs insisted upon by host governments—to countries like Burundi, Liberia, southern Sudan, and Afghanistan—have been strongly disputed by some agencies.

A second reason why refugees do not return, even where peace agreements have held and security is not a major concern, is because economic conditions in home countries devastated by years of conflict make the reconstruction of livelihoods very difficult. Roads and other transportation infrastructure are destroyed, and access to land is prevented by leftover problems from the war, such as mines or unexploded ordinance. At the village level, displacement and loss of life means social networks are disrupted or destroyed. In addition, most returnees lack the financial capital needed to re-establish their businesses or farms in their home countries. Given these problems, it is difficult for returnees to restart their livelihoods, and refugees often delay their return journey—preferring to wait until they can gather sufficient resources to ensure that they can put together a life when they return.

There are other reasons why refugees in protracted situations delay returning home. For some, it is the prospect of overwhelming family obligations in the home country. One Liberian refugee at Buduburam camp in Ghana, said,

> "I stay here because if I go home there are many people to take care of. My sister and brother have many children and they will ask me to help them. They think that because I am in Ghana I have more money to help. I want to help them but how can I? In Liberia you can work for two weeks or a month and when you go to collect your pay there is no money."[16]

For others, the lives they have constructed during their exile—even if they have been in a refugee camp—are better than the ones to which they would return in their home country. Even in camps, most refugees are fairly safe, with access to schools and health facilities, and some opportunities to pursue livelihoods—none of which is guaranteed in their home country. Some refugees remain in camps and hold onto their refugee status, so that they can remain eligible for resettlement in third countries like the United States or Europe. Last, and by no means least, many refugees have very bad memories of their homeland: including the loss of relatives and their own devastating ordeals of flight—any of these are enough to make refugees unwilling to ever return.

Refugees with *prima facie* status often find themselves in a precarious legal position when the civil war or conflict in their home country ends. Although UNHCR stipulates that all returns should be voluntary, the situation depends on the host government's position. In some countries, the government decides that refugees should return, and requires that those wishing to remain in the host country regularize their immigration papers, and either qualify as Convention refugees (prove their eligibility as individual refugees rather than *prima facie* ones) or risk being deported.[17] In host countries that are slow to execute determination procedures or other immigration requirements, long-term refugees usually continue living as *de facto* refugees—hoping the government will leave them alone—but in a precarious legal situation.

REFUGEE LIVELIHOODS

The study of refugee livelihoods is part of the body of research on livelihoods in zones of prolonged conflict and instability.[18] There are multiple strands of this research, including frameworks for understanding the context,[19] policy analysis regarding humanitarian assistance,[20] anthropological accounts of conflict-affected diasporas and their networks,[21] and the role of humanitarian assistance—both in supporting conflict reduction and peace capacities,[22] and in contributing to the conflict.[23] Much of this livelihoods research is useful for analyzing and understanding the economic experience of refugees, and there is now a growing body of research on "displaced livelihoods"—the experience of forced migrants and the role of migration in livelihoods.[24]

The economic impact of conflict and displacement on a household can be understood using an assets framework. Each household has a portfolio of assets, or types of capital, which are the things it needs, uses, and has access to, in order to pursue livelihoods.[25] Assets include different types of capital:

- Natural capital (land, water, forests);
- Physical capital (livestock, equipment, infrastructure like roads, buildings);
- Human capital (education and skills, life experience, health);
- Social capital (community trust and knowledge, networks);
- Financial capital (stocks and flows) which include:
  - Regular inflows of money through earned income, state transfers (for example pensions), and remittances;
  - Savings, in the form of cash, bank deposits, or liquid assets like livestock and jewelry; and
  - Credit, including access to credit institutions.

In conflict zones—like southern Sudan, eastern Congo, Afghanistan, and Burma—from which people are eventually displaced, all forms of household capital are seriously compromised. Assets are stolen or destroyed ("stripped"), and access to them is blocked or endangered. Physical assets like cattle, harvests, or transportation equipment is stolen or destroyed, both by raiding militias and as a result of a widespread instability, increased crime, and breakdown of law and order. Access to physical and natural capital like street markets, businesses, farms, or grazing land, is reduced because of the dangers associated with travel. People on the roads risk being caught in the crossfire between armed groups and encounters with armed roadblocks or roving gangs of bandits. Mines are a particular danger and threat to livelihoods; they are often laid in random or unanticipated ways, including in roads and fields. The dangers of travel mean reduced contact with markets and vendors, and decreased circulation of goods, services, and money. Availability of and access to social services—such as health or education—is also reduced, as personnel flee and sites come under attack. For example, in the northeastern Congo, near Bunia, it is common for hospitals to be assailed because they treat both sides of the ethnic conflict.

When people flee their homes in conflict zones, they have often lost everything that enables them to earn their own living. Whether they become internally displaced or cross the border to become refugees, they use up their last resources to finance the journeys. For example, most Afghan refugees who came to Pakistan during the late 1990s had been internally displaced in Afghanistan for months, as a result of both drought and the conflict. Many had been impoverished by the need to give the Taliban cash to avoid being forcibly recruited, or by damage to their property or livelihoods through war, leaving no resources with which to survive the current severe drought. They arrived impoverished, having had to sell everything they had left to pay for the journey to Pakistan.[26]

The constraints and challenges facing refugees are similar to those of all people, whether displaced or not, trying to survive in conflict zones. Their economic activities tend to be based in the informal sector, oriented towards generating quick cash, and characterized by low financial risk.[27] The following kinds of cash-generating activities are common:

- Buying and selling goods like firewood, charcoal, vegetables, prepared food, cigarettes, and sweets, on a daily basis (hawking);
- Services provided by hair dressers/beauticians, mechanics, food preparation, construction, telephone booths (where individual calls on a cell phone are sold), and courier services (including carrying money and other goods between town and villages);
- Special services by and for refugees like language tutoring or interpreting.

Income level depends on whether a person owns the small business or works for the owner, and on the cost of the credit needed to jumpstart the business. These activities generate small, irregular sums of money—which for many are insufficient and must be supplemented by other kinds of work—sometimes including high-risk activities, like prostitution or smuggling. In conflict zones where there is also commercial resource extraction (legal or illegal), like mining, logging, or oil extraction, many people also derive livelihoods from these industries.

In our livelihoods research conducted during the course of the Alchemy Project,[28] almost all of the economically active refugees with whom we worked were engaged in informal, sector-based, small enterprises of some kind—often supplemented with wage work, such as part-time employment with aid agencies (as teachers or translators or program staff). In camps, most refugees obtained some income by selling food rations (often the only source of cash income) or with "piecework" on local farms or households when the opportunity arose. Many tried to start a small business with cash left over after household needs were met, but for most, this amount was insufficient to start a sustainable business without a supplementary loan. In camps where cultivatable land was available or could be negotiated from the local community (usually by UNHCR), refugees engaged in agriculture on a small scale, sometimes harvesting enough to sell in local markets.

One of the most marked effects of forced displacement is the need to shift or diversify livelihoods. For most displaced people the only real income-earning possibility lies in petty trade. Most refugees have no access to farmland (or rangeland for pastoralists), and displaced people are obliged to become entrepreneurs, since any form of employment except odd jobs is usually hard to find. Very few refugees find formal wage employment, and those who do find it mainly with aid agencies. In urban areas and refugee camps, few of those with professional skills like nursing or teaching are able to utilize them, despite the need for these occupations in many host countries. The move toward non-farm activities like trading is very important, especially for women.[29] Displaced pastoralists, deprived of their cattle and rangeland by conflict, and settled in camps or villages, turn to other sources of income, like fishing or dairies. For example, in southern Sudan, displaced pastoralists like the Mundari people have discovered that the plentiful fish in the lakes and rivers can provide a livelihood. The Mundari traditionally had a disdain for fish as a food and for anyone who worked with fish, but the loss of their herds and the realization that fish is an important commodity have encouraged many to take up fishing as a livelihood.[30] In northeastern Kenya, displaced Somali pastoralists who have settled near the town of Wajir have started in the dairy business, and cooperatives of women sell milk in roadside stalls.[31] Urban migration by refugees is also a livelihood response, but refugees in urban areas face many occupational difficulties, which are magnified by their lack of legal status and the absence of much official assistance. We will return to this discussion in Chapter Three.

THE NEED FOR CASH AND CREDIT

The losses and dislocations from conflict and the ensuing displacement mean that one of the most serious needs for displaced people is access to cash and credit. Cash can only be obtained by engaging in economic activities, but cash or credit is needed in order to jumpstart these activities. Refugees also need cash for other purposes: to meet basic needs, to pay for transportation to the capital to keep their papers in order, and to pay their debts before they can begin reconstructing their livelihoods. In refugee camps, many basic needs are met through relief programs, but not all are, and not usually for as long as the refugees need them. For example, in many camps, firewood for cooking is not provided as part of the ration, and refugees must either buy it from local vendors (for which they need cash), or leave the camp to find it in the bush, often quite a risky venture. For refugees not living in camps, both basic needs and the means to restart one's livelihood require cash or credit.

There are few sources of credit for refugees. In most host countries, refugees do not have access to savings and loans facilities of formal banks and credit institutions, and without bank accounts they lack both credit and a safe place to keep savings. One of the biggest problems faced by displaced people trying to save money is the insecure environment and lack of safe facilities, especially in urban areas. Refugees can borrow money from moneylenders, but their rates are very high. Displaced people must establish access to new sources of financial capital, either through tapping into home community networks that become re-established in new places, or by trying to access local credit networks and community banks. Community-based rotating savings and credit associations (ROSCAs) can be established in refugee camps, but these groups often require that members be solvent or have a source of income before they can join. Perhaps the most fortunate refugees in first asylum countries are those with family in other countries, especially the West, who send remittances. For those lucky few, remittances are a lifesaving source of income, but for those refugees in third countries who must send them, this obligation can be a serious drain on their income. We return to these issues in later chapters. First, we consider the context in which refugees pursue livelihood strategies.

THE INSTITUTIONAL CONTEXT OF DISPLACED LIVELIHOODS

The ability of refugees in protracted situations to pursue livelihoods is both constrained and enabled by social, political, and institutional factors at the global, national, and local levels. At the global level, there are the *rights*—especially social and economic rights—assigned to refugees by international laws and agreements, plus the international expectation that refugees should receive humanitarian aid, protection, and advocacy from international organizations like UNHCR and nongovernmental organizations. At the national level, there is the *host government's policy* towards refugees, which may or may not be in line with the government's international obligations. At the local level, there is the host community in which refugees settle, which brings with it many factors affecting refugee livelihoods—including the response of the local authorities, local security, economic problems, and the attitudes of the local population. Here we briefly consider each of these components, and then explore them in more detail in the next two chapters, as they play out in camp and urban settings.

The Rights of Refugees to Engage in Economic Activities

The economic rights of refugees to pursue livelihoods are clearly set forth in the principle international instrument pertaining to refugees, the United Nations Convention Relating to the Status of Refugees, adopted in Geneva on 28 July 1951, and commonly referred to as the 1951 Convention (see Appendix A for the full text).[32] According to Articles 17 and 18 (Wage-Earning Employment and Self-Employment), the Contracting State shall accord to refugees lawfully staying in their territory:

> "the most favourable treatment accorded to nationals of a foreign country in the same circumstances, as regards the right to engage in wage-earning employment."

and

> "… treatment as favourable as possible and, in any event, not less favourable than that accorded to aliens generally in the same circumstances, as regards the right to engage on his own account in agriculture, industry, handicrafts, and commerce, and to establish commercial and industrial companies.

In addition, the Convention requires that Contracting States give refugees the right to:

- Practice a liberal profession (Article 19);
- Choose their place of residence to move freely within its territory (Article 26);
- Obtain travel documents for the purpose of travel outside their territory (Article 28).

Other rights relating to refugees' economic activities include the imposition of taxes: Contracting States should "not impose upon refugees duties, charges, or taxes, of any description whatsoever, *other or higher than those which are or may be levied on their nationals* in similar situations." (Article 29, emphasis added). But the Convention does not forbid imposing fees or "charges in respect of the issue to aliens of administrative documents including identity papers." Refugees should also be permitted to "transfer assets which they have brought into its territory, to another country where they have been admitted for the purposes of resettlement" (Article 30). In general, the Convention requires that the Contracting States "shall as far as possible facilitate the assimilation and naturalization of refugees" (Article 34).

In addition to these rights, refugees are entitled to humanitarian assistance, but as discussed earlier, this assistance declines precipitously in protracted situations. Funding that is available during emergencies is cut off after a period of time, and soon only food rations for the most vulnerable are available, and even those eventually cease.[33] The reasons for cuts in the level of humanitarian assistance are both budgetary and substantive. UNHCR often has difficulty allocating funds to protracted situations, because most donors want humanitarian assistance directed at emergencies. But in addition, UNHCR and the host government sometimes use reduced rations to discourage the long-term presence of refugees and encourage repatriation. Whatever the reason, the lack of adequate assistance has significant implications for how refugees survive. The reluctance of donors to continue funding once the emergency phase has ended means UNHCR must triage its funding of long-term refugee situations. For every refugee situation, the level of assistance depends on the willingness and size of donor states' contributions. Low levels of funding require UNHCR to come up with alternative ways to support refugees, usually by encouraging self-sufficiency or self-reliance. We will return to this issue in Chapter Five.

Host Government Policy Regarding Refugees' Economic Activities

The economic rights assigned refugees by the 1951 Convention are clear, but to be effective they need to be implemented by host governments, and this implementation often fails to take place.

Every host country has (or is supposed to have, according to international refugee law) national refugee legislation, which sets out the country's official response to refugee arrivals and the conditions of their stay, including their freedom of movement and right to work. In many host countries, the rights of refugees to be economically active are ignored or overruled, or at best practiced irregularly. It is increasingly common for host governments to restrict all kinds of economic activities by refugees outside designated camp areas, in an effort to discourage permanence and encourage repatriation. If legislation does not exist, host governments usually issue regulations concerning where refugees should live, and their freedom to move around, seek work, and access social services. In recent years, an increasingly restrictive climate has prevailed in many key host countries.

A key problem in developing countries is that many host countries do not have specific laws pertaining to refugees, nor a clearly articulated refugee policy. When there is such a policy it is often unevenly or irregularly implemented, and some host countries, like Kenya, leave all refugee matters to UNHCR. In most countries, there are regulations on refugees' economic activities, usually restricting them to designated zones, or to areas within a designated distance of the camps. When these zones are in isolated areas, refugees have difficulty establishing livelihoods, particularly because of the resources they need to travel to markets to trade their goods.

Two of the main reasons for host governments' resistance to refugees' economic activities are security problems and resource burdens. During the 1980s, many host governments—particularly in Africa—cited the limited capacity of their national economies to absorb refugees as the primary reason for their desire that refugees should be fully taken care of by aid agencies, rather than be allowed to support themselves. Since the 1990s, security concerns have added an equally powerful reason to keep refugees segregated from the local community. Even when government policies are in place to assist refugees with economic activities, such as the Self-reliance Strategy in Uganda, security problems can overwhelm them. In northern Uganda, chronic violence and conflict between government forces and the rebel Lord's Resistance Army has severely disrupted the lives of both long-term Sudanese refugees living there and the local population. In Adjumani, for example, many refugees had become self-sufficient in terms of food production, but the upheavals from attacks and violence have caused refugees to flee their fields, and become once again dependent on direct assistance.[34] Faced with domestic economic problems of unemployment and poverty, together with security threats, few host governments are willing to be generous to refugees, preferring to keep them in camps where international relief agencies can take care of them and ensure they return to their home countries as soon as possible. That return is unlikely to occur soon nevertheless does not incline them to allow refugees their rights to economic freedom.

The Local Response: The Relationship Between the Local Population and the Refugees

A third factor affecting the context for refugee livelihoods is the host community and its local authorities. Many refugee-hosting areas are in remote locations, at a distance from the national capital, and the reach of the central government into these areas is weak, so it is often local or provincial authorities that decide how strictly to implement national policy. As outsiders and "guests," the ability of refugees to work and move around freely outside of camps is contingent upon the good will and cooperation of most of the local population, their leaders, and the local authorities. In the absence of this good will, refugees encounter hostility, antagonism, and even threats, and the host community is more likely to call on the national government to clamp down on refugees. When the local community accepts refugees, they are better able to hide from authorities, face fewer security threats, and are more able to pursue livelihoods. In some host countries, official policies of encampment are undermined or subverted by local chiefs and villagers who collaborate in enabling refugees to settle in the community.[35] Refugees' ability to pursue livelihoods depends on who benefits and who loses from their presence, and on whether the interests of the most powerful actors are being sufficiently served, or at least not subverted. There are multiple actors, or stakeholders, in a host area—including wealthy farmers and businessmen, poor peasants, and local authorities, such as chiefs and village leaders—each with varying interests in refugees and different degrees of power to block or enable refugees' economic activities.

One of the key issues mediating the relationship between the host community and refugees is *access to land*. Where refugees live in camps or settlements, their access to farm land is usually negotiated by either the government or UNHCR, but refugees must also have access to the commons to obtain basic necessities like firewood or construction timber, or grass for grazing if they want to keep livestock. Where land is scarce, tensions occur. An example is the case of Nakivale Refugee Settlement in western Uganda, which began in 1960 in response to an influx of Batutsi refugees fleeing the Bahutu regime that had taken power in Rwanda. The land for the settlement was acquired from the local king by the colonial government in exchange for other land. The Nakivale land was close to the border with Rwanda and had a low population of nationals because of infestation with tsetse fly. Nakivale has since hosted a wide diversity of refugee nationalities, and, as land constraints have grown in Uganda, tensions between refugees and nationals over access to the land in the Nakivale area has become a critical issue.[36]

By contrast, when land is abundant, sufficient for people to grow their own food, and the settlement is far from insecure borders, the situation is often calmer and less tense. Sarah Dryden Peterson contrasts the situation in Nakivale with that in Kyaka II Refugee Settlement in Kyenjojo District in western Uganda, where refugees live in harmony with locals and where everyone is able to grow [his or her] own food.[37] Similarly, in Zambia's western province, Angolan refugees have lived in peace for many years among Zambians, who regard them as hard workers, able to bring more land under production. This region of Zambia is relatively undeveloped and land—while not very fertile—is abundant. Most importantly, the locals do not perceive there to be security problems linked to the Angolans.

Security problems are serious obstacles to economic activity, making movement outside the camps dangerous, and affecting life inside the camps. On the part of the host community, initial sympathy and willingness to help the refugees often turns into resentment when they are perceived to create or aggravate security or economic problems. These threats and the resulting resentment increase when refugee numbers continue to grow or with new waves of arrivals. However, while security and resource burdens are real problems in many host areas, refugees are often blamed for pre-existing social or economic problems. Many host countries today are experiencing a range of rapid and disorienting economic, social, and political changes that have resulted in rises in crime and insecurity or declining standards of living. Such changes include the imposition of structural adjustment programs, proximity to conflict zones and/or involvement in the conflict, and public health crises like HIV-AIDS. In this context, refugees often become scapegoats and are more vulnerable and more likely to lack protection of their rights, including the right to work. This is illustrated in case of South Africa, currently struggling through a period of transition and stress as it recovers from the apartheid years. High levels of unemployment and a struggling economy, elevated crime rates, and widespread insecurity have led to harassment of migrants, among whom there are many urban self-settled refugees. In many host countries, local people believe that the presence of refugees is linked to the rise in criminal activity, delinquency, street prostitution, and drug proliferation. But many of these countries were already experiencing rising poverty, unemployment, and other structural economic problems that were not caused by refugees. While refugees can aggravate the social dislocations associated with this poverty, it is unlikely that they are responsible for them. The economic and social benefits to host communities of hosting refugees can outweigh the costs, particularly if policies are set up so as to take advantage of the refugees' presence.[38]

NOTES

1. This book focuses on the experience of refugees, and does not address the larger problem of internally displaced people. Although the economic problems of IDPs are often similar to those of refugees, the policy context and politics of IDP situations are very different and will not be addressed in this book.

2. Executive Committee of the High Commissioner's Programme, "Protracted Refugee Situations" Standing Committee 30th Meeting, 10 June 2004; available at www.unhcr.ch.statistics. See also Jeff Crisp and Damtew Dessalegne, "Refugee Protection and Migration Management: The Challenge for UNHCR," (working paper, New Issues in Refugee Research, no. 64, UNHCR, 2002); Jeff Crisp "No Solutions in Sight: The Problem of Protracted Refugee Situations in Africa," (working paper, New Issues in Refugee Research, no. 75, UNHCR, 2002).

3. The official UN figure was 175 million international migrants in 2002, but some experts, including the Global Commission for International Migration, think this is an undercount and think 200 million is a closer estimate (www.gcim.org).

4. The 1951 UN Convention defines a refugee as any person who: "owing to a well-founded fear of being persecuted for reasons of race, religion, nationality, membership of a particular social group or political opinion, is outside the country of his nationality and is unable or, owing to such fear or for reasons other than personal convenience, is unwilling to avail himself of the protection of that country." In 1969, the Organization of African States enlarged that definition for African states so as to include persons who: "owing to external aggression, occupation, foreign domination or events seriously disturbing public order in either part or the whole of his country of origin or nationality, is compelled to leave his place of habitual residence in order to seek refuge in another place outside his country ..." For full definitions see Appendix A which contains the text of the 1951 Convention, and UNHCR's Web site: www.unhcr.ch.

5. Even those who have undergone full determination and have legal refugee status may find their actual rights and residence status to be insecure and incomplete. Not all host countries signatory to the Convention have implemented the Articles of the Convention. See Jennifer Hyndman and B.V. Nylund, "UNHCR and the Status of *Prima Facie* Refugees in Kenya," *International Journal of Refugee Law* 10(1/2) (1998): 21–48.

6. Bonaventure Rutinwa, "*Prima Facie* Status and Refugee Protection," (working paper, New Issues in Refugee Research, no. 69, UNHCR, 2002).

7. Rutinwa, "*Prima Facie* Status," 1.

8. UNHCR, "Global Refugee Trends: Overview of Refugee Populations, New Arrivals, Durable Solutions, Asylum-Seekers and Other Persons of Concern to UNHCR"; available at www.unhcr.ch/cgi-bin/texis/vtx/statistics.

9. See Rutinwa, "*Prima Facie* Status," 1.

10. Tom Kuhlman, *Responding to Protracted Refugee Situations: A Case Study of Liberian Refugees in Côte d'Ivoire*, report for UNHCR Evaluation and Policy Unit, 2002, 11.

11. Sarah Dryden-Peterson and Lucy Hovil, "Local Integration as a Durable Solution: Refugees, Host Populations and Education in Uganda," (working paper, New Issues in Refugee Research, no. 93, UNHCR, 2003), 6.

12. *UNHCR Statistical Handbook* 2001 (Geneva: UNHCR, 2001), 38; available at www.unhcr.ch/cgi-bin/texis/vtx/statistics.

13. See Bela Hovy, "Statistically Correct Asylum Data: Prospects and Limitations," (working paper, New Issues in Refugee Research, no. 37, UNHCR, 2001); and Jonathan Bascom, *Losing Place: Refugee Populations and Rural Transformations in East Africa* (New York: Berghahn Books, 1998), 26. For example in Uganda, at the end of 2002, the UNHCR reported a national total of 197,082 refugees, primarily from Sudan, Democratic Republic of Congo (DRC), and Rwanda, who were registered with UNHCR and who living in settlement areas. However, according to Dryden-Peterson and Hovil (5) "In addition to this number, conservative estimates place the number of self-settled refugees in the country at approximately 50,000. In reality, the number is probably far higher. Furthermore, there are 10,000 refugees registered with the Office of the Prime Minister as self-sufficient urban refugees and it is estimated that 5,000 to 10,000 others live in Kampala without assistance or protection."

14. Rather than calling countries "post-conflict," a preferable term might be "post-peace accord" which describes the situation, but does not imply that conflict is over.

15. Shelly Dick, "Liberians in Ghana: Living without Humanitarian Assistance," (working paper, New Issues in Refugee Research, no. 57, UNHCR, 2002), 40.

16. Dick, "Liberians in Ghana," 49.

17. Dick, "Liberians in Ghana," 42.

18. G. M. Hamid, "Livelihood Patterns of Displaced Households in Greater Khartoum," *Disasters* 16 (1992): 230–239; Sue Lautze, E. Stites, N. Nojumi, and F. Najimi, "Qaht-E-Pool 'A Cash Famine': Food Insecurity in Afghanistan 1999–2002," (28 October 2002); available at famine.tufts.edu/pdf/cash_famine.pdf; Mark Vincent and Birgitte Sorensen, *Caught Between Borders: Response Strategies of the Internally Displaced* (London and Sterling, VA: Norwegian Refugee Council and Pluto Press, 2001); and T. Wilson, *Microfinance during and After Armed Conflict: Lessons from Angola, Cambodia, Mozambique and Rwanda* (Durham, UK: Concern Worldwide and Springfield Centre for Business in Development, 2002).

19. These include political analyses such as Joanna Macrae and Anthony Zwi, eds. (with Mark Duffield and Hugo Slim), *War and Hunger: Rethinking International Responses to Complex Emergencies* (London: Zed Books in association with Save the Children Fund (UK), 1994); more policy-oriented frameworks such as DFID's Sustainable Livelihoods model (www.livelihoods.org), and the recent work that emphasizes the importance of vulnerability and risk and downplays the importance of sustainability in a livelihoods framework, for example Helen Young et al., *Nutrition and Livelihoods in Situations of Conflict and other Crises* (Medford, MA: Feinstein International Famine Center, Tufts University, 2002) and Adam Pain and Sue Lautze, *Livelihoods in Afghanistan* (Kabul: Afghanistan, Afghanistan Research and Evaluation Unit, 2002).

20. Recommendations concerning livelihood interventions in conflict and displaced situations include those concerned with providing shelter and access to productive assets as a means to support livelihoods, see S. Ellis and S. Barakat, "From Relief to Development: The Long-Term Effects of 'Temporary' Accommodation of Refugees and Displaced Persons in the Republic of Croatia," *Disasters* 20 (1996): 111–124; R. Green, "Regaining and Securing Access to Common Property Resources," in *Risks andReconstruction: Experiences of Resettlers and Refugees,* eds. Michael M. Cernea and Christopher McDowell (Washington, DC: World Bank, 2000), 253–290; and a very large literature on food security (for a review see Young et al., *Nutrition and Livelihoods*).

21. Many of these studies emphasize how different networks underpin and enable people's pursuit of livelihoods in conflict. See Janet MacGaffey and Remy Bazengguissa-Ganga, *Congo-Paris: Transnational Traders on the Margins of the Law* (Indiana: James Currey/Indiana University Press, 2000) for their study of Congolese traders in Paris, and Cindy Horst, "Vital Links in Social Security: Somali Refugees in the Dadaab Camps, Kenya," (working paper, New Issues in Refugee Research, no. 38, UNHCR, 2001) for her account of Somali networks.

22. This strand of research is exemplified in Mary Anderson's work and her Local Capacities for Peace Project which explores how humanitarian aid can help communities find and strengthen the peace capacities ("peace connectors") in their societies. See Mary B. Anderson, *Do No Harm; How Aid Can Support Peace—or War* (Boulder, CO: Lynne Rienner Publishers, Inc., 1999).

23. Marl Duffied, *Shifting Sands: The Search for 'Coherence' Between Political and Humanitarian Responses to Complex Emergencies,* Humanitarian Policy Group Report 8 (London: ODI, August 2001); D. Keen, "A Disaster for Whom? Local Interests and International Donors During Famine among the Dinka of Sudan," *Disasters* 15 (1991): 58–73; and J. Goodhand and D. Hulme, "Understanding Conflict and Peace-Building in the New World Disorder," *Third World Quarterly* Vol. 20(1) (1999): 13–26.

24. See for example, M. Cernea, "The Risks and Reconstruction Model for Resettling Displaced Populations," *World Development* 25 (1997): 1569–1587; A. De Haan, "Livelihoods and Poverty: The Role of Migration—A Critical Review of the Migration Literature," *The Journal of Development Studies* 36 (1999): 1–47; K. Ogden, "Coping Strategies Developed as a Result of Social Structure and Conflict: Kosovo in the 1990s," *Disasters* 24 (2000): 117–132; Dick, "Liberians in Ghana"; Karen Jacobsen, "Livelihoods in Conflict: The Pursuit of Livelihoods by Refugees and the Impact on the Human Security of Host Communities," (expert working paper, Center for Development Research Study: Migration-Development Links: Evidence and Options, February 2002).

25. This section draws on the discussion of this framework and the different types of capital in Pain and Lautze, *Livelihoods in Afghanistan,* 9–14. See also www.livelihoods.org/info/info_guidancesheets.html#11.

26. U.S. Committee for Refugees (USCR), "Pakistan: Afghan Refugees Shunned and Scorned," (Washington, DC, September 2001); available at www.refugees.org/world/articles/pakistan_introduction_2001.htm.

27. Wilson, *Microfinance,* 1.

28. Karen Jacobsen, "Supporting Displaced Livelihoods with Microcredit and Other Income Generating Programs: Findings from the Alchemy Project, 2001–2004," Feinstein International Famine Center, Tufts University. November 2004; available at www.famine.tufts.edu.

29. Grace Carswell, "Livelihood Diversification in Southern Ethiopia," (working paper, Institute of Development Studies, no. 117, 2000).

30. *Alchemy Project Annual Report 2002,* Alchemy Project, Feinstein International Famine Center, Tufts University, Medford, MA, 2002; available at famine.tufts.edu/index.html?id=18.

31. Maitri Morarji, *Alchemy Project Field Assessment: Arid Lands Development Focus, Wajir, Kenya,* Alchemy Project Country Report No. 6 (August 2004); available at www.famine.tufts.edu.

32. For a discussion of these rights, and several relevant articles, see USCRI, *World Refugee Survey,* 2004, (Washington, DC, 2004); available at www.refugees.org/wrs04/main.html.

33. Shelly Dick (23–24) cites the case of Liberian refugees in Ghana: "By August 1996 when Liberia's civil war officially ended, Ghana was said to be providing asylum for an estimated 17,000 Liberians … Up to that point the humanitarian aid regime was in full operation providing food rations, education, health care and other basic needs for the refugees … as of 1997 assistance was greatly reduced. By 1998, the loan scheme was discontinued and food rations were only distributed to the most vulnerable refugees … As of 30 June 2000 even food rations for vulnerable refugees ceased and all humanitarian assistance … was withdrawn from Liberians according to UNHCR regional policy."

34. As reported by Dryden-Peterson and Hovil (9), an extreme case of security threat was the Achol-Pii Refugee Settlement in Pader District, Uganda. In July 1996, the Lords Resistance Army (LRA) attacked the settlement killing over 100 unarmed refugees and wounding several others. After a passionate appeal to the government of Uganda to relocate them to the southern parts of the country, the Government responded that the refugees had no right to decide where to be housed and that if they were tired of government's hospitality, they should go back to their country of origin. Unable to return to Sudan, the majority remained in Achol-Pii. Despite numerous reports warning of an imminent attack on the settlement in 2002, the government did not act. On August 5, 2002, the LRA again attacked Achol-Pii Refugee Settlement killing more than 20 refugees, injuring several others, and displacing 23,000.

35. Oliver Bakewell, "Repatriation and Self-Settled Refugees in Zambia: Bringing Solutions to the Wrong Problems," *Journal of Refugee Studies* 13, no. 4 (2000): 370.

36. Dryden-Peterson and Hovil, "Local Integration," 13.

37. Dryden-Peterson and Hovil, "Local Integration," 17.

38. See, among others, Karen Jacobsen, "The Forgotten Solution: Local Integration for Refugees in Developing Countries," (working paper, New Issues in Refugee Research, no. 45, UNHCR, 2001); Dryden-Peterson and Hovil, "Local Integration," 7; Tania Kaiser, *A Beneficiary-Based Evaluation of the UNHCR Programme in Guinea,* report for UNHCR Evaluation and Policy Analysis Unit, 2001; Crisp, "No Solutions"; Barbara Harrell-Bond, "Toward the Economic and Social 'Integration' of Refugee Populations in Host Countries in Africa," (conference, Stanley Foundation, "Refugee Protection in Africa: How to Ensure Security and Development for Refugees and Hosts," Entebbe, Uganda, November 2002).

STUDY QUESTIONS

1. How would you characterize the migration patterns of most forcibly displaced people?
2. A second reality of refugee situations, not captured on TV images, is the protracted nature of displacement. What contributes to this protracted situation?
3. What distinguishes refugees from migrants?
4. Who are refugees?
5. How do most refugees travel?
6. A significant proportion of refugees stay away from camps or official settlement sites. What do they do instead and what is it like?
7. Which generally has the higher population numbers, self-settled refugees or refugees in camps and official settlements?
8. What are some of the ways refugee households use camps as part of a broad pattern of survival?
9. Is there a clear segregation between refugees in camps and the local people?
10. Once the war is over, peace accords have been signed, and perhaps, governments even call for refugees to return, why do many refugees still not go home?
11. List the types of capital or assets households need in order to pursue livelihoods.
12. When people flee their homes in conflict zones, what often happens to their capital and assets?
13. Why are most refugees obliged to become entrepreneurs?
14. Internationally, which three Articles of the 1951 Convention specifically protect the right of refugees to work in the host country?
15. Are these Articles commonly followed in the host country? Why or why not?
16. Why would host countries prefer for refugees to stay in camps?
17. How does distance from the national capital affect local policies towards refugees?
18. Explain why one of the key issues mediating the relationship between the host community and refuges is access to land.
19. Under what conditions do refugees often become scapegoats?

Chapter 7 Snapshot
Screaming at The Moptops: Convergences Between Tourism and Popular Music

Music can enhance tourism. In fact, "music sounds, scenes and performance events have encouraged people to visit geographical places in person, or to travel to other places in an imaginary sense" (104). It doesn't take long, when hearing Hawaiian music, to feel yourself whisked off to the Islands in your imagination, or upon hearing steel drums to feel yourself slipping into the Caribbean. It's difficult to think of a trip to New York City without taking in a Broadway play, or going to Southern California without having the experience of listening to beautiful music under the stars at the Hollywood Bowl. Not only can music represent place through images and emotions, place can also "represent the lives and work of popular musicians" (104). All we have to do is think of Elvis Presley, and Graceland comes to mind; Dolly Parton and Dollywood or the Grand Ole Opry. This article uses a Beatles tribute band called The Moptops to explore the relationship between music and cultural tourism in the Beatles' hometown of Liverpool, and to investigate some of the ways that music influences place.

TOURISM AND POPULAR MUSIC EVENTS

Liverpool was the origin of The Beatles and it has attracted fans and tourists since the 1960s; in fact, The Beatles "were perhaps the first band to make their local origins a part of their global success" (59). Many of the Beatles' songs make references to places in and around Liverpool. There are Beatles tribute bands all over the world, including Sweden, Japan, and Argentina, but none inspire fans as much as the tribute bands that perform in Liverpool. Fans want to know "more about the Beatles' connections with Liverpool and to celebrate and commemorate those connections" (105). For example, there was an informal Beatles convention organized by local fans that was taken over by Cavern Club Tours (CCT) in 1986 (the Cavern Club is where the Beatles used to play, but the original building has been torn down). By 1995 this convention became one of the most important annual tourist attractions in the region. "Other commercial organisations directly involved with Beatles tourism in Liverpool at the time of The Moptops performance included the Beatles Story Museum, the Beatles Shop selling Beatles recordings and merchandise, and a few individual entrepreneurs" (105). There were other affiliated businesses as well: a hotel and private-sector businesses which launched the Cavern Quarter Initiative in 1993. "This initiative involved the development of a music heritage quarter around Mathew Street, and aimed to physically transform and gentrify the area through place marketing and the development of tourism, retail and entertainment" (105). This region was beginning to take on the image of a heritage center because The Moptops "were designed to re-enact and recreate the local past through repertoire, stage dress, performance gestures and movements" (106). According to author Sara Cohen, "The Beatles may be regarded as a product of Liverpool but the city has also been a product of the Beatles and their music" (106).

TOURISM AND MUSIC INSTITUTIONS AND POLICIES

The city of Liverpool was not always seen so brightly. "During the 1980s and early 1990s, in particular, the city became known in Britain as much for urban decline as for football and the Beatles" (106). In fact, "the British media used the city as a symbol not just of urban decay but of everything wrong with the nation's cities, representing the city through narrow, ugly stereotypes" (106). Some people saw Liverpool's association with The Beatles as a way to promote Liverpool to the world, while others "associated the Beatles, and popular music generally, with drugs, deviancy and rebellion" (107). Beatles tourist entrepreneurs however, did not give up, continuing to lobby the city for their financial support and recognition. "To strengthen their argument they likened the connection between Liverpool and the Beatles to that between Stratford and Shakespeare ..., thus elevating the Beatles to the status of high culture" (107). It wasn't just the persistence of these hard-working entrepreneurs; timing played a big part in what was going to happen to Liverpool. There was a new movement among Britain's cities to emphasize art and culture as contributing to economic development. Tourism was becoming one of the world's largest international industries, replacing traditional manufacturing. In fact, these trends were not only occurring in Great Britain but in many other British and North American cities. "New Orleans' infamous jazz musicians and scene had attracted visiting jazz fans since the early 1940s, but the city's policy-makers associated jazz with prostitution and gambling. Only in the 1990s did they begin to promote jazz tourism" (108). Elvis Presley's Graceland was opened to the public in Memphis, providing "gift shops and themed restaurants, and the city's Beale Street, site of Sun Studios where Elvis first recorded, was rebuilt and marketed to visitors as the 'birthplace of the blues'" (108). In Britain, the notion of heritage and culture began to encompass the popular and more recent past and the everyday. In 1995 "Britain's National Trust announced that it would be purchasing the former Liverpool home of Sir Paul McCartney (only recently knighted) to develop it as a visitor attraction. In 1997, England's Historical Buildings and Monuments Commission ... erected a plaque on the former London residence of rock guitarist Jimi Hendrix. In 1998, the English Tourist Board published *Rock and Popular Map of Britain: One Nation One Groove*, as a guide to places that have inspired British popular musicians, and by 2003, Britain's National Trust also purchased John Lennon's Liverpool home (108). "As a tour operator, however, one of CCT's primary aims was to encourage Beatle fans and audiences from outside the city to visit Liverpool, thus turning fans into tourists" (108).

CONVERGENCE BETWEEN TOURISM AND MUSIC IDEOLOGIES

There was a serious interest in Beatles history. However, was the Liverpool that was being marketed as the birthplace of the Beatles authentically Liverpool or a contrived Liverpool? It is clear, as Thomas S. Bremer (*Sacred Spaces and Tourist Places*) has pointed out, that tourists require that places be commodified (be considered a commodity presented in the marketplace) to respond to touristic needs; hotels, restaurants, easy access places, language translations, souvenir shops, and so on. That is, tourists "serve as consumers in a marketplace of aesthetically pleasing experiences" (Bremer: 71). But is this authentically Liverpool as the Beatles experienced it … or even as the Beatles *made* it? Recall Mike Crang, (*Place or Space?*) commenting that "locals may find themselves dealing with tourists to such an extent that they end up trying to look more 'authentic' than otherwise. They act so as to confirm touristic impressions of what a local should look like" (Crang: 57) or of what Liverpool as a tribute town to the Beatles should look like. "…[T]hroughout Beatles Week they and other city visitors debated the accuracy of the continual stories being told about the Beatles; the authenticity of Beatles-related artefacts up for auction, or of Beatle sites; whether the Beatles should be used to represent and promote Liverpool or whether the city was 'more than the Beatles'" (109). The original Cavern Club had been torn down, but a new one was replicated somewhat further down Mathew Street from the original site. There were various viewpoints about the authenticity of the Cavern Club; "some visitors were unaware that the original Cavern Club no longer existed, others criticized Liverpool for demolishing the original saying they would have preferred to have seen 'the real thing'", others "knew that the replica Cavern Club had been rebuilt further along Mathew Street", and still "other fans felt that if they couldn't see the original Cavern club then the reconstruction of it in both Mathew Street, and in the Beatles Story museum in Liverpool's docklands area, were the next best thing and helped them to feel closer to the Beatles" (110). Still, "many were concerned that if Beatles tourism was over-commercialised the city could become a 'tacky', 'artificial', 'plastic' 'themepark', Disneyland or Graceland being commonly referenced as negative illustrations of what Liverpool could become" (111). "Both examples, but particularly the former, have become familiar symbols of the Americanisation of the service economy, of the commercial and inauthentic, and of fake culture with little grounding in reality" (111). Is the authenticity of local culture being destroyed through the commercialization of the Beatles in what was being perceived as a "heritage quarter" or has this gentrification provided a stronger cultural identity for Liverpool?

CONCLUSION AND DISJUNCTURE

"Music-makers in other post-industrial cities have shared similar attitudes and experiences, and the questions 'whose culture? Whose heritage?' are familiar to cultural tourism in general" (113). "In New Orleans jazz musicians regularly perform for tourists, but this relationship is often regarded as exploitative … and 'real' New Orleans music-making has been considered as that which exists beyond the earshot of tourists and outside the city tourist areas" (113).

The Beatles left Liverpool actually very early in their careers. Many local music-makers are not enthusiastic about the elevation of the Beatles' culture in Liverpool, overshadowing more contemporary popular music. Some actually resented the Beatles heritage efforts. The Cavern Quarter Initiative gentrified the area along Mathew Street, but inevitably this gentrification began raising rents in this area, forcing out many small music businesses. "Many other music practitioners also argued the Liverpool should promote a vibrant, alive musical culture rather than the dead or sterile" (113).

7. Screaming at The Moptops

Convergences Between Tourism and Popular Music

By Sara Cohen

INTRODUCTION

On 23 August 1996, four young men took to the stage in a large bar room located in the basement of a grand but rather jaded hotel in Liverpool, a post-industrial maritime city on the northwest coast of England. Each wore a grey round-collar jacket, white shirt, black tie, pointed black patent boots and a black wig. Together they performed a series of Beatles songs on instruments similar to those of the original and infamous Beatles, including Paul McCartney's notorious left-handed bass. Their vocal and instrumental sounds, stage movements and gestures, were closely modelled on those of the original band members, hence 'Ringo' moved his head rhythmically from side to side behind his drumkit which displayed in large black letters the band's name, The Moptops. 'George' kicked up his feet in a familiar quirky, knee-jerk style, and the heads of 'Paul' and 'John' met as they leant into one of the microphones, shaking their dark heavy fringes. The bar contained around two hundred people. Some wandered around the darkened perimeter walls looking rather lost and lonely. Others queued to buy drinks or stood further forward sipping their drinks and chatting in groups of two or three. Towards the centre of the room a large attentive group of mostly young women gathered around the spot-lit stage. Amongst them were those who sang along and danced enthusiastically or screamed at the band, gesticulating wildly at each song. Following the final encore some giggled excitably as they queued backstage to demand autographs, but the band were soon ushered away by the event's organisers.

The Moptops performance is used in this chapter as a starting point for an exploration of convergences between music and tourism.[1] Music and tourism have always converged in some way. Music sounds, scenes and performance events have encouraged people to visit geographical places in person, or to travel to other places in an imaginary sense (Cohen 1998). Music has also been used to represent and market places to potential visitors because of its ability to connect places with particular images and emotions. In addition, music has influenced visitors' experiences of places, because of its central role in local leisure and entertainment venues. This chapter focuses on a specific form of niche tourism based on visits to locations significant to the lives and work of popular musicians, using the case of Beatles tourism in Liverpool as an example. The main aim is to explore the increasing role and significance of cultural tourism[2] in British and North American post-industrial cities during the 1980s and 1990s, and the growing emphasis on, and legitimation of, popular music as part of this process. It examines how this involved convergences between popular music and tourism events, industries and policies, and highlights convergences and similarities between discourses of and about popular music and tourism. The chapter ends by highlighting significant disjunctures between tourism and popular music cultures in order to offer a better perspective on their intertwining.[3]

TOURISM AND POPULAR MUSIC EVENTS

Many events could be categorised in terms of music or tourism or a combination of both. They include eighteenth-century classical concerts or operas that attracted elite audiences on the Grand Tour, twentieth-century club nights in Ibiza that have attracted young, pleasure-seeking backpackers (Connell and Gibson 2002: 231–232), Broadway shows and seaside pantomimes used to promote package holidays and weekends, and the Moptops performance which brought together social and occupational groups involved with music and tourism.

The Moptops were a professional Beatles tribute band from Britain. Tribute acts are so called because they model themselves on other well-known performers, attempting to recreate their performances. During the mid-1990s the popularity of tribute acts became widespread in Western Europe, North America and Australia, and have become a familiar feature of tourist attractions based on a few specific popular musicians, most notably Elvis Presley, Dolly Parton and the Beatles. The Moptops' performance was part of the 'Welcome Party' for Beatles Week, an annual celebration of the Beatles staged every August in Liverpool. Beatles Week involved a convention based in a local hotel, aimed at Beatles fans, particularly those from outside Liverpool, and events related to the convention such as the sale and auction of Beatles memorabilia, Beatles-related exhibitions, talks on the Beatles, and numerous performance events and competitions involving visiting professional and amateur Beatles tribute acts from all over the world, from Sweden's Lenny Pane to The Parrots from Japan and The Beat from Argentina.[4] Most tribute musicians, including members of The Moptops, declared themselves to be strong Beatles fans saying that they performed largely out of love and admiration for the Beatles and their music. Many performed alongside tribute acts for other artists at the Mathew Street Festival which marked the official end of Beatles Week, and involved performances by musicians on outdoor stages and in bars and pubs across Liverpool city centre.

The audience for The Moptops included some Beatles fans and musicians from Liverpool, but largely consisted of visiting fans, an extremely diverse group in terms of age, class, gender and nationality, representing varying degrees of interest in the Beatles. There were those whose interest in the Beatles was fairly casual, plus many ardent fans who said that they 'lived and breathed the Beatles every day' planning much of their lives around Beatles-related activities and events. Some had accumulated vast collections of Beatles recordings, artefacts and knowledge, some ran Beatles fanclubs or wrote for Beatles fanzines. Many regularly attended Beatles conventions in Europe and North America but said that the Liverpool convention was particularly significant because Liverpool as the birthplace of the Beatles had influenced and inspired the band and their musical creativity. For some this was their first visit to Liverpool but other fans were referred to as 'returnees' because they returned to the city to attend the convention every year. Fans attended the Liverpool convention to learn more about the Beatles' connections with Liverpool and to celebrate and commemorate those connections. They believed that by visiting the city that had inspired the Beatles they might feel closer to the band or experience something of their 'aura'. Plus, they wanted to meet and interact with other fans to establish and maintain friendships and social networks. The Beatles and their music had attracted visitors to Liverpool since the 1960s. They were perhaps the first band to make their local origins a part of their global success. They connected themselves to Liverpool in interviews, through lyrical compositions, and were associated with a Liverpool scene and sound (Cohen 1994, 2003c; Connell and Gibson 2002: 98).

The Moptops' performance event was organised by Cavern City Tours (CCT) then Liverpool's only city-based tour operator. The company launched in 1983 as a specialist in Beatles tours, and had driven the commercial development of Beatles tourism in Liverpool as its most central player. CCT organised Beatles package weekends and ran a daily 'Magical Mystery' coach tour around Liverpool sites of Beatles significance. In 1986 it took over as the main organiser of Liverpool's annual Beatles convention (this began as an informal event organised by local fans but was later run by the regional county council), an event officially recognised in 1995 as the region's second most important annual tourist attraction. By 1993 CCT had four full-time employees and had staged the first annual Mathew Street Festival. Throughout the 1990s CCT continued to extend Beatle-related tourism and leisure activities. The company took over ownership of the Cavern Club, made famous by the Beatles who performed there on a regular basis between 1961 and 1963, and also launched the Cavern Pub. Both club and pub were located in Mathew Street and CCT planned to develop a Beatles theme hotel and restaurant nearby. By 2002 CCT had 150 employees, including part-time bar staff (Kaijser 2002).

Other commercial organisations directly involved with Beatles tourism in Liverpool at the time of The Moptops performance included the Beatles Story museum, the Beatles Shop selling Beatles recordings and merchandise, and a few individual entrepreneurs. The directors of CCT referred to those businesses as Liverpool's 'Beatles Industry'. Beatles tourism in Liverpool was thus a small-scale, private-sector affair, although according to the statistics of the regional tourist authorities, in 2002 it contributed £20m to the region's economy. There were also businesses which were more indirectly involved with Beatles tourism, including the hotel that hosted the Beatles convention, and a group of private-sector businesses based in or around Mathew Street, some of which had launched the Cavern Quarter Initiative in 1993. This initiative involved the development of a music heritage quarter around Mathew Street, and aimed to physically transform and gentrify the area through place marketing and the development of tourism, retail and entertainment.

Despite some rivalries between the commercial operators involved with Beatles tourism, they formed a close-knit group drawing upon similar phrases, anecdotes and arguments when they discussed Beatles tourism. Many were Beatles fans driven also by the commercial potential of the Beatles' connection with Liverpool, arguing that for many people Liverpool was synonymous with the Beatles, and that this was something the city should capitalise upon by making the Beatles the focus of organised tourism, and by protecting and preserving city buildings with connections to the Beatles. They categorised city visitors according to their interest in the Beatles and their corresponding economic impact. CCT, for example, distinguished between 'fans' who visited Liverpool on a 'once in a lifetime' Beatles 'pilgrimage', 'fanatics' or 'die-hards' who visited Liverpool repeatedly from all over the world, and 'general interest' visitors who visited the city for other reasons besides the Beatles (Dave Jones, Personal Communication, April, 1994).

The Moptops' performance event thus involved tourist entrepreneurs, musicians and music fans, and was also perceived in terms of both tourism and music. In one sense, for example, the Moptops were a musical tribute to a globally successful pop band, members of their audience comparing their performance with other popular music events involving tribute bands or the Beatles. Simultaneously, however, some audience members also related the event to tourist events experienced during visits to other places, The Moptops being likened to a heritage centre because they were designed to re-enact and recreate the local past through repertoire, stage dress, performance gestures and movements.[5] The Moptops performance event could thus be perceived as involving a musical representation or construction of Liverpool for city visitors, because of the close connection between the Beatles and the city where they were born and brought up. The Beatles may be regarded as a product of Liverpool but the city has also been a product of the Beatles and their music. Liverpool features in several Beatles songs, and the Beatles' wit, their 'scouse' accent and characteristic nasal tones (Belchem 2000), and their jangly guitars and melodic, male vocal harmonies have been used to signify Liverpool in various contexts, to promote and market Liverpool as a tourist destination.

TOURISM AND MUSIC INSTITUTIONS AND POLICIES

By bringing together groups and interests, activities and events involved with tourism and music, The Moptops' performance exemplifies the growth of cultural tourism in British and North American cities during the 1980s and 1990s. It also points to increasing convergences between tourism, the arts and other cultural industries, and between cultural and economic policies.

Liverpool has always attracted visitors because of its maritime heritage, grand architecture and waterfront, and its impressive array of museums and galleries. Throughout the twentieth century, however, Liverpool experienced a series of economic slumps far more severe than those experienced by other British cities. During the 1980s and early 1990s, in particular, the city became known in Britain as much for urban decline as for football and the Beatles. The British media used the city as a symbol not just of urban decay but of everything wrong with the nation's cities, representing the city through narrow, ugly stereotypes. Liverpool's economic and image problems contributed to a long-running ambivalence within the city to the idea of promoting the Beatles as a local tourist attraction. According to the director of the Merseyside Tourism and Conference Bureau, there were 'those who feel that Liverpool shouldn't have to rely on four lads—there's more to it than that', and 'those who feel that the Beatles were local lads who made good and then turned their backs on the city' (Pam Wilsher, Personal Communication, 4 October 1993).

As a symbol of rock culture's conventional dreams of escape from the local, the Beatles served to highlight perceptions of Liverpool as a shrinking city in decline. Tourist slogans and banners proclaimed 'From Liverpool to the World', and 'Liverpool—the 5th Beatle' concealed deep, long-running tensions within the city. Additionally, some policy-makers associated the Beatles, and popular music generally, with drugs, deviancy and rebellion. During the 1980s tourism and city re-imaging were not on the agenda of Liverpool City Council which was dominated between 1983 and 1987 by an extreme Trotskyist faction, the Militant Tendency, which prioritised local taxation and housing policies, regarded culture and tourism as peripheral concerns, and entered into a direct confrontation with central government, threatening to bankrupt the city.

Throughout the 1990s CCT and other Beatles tourist entrepreneurs lobbied city policy-makers for financial investment and recognition, arguing that the Beatles were an important resource for the city and a potential tool for its regeneration. They complained of a lack of local support for their important and unacknowledged role in the promotion, marketing and regeneration of Liverpool and in the preservation of its heritage. To strengthen their argument they likened the connection between Liverpool and the Beatles to that between Stratford and Shakespeare (Dave Jones addressing a meeting of the Merseyside Music Industry Association in 1994), thus elevating the Beatles to the status of high culture. Through promotional literature CCT informed clients, largely Beatles fans, about their ongoing struggle with city policy-makers, but here their emphasis was slightly different, highlighting the value of the Beatles as city heritage and criticising city policy-makers for their unwillingness to preserve and promote that heritage and to pay the Beatles the respect they so obviously deserved. Meanwhile CCT suggested to local music-makers that the Beatles could be used as a 'seed' for the promotion of the city's music more generally. They argued, for example, that the Mathew Street festival need not necessarily be associated with one narrow aspect of Liverpool's musical past but could be broadened out to incorporate other music genres and styles. As part of their efforts to develop Beatles tourism in Liverpool CCT thus operated as intermediaries between policy-makers, music-makers and fans, tailoring the way that they interpreted connections between the Beatles and Liverpool in a manner suited to each group.

Several factors combined, however, to encourage Liverpool policy-makers to pay more attention to Beatles tourism and to cultural tourism more generally. First, following Britain's economic decline during the late 1970s and early 1980s, The Greater London Council had pioneered a new strategy for the regeneration of Britain's cities emphasising the contribution of art and culture to local economic development, that connected, for the first time in Britain, cultural and economic policy. The strategy was supported by high-profile research (see Myerscough 1988) that emphasised the role of art and culture in generating local employment and improving the image of cities, thus helping to attract visitors and investment that would enable them to reassert or increase their influence on 'the world stage' (Massey 1999: 122).

Tourism, which was fast becoming the world's largest international industry, thus became increasingly perceived as a replacement for traditional manufacturing industries, and increasingly prioritised in urban regeneration. In 1987 a new City Council in Liverpool had adopted a more realistic attitude to local economic development, following the line that money spent on housing would never be recovered but that investing in the city as a cultural attraction would bring economic returns. In 1993 the Council appointed its first ever tourism officer. Cultural tourism was also promoted as a local development strategy by the European Union. The emphasis on the role of culture and tourism in the development of Liverpool's economy thus increased in 1994 when Merseyside was awarded Objective One status, the European Union's highest funding category reserved for its poorest regions. Nine years later Liverpool won its bid to become European Capital of Culture 2008. In 1997 the head of the Council's Department of Leisure Services declared that by 2000 Liverpool would be a 'shrine' to the Beatles (Robbie Quinn speaking at University of Liverpool in March). On 14 December 1999, Paul McCartney performed at the Cavern Club for the first time since 1963. The event was a huge coup for CCT, the local media emphasising the positive world-wide publicity it had given the city (while also providing huge publicity for McCartney's latest album) and quoted City Council officers that the city was now determined to make more of its Beatles connections. In 2001 Liverpool's Speke airport was renamed the 'John Lennon Airport' and marketed through the rather trite slogan 'Above us only sky'.

The Moptops performance event was thus staged at a time when many Liverpool policy-makers had turned to, or were being forced into considering, the economic benefits of tourism and the arts and cultural industries (Cohen 1991b, 2002), and it occupied a rather ambiguous position at the intersection of policies aimed at art, culture and the media and those aimed at tourism. There were similar developments in many other British and North American post-industrial cities. New Orleans' infamous jazz musicians and scene had attracted visiting jazz fans since the early 1940s, but the city's policy-makers associated jazz with prostitution and gambling. Only in the 1990s did they begin to promote jazz tourism. Their interest was prompted by the sudden collapse of the city's oil industry during the mid-1980s, and by the success of the New Orleans Jazz & Heritage Festival. In Memphis the former home of Elvis Presley, Graceland, was opened to the public complete with gift shops and themed restaurants, and the city's Beale Street, site of Sun Studios where Elvis first recorded, was rebuilt and marketed to visitors as the 'birthplace of the blues' (see Connell and Gibson 2002: 246–7). In Britain Sheffield was the first City Council to develop an arts and cultural industries strategy following the rapid and dramatic decline of the city's steel industry in the early 1980s. The strategy involved long-term planning for, and launch of, the ill-fated tourist attraction The National Centre for Popular Music (Brown, Cohen and O'Connor 1998).

The growth of Beatles tourism in Liverpool can also be connected to that of a broader commercial heritage industry in Britain which emerged during the 1980s, provoking much scholarly debate (see, for example, Hewison 1987; Urry 1995; Wright 1985). This industry involved the promotion of nostalgia and the transformation of urban industrial sites into heritage centres aiming to bring the past to life in an entertaining manner, and to contribute to local economic development. It also challenged traditional notions of heritage which in Britain had tended to be rather narrowly defined, associated with the tastes and values of a conservative establishment. It thus helped to promote a British trend during the 1980s and 1990s towards broader, more pluralist notions of heritage and culture which encompassed the popular and more recent past and the everyday. This trend affected even the most notoriously conservative of institutions which had hitherto shown little interest in popular culture. Hence in 1995 Britain's National Trust announced that it would be purchasing the former Liverpool home of Sir Paul McCartney (only recently knighted) to develop it as a visitor attraction. In 2003 it did the same for John Lennon's Liverpool home. Similarly, in 1997 English Heritage, England's Historic Buildings and Monuments Commission, honoured a popular musician for the first time by erecting a plaque on the former London residence of rock guitarist Jimi Hendrix. In 2001 another plaque was unveiled on the former Liverpool home of John Lennon. In 1998 the English Tourist Board published *Rock and Pop Map of Britain: One Nation, One Groove,* a guide to places that have inspired British popular musicians. Popular music thus became legitimised as local and national heritage-based tourism.

These convergences between tourism and cultural policy increased the interlinking of music and tourism industries. CCT, for example, was a tour operator that also acted as a music agent and promoter and as a fan club. It arranged Beatles-related music events through its extensive contacts with musicians and music businesses, managed leisure facilities and organised music activities for local people and visitors. Additionally, it organized events specifically for Beatles fans, promoting meetings between fans that enabled the development of fan networks and communities. In some of its literature circulated to clients CCT promoted itself as a company acting on behalf of fans and in their interests. In fact, in 1995 CCT announced plans to launch 'the first official world-wide Beatles fan club'. As a tour operator, however, one of CCT's primary aims was to encourage Beatle fans and audiences from outside the city to visit Liverpool, thus turning fans into tourists. Meanwhile one of the main organisers of the official Liverpool Beatles fanclub explained: 'We act like a tourist office really. We are very conscious of the image of the city and we try our best to include in our literature items about what's going on in the city' (Jean Catharell, Personal Communication, 30/8/96). During Beatles Week the club organised gatherings and walking tours of the city for its members. In 1996 CCT tried unsuccessfully to obtain Objective One funding for the Mathew Street festival by defining it as a music/cultural event. At the same time, local music organisations seeking similar funding or support were pushed into justifying themselves in terms of tourism. Directors of the dance 'superclub' Cream, for example, emphasised the club's success in regularly attracting to Liverpool large numbers of club-goers from outside the city who spent money on local facilities and resources.

CONVERGENCE BETWEEN TOURISM AND MUSIC IDEOLOGIES

The Moptops' performance event provoked certain discussions and debates amongst the social and occupational groups involved common to Beatles tourism, indicating similarities between discourses typical of tourism and popular music. It thus highlighted convergences between music and tourism groups and events, institutions and policies, plus between music and tourism ideologies.

The relative merits of the Moptops and other Beatle tribute bands performing during Liverpool's Beatles Week were debated at length by Beatles fans and by musicians, often raising the ideological distinction between representation and reality familiar to discourses of both tourism and media cultures. Distinctions are commonly drawn, for example, between tourist attractions perceived as 'contrived' or 'artificial' and those perceived as 'genuine' or 'authentic' (Stokes, 1999). The search for the real, authentic Beatles Liverpool was clearly something that motivated many fans to visit the city, and throughout Beatles Week they and other city visitors debated the accuracy of the continual stories being told about the Beatles; the authenticity of Beatles-related artefacts up for auction, or of Beatle sites; whether the Beatles should be used to represent and promote Liverpool or whether the city was 'more than the Beatles' (Cohen 1997).

Similar debates were provoked as the tribute acts were inevitably compared with the original. Among The Moptops' audience were some male, British fans in their thirties, clearly irritated by Beatles tribute artists, saying they would have preferred to see 'the real thing', stressing the emphasis of earlier Liverpool conventions on video screenings of performances by the original Beatles. Other fans expressed concern about musicians who appeared to be too self-important, deluding themselves into believing that they were the Beatles, and about Beatles fans who acted as if those musicians were the real thing. Others in the audience were more concerned about how accurately The Moptops and other tribute artists had managed to recreate the original Beatles and some, along with the musicians involved, enjoyed the opportunity the bands offered to explore the tensions between musical sameness and difference. Some artists were admired for their close physical resemblance to the original Beatles, some for their skill in mimicking the Beatles' performance styles and sounds, others for the way they had somehow managed to capture the spirit of the original Beatles. As one fan put it: 'they don't try to imitate but they have the feel'.

Some of the young women who had queued backstage for The Moptops, however, were not concerned to relate the tribute bands to the original in order to judge how well they matched up, saying that attending their performances was the closest they would ever get to the real Beatles. The Moptops were thus appreciated as a vehicle that could lead to a better understanding and appreciation of the original. One small group of fans said that they liked to fantasise that The Moptops and other Beatles tribute bands actually were the original, to lose themselves in the performance and in the excitement of the event. Many obviously enjoyed the fun of the pretence thus participating with the musicians in recreating the 1960s through both mimicry and parody. With much fluttering of hands and rolling of eyes a group of George fans from Portsmouth talked about how excited they had been to meet members of the American Beatles tribute band 1964, how they had repeatedly requested 'George' to demonstrate his stage moves, and how they argued with another convention-goer who questioned the merits of the band ('He obviously wasn't a George fan'). A group of Liverpool women from a local insurance company managed to attend an afternoon performance by a Beatles tribute band in the Cavern Club by telling their boss they were sick. It reminded them of when they used to skip school to go to the original Cavern, giggling when they discussed what their husbands might think and how they might even find a new one at the performance event ('I'll take that George in the Cavern Beatles'—giggles all round).

The Cavern Club provoked similar debates. Some visitors were unaware that the original Cavern Club no longer existed, others criticised Liverpool for demolishing the original saying they would have preferred to have seen 'the real thing'.[6] Some knew that the replica Cavern Club had been rebuilt further along Mathew Street than the site of the original, in the 'wrong' place. Other fans felt that if they couldn't see the original Cavern Club then the reconstructions of it in both Mathew Street, and in the Beatles Story museum in Liverpool's docklands area, were the next best thing and helped them to feel closer to the Beatles. One of the Beatles Week coach trips toured sites from the video for the Beatles' 'Free as a Bird' single released in 1996. At one point the coach stopped at a cluster of old, derelict and disused warehouses, one of which had appeared in the video as the original Cavern Club. A poster advertising the Cavern Club was displayed on its crumbling wall, ripped and worn-looking as though it had been there for years. The 'George fans' from Portsmouth lined up eagerly beneath the poster pretending that they were in the famous Cavern Club queue and urging the rest to join them or photograph them.

Tourism and music commonly raise debates about the representation and authenticity of culture and also about its commodification. Music is a product of what is often regarded as the most commercial and exploitative of cultural industries (Cohen 2002), many popular music genres promoting strong notions of authenticity, emphasising sincerity and honesty of creative musical expression in the face of perceived commercial restrictions and exploitation (Frith 1981; Becker 1997; Cohen 1991a; Negus 1995). Tourism is also commonly associated with the circulation of money, thus provoking concerns about the commercialisation of local culture through tourism and the consequent destruction of local authenticity. Both music and tourism industries exploit these perceived tensions between creativity and commerce, connecting their products with notions of authenticity in order to obscure the commercial transactions involved and increase sales (see Stratton, 1982a, b, on the music industry).

Cavern City Tours, for example, were anxious to promote themselves as guides to authentic local Beatles sites and experiences. The Moptops PR leaflet stated, 'All the members of the band are sound-a-like actors/musicians and provide authentic action and dialogue. … Authentic Beatles sound recreated live on stage!' There was, however, a fear amongst tourist entrepreneurs, musicians and fans involved with Beatles tourism that its commercial development could destroy the authenticity of Liverpool culture. Many were concerned that if Beatles tourism was over-commercialised the city could become a 'tacky', 'artificial', 'plastic' 'themepark', Disneyland or Graceland being commonly referenced as negative illustrations of what Liverpool could become. Both examples, but particularly the former, have become familiar symbols of the Americanisation of the service economy, of the commercial and inauthentic, and of fake culture with little grounding in reality. Beatles tourist entrepreneurs needed to negotiate a tension between their desire to commercially develop Beatles tourism, and their need to promote local authenticity. Similarly, many Beatles fans were critical of the idea of 'cashing in' on the Beatles, and of commercial developments that they regarded as a threat to authentic Beatles Liverpool. At the same time they wanted better organised Beatles events in terms of local facilities and resources, and for Liverpool to make more of an effort to commemorate and pay tribute to the Beatles by preserving Beatles sites and promoting the Beatles as city heritage.

These ideological distinctions between representation and the real, authenticity and commerce, have been raised by other attractions that combine both music and tourism. Fears have been expressed, for example, that tourism based around traditional and so-called 'world' music will end up destroying local music traditions, staging authenticity and inventing tradition, although others have welcomed such tourism as a means of preserving local music traditions, promoting local identity and pride and contributing to local economies. As Stokes (1999) points out, such debates typify tourism and inform people's understanding of what it is.

There were similarities and convergences between some discourses characteristic of the cultures of popular music and tourism, and also between discourses about popular music and tourism. For example, because they have been regarded as overtly commercial, both tourism and popular music have attracted a familiar mass culture critique. Music fans and tourists have been negatively stereotyped in popular and scholarly literature, being commonly perceived as unthinking, manipulated masses, or commercially exploited dupes (see Adorno 1990; Jenson 1992, on perceptions of fans). Such perceptions may help to explain the devaluing and trivialisation of tourism and popular music, and why popular music and tourism studies have been relatively marginalised within the academy (see Crick 1989 on negative perceptions of tourism within the social sciences). Members of The Moptops' audience were aware of such stereotypes and tried to distance themselves from them. Some refused to be labelled as 'fans' feeling that the way that fandom was perceived did not match their own experience (see also Cavicchi 1998); some also disliked being referred to as 'tourists': 'I'm not a tourist, I guess. I'm here because of the Beatles and if I don't have the time to visit any tourist sites then too bad, they'll have to wait until another time' (David Riesman from the USA, Personal Communication, 1996). As in other parts of Britain, local policy-makers used the term 'visitor' rather than 'tourist', to escape such negative stereotypes and to broaden out from the narrower implications of 'tourist' and encourage those travelling to the city on business, or to see family and friends, to visit city attractions.

Tourism and popular music fandom have also been debated in terms of religion (see, for example, MacCannell 1976, on tourism). Hence Stokes (1999: 150) highlights the way that tourism has commonly been connected with pilgrimage, and music tourism has been 'framed in a religious idiom'. While many significant and insightful ideas and theories have emerged from this work, popular notions of tourism and popular music fandom as religion have again raised negative images of tourists and fans as devoted, passive and uncritical followers. In Liverpool Beatles fans were often stereotyped as obsessive, religious fanatics. A local newspaper article about the barber shop mentioned in the song 'Penny Lane' quoted Tony, the shop's owner, describing how the shop had become 'a mecca for Beatles fans from across the world': 'We get about 100 people per day visiting the shop purely through the Beatles connection. And we also get people picking away at the window frames to get a souvenir. They believe the spirits of people are trapped in the fabric of the building which is why they go at the windows' (*Merseymart* 30 January 1997). Many Beatles fans at Beatles Week certainly described their visit to Liverpool as a 'pilgrimage'. Some also referred to the community of Beatles fans as a 'congregation', highlighting the spiritual, sacred nature of connections between Liverpool and the Beatles and telling how they had become 'born again' fans. However, as Cavicchi (1998) argues, religious metaphors and language are used by fans to stress parallels between fandom and religion rather than to suggest that fandom actually is a religion.

CONCLUSION AND DISJUNCTURE

This chapter used a Beatles tribute band performance to explore the interrelation of popular music and tourism events, institutions and policies in British and North American post-industrial cities, to highlight convergences and parallels between the discourses that they provoked. In particular it drew attention to the growth of popular music tourism during the latter decades of the twentieth century, involving a proliferation of festivals, tours, museums, heritage quarters, and a range of different musical styles. Similar initiatives have emerged in cities not so well known for their music, or with no obvious connection to the heritage concerned. Beatles tourism, for example, exists not just in Liverpool, London and New York, but also in Prague (Connell and Gibson 2002:285); there are now Cavern Clubs in Tokyo and Brazil. In their race to market local distinctiveness (Robins 1991), cities compete with each other to lay claim to the same music heritage title or initiative. Popular music heritage also flourishes outside the city, as illustrated by heritage theme parks and towns such as Dollywood and Branson. The music industry colludes with these developments by promoting music nostalgia to sell products, and by recycling musical trends for younger audiences.

I want to end, however, by emphasising that The Moptops performance event could also help to draw attention to disjunctures between music and tourism. There is little space here to develop this discussion adequately, but in Liverpool although popular music and tourism have converged through the Beatles, they have been more commonly regarded as entirely separate or as incompatible and conflicting. The widespread availability and appeal of commercial popular music can certainly sit rather uneasily alongside efforts of the tourism industry to promote it as local culture. Visiting Beatles fans who participated in The Moptops' performance seemed extremely knowledgeable about the Beatles and their music speaking at length about the huge significance of the Beatles to their lives and their sense of self. The Beatles were so commercially successful that their music reached and touched all sorts of people from all over the world. They became a symbol of global culture, part of everyone's heritage and the ultimate 'Music of the Millennium' (Channel 4, 1998). The Beatles' global success was celebrated with pride by Beatles tourist entrepreneurs, yet at the same time, the Beatles departure from Liverpool relatively early on in their career, challenged their efforts to promote the Beatles as Liverpool's own and to interpret and present them from a local perspective (Kaijser 2002).

Additionally, Beatles tourist entrepreneurs complained that most Liverpool residents were uninterested in, or even hostile to, their efforts to promote the Beatles as a tourist attraction. This may have been an exaggeration, but it was certainly true of many local music-makers with little involvement with Beatles tourism who attracted little recognition from policy-makers concerned with its development. Many were undoubtedly proud of the Beatles and their musical achievements, but some resented the dominance of Beatles heritage, the way it obscured or excluded other local music heritages,[7] or regarded tourism as a threat to, or even antithesis of, what music should be about. The Cavern Quarter Initiative, for example, helped to regenerate Mathew Street and its surrounding area, but the inevitable rise in rent and rates forced some small music businesses out of the area (see Zukin 1989, for account of a similar process in US cities). For those businesses, the commercial exploitation and institutionalisation of Liverpool music as heritage-based tourism sat uneasily with familiar rock ideology where music was associated with creativity, with the contemporary and everyday, with a rebellious, anti-establishment stance, with subcultures and the authenticity of 'the street', and with change rather than stasis. Many other music practitioners also argued that Liverpool should promote a vibrant, alive musical culture rather than the dead or sterile.

Music-makers in other post-industrial cities have shared similar attitudes and experiences, and the questions 'whose culture? whose heritage?' are familiar to cultural tourism in general. In New Orleans jazz musicians regularly perform for tourists, but this relationship is often regarded as exploitative (Atkinson 1996a) and 'real' New Orleans music-making has been considered as that which exists beyond the earshot of tourists and outside the city tourist areas. The city's Arts and Tourism Partnership formed during the mid-1990s to bridge the gap between arts and tourism cultures. It found, however, marked differences between the approach, motivation and even language of those involved with these cultures, which made linking the two a formidable task. Consequently, one of its initiatives involved the production of 'Flip Tips', a dictionary which translated the language of the arts into that of tourism, and vice versa, to promote understanding between those involved (Atkinson 1996b).

Finally, The Moptops' performance event problematises the familiar association of tourist culture with the visual 'gaze' and the way visual culture has been prioritised over the aural within Western society. Beatles fans participating in that event insisted that for them the most important thing was 'the music'. They described Beatles music as a powerful force, emphasising its significance at key moments in their lives, and the way that it acted as a focus, frame or backdrop to more mundane rituals and routines. They referred to music's ability to unite people, overcoming social and national divisions, to its emotional effects and its ability to move listeners and transport them from one state of being to another. For these fans the music was clearly something special plus something valued for its relevance to the ordinary and everyday. As a non-verbal, non-depictive medium with a temporal and physical dimension (De Nora 2000:159), music was strongly perceived as penetrating personal, interior worlds and feelings, connecting with individual sense of self. It was also valued for its sociability, the way that it encourages social interaction and the construction of collective identity. Fans clearly expressed rather essentialist and romantic notions of music, evident in the way that they suggested an organic connection between the Beatles' music and Liverpool. At the same time, their discussions highlighted the significance of listening and of sonic constructions of geographical place.

NOTES

1. Those involved with tourism employ numerous definitions of it, many academic researchers on tourism finding it difficult to define it in any analytically useful way (see, for example, Stokes 1999; Abram, Waldren and Macleod 1997). There is some consensus, however, that tourism can be regarded as undertaken by temporarily leisured people who voluntarily visit a place away from home for the purpose of experiencing change (Boissevain 1996, 3 quoting Valerie Smith).

2. 'Cultural tourism' covers a broad range of activities and cultural forms, but generally involves an emphasis on the tourist dimension of arts, cultural events and activities, marking a trend towards organised tourism based around more specialist interests, including heritage and nostalgia, rather than standard, packaged tours.

3. The chapter draws upon ethnographic research conducted in Liverpool between 1995 and 1997 by myself and Connie Atkinson, for a comparative project on popular music, tourism and urban regeneration in Liverpool and New Orleans. I would like to thank the Economic and Social Research Council in Britain for supporting and funding this project.

4. One hundred and thirty-four bands performed, mostly as tribute or 'cover' acts (the latter being acts who perform their own versions of songs associated with other artists).

5. They aimed, according to their manager, Mr. B. T. Blackburn, to 'recreate the magic of the Beatles' (Moptops PR leaflet).

6. At the 1996 Liverpool Beatles auction a brick claimed by the event's organisers to be from the original Cavern Club with attached plaque that explained its history was open for bids.

7. Liverpool's Capital of Culture bid of 2003 downplayed the Beatles connections in favour of emphasising the city's cultural diversity and some of its less familiar or dominant cultural attractions and heritages.

BIBLIOGRAPHY

Abram, S., Waldren, J., and Macleod, D.V.L. (eds) (1997) *Tourists and Tourism: Identifying with People and Places,* Oxford and New York: Berg.

Adorno,T.W. (1990) 'On Popular Music', in S. Frith and A. Goodwin (eds) *On Record,* New York: Pantheon

Atkinson, C. (1996a) 'Shakin' Your Butt for the Tourist: music's role in the identification and selling of New Orleans', in D. King and H. Taylor (eds) *Dixie Debates: Perspectives on Southern Cultures,* London: Pluto.

Atkinson, C. (1996b) 'Art for Tourism's Sake?', Paper presented at the Institute of Economic Studies, University of Birmingham, Nov. 7.

Becker, H. (1997) 'The Culture of a Deviant Group: the "jazz" musician', in K. Gelder and S. Thornton, *The Subcultures Reader.* London: Routledge.

Belchem, J. (2000) *Merseypride: Essays in Liverpool Exceptionalism,* Liverpool: University of Liverpool Press.

Boissevain, J. (ed) (1996) *Coping with Tourists: European Reactions to Mass Tourism,* Providence, RI: Berghahn Books.

Brown, A., Cohen, S. and O'Connor, J. (1998) *Music Policy in Sheffield, Manchester and Liverpool: A Report for Comedia,* Manchester Institute of Popular Culture, Manchester Metropolitan University, Manchester, and Institute of Popular Music, Liverpool.

Cavicchi, D. (1998) *Tramps Like Us: Music and Meaning Among Springsteen Fans,* New York: Oxford University Press.

Cohen, S. (1991a) *Rock Culture in Liverpool: Popular Music in the Making,* Oxford: Oxford University Press.

———(1991b) 'Popular Music and Urban Regeneration: The Music Industries on Merseyside', *Cultural Studies,* Vol. 5 (1991), pp. 332–346.

————(1994) 'Mapping the Sound: identity, place, and the Liverpool Sound', in M. Stokes (ed.) *Ethnicity, Identity: The Musical Construction of Place*, Oxford: Berg, pp. 117–134

————(1997) 'Popular Music, Tourism, and Urban Regeneration'. In S. Abram, J. Waldren and D. McLeod (eds) *Tourists and Tourism: Identifying With People and Places*, Oxford: Berg., pp. 71–90.

————(1998) 'Sounding Out the City: Music and the Sensuous Production of Place'. In A. Leyshon, D. Matless and G. Revill (eds) *The Place of Music: Music, Space and the Production of Place*, New York: Guilford Press, pp. 269–290.

————(2002) 'Paying One's Dues: The Music Business, the City and Urban Regeneration', in M. Talbot (ed.) *The Business of Music*, Liverpool: University of Liverpool Press, pp. 263–291.

————(2003a) 'Tourism', *Continuum Encyclopedia of Popular Music of the World*, London: Continuum.

————(2003b) 'Heritage'. *Continuum Encyclopedia of Popular Music of the World*. London: Continuum.

————(2003c) 'Local Sound'. *Continuum Encyclopedia of Popular Music of the World*. London: Continuum.

Connell,J. and Gibson,C. (2002) *Sound Tracks: Popular Music, Identity and Place*. London: Routledge.

Crick, M. 1989. 'Representations of International Tourism in the Social Sciences: sun, sex, sights, savings, and servility'. *Annual Review of Anthropology* 18: 307–344.

De Nora, T. (2000) *Music in Everyday Life*. Cambridge: Cambridge University Press.

Frith, S. (1981) 'The Magic that can set you Free: the ideology of folk and the myth of the rock community'. In *Popular Music* 1. Cambridge: Cambridge University Press.

Hewison, R. (1987) *The Heritage Industry: Britain in a Climate of Decline*. London: Methuen.

Jensen, J. (1992) 'Fandom as Pathology: The Consequences of Characterization.' In Lisa A. Lewis (ed.) *The Adoring Audience: Fan Culture and Popular Media*. London and New York: Routledge, pp. 9–29.

Kaijser, L. (2002) 'Beatles Tourism in Liverpool'. Paper presented at the Institute of PopularMusic, University of Liverpool on 10 December.

MacCannell, Dean. (1976) *The Tourist. A New Theory of the Leisure Class*. New York: Schocken

Massey, D. (1999) 'Cities in the world'. In D. Massey, J. Allen and S. Pile, (eds) *City Worlds*. London: Routledge, pp. 99–156.

Myerscough, J. (1988) *The Economic Importance of the Arts in Britain*. London: Policy Studies Institute.

Negus, K. (1995) 'Where the Mystical Meets the Market: creativity and commerce in the production of popular music'. *The Sociological Review*, 43 (2): 316–341.

Robins, K. (1991) 'Traditions and Translation: National Culture in its Global Context', in Corner, J. and Harvey, S. (eds) *Enterprise and Heritabe: Crosscurrents of National Culture*, London: Routledge.

Stokes, M. (1999) 'Music, Travel and Tourism: An Afterword.' *The World of Music*, 41 (3): 141–56.

Stratton, J. (1982a) 'Reconciling Contradictions: the role of the artist and repertoire person in the British music industry', *Popular Music and Society*, .8 (2): 90–100.

————(1982b) 'Between Two Worlds: art and commercialism in the record industry', *The Sociological Review*, 30: 267–285.

Urry, J. (1990) *The Tourist Gaze: Leisure and Travel in Contemporary Societies*. London and Newbury Park: Sage Publications.

————(1995) *Consuming Places*. London: Routledge.

Wright, P. (1985) *On Living in an Old Country*. London: Verso.

Zukin, S. (1989) *Loft Living: Culture and Capital in Urban Change*. Piscataway, NJ: Rutgers University Press.

STUDY QUESTIONS

1. What are some of the ways music can enhance tourism?
2. Give some examples of "tribute acts."
3. What is the Cavern Quarter Initiative of 1993?
4. During the 1980s and 1990s, what was the general perception of Liverpool and how did the perception of the Beatles contribute to this view?
5. What factors combined to encourage Liverpool policymakers to pay more attention to Beatles tourism and to cultural tourism more generally?
6. What other examples can you find of the intersection of the economic benefits of tourism, the arts, and cultural industries?
7. Characterize the growth of Beatles tourism in Liverpool between the 1980s and 1990s.
8. Popular music became legitimized as a local and national heritage-based tourism in the 1980s with the recognition of specific sites. Which ones were they?
9. What debate did the Cavern Club provoke?
10. Explain the debate about the representation and authenticity of culture and its commodification; what worried some about Beatles tourism?
11. What is the controversy surrounding tourism based around traditional and so-called "world" music?
12. Where else can you find evidence of Beatles tourism and why is this significant?
13. Beatles tourist entrepreneurs complained that most Liverpool residents were uninterested in, or even hostile to, their efforts to promote The Beatles as a tourist attraction. What were some reasons for the hostility?
14. Music makers in other post-industrial cities have shared similar attitudes and experiences, and the questions, "whose culture?" and "whose heritage?" are familiar to cultural tourism in general. How does this statement apply to New Orleans jazz?
15. How does music contribute to a geographical sense of place?

Chapter 8 Snapshot
Women, Islam, and the New Iraq

The reason I included this article is that so often we are tempted to think of Islam as a monolithic ideology governed by a fundamentalist interpretation of sharia law. There also is a perception that it is a religion with an inability to change with the times, and that women represent a passive and permanent underclass. This article will challenge all of these assumptions, and, as a matter of fact, you might come to be very surprised at what you will learn about Islam and the development of Iraq's constitution that you may not have known before.

THE IMPACT OF SHARIA

Women have been concerned about their status in the new Iraq and have seen the development of Iraq's constitution as a clear opportunity to safeguard their rights legally. But there are some seeming contradictions, or at least ambiguities that have caused some concern. For example, Isobel Coleman points out that "Article 14 of Iraq's new constitution … states that Iraqis are equal before the law 'without discrimination because of sex.' Yet the constitution also states that no law can be passed that contradicts the 'established rulings' of Islam" (123). These established rulings of Islam are based in sharia law, and according to "Isam al-Khafaji, an Iraqi scholar, the document 'could easily deprive women of their rights.'" In addition, "Yanar Muhammad, a leading secular activist and the head of the Organization of Women's Freedom in Iraq, worries that the Islamic provision will turn the country 'into an Afghanistan under the Taliban, where oppression and discrimination of women is institutionalized'" (123).

Is it possible that women could be accorded a modern role in Iraqi society if the core of its very constitution is founded on sharia law? Can women be successful at improving their status within sharia law or should they lobby for the constitution to be based on secular law instead? Is there room within sharia law for more modern interpretations or is it set in stone? You might be surprised to learn that sharia law is actually "open to a wide range of understanding, and across the Islamic world today, progressive Muslims are seeking to reinterpret its rules to accommodate a modern role for women" (123). In fact, in many Islamic countries, "reformers have largely abandoned attempts to replace sharia with secular law, a route that has proved mostly futile … . Instead, they are trying to promote women's rights within an Islamic framework" (124).

Why is this issue of women's rights under the law an important issue? Iraq is working to develop a strong democratic society, and that means equal representation of all its people. "Allowing a full social, political, and economic role for women in Iraq would help ensure its transition to a stable democracy" (124). Working within sharia law would seem to be less disruptive culturally for the country … and the region, and it meets the mindset of those that see sharia law as the very foundation of Iraq's constitution. Is there any precedent where there has been discussion or discourse about the interpretation of sharia law? Not so much in modern times, but there has been in times past.

RETHINKING THE LAW

We should really start here by going over some basic terms. An *ulama* is a religious scholar, Sunna is the recorded traditions or customs of the Prophet Muhammad, *fiqh* is jurisprudence, and *ijtihad* is scriptural interpretation and discourse. Sharia is "the body of Islamic law that was developed by religious scholars *(ulama)* after the death of the Prophet Muhammad" (124). Similar to the Mosaic law that forms the basis of the Judeo-Christian traditions, sharia is "meant to provide moral and legal guidance to Muslims" (124). It is "based on the Koran and the Sunna" (124). Although the Koran includes about 80 verses covering legal issues of concern to women like inheritance, polygamy, and divorce, "neither the Koran nor the Sunna cover most day-to-day issues" (124). This is where *ijtihad* come in. After the death of Muhammad, "the *ulama* created other means" to address day-to-day issues; that is, "as a last measure, qualified legal scholars could study a question, apply independent reasoning *(ijtihad)*, and issue a nonbinding fatwa" (124). Then, in the eleventh century, "to consolidate their control, the Sunni *ulama* crystallized their legal judgments into various schools of Islamic jurisprudence and banned *ijtihad*" (124). What this means is that the Sunni *ulama* shut down the possibility of independent interpretation, "the traditionalists imposed their own conservative positions on mainstream Islamic jurisprudence, and these have remained largely frozen for almost a millennium" (124).

It would seem that any progress to making Islam more responsive to women's rights in this day and age would be a daunting task. However, there are several scholars who are working very hard to make important changes. "Islamic feminists now seek to revive the equality bestowed on women in the religion's early years by rereading the Koran, putting the Scriptures in context, and disentangling them from tribal practices" (124). So where do these scholars find the leverage within sharia law to lobby for more progressive interpretations? "The Koran, like the Bible … includes many multilayered, seemingly contradictory passages, and Islamic feminists tend to emphasize different verses than the traditionalists" (125). Author Isobel Coleman uses the example of polygamy to explain:

> One verse of the Koran says, "Marry those women who are lawful for you, up to two, three, or four, but only if you can treat them all equally." Later in the same chapter, however, the Koran reads, "No matter how you try you will never be able to treat your wives equally." Many Muslim scholars today read the two

verses together, as an effective endorsement of monogamy. Many tribal communities, on the other hand, focus on the former verse alone and cite it as a justification for having multiple wives (125).

What this means is that sharia law isn't inherently anti-women's rights, but it does suggest "that the question of who gets to interpret sharia is critical—especially on areas such as gender equality, where the letter of the law is vague" (125). Moroccan writer Fatema Mernissi and Pakistani scholar Riffat Hassan are considered to be pioneers of Islamic feminism who also are "pursuing rights for women within an Islamic discourse; … Their movement already spans the globe, is growing, and is increasingly innovative" (125). You can read about other such movements in the next article, *Applying Islamic Principles in the Twenty-First Century,* by David R. Smock.

In 1959, Iraq enacted a personal-status law that "provided women with some of the broadest legal rights in the region" (125). It changed the marriage age to 18, prohibited polygamy, prohibited arbitrary divorce, and equalized the inheritance laws between men and women (125). In addition, "under secular, albeit brutal, Baathist rule, Iraqi women made significant advances in numerous areas, including education and employment" (126). When Saddam Hussein was deposed in 2003, Shiites made clear that they wanted a more conservative Islamic state, and one of the first things they wanted to reverse was the 1959 personal-status law. Instead, they wanted to put into place Resolution 137 "which canceled Iraq's existing family laws and placed all such issues under the rules of sharia" (126). Although the vote took place behind closed doors,

> women's organizations and moderates across the country quickly mobilized against the new regulation. They held rallies, press conferences, and high-level meetings with the American authorities to make their concerns known. They even gained the support of several moderate Islamic clerics. L. Paul Bremer, the head of the coalition Provisional Authority, ultimately vetoed the IGC's [the US-appointed Iraqi Governing Council] resolution. But the intentions of Iraqi's powerful conservative Shiite leaders –to broadly assert sharia over a whole range of legal questions—had been made clear (126).

MOSQUE AND STATE

The determination that put forward Resolution 137 was the same determination brought to bear on the forging of Iraq's new constitution. "Sharia quickly became one of the most contentious issues facing the drafting committee"(126). Iraq under Saddam Hussein was a secular state meaning that religion did not play a role in government. "Moderate Shiite leaders such as Grand Ayatollah Ali al-Sistani insisted that they did not want to replicate Iran's theocratic system (in which clerics run most aspects of the government). But after years of brutal suppression by Saddam, the Shiites were nonetheless determined to give Islam a central role in Iraq's reconstituted state … [while] the Kurds and secular Sunnis were equally adamant about keeping religion out of government"(126). However, the polls supported Islam as part of Iraq's constitution; "the real debate was over how much weight to give it" (127). In the final version of the constitution, Article 2 "makes Islam the official religion of the state, cites it as a basic source of legislation, and says that no law can be passed that contradicts its 'undisputed' rulings" (127). This brings us back to the discussion of inherent contradictions in Iraq's constitution; however, in regards to Article 2, "interpreting this provision will fall to the Supreme Court …" (127).

Article 39 of Iraq's constitution deals with personal-status law. It basically says that Iraqis are "'free in their personal status according to their religions, sects, beliefs, or choices, but leaves it up to subsequent legislation to define what this means" (127). Some are concerned that this might lead to a "confusing but relatively benign system (not unprecedented in the region), under which Iraqis with legal questions could choose among different codes and court systems—Sunni, secular, or Shiite—depending on which they thought would give them the most favorable treatment" (127). Others are worried that Article 39 will lead instead "to an Iranian-style theocracy, which would severely limit women's rights in particular" (127). In regard to women's rights in Iran, after the Iranian Revolution,

> Iran's new government quickly suspended the country's progressive family law, disallowed female judges, and strongly enforced the wearing of the hijab. Within a few months, sharia rulings lowered the marriage age to nine, permitted polygamy, gave fathers the right to decide who their daughters could marry, permitted unilateral divorce for men but not women, and gave fathers sole custody of children in the case of divorce (127).

Over the years some of the harshest of these provisions have been softened somewhat, but still, Iranian theocracy is not a model many Iraqis want to follow... especially many of Iraq's women.

LEARNING FROM OTHERS

Fortunately, there are other models of moderate Islamic governments. For example, Morocco "recently revised its personal-status code (*moudawana*) but claimed to be doing so on Islamic grounds. Morocco's nongovernmental organizations "pushed to raise the marriage age from 15 to 18, abolish polygamy, equalize the right to divorce, and give women the right to retain custody of their children" (128). In October 2003, Morocco's king "formally presented parliament with a set of sweeping revisions to the family law, defending the changes with copious references to the Koran. In fact, both religious and secular supporters of the reforms used the language of religion and Islamic jurisprudence to advocate gender equality, and despite conservative opposition, parliament approved the changes" (128).

Indonesia, and an organization known as Women Living Under Muslim Laws, working in Algeria provide additional examples illustrating how positive change can come from within Islam (128–129). This section will go very nicely with the next chapter, *Applying Islamic Principles in the Twenty-First Century*, by David R. Smock.

TURNING NUMBERS INTO INFLUENCE

During the drafting process of the constitution, Iraqi women were marginalized. The constitutional committee had 55 members, and about half of these came from the Shiite United Iraqi Alliance (UIA). Twenty-five percent of the committee was composed of the Democratic Patriotic Alliance of Kurdistan. There were only eight women on the committee, five were from the UIA, two were Kurdish, and one was an independent (127). However, according to Iraq's new constitution, a full 25 percent of the seats in parliament is reserved for women, but this doesn't mean that more legislation will be passed that is favorable to women, because "nearly half of the women elected had run on the UIA list, and they have toed their party's conservative Shiite line" (129). Some women wanted to push the quota closer to 40 percent, while many conservatives wanted the quota struck from the constitution altogether. "In the end, the quota did make it into the final draft of the constitution which will give women in Iraq one of the highest levels of representation in the world (after all, women make up less than 15 percent of the U.S. Congress)" (129). Many of the women occupying these seats are conservative, so they will be unlikely to support progressive legislation; "over time, however, these same legislators may start advancing women's rights within an Islamic context" (129).

As we saw earlier in considering the contradictions or ambiguities in Iraq's constitution, the ones who will be making those legal decisions will be critical to the future of women in Iraq; and "having the right judges on the bench will determine the formal rights of Iraqi women over the long term, in the short term religious vigilantes, who are forcing their own fundamentalist views on Iraq's besieged population, are having the greatest impact" (130). These vigilantes are "imposing stringent restrictions ... such as requiring women to wear full-length veils, forbidding music and dancing, and enforcing strict segregation of the sexes in public" (130). So even as Iraq is working through the development and strengthening of its constitution and considering modifications within sharia law, there also are others who are taking the law into their own hands. Isobel Coleman sums up the situation this way: "... the greatest danger to Iraqi women stems not from any legal restrictions, but from lawlessness" (130).

FRIENDS IN HIGH PLACES

This section is about recommendations to the U.S. regarding ways it can strengthen democracy in Iraq by strengthening the position of women in Iraqi society. More importantly, however, is to understand all of the ways in which, by empowering women, an entire country can be stabilized and empowered.

8. Women, Islam, and the New Iraq

By Isobel Coleman

THE IMPACT OF SHARIA

Article 14 of Iraq's new constitution, approved in a nationwide referendum held on October 15, states that Iraqis are equal before the law "without discrimination because of sex." Yet the constitution also states that no law can be passed that contradicts the "established rulings" of Islam. For this reason, the new document has been condemned by critics both inside and outside Iraq as a fundamental setback for a majority of Iraq's population—namely, its women. According to Isam al-Khafaji, an Iraqi scholar, the document "could easily deprive women of their rights." Yanar Muhammad, a leading secular activist and the head of the Organization of Women's Freedom in Iraq, worries that the Islamic provision will turn the country "into an Afghanistan under the Taliban, where oppression and discrimination of women is institutionalized."

These criticisms are not without merit, and the ambiguity of the new constitution is a cause for concern. The centrality of Islamic law in the document, however, does not necessarily mean trouble for Iraqi women. In fact, sharia is open to a wide range of understanding, and across the Islamic world today, progressive Muslims are seeking to reinterpret its rules to accommodate a modern role for women.

Iraq's constitution does not specify who will decide which version of Islam will prevail in the country's new legal system. But the battle has already begun. Victory by the progressives would have positive implications for all aspects of the future of Iraq, since women's rights are critical to democratic consolidation in transitional and war-torn societies. Allowing a full social, political, and economic role for women in Iraq would help ensure its transition to a stable democracy. Success for women in Iraq would also reverberate throughout the broader Muslim world. In every country where sharia is enforced, women's rights have become a divisive issue, and the balance struck between tradition and equality in Iraq will influence these other debates.

In many Islamic countries, reformers have largely abandoned attempts to replace sharia with secular law, a route that has proved mostly futile. Instead, they are trying to promote women's rights within an Islamic framework. This approach seems more likely to succeed, since it fights theology with theology—a natural strategy in countries with conservative populations and where religious authority is hard to challenge. Now that the United States has helped midwife an Islamic state in Iraq, U.S. officials would, for similar reasons, be wise to move beyond their largely secular interlocutors. If Washington still hopes to create a relatively liberal regime in Iraq, it must start working with progressive religious Muslims to advance the role of women through religious channels.

RETHINKING THE LAW

Sharia is the body of Islamic law that was developed by religious scholars (*ulama*) after the death of the Prophet Muhammad. Meant to provide moral and legal guidance to Muslims, sharia is based on the Koran and the Sunna (the recorded traditions or customs of the Prophet). The Koran has about 80 verses concerning legal issues, many of which refer to the role of women in society and to important family issues, such as marriage, divorce, and inheritance.

Because neither the Koran nor the Sunna cover most day-to-day issues, however, after the death of the Prophet the *ulama* created other means for addressing them. As a last measure, qualified legal scholars could study a question, apply independent reasoning (*ijtihad*), and issue a nonbinding fatwa. In the eleventh century, however, to consolidate their control, the Sunni *ulama* crystallized their legal judgments into various schools of Islamic jurisprudence and banned *ijtihad*. With the gates of independent interpretation closed, the traditionalists imposed their own conservative positions on mainstream Islamic jurisprudence, and these have remained largely frozen for almost a millennium.

Some scholars, however, have continued to search for Islamic answers to the questions of modern life. Contrary to the claims of secularists who deny the compatibility of Islam and modern notions of women's rights, Islamic attitudes on the question actually vary quite widely. According to "Islamic feminists," Islam is actually a very progressive religion for women, was radically egalitarian for its time, and remains so in some of its Scriptures. They contend that Islamic law has evolved in ways that are inimical to gender equality not because it clearly pointed in that direction, but because of selective interpretation by patriarchal leaders and a mingling of Islamic teachings with tribal customs and traditions. Islamic feminists now seek to revive the equality bestowed on women in the religion's early years by rereading the Koran, putting the Scriptures in context, and disentangling them from tribal practices.

Among the pioneers of Islamic feminism are the Moroccan writer Fatema Mernissi and the Pakistani scholar Riffat Hassan—although neither is entirely comfortable with the label. In fact, many religious progressives prefer to distance themselves from the term "feminism" and the Western cultural baggage it brings. These scholars simply see themselves as Muslims pursuing rights for women within an Islamic discourse. Their movement already spans the globe, is growing, and is increasingly innovative. Many of its leading lights are actually men, distinguished Islamic scholars such as Hussein Muhammad in Indonesia, whose high status gives them particular credibility.

The Islamic feminists tend to focus their work on the sensitive area of family law, since it is the area of jurisprudence that has the greatest impact on women's daily lives—and since it also leaves much room for interpretation. Take, for example, the Koran's stipulations on inheritance. One contested verse states that on her parents' death, a daughter should receive half of what her brother inherits. Progressives, however, point out that at the time of the Prophet, giving a woman any inheritance was a radical departure from Arab practice. (Indeed, it was a radical notion in much of the West as well until the twentieth century.) The progressives also note that the rule made sense in traditional Islamic societies, where women had no financial obligations, only financial rights. But today, they argue, when many Muslim women do earn a living and men do not always provide the necessary support, it is important to adapt the law to changing circumstances.

The Koran, like the Bible, also includes many multilayered, seemingly contradictory passages, and Islamic feminists tend to emphasize different verses than the traditionalists. On the sensitive subject of polygamy, for example, one verse of the Koran says, "Marry those women who are lawful for you, up to two, three, or four, but only if you can treat them all equally." Later in the same chapter, however, the Koran reads, "No matter how you try you will never be able to treat your wives equally." Many Muslim scholars today read the two verses together, as an effective endorsement of monogamy. Many tribal communities, on the other hand, focus on the former verse alone and cite it as a justification for having multiple wives.

The rules on veiling are similarly inconclusive. Progressive Muslims point out that nowhere does the Koran actually require the veiling of all Muslim women. Veiling was simply a custom in pre-Islamic Arabia, where the hijab was considered a status symbol (after all, only women who did not have to work in the fields had the luxury of wearing a veil). When the Koran mentions veils, it is in reference to Muhammad's wives. The "hijab verse" reads, "Believers, do not enter the Prophet's house … unless asked. And if you are invited … do not linger. And when you ask something from the Prophet's wives, do so from behind a hijab. This will assure the purity of your hearts as well as theirs." In the Prophet's lifetime, all believers (men and women) were encouraged to be modest. But the veil did not become widespread for several generations—until conservatives became ascendant.

What all this suggests for Iraq is that sharia is not inherently inimical to women's rights. It also suggests that the question of who gets to interpret sharia is critical—especially on areas such as gender equality, where the letter of the law is vague.

For nearly 50 years, Iraq's personal-status law provided women with some of the broadest legal rights in the region. The law, enacted in 1959, included several progressive provisions loosely derived from various schools of Islamic jurisprudence. It set the marriage age at 18 and prohibited arbitrary divorce. It also restricted polygamy, making that practice almost impossible (the code required men seeking a second wife to get judicial permission, which would only be granted if the judge believed the man could treat both wives equally). And it required that men and women be treated equally for purposes of inheritance. When he was challenged by clerics over this provision, Abdul Karim Kassem, the Iraqi prime minister at the time, responded that the verse in the Koran calling for a daughter's inheritance to be half that of a son's was only a recommendation, not a commandment.

Religious scholars were unhappy with the code from the beginning, largely because it imposed a unified standard on Iraq's population without allowing for the differences among its various religious sects. Shiite clerics, in particular, viewed it as another aspect of unwanted Sunni oppression. But the legislation played an important role in modernizing the role of women in Iraqi society. Under secular, albeit brutal, Baathist rule, Iraqi women made significant advances in numerous areas, including education and employment.

With the overthrow of Saddam Hussein in March 2003, Shiite leaders quickly made clear that they expected the new Iraq to be an Islamic state. One of their first priorities was to try to annul the personal-status law. In December 2003, a conservative contingent on the U.S.-appointed Iraqi Governing Council (IGC) voted behind closed doors for Resolution 137, which canceled Iraq's existing family laws and placed such issues under the rules of sharia. Abdul Aziz al-Hakim, the Shiite leader of the powerful Supreme Council for the Islamic Revolution in Iraq (SCIRI), held the rotating chairmanship of the IGC at the time of the vote.

Resolution 137 was worryingly vague about exactly what form of Islamic regulation would replace the old legislation, although the decree seemed to imply that each Islamic community would be free to impose its own rules on issues such as marriage, divorce, and other important family matters. This ambiguity worried not only women's groups, but also those who feared that such an Islamic free-for-all would exacerbate sectarian tensions.

Women's organizations and moderates across the country quickly mobilized against the new regulation. They held rallies, press conferences, and high-level meetings with the American authorities to make their concerns known. They even gained the support of several moderate Islamic clerics. L. Paul Bremer, the head of the Coalition Provisional Authority, ultimately vetoed the IGC's resolution. But the intentions of Iraq's powerful conservative Shiite leaders—to broadly assert sharia over a whole range of legal questions—had been made clear.

MOSQUE AND STATE

This determination was soon directed at a new target: Iraq's constitution. Sharia quickly became one of the most contentious issues facing the drafting committee. Moderate Shiite leaders such as Grand Ayatollah Ali al-Sistani insisted that they did not want to replicate Iran's theocratic system (in which clerics run most aspects of the government). But after years of brutal suppression by Saddam, the Shiites were nonetheless determined to give Islam a central role in Iraq's reconstituted state. In an August 2003 statement, Sistani announced, "The religious constants and the Iraqi people's moral principles and noble social values should be the main pillars of the coming Iraqi constitution."

The Kurds and secular Sunnis were equally adamant about keeping religion out of government. Speaking to a reporter in early 2005, Kurdish leader Jalal Talabani (shortly before he became president of Iraq) insisted, "We will never accept any religious government in Iraq. Never. This is a red line for us. We will never live inside an Islamic Iraq." Maysoon al-Damluji, president of the Iraqi Independent Women's Group, worried that "the interpretation of sharia law will take us backward." But with polls showing that a majority of Iraqis endorsed sharia, there was never really any question of whether Islam would be in the constitution; the real debate was over how much weight to give it.

Secular Iraqi women were marginalized during the drafting process. The composition of the constitutional committee reflected the results of the January 2005 national elections: about half of its 55 members came from the Shiite United Iraqi Alliance (UIA), and another quarter came from the Democratic Patriotic Alliance of Kurdistan. Of the eight women on the committee, five represented the UIA, two were Kurdish representatives, and only one, Dr. Rajaa al-Khuzai, was an independent.

The committee spent months arguing over whether Islam would be *the* source of legislation for the country (as the religious parties wanted) or *a* source (a compromise sought by the Kurds and other secularists). The disagreement had not been resolved by the time the original August 15 deadline passed, and the debate spilled over into the extension period. Conservative Shiite leaders remained intransigent and threatened to scuttle talks if Islam did not get a central place in the constitution. As the arguments dragged on, U.S. Ambassador Zalmay Khalilzad finally intervened to avoid a stalemate. To gain concessions in other areas, he supported provisions that strengthened Islam's influence. Ultimately, the Kurds acquiesced too, both because they had other priorities to defend and because they recognized that conservative Shiites were not going to capitulate.

Article 2 of the final version of the constitution makes Islam the official religion of the state, cites it as a basic source of legislation, and says that no law can be passed that contradicts its "undisputed" rulings. Interpreting this provision will fall to the Supreme Court, which the new constitution says may include clerics; their number and method of selection were not specified, but will be defined by a subsequent law that must be approved by a two-thirds majority of parliament.

Secularists and women's advocates are also worried about Article 39, the section dealing with personal-status law. As foreshadowed by the battle in the IGC, Article 39 deems Iraqis "free in their personal status according to their religions, sects, beliefs, or choices," but leaves it up to subsequent legislation to define what this means. If Shiite leaders truly meant for the provision to give Iraqis the freedom of choice—allowing Shiites to live under Shiite law and Sunnis to live under Sunni law—then the progressive 1959 code may also be kept on the books for those who want it. Allowing such freedom could lead to a confusing but relatively benign system (not unprecedented in the region), under which Iraqis with legal questions could choose among different codes and court systems—Sunni, secular, or Shiite—depending on which they thought would give them the most favorable treatment.

Many secular Iraqis worry, however, that Article 39 will lead instead to an Iranian-style theocracy, which would severely limit women's rights in particular. Adnan Pachachi, the former Iraqi foreign minister and a secular Sunni leader, told *The New York Times* in August that although he agreed with much of the new constitution, he was troubled by its more overtly Islamic provisions. "They want to inject religion into everything, which is not right," he said. "I cannot imagine that we might have a theocratic regime in Iraq like the one in Iran. That would be a disaster."

Indeed, Iran's theocracy has been a disaster on multiple fronts, including women's rights. In the aftermath of the 1979 revolution, Iran's new government quickly suspended the country's progressive family law, disallowed female judges, and strongly enforced the wearing of the hijab. Within a few months, sharia rulings lowered the marriage age to nine, permitted polygamy, gave fathers the right to decide who their daughters could marry, permitted unilateral divorce for men but not women, and gave fathers sole custody of children in the case of divorce. Over the intervening years, Iranian activists, including some conservative religious women, have managed to soften some of the harshest inequalities. But anything approaching the Iranian system would still represent a major setback for Iraq's women.

Skeptics might wonder whether the legal debate in Iraq really matters. After all, most Middle Eastern countries have elegant constitutions guaranteeing many rights and freedoms to their citizens, yet lack the sorts of strong institutions that could defend those rights with any consistency. And indeed, Iraq may slide down this path over time. In the short term, however, the heavy U.S. presence there ensures that the political process will emphasize constitutional provisions and the rule of law. Moreover, according to an analysis by Nathan Brown, a George Washington University professor and a constitutional expert, Iraq's constitution has fewer loopholes for limiting basic freedoms than those of Iraq's neighbors. The new document also designates certain institutions, such as the Human Rights Commission and the Federal Supreme Court, to defend individual rights. Although the structural details of these bodies remain to be determined by Iraq's legislature, there is still reason to hope they will effectively defend Iraqis' freedoms.

LEARNING FROM OTHERS

No matter how effective such institutions turn out to be, the fact remains that the new constitution makes sharia supreme in Iraq. If moderates hope to advance women's rights, therefore, they will have to do it within an Islamic framework.

Fortunately, there are good precedents for such a process. Morocco, for example, recently revised its personal-status code (*moudawana*) but claimed to be doing so on Islamic grounds. The reforms were the result of over a decade of pressure from progressive Moroccan nongovernmental organizations (NGOS), which pushed to raise the marriage age from 15 to 18, abolish polygamy, equalize the right to divorce, and give women the right to retain custody of their children. Such efforts were opposed by religious groups. But Morocco's modernizing young king, Muhammad VI (who claims to be a direct descendent of the Prophet), backed the reformers and appointed a committee to examine potential changes to the *moudawana*. In October 2003, he formally presented parliament with a set of sweeping revisions to the family law, defending the changes with copious references to the Koran. In fact, both religious and secular supporters of the reforms used the language of religion and Islamic jurisprudence to advocate gender equality, and despite conservative opposition, parliament approved the changes.

Indonesia provides another example of how progressive change can come from within Islam. A group called Fatayat, the women's wing of the country's largest grass-roots organization (known as Nahdlatul Ulama), now trains its members in Islamic *fiqh* (jurisprudence) so that they can hold their own in religious debates. An NGO known as P3M (the Indonesian Society for Pesantren and Community Development) also uses *fiqh* to encourage Indonesia's many *pesantren* (religious schools) to promote women's reproductive health and family planning. And Musdah Mulia, the chief researcher at Indonesia's Ministry of Religious Affairs, caused a sensation in 2004 by calling for important changes to sharia in areas such as marriage, polygamy, and the wearing of the hijab—changes that she defended through meticulous references to Islamic jurisprudence. Her controversial recommendations have not yet been enacted, but they have sparked an important debate across Indonesian society that may eventually lead to significant changes.

An organization known as Women Living Under Muslim Laws (WLUML) provides another, transnational example of how women are pushing for change from within Islam. Founded in 1984 to oppose the harsh interpretation of sharia emerging in Algeria, WLUML functions by giving information on progressive Islamic systems around the world to local activists, who use the information to fight for greater freedoms. The network remains up and running today, providing women's groups around the world with powerful Islamic justifications for gender equality.

TURNING NUMBERS INTO INFLUENCE

In Iraq, unlike in many other Muslim nations, women will have a strong advantage in their fight for equality: namely, a provision in the new constitution that guarantees them 25 percent of the seats in parliament. This quota is the product of intense lobbying by women's groups, who feared being left out of the new Iraqi politics. It also has some grounding in Iraqi history. The Baathists gave women the vote and the right to run for office in 1980; within two decades, women had come to occupy 20 percent of the seats in Iraq's rubber-stamp parliament (compared to a 3.5 percent average in the region) and some prominent cabinet positions. After the invasion, U.S. policymakers were sympathetic to women's concerns that they would lose their political position in an election process dominated by conservative Shiites. Washington also wanted to support Iraqi women without directly challenging religious convictions. Instituting a quota seemed a good way to do both.

The process started with the Transitional Administrative Law, the interim constitution issued by the Americans and the IGC in 2004, which stated that women should constitute no less than a quarter of the members of the National Assembly. In the run-up to the January 2005 elections, political parties were required to field electoral slates on which every third candidate was a woman. As a result, women captured 31 percent of the seats.

At the time of the elections, some Western commentators pointed to this high level of female representation as evidence that a grand social and cultural transformation was under way in Iraq. With so many women in parliament, they reasoned, Iraq's new government would have to take a progressive stance on women's rights in drafting the new constitution and limit the role of religion. But assuming that merely having women in government would produce liberal legislation was a mistake. After all, nearly half of the women elected had run on the UIA list, and they have toed their party's conservative Shiite line.

When the constitution-drafting process began, progressive women, sensing that they would lose the battle over Islam, focused on holding on to their 25 percent quota in parliament. Several women leaders actually hoped to expand the quota (a few mentioned 40 percent as their goal) and apply it to other decision-making positions as well. But conservatives responded by attempting to have the quota phased out altogether after two rounds of elections. In the end, the quota did make it into the final draft of the constitution, which will give women in Iraq one of the highest levels of representation in the world (after all, women make up less than 15 percent of the U.S. Congress). Many of these seats may continue to be filled by female conservatives unlikely to support progressive legislation on women's issues in the near term. Over time, however, these same legislators may start advancing women's rights within an Islamic context.

The future of Islamic feminism in Iraq will depend on politicians such as Salama al-Khafaji, a dentist turned politician who is also a devout Shiite. After losing her son in an ambush, Khafaji was rated the most popular female politician in Iraq in a survey conducted in June 2005 (and was ranked the 11th most popular politician overall). As a member of the IGC, she incurred the wrath of secular women's groups by voting for Resolution 137. But Khafaji (who has pursued her political ambitions despite the objections of her husband, who divorced her as a consequence) defended her position by arguing that Islamic rules actually provide better protection to women in divorce and custody proceedings than does secular law. Khafaji sees herself as a positive force for change on women's issues; as she told a journalist last November, "I have Islamic ideas on justice, but I am moderate." And her ability to work with both secular and Islamic parties could make her an effective legislator.

The status of women in the future Iraq will also depend in large part on the strength of the country's judicial system. Here, too, there is reason for guarded optimism; although Iraq's court system needs significant reform, it does include many qualified lawyers and judges (although their expertise lies mostly in secular law, not sharia). Iraq also has a tradition of women serving as judges. The country's first female judge, Zakia Hakki, was appointed in 1959 (she is currently a prominent member of parliament). Today, women are widely accepted as judges in the Kurdish north and in the more secular parts of Baghdad.

But keeping women on the bench elsewhere will not be easy, as the story of Nidal Nasser Hussein illustrates. In 2003, the U.S. authorities appointed her the first female judge in the Shiite holy city of Najaf. The decision was met with widespread outrage. Several senior clerics quickly issued fatwas saying that under Islamic law only men can be judges, and angry protesters showed up at her swearing-in ceremony. In the face of such unexpected opposition, the senior U.S. commanding officer in Najaf decided to delay Hussein's appointment indefinitely, and she has yet to take her seat on the bench. As conservatives consolidate their control in the Shiite south, such conflicts are likely to intensify. Iraqi women should respond by invoking Islamic scholars who argue in favor of female judges.

Although having the right judges on the bench will determine the formal rights of Iraqi women over the long term, in the short term religious vigilantes, who are forcing their own fundamentalist views on Iraq's besieged population, are having the greatest impact. Over the past two years, various towns in both Shiite and Sunni areas have fallen into the hands of extremists who are imposing stringent restrictions there, such as requiring women to wear full-length veils, forbidding music and dancing, and enforcing strict segregation of the sexes in public. Many of these vigilantes are unemployed, undereducated followers of demagogues such as Muqtada al-Sadr. But at least some are reportedly also members of the police force in several southern cities (notably Basra). As their activities suggest, the greatest danger to Iraqi women stems not from any legal restrictions, but from lawlessness.

FRIENDS IN HIGH PLACES

Although the status of Iraqi women will ultimately depend on Iraqis themselves, the United States can still play a constructive role. Washington should start by identifying and cultivating Islamic feminists within Iraq's mainstream religious parties. These women (and men) may not want to cooperate with the United States at first, and some of them will hold anti-American views. But these individuals wield far more political influence than the secular but marginalized Iraqi leaders who are popular in Washington, and the United States must learn how to work with them.

Indeed, the United States should work with Iraqi women across the religious spectrum in order to cultivate new leaders. Thanks to the quota system, there is no question that Iraqi women will continue to play a significant role in national politics in the years ahead, and Washington should help ensure that it is a moderating one. Most of the women elected to parliament will be new to politics. The United States should provide them with technical training (through organizations such as the National Democratic Institute for International Affairs, an NGO that provides practical assistance to leaders advancing democracy) and help them to network across sectarian lines. Iraqi politicians should also be encouraged to work with their more moderate Iranian counterparts. The current U.S. policy of excluding Iranian parliamentarians and activists from U.S.-funded conferences in the region is counterproductive and should be abandoned.

The United States should also assist with judicial reform. This means not only helping the courts modernize technologically, but also training judges, especially women, in modern Islamic jurisprudence. These training programs could be developed in partnership with the leading institutions of Islamic jurisprudence throughout the region, and they should be open to judges from across the Muslim world.

To help women defend their rights, Washington should also educate Iraqis about what their rights are—both under the new constitution and under sharia. A recent Freedom House report assessing women's rights in 17 Arab countries found that with the exception of Saudi Arabia, each has a constitution that formally mandates gender equality. The problem in these countries, however, is that the governments make little effort to inform the people of their rights. To avoid such a scenario in Iraq, the United States should support educational programs and a nationwide media campaign to promote better understanding of Iraqis' freedoms, under both the constitution and other laws. Washington should also encourage open dialogue on various interpretations of sharia governing personal-status laws. Religious scholars and international Islamic groups, such as Sisters in Islam and WLUML, should be invited to join and inform the discussions, which should be widely broadcast through media outlets such as Radio Al-Mahabba (a U.S.-funded Iraqi station dedicated to raising awareness on women's rights).

In the long term, female education may be the best way to advance the status of women. During the difficult decade of the 1990s, school-enrollment rates for girls in Iraq declined significantly, making Iraq one of the few countries in the world today where mothers are generally better educated than their daughters. Although reliable literacy figures are hard to come by, most observers agree that Iraq now has one of the worst gender literacy gaps in the world. As Iran, with its female literacy rate of more than 70 percent, has shown, educated women inevitably become effective advocates for their own rights. The United States should therefore champion female education in Iraq at all levels—primary, secondary, and tertiary—and promote adult-literacy programs for women.

In the next year, a new Iraqi parliament will be elected with the power to write laws that will shape the country for the next generation. Washington must therefore do everything it can to aid Iraqi women's groups and programs designed to help women leaders there. Efforts such as the U.S.-funded legal-education program at the University of Baghdad, where women make up 40 percent of the participants in rule-of-law seminars, should be expanded to other universities and cities across Iraq. Washington should also consider establishing a women's college in Baghdad, which could become a center of learning and critical thinking for the entire region.

The United States should also start channeling a significant portion of its reconstruction dollars to Iraqi businesswomen. Economic empowerment is a good way to boost the status of women. Despite the enormous sums of American aid flowing into Iraq, the U.S. mission in Baghdad has so far resisted having an adviser on gender issues on the ground in Iraq—where programs to support women are actually implemented. As a result, its many gender initiatives have not been nearly as effective as they could have been.

Although the United States has now missed this and several other important opportunities to promote the role of women in post-Saddam Iraq, the imposition of sharia there was virtually inevitable. But the resurgence of Islamic law in Iraq need not be a disaster for women. Although it may well mean a short-term setback in certain rights enjoyed under Saddam, in the long run, Iraqis may manage to build a more equitable society that accommodates both Islamic principles and a modern role for women. This outcome is far from guaranteed, but it is also not too much to hope for.

STUDY QUESTIONS

1. In what way is Iraq's new constitution ambiguous in relation to women?
2. Why do some believe this does not necessarily mean trouble for Iraqi women?
3. Why is the status of women an important issue in Iraq?
4. What approach have reformers largely abandoned and which one are they trying to promote—and why?
5. Where does sharia law come from?
6. What happened in the 11th century that affected the direction of sharia law, and what was the result?
7. What is the position of "Islamic feminists" on Islam?
8. What is the contradiction in the Koran about polygamy?
9. Where did the tradition of the veil come from?
10. What were some of the more progressive provisions in Iraq's personal-status law of 1959?
11. What became the most contentious issue in drafting Iraq's modern constitution, what was the committee's argument, and what was the outcome?
12. What is Article 2 of the final version of the Iraqi constitution?
13. Why are secularists and women's advocates worried about Article 39?
14. If moderates hope to advance women's rights in Iraq, they will have to do it within an Islamic framework. In what ways is Morocco a good example?
15. How is Indonesia approaching progressive change?
16. What advantage do Iraqi women have in their fight for equality and why is that equality not assumed?
17. Although in the long term the future of women's rights in Iraq will depend on its politicians and judges, what are some short term concerns?

Chapter 9 Snapshot
Applying Islamic Principles in the Twenty-first Century: Nigeria, Iran, and Indonesia

I selected this article because I wanted to continue our discussion of Islam from a slightly different perspective. In the last article we looked at ways Iraq has been struggling with updating women's rights as they are protected under their new constitution and in civil law, yet also supported by sharia law and the process of *ijtihad*. Iraq, however, is not the only Islamic country that is engaging in such discourse (conversations) about the role of shari'ah law, especially as it relates to democracy, human rights, rule of law, and pluralism. In this article we will read about three more countries, Nigeria, Iran, and Indonesia that are also engaging in this dialog and we will get an insight as to how each of these countries is working out their concerns regarding reform and liberalism in different ways. Our author, David R. Smock, characterizes this as a dialog between a literal versus an interpretive approach to reading the Qur'an, and between "'text-proof' versus 'rational proof'" of fundamental and liberal interpretations of Shari'ah. (140). This article is a report of several of the conference presentations made in these countries.

Just a brief note about spelling before we continue. You will notice that in this article Islamic law is spelled "shari'ah" while in the last article it was spelled "sharia." You will also see in this article that Islam's holy book is spelled "Qur'an" while in the last article it was spelled "Koran." This is an example of transliteration. When translating languages with different alphabets, like Arabic to English or Hebrew to English, the spelling is imprecise because of the lack of the same letters. In these cases, the translated word can be spelled in a variety of ways as long as the pronunciation of that word is the same as the original.

SHARI'AH, JUSTICE AND IJTIHAD IN NIGERIA

Nigeria is a very complex country with well over 200 languages representing distinct ethnic groups and religious traditions. When 300 Muslim scholars from inside and outside Nigeria met in 2004, they wanted to discuss "how shari'ah can be interpreted through ijtihad to meet changing needs and provide justice in Nigeria" (140). As we learned in the last article, "… like the Hebrew Bible, the Holy Qur'an contains commandments that Muslims must follow and apply in their daily lives" (140). It includes references to the Five Pillars of Islam, including praying and fasting. In all, the Qur'an includes approximately 80 verses that addresses "political, economic, and social matters such as inheritance, interest, and economic justice as well as punishments for crimes such as theft, adultery, and drinking alcohol" (140). These writings are also supported by the Sunnah, the traditions of the Prophet Mohammad, and various interpretations of these writings by Islamic scholars. "Throughout history, Muslim jurists and scholars have had divergent opinions about many issues, and the process of ijtihad has been essential to adapting Islamic jurisprudence (shari'ah) to changing needs and realities" (140).

Shari'ah law has become an increasingly divided issue in Nigeria, primarily between fundamentalist (traditionalist) and modernist (liberal) interpretations of the law. The traditionalists believe the letter of the law should be followed precisely (e.g. cutting off the hand of a thief, stoning as a punishment for adultery), while "modernists believe that this interpretation does not represent the spirit of the Qur'anic teaching and, more important, that shari'ah has always been subject to multiple interpretations in light of the ever-changing needs of society" (140). Traditionally, it has fallen to Islamic jurists and scholars, practicing ijtihad (scriptural interpretation), "which is based not only on the Qur'an and sunnah, but also on reason, deduction, and prioritization" (140).

Nigeria is a country of mixed religious adherents; the northern states are primarily Islamic, while further south and east, we find mostly Christian and indigenous religions. "Twelve northern states, under pressure from their populations, recently adopted or reintroduced the criminal component of shari'ah. While this step has enjoyed broad public support from the Muslim populations in these states, Christians living there and in other parts of the country have felt threatened" (141).

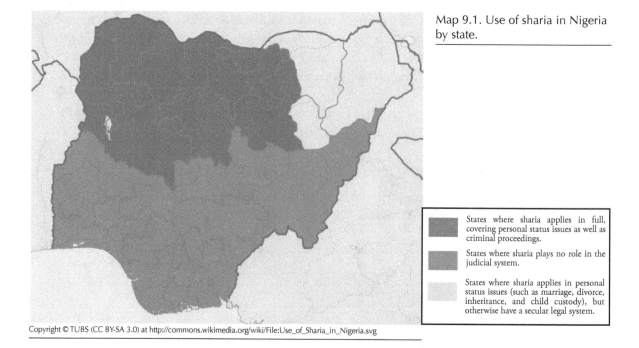

Map 9.1. Use of sharia in Nigeria by state.

States where sharia applies in full, covering personal status issues as well as criminal proceedings.

States where sharia plays no role in the judicial system.

States where sharia applies in personal status issues (such as marriage, divorce, inheritance, and child custody), but otherwise have a secular legal system.

The purpose of the conference in Nigeria was to consider if Islamic law would work within a plural democratic setting (140; also see p. 140–141 for the three objectives of the conference). This 2004 conference was sparked by an incident involving a woman, Amina Lawal, who was convicted of adultery and sentenced to stoning although the man, having denied having sexual relations with Amina Lawal, was released. "Although the decision was eventually overturned by the court of appeals, the case generated fierce debate about the suitability of Islamic law in modern societies" (141). Islamic societies are very different today than when Islamic law was written and many scholars feel it is time to have a reasoned debate.

One of the topics of great interest has to do with the distinctions between the moral and legal issues within Islamic law; "which parts of shari'ah are moral—and hence fall within the realm of education and voluntary compliance—and which parts are legal and therefore must be enforced by society" (142).

How far can the state intrude into individual privacy or police individual morality? Other questions addressed the limits of shari'ah in light of globalization: how can shari'ah be adapted to modern society without losing its distinctively Islamic identity, and how shall the rich and powerful be held accountable to the same laws and justice as the weak and the poor (142).

There were quite a wide range of topics presented at the conference that sparked debate and dialog. The important point here is that the debate "concerning how Islamic norms and heritage relate to modern society" is continuing, that "radical notions will not go unchallenged and that claims to exclusive authenticity by extreme voices will be addressed" (142).

There was more opening of dialog at this conference than there were definitive answers, and David Smock cautions that Westerners should be aware of this debate within Islam and its meaning for shari'ah rather than just dismissing shari'ah "with alarmist condemnations. Everyone surely has the right to be critical "of practices they deem immoral, inhumane, and degrading to human dignity, no culture or religion has the right to dismiss the capacity of another to develop its own moral and legal systems through an open process and dialogue" (143)

REFLECTIONS ON ISLAM AND DEMOCRACY IN IRAN

Such conversations have been going on in Iran, as well, although not without some struggle. A conference was to be held in 2004, having to do with the compatibility of Islam and democracy. Hosted by the Center for the Study of Islam and Democracy, the conference leaders wanted a diversity of opinions represented and, although they were able to get a group of modernist Iranian ulama to attend the meeting at Ferdowsi University of Mashhad, they were having more trouble getting traditionalist Iranian ulama to attend. "There was constant risk that the conference would be derailed at the last minute, mainly because it was to be the first of its kind in the country" (144). Twice the conference was postponed, and an extremist group, Ansar-I Hizb Allah, "supporting clerical rule in Iran had threatened to disrupt the proceedings" (144). Just days before the conference was to begin, "Ansar-I Hizb Allah had demanded that five prominent scholars, who formed the liberal group in support of democratic governance in Iran, be barred from participating. The group had also threatened the lives of these five scholars …" (144).

The first day of the conference in Mashhad was tense. But there were good discussions that were "open and critical of the role religion was playing in Iranian politics. The participants were unanimous in feeling that unchecked state religiosity could lead to a dangerous and tyrannical system of governance, as the events of the past few years had indicated" (144). They "spoke about secularism and the problems posed by the fact that in modern democratic society, religion is privatized and its scope limited to spiritual and moral well-being" (144). However, one of the other ideas brought out on this first day was that to develop peaceful coexistence between people of different faiths, faith communities had to let go of the attitude that they have exclusive control of the truth (145).

The second day of the conference was held at the Ministry of Higher Education and Scientific Research in Tehran, and the scholars who were prevented from the meeting in Mashhad were able to attend. This was a much more relaxed conference. During these meetings participants were not debating whether religion and democracy were compatible; they already accepted this point as a given. They also agreed that in a country like Iran, religion "cannot be eliminated from the public square" (145). Some of the discussions acknowledged that "Islamic democracy has to be based on a minimalist-rationalist reading of Islam" while other participants were concerned that "human freedom, having private and public dimensions, should not be exercised in a way that causes harm to others or threatens other people's moral values" (145).

PEACE EDUCATION IN ACEH, INDONESIA

Indonesia is the most populous Islamic country in the world, with approximately 202.9 million identified as Muslim (88.2% of the total population) as of 2009 and Aceh "is still among Indonesia's most religiously conservative and observant provinces" (146). Aceh is a special province on the northwest tip of Sumatra. The ulama of Aceh

> have been the principal initiators of religious, academic, and cultural life, giving them a special place within Acehnese society. While they continue to play a dominant role as the guardians of faith and values, the contemporary ulama are facing a serious challenge. They must respond to the fast-changing global information age on the one hand and uphold the Prophet's legacy on the other hand (146).

One of the areas the ulama felt they could influence with the most long-lasting effect is the madrassas (Islamic schools) "or, as they are known in Indonesia, pesantrens (private Islamic boarding schools)" (146). So, along with Acehnese scholars and educators, the ulama "organized the Peace Education Program, supervised by the leaders of the Consultative Council of Ulama of Aceh" (146). There were also international partners supporting this program, Nonviolence International, the United States Institute of Peace, and the Canadian International Development Agency (146). Their primary goal was to develop a foundational core and expectation of peace; in fact, because they view peace as inherent to Islam (146).

However, besides addressing ways Islam must keep up with a globalizing world and a modernizing society, Aceh has been struggling for independence from Indonesia in a war that only ended in 2005, giving Aceh more autonomy. In the 30 or so years of fighting, over 15,000 people have been killed and both sides have been guilty of human rights abuses (http://www.bbc.co.uk/news/world-asia-22198860. Accessed 6/23/2013). "Aceh's prolonged conflicts, rooted in communal violence and severe human rights abuses, compel the ulama to seek methods of resolving violence and conflict" (146).

The Peace Education Project was initiated during the war, in early 2003, and was developed to complete two goals. The first goal was to create a peace education manual and the second was to see this manual implemented in at least a pilot program in selected pesantrens (146–147). The manual

Map 9.2. Locator map of Aceh showing provincial boundaries.

promotes a positive, comprehensive peace, encompassing peaceful relations with God the Creator, with oneself, with one's fellow humans, and with the environment. The curriculum teaches communal peace in accordance with a positive Islamic approach, namely the absence of war and discrimination, as well as the necessity for justice (147).

The manual was completed in 2005 and "covers a wide range of critical topics, including democracy, pluralism, human rights, conflict and neutralization of violence, emotion management, leadership, natural resources, and conflict resolution" (147). Many of the pesantren leaders have expressed interest in implementing this manual as soon as teachers are trained. In addition, other parts of Indonesia and other Muslim countries have shown an interest in this manual and its curriculum. "It is being translated into English and Arabic and will be disseminated for use in places that face similar challenges of interpreting Islamic principles to address rapidly changing global realities" (147). Most importantly, the intent of this manual and its curriculum "emphasizes that peace is neither subjugation to inequitable situations nor a passive acceptance of injustice, discrimination, and war" (147). and that peace is an inherent characteristic fully consistent with Islamic principles.

CONCLUSION

The three countries in this article add an additional dimension to some of the changes taking place in the Islamic world, as we saw in the previous article on Iraq.

Nigerian jurists, scholars, and clerics are engaged in an ongoing dialogue among themselves, with the international Muslim community, and with Nigerian Christians about the appropriate scope of—and limitations on—shari'ah in northern Nigeria. Iranian clerics and scholars are grappling with the proper balance between Islam and democracy … Iran is still evolving, and liberal scholars and clerics, while sometimes silenced, speak out. The ulama in Aceh had enthusiastically supported a project to introduce peace studies in Achenese religious schools, emphasizing peace, democracy, and pluralism. The ulama have been supportive because the teaching materials are all based on Islamic texts (147).

The Islamic world cannot be stereotyped, and it is not static; numerous countries are striving to see how Islam and the application of Islamic principles can be adapted to modern realities and are subject to intense debate.

9. APPLYING ISLAMIC PRINCIPLES IN THE TWENTY-FIRST CENTURY

Nigeria, Iran, and Indonesia[1]

By David R. Smock

This report describes three projects that illustrate how Muslim scholars in three countries are addressing critical contemporary issues from an Islamic perspective. In Nigeria, more than 300 Muslim scholars and clerics engaged in a critical examination of shari'ah as it is being adopted and modified in Nigeria's northern states. In Iran, Iranian scholars, clerics, and others convened to address the relationship between Islam and democracy in that country. In Indonesia, a team of scholars has written a manual based on Islamic sources for religious schools on the topics of peace/violence, democracy, rule of law, conflict resolution, human rights, and pluralism.

The debates among scholars and clerics in these three countries, as in other Muslim countries, on issues such as shari'ah and ijtihad (scriptural interpretation) are spirited. Resistance to reform and liberalism is particularly strong in Iran, but also in Nigeria. Those adhering

1. A priority of the Religion and Peacemaking program of the United States Institute of Peace has been to support Muslim efforts to reinterpret Islamic principles for the twenty-first century. The Initiative has organized workshops on Islamic perspectives on peace and violence, on Islam and democracy, and, most recently, on ijtihad (scriptural interpretation). This report describes Initiative-supported conferences in Nigeria and Iran to enable Muslim scholars to grapple with how faithful Muslims can respond to a range of contemporary issues. In Indonesia, a project yielded a peace-focused teaching tool based on Islamic principles. This report summarizes the three projects and offers salient points raised by some of the conference participants.

to literal interpretations of the texts challenge those adopting a more rational/interpretive approach. "Text proof" versus "rational proof" approaches divide the ulama in Iran and Nigeria into traditionalist and rationalist camps, with the majority leaning toward the former.

The projects in Nigeria and in Iran were cosponsored by the Center for the Study of Islam and Democracy (CSID), based in Washington, D.C. CSID arranged for scholars of Islam from the United States and elsewhere to make presentations at the two conferences. The Indonesian project was cosponsored by Nonviolence International.

SHARI'AH, JUSTICE, AND IJTIHAD IN NIGERIA

CSID, in collaboration with the Centre for Islamic Legal Studies in Zaria, Nigeria, and the London-based International Forum for Islamic Dialogue (IFID), organized a three-day conference in July 2004 titled "Implementation of the Shari'ah in a Democracy: The Nigerian Experience." The conference was funded by the United States Institute of Peace and the U.S. State Department. Three hundred Muslim scholars and leaders from inside and outside of Nigeria discussed how shari'ah can be interpreted through ijtihad to meet changing needs and provide justice in Nigeria.

Radwan Masmoudi, president of CSID, explained that, like the Hebrew Bible, the Holy Qur'an contains commandments that Muslims must follow and apply in their daily lives. These commandments address not only purely religious issues such as praying and fasting, but also political, economic, and social matters such as inheritance, interest, and economic justice, as well as punishments for crimes such as theft, adultery, and drinking alcohol. These Qur'anic teachings are supplemented by the tradition of the Prophet Mohammad (sunnah) and by the long history of scholars' interpretations. Throughout history, Muslim jurists and scholars have had divergent opinions about many issues, and the process of ijtihad has been essential to adapting Islamic jurisprudence (shari'ah) to changing needs and realities.

The Tension between Fundamental and Liberal Interpretations of Shari'ah

Traditionalists believe legal punishments (hudud) prescribed in the Qur'an—such as for stealing and adultery—must be applied literally (e.g., cutting off the hand of the thief) in order to obey God's commandments, said Masmoudi. Modernists believe that this interpretation does not represent the spirit of the Qur'anic teaching and, more important, that shari'ah has always been subject to multiple interpretations in light of the ever-changing needs of society. To address the changing needs of their societies, Muslim jurists and scholars have relied on a well-established process of innovation (ijtihad), which is based not only on the Qur'an and sunnah, but also on reason, deduction, and prioritization. Imam Abu Hamid al-Ghazzali, a renowned twelfth-century scholar and theologian in Sunni Islam, presented this guidance about the overarching purpose of shari'ah: "The purpose of the law [shari'ah] for human beings is fivefold: the preservation for them of their religion, soul, intellect, offspring, and property."

Shari'ah has become a very divisive issue in Nigeria. Simmering discontent among the various segments of Nigerian society has resulted in violent outbursts—sometimes appearing as religious fervor and other times dressed in ethnic prejudice—but all underscoring the country's imperfect federal structure. Twelve northern states, under pressure from their populations, recently adopted or reintroduced the criminal component of shari'ah. While this step has enjoyed broad public support from the Muslim populations in these states, Christians living there and in other parts of the country have felt threatened.

Masmoudi concludes that objective examination of the relationship among shari'ah, justice, and sustainable plural democracy is essential. The need to bring together scholars and experts on Islam, politics, governance, and democracy to assess how to accommodate and harmonize the assertion of Islamic law within a plural democratic setting led him to convene the conference. This conference had the following objectives:

- Promote an interpretation of shari'ah that is modern and compatible with universal human rights, pluralism, and democracy, while remaining genuinely Islamic
- Discuss shari'ah's true meaning, its various forms, and its Islamic roots
- Encourage efforts at Islamic reformation (ijtihad) to solve the political, economic, and social problems of the Muslim world.

In addition, the conference discussed the broader subject of democracy and political pluralism, covering such topics as independence of the judiciary, women's participation, responsibility and freedom of the press, rights of minorities, good governance, freedom of worship, and social justice.

The Case of Amina Lawal

In Nigeria, the debate about shari'ah implementation reached a peak in 2002, when a shari'ah court sentenced a young woman, Amina Lawal, to death after she was convicted of adultery. The case generated great interest, and the court's decision met with international protest and condemnation.

Many Westerners saw death as an excessive punishment for an act that falls within the realm of private choice in most countries. Many Muslims also opposed the shari'ah court's ruling, and reputable Muslim scholars and jurists found many flaws in its judgment. The court did not, for instance, give sufficient attention to ensuring due process: among other issues, it accepted a forced confession the police took from the accused and it released the man, who denied having sexual relations with the woman, without any punishment. Although the decision was ultimately overturned by the court of appeals, the case generated fierce debate about the suitability of Islamic law in modern societies.

As Masmoudi points out, the challenge facing modern Muslim societies is how to reapply the principles of shari'ah in social, economic, and political contexts that are markedly different from those that existed during its original development. The question is debated in academic and intellectual circles in Muslim societies. But in the absence of an open political debate, little has been done to educate the public on these issues, or to determine the relevance of shari'ah to contemporary cultural and legal practices. In addition, there is a significant debate in academic and religious quarters about the historicity, and even the authenticity, of certain historical pronouncements of shari'ah laws. For example, some scholars contend that stoning and punishments for apostasy have no basis in the Qur'an, while other Muslim jurists claim that these interpretations of shari'ah were meant only for a particular time and place in Islamic history.

Morality vs. Legality

Many Muslims scholars and jurists are profoundly concerned about the literal and uncritical application of ancient shari'ah rules, as well as the lack of clear delineation between the moral and the legal in Islamic law. Which parts of shari'ah are moral—and hence fall within the realm of education and voluntary compliance—and which parts are legal and therefore must be enforced by society? Also, there are intense debates on the issue of state intrusion into individual privacy and on the extent to which the state should be allowed to police individual morality. Questions also arise about due process and rules of evidence in shari'ah courts. To what extent can courts rely on circumstantial evidence to convict a person of a crime?

At the conference's opening session, chaired by Nigerian Chief Justice Muhammad Lawal Uwais, the governors of the northern states of Kano, Bauchi, and Zamfara delivered keynote addresses. Other attendees included several prominent judges from Islamic courts, academicians, and government officials. In his address, the governor of Bauchi State posed several challenging questions:

- In the light of globalization, how do we determine the limits within which we will implement shari'ah so that non-Muslims are also accommodated?
- How do we evaluate the changes in shari'ah without losing our distinct identity as Muslims?
- Shari'ah does not only apply to the weak and the poor, while we turn a blind eye to the rich and powerful. How can we create a spiritual policeman or a spiritual judge?

Conference Presentations

Dr. Najah Kadhim of IFID observed that of the Qur'an's thousands of verses, only a handful deal with shari'ah, so there is considerable room for flexibility and interpretation. Professor Abdelaziz Sachedina of the University of Virginia reminded the audience that shari'ah was formulated in a transnational world and by a transnational people. Muslims have inherited a diverse tradition, which must be rethought if it is to work for the modern nation-state. "You and I have a responsibility as Muslims," he said, "to clarify what we mean by shari'ah."

Saudatu Mahdi presented a paper titled "Shari'ah and Women in Nigeria: The Expectations." Mahdi asserted that Nigerian women expect the Nigerian implementation process to draw from the broadest and most tolerant understanding of the shari'ah's tenets. Moreover, she said, the entire Muslim world, as well as the world at large, is watching how Nigeria handles the implementation of shari'ah. Her presentation included both detailed recommendations, including the repeal or modification of specific laws, and a general discussion of women's rights in an Islamic state.

Does shari'ah as implemented meet the people's socioeconomic needs? This was the foremost question raised in Baffa Aliyu Umar's paper: chiefly, how shari'ah provides a basis for the social, political, and economic life of both Muslims and non-Muslims. Umar asserted that even the smallest of social programs, appropriately aimed at people's most pressing needs, improves the shari'ah system as a whole.

As the debate at the conference reveals, the scope of the contending perspectives is wide, particularly concerning how Islamic norms and heritage relate to modern society. Masmoudi asserts that the debate must continue, as openness and dialogue are the best guarantors that radical notions will not go unchallenged and that claims to exclusive authenticity by extreme voices will be addressed. Open debate and the freedom to put popular choices to the test of time (as long as they do not infringe on human rights and human dignity) have been crucial for the maturation of Western democracy. The maturation of Islamic democracy and law requires similar time and space, he said.

Recommendations

Many questions remained unanswered, underscoring the importance of organizing more international discussions of the variety of interpretations and the complexity of applying shari'ah in modern Muslim societies. The exchange between local and international Muslim scholars was particularly stimulating and should continue in follow-up meetings.

Western societies and policymakers, Masmoudi pointed out, should appreciate that Muslim societies and lawmakers have every right to reconcile their legal system with their moral values. Instead of voicing alarmist condemnations of shari'ah, Westerners should pay closer attention to the lively debate on law and morality within Muslim societies. While all human beings, regardless of nationality and religion, have the right to be critical of practices they deem immoral, inhumane, and degrading to human dignity, no culture or religion has the right to dismiss the capacity of another to develop its own moral and legal systems through an open process and dialogue.

REFLECTIONS ON ISLAM AND DEMOCRACY IN IRAN

In recent years, attempts to engage Iran in a productive dialogue regarding developing a constitutional democracy have been thwarted by internal Iranian politics and external negativism, particularly from the United States. For almost a decade, a number of American foundations have led delegations to meet with Iranian religious leaders and other political activists to discuss political reform. Such meetings became possible after the election of reformist president Muhammad Khatami. However, none of these foundations was seen as empathetic to the Iranian political intricacies by the Iranians themselves. Most were regarded as American agents intrinsically opposed to Islam and anything Islamic.

The Center for the Study of Islam and Democracy, with its mission to search for the compatibility between religion and democratic politics, took a special interest in the Iranian experiment. Then-chair of the CSID board Abdulaziz Sachedina was in Iran in the summer of 2002 when Radwan Masmoudi suggested that he submit a proposal to hold a conference at his alma mater, Ferdowsi University of Mashhad (FUM). The story of how this conference was planned and executed helps elucidate the complexities that surround debate about religious and political change in Iran.

The subject of democracy and religion has been controversial in the Islamic Republic of Iran since its establishment under the late Ayatollah Khomeini. The government has been divided on the exact nature of the Islamic state from its inception, dating to the 1978–79 constitutional debates. With the rise of anti-Americanism as a vehicle to keep the religious establishment in power, the Iranian academic establishment has become extremely sensitive about being seen as encouraging American interference in Iran's internal politics.

Confronting the Obstacles

FUM welcomed the opportunity to collaborate with CSID and took precautions to avoid potential problems. FUM applied for official permission to hold the conference in Mashhad; the request was approved at the highest level in Tehran. CSID was committed to including both proponents and opponents of constitutional democracy in Iran. It was relatively easy to enlist the participation of secularist-modernist academicians such as Dr. Abdol Karim Soroush and his group of Iranian thinkers. The critical task for CSID/FUM was to get the traditionalist ulama, who oppose democracy as a Western imperialist ploy, to participate. For that purpose, Dr. Hassan Jamshidi, who has excellent connections to the traditionalists, was appointed as a "shuttle diplomat" to get as many members of the conservative ulama on board as possible. Thanks to his efforts, the conference was able to enlist well-known figures whose views about the role of clergy and Islam in a modern nation-state were important to the debate.

There was constant risk that the conference would be derailed at the last minute, mainly because it was to be the first of its kind in the country. Twice, parliamentary elections—resulting in hard-liners' forming the majority—postponed the conference. They also served as a warning to CSID that antidemocratic forces connected with the religious establishment might pressure the university to cancel the event.

The final date of December 1–2, 2004, was mutually approved by CSID and FUM. During the last week of November, Dr. Ali Yousefi, the FUM-appointed conference director, informed Sachedina that Ansar-i Hizb Allah, an extremist group supporting clerical rule in Iran, had threatened to disrupt the proceedings. The university, in consultation with the government officials in Tehran, nevertheless decided to proceed with the conference.

As soon as the CSID delegation, made up of Masmoudi, Sachedina, and Antony Sullivan, arrived in Mashhad the morning of November 30, they learned that Ansar-i Hizb Allah had demanded that five prominent scholars, who formed the liberal group in support of democratic governance in Iran, be barred from participating. The group had also threatened the lives of these five scholars, including Soroush and Dr. Mohsin Kadivar, a liberal cleric.

The First Day of the Conference

CSID and FUM moved quickly to arrange for alternative programs in Mashhad and Tehran, where a number of key participants had been asked to stay until further instructions from the conference organizers. On December 1, the CSID delegation met with several faculty members in the Theology School and Faculty of Arts and Humanities. In the evening, some scholars who were already in Mashhad met for about three hours at FUM to present their views and discuss issues connected with democratization. The atmosphere was tense, but the discussions were open and critical of the role religion was playing in Iranian politics. The participants were unanimous in feeling that unchecked state religiosity could lead to a dangerous and tyrannical system of governance, as the events of the past few years had indicated.

In addition to Masmoudi and Sachedina, the Iranian group was led in discussion by Professor Mohammad Mojtahed Shabestari, a member of the clerical establishment; Professor Gholam Abbas Tavassoli, and Drs. Mohammad Reza Beheshti and Arjomand. They spoke about secularism and the problems posed by the fact that in modern democratic society, religion is privatized and its scope limited to spiritual and moral well-being. There were also interesting exchanges about critical conceptual clarity concerning the meaning and nature of democracy and its cultural relativity.

Dr. Beheshti's presentation raised important issues in the emerging intercultural dialogue among world religions. Peaceful coexistence among peoples of different religions depends on changing faith communities' attitudes that they have exclusive control of the truth. The unique aspect of this frank exchange among Iranian thinkers was the total absence of anti-American rhetoric. The entire discussion demonstrated sophisticated understanding of the issues related to developing democratic freedoms within the framework of a secular state that respects the wisdom of religion in both its internal and external policies.

The Second Day of the Conference

On December 2, the scholars who had been prevented from traveling to Mashhad met with twenty-five other participants at the Ministry of Higher Education and Scientific Research in Tehran to present their papers and discuss the compatibility of Islam and democracy in Iran. The Tehran meeting compensated for all that was lacking in the Mashhad meeting. The atmosphere was relaxed and the participants contributed extremely well in terms of quality and transparency. The issue that dominated the afternoon was not whether religion and democracy are compatible. That was taken as a given, as was recognition that religion in a country like Iran cannot be eliminated from the public square.

Soroush argued that Muslim sensibilities are offended when liberal democracy tolerates or encourages immoral social behavior. Iranians must search for political democracy; they need an accountable government that creates laws for individual Iranians as citizens, not as believers.

Dr. Reza Eslami contended that no true reform could ignore the critical need to make the official religion more inclusive in order to guarantee the human rights of all citizens, regardless of their faith. Dr. Forough Jahan-bakhsh, the only woman participant in the session, underscored the paradigm shift in the Muslim modernist discourse on religion and democracy and the obstacles confronting the reformers advocating democratic governance for Iran. Dr. Mohsen Kadivar spoke about various twentieth-century readings of the Islamic tradition. In some important ways, Kadivar took Mohammad Mojtahed Shabistari's relativism in the religious readings a step further by providing an alternative paradigm for democratic governance to become deeply ingrained in the Iranian political processes.

Dr. Ali Paya's model of democracy argued for an efficient political system responsive to the needs of modern citizens searching to implement the best in society. Islamic democracy can compare favorably with the best Western democracies if it represents the social, religious, political, economic, legal, educational, and human aspirations of Islamic societies. Yet Islamic democracy has to be based on a minimalist-rationalist reading of Islam.

Two of the papers submitted in writing that could not be presented in person—both by traditionalist scholars—deserve special mention. Ayatollah Mohamed Jannati questioned whether freedom and equality—the two pillars of human rights—are compatible with human nature and with "divine religions" in which human rights are based on natural law. He believes freedom is the sum of rights recognized for human beings, who are free to accept them. However, human freedom, having private and public dimensions, should not be exercised in a way that causes harm to others or threatens other people's moral values. In Islam, freedom is not absolute; it is delimited by the law that regulates mutual rights and duties to others.

Ayatollah Amid Zanjani's paper critically assessed the crisis over democracy in the Muslim world, which either totally rejects or conditionally accepts democratic governance. His prescription for democratic politics is to adopt a middle path: no people, including Iranians, should adopt alien systems of governance without ensuring their cultural and religious legitimacy.

PEACE EDUCATION IN ACEH, INDONESIA

The Gate of Mecca

Aceh, on the northern tip of the island of Sumatra, was once known as the Gate of Mecca for its contribution to the development of Islamic spiritual scholarship and Indonesian-Malay civilization. Today, Aceh is still among Indonesia's most religiously conservative and observant provinces. The ulama have been the principal initiators of religious, academic, and cultural life, giving them a special place within Acehnese society. While they continue to play a dominant role as the guardians of faith and values, the contemporary ulama are facing a serious challenge. They must respond to the fast-changing global information age on the one hand and uphold the Prophet's legacy on the other hand. The tension between these two expectations puts tremendous pressure on the ulama and on the headmasters of the madrassas (Islamic schools) or, as they are known in Indonesia, pesantrens (private Islamic boarding schools).

The Peace Education Program

To address this challenge, a team of Acehnese scholars, ulama, and educators, led by Asna Husin, organized the Peace Education Program, supervised by the leaders of the Consultative Council of Ulama of Aceh. The international partners for this program are Nonviolence International, the United States Institute of Peace, and the Canadian International Development Agency. As one ulama put it, "Peace education is empowering our leadership." The ulama embrace this program because they view peace as inherent to Islam. Peace and security from that which negates human dignity are essential components of Islam, as the very name "Islam" (submission to the will of God) connotes. Promoting Islam and peace as well as maintaining security are central duties of every believer, and especially of the ulama. The ulama can claim to be "heirs of the prophets" only if they are equipped with knowledge and use it to benefit their communities. The ulama of Aceh seek to reinforce Islamic peace and promote communal good and justice.

A Province in Conflict

As Husin explains, Aceh's prolonged conflicts, rooted in communal violence and severe human rights abuses, compel the ulama to seek methods of resolving violence and conflict. They recognize that most Acehnese look to them for moral and practical guidance in the context of communal bloodshed and the growing political and social isolation of the Acehnese within Indonesian society. This is not an easy task, since the ulama are caught between the struggle of Free Aceh Movement (GAM) to achieve independence for Aceh, lawless gangs, and various police and military forces, in addition to suffering the demoralizing effects of corrupt political leadership. Finally, the tsunami of December 26, 2004, destroyed two-thirds of the provincial capital of Banda Aceh, sweeping away the coastal cities of Meulaboh and Calang and killing more than 245,000 inhabitants. The tragedy greatly intensified the challenges the ulama face and increased their awareness of their responsibilities.

The New Curriculum

The Peace Education Project, initiated in early 2003, is helping Aceh's ulama to address contemporary challenges and apply Islamic principles to contemporary realities. The project has had two phases: the creation of a peace education manual and its pilot implementation in selected pesantrens. By early 2005 the project had finished developing the peace manual, Kurikulum Pendidikan Damai: Perspektif Ulama Aceh (Peace Education Curriculum: Perspective of the Ulama of Aceh). This 385-page training book, which presents peace education from an Islamic and Acehnese perspective, is being used both to train ulama and as a resource for teaching in Aceh's pesantrens. It promotes a positive, comprehensive peace, encompassing peaceful relations with God the Creator, with oneself, with one's fellow humans, and with the environment. The curriculum teaches communal peace in accordance with a positive Islamic approach, namely the absence of war and discrimination, as well as the necessity for justice. It emphasizes that peace is neither subjugation to inequitable situations nor a passive acceptance of injustice, discrimination, and war.

This curriculum, according to Husin, takes advantage of the power of play in education and actively engages learners with a "playing for learning" methodology. It incorporates various game strategies, humorous teaching stories, and classical wisdom, along with drawings and illustrations. The "thinking for reviving" methodology is a cornerstone technique. This teaching/learning method is critical to ulama empowerment, because it permits the primordial values of Islam to be revitalized in a way that meets the challenges of contemporary global realities.

The manual is a product of serious research into the Islamic intellectual wellsprings, including the Qur'an, prophetic tradition, the history of Islam, and the work of the classical ulama and contemporary scholars—with the focus on peace, conflict, and violence. The study of non-Muslim sources is integral to the manual. It also incorporates Acehnese moral values and traditional wisdom, along with indigenous mechanisms for conflict management. In adopting such peace education principles as rights and responsibilities, this peace initiative is consistent with Islamic principles.

The manual covers a wide range of critical topics, including democracy, pluralism, human rights, conflict and neutralization of violence, emotion management, leadership, natural resources, and conflict resolution. That the project team has been able to address such important and potentially sensitive topics in a way that satisfies the ulama and also stretches their thinking is a credit to Husin and her team. Husin indicates that it is still too early to assess the impact of the project. Nevertheless, the manual has generated awareness among the ulama of the need for new approaches to contemporary realities while still maintaining their religious pride and scholarship. Many educational leaders from the pesantrens/dayahs have expressed their willingness to implement the curriculum in their institutions, once their teachers are properly trained.

The ulama have demonstrated a strong sense of ownership of this manual, both because a number of them were members of the curriculum team that helped review the draft and because its content fully accords with Islamic values and principles. This does not imply that no controversial issues are raised, but such topics as gender are dealt with from a solid religious foundation. More important, this curriculum helps the ulama take responsibility and leadership at a time when Aceh stands in great need of such guidance. They thereby become worthy heirs of the prophets. This manual has generated considerable interest both in other parts of Indonesia and in other Muslim countries. It is being translated into English and Arabic and will be disseminated for use in places that face similar challenges of interpreting Islamic principles to address rapidly changing global realities.

CONCLUSION

Northern Nigeria, Iran, and Aceh are typically characterized as places gripped by rigid religious ideologies and practices. Northern Nigerian states have adopted very conservative versions of shari'ah. Iran is governed by conservative clerics. Some movements in Aceh agitate for more thorough going Islamic forms of government. But the three projects described in this publication add another dimension to the picture:

- Nigerian jurists, scholars, and clerics are engaged in an ongoing dialogue among themselves, with the international Muslim community, and with Nigerian Christians about the appropriate scope of—and limitations on—shari'ah in northern Nigeria.
- Iranian clerics and scholars are grappling with the proper balance between Islam and democracy, as heard in the presentations at the CSID workshop and in other forums. Iran is still evolving, and liberal scholars and clerics, while sometimes silenced, speak out.
- The ulama in Aceh have enthusiastically supported a project to introduce peace studies in Achenese religious schools, emphasizing peace, democracy, and pluralism. The ulama have been supportive because the teaching materials are all based on Islamic texts.

In these projects in Nigeria, Iran, and Indonesia—as well as in Muslim communities worldwide—Islam and the application of Islamic principles to modern realities are under active review and subject to intense debate. This dialogue is also carried on internationally, as indicated by the involvement of Muslim scholars from the United States and other countries in the discussion of shari'ah in Nigeria and of Islam and democracy in Iran. The Institute has been pleased to be able to play a supportive role in these projects, as well as with comparable projects in other countries.

STUDY QUESTIONS

Nigeria
1. What was the goal of the Nigerian conference?
2. Characterize the differences between traditionalists and modernists.
3. What evidence is there that shari'ah has become a divisive issue in Nigeria?
4. What were the three objectives of the Nigerian conference?
5. Who was Amina Lawal and why was her case important?
6. What is the challenge facing modern Muslim societies?
7. What is the issue regarding morality versus legality?
8. What three challenging questions did the governor of Baluchi State pose?
9. What do women in Nigeria expect when it comes to shari'ah?
10. Why is it critical that the debate concerning Islam's norms and heritage relative to modern society continue?

Iran

1. What is the mission of the Center for the Study of Islam and Democracy?
2. It was relatively easy to enlist the participation of secularists-modernists in the conference, but Dr. Hassan Jamshidi was given the role of "shuttle diplomat" to do what? Was he successful?
3. Who were the Ansar-i-Hizb Allah and what role did they play in the conference?
4. On the first day of the conference, on what could all participants agree? And what was the clerical response?
5. What was the point Dr. Bishiti made regarding the emerging intercultural dialogue among world religions?
6. On the second day of the conference, what was taken as a given?
7. In what way did Soroush and Kadivar advocate a similar position?
8. What was Dr. Paya's model of democracy?
9. What was the traditionalists' position?

Indonesia

1. How would you characterize Aceh today, and what struggle do the contemporary ulama face?
2. What is the position of the ulama regarding the Peace Education Program and why?
3. What are some of the social and political challenges that threaten the peace in Aceh and what is the role of the ulama?
4. How would you describe peace education from an Islamic and Acehnese perspective?
5. The Peace Education Manual has been accepted as being consistent with Islamic principles. What resources were consulted in the development of the Manual?
6. How have the ulama responded to the Peace Education Manual?
7. Is there any interest in this Peace Education Manual outside of Aceh?
8. How would you characterize the similarities in approach by Northern Nigeria, Iran, and Aceh? Give examples.
9. Where has there been at least some dialog concerning moderate reform in these places: Northern Nigeria, Iran, Aceh?

Chapter 10 Snapshot
Electoral Geographies

I chose this article for the collection because it so clearly makes a connection between demographics, spatial distributions, and the power of a democracy. The power of a democracy comes with voting and our representation in government at all spatial scales from the local elections in our communities, to state or national elections, and even supranational representation. How do we decide who can vote? What kind of voting system is the most fair and inclusive, and how shall we determine how places and the people who live there (constituencies) are to be represented? How can our voting system guarantee that every voter has a voice?

VOTING, THE WIDENING FRANCHISE, AND THE GROWTH OF ELECTORAL GEOGRAPHY

If we look at the history of the voting franchise (who is allowed to vote), we can see that there have been several stages. Answering the question of who is eligible to vote also addresses what it means to be a citizen; race, property ownership, and gender were the first characteristics that defined a citizen, so white men who owned property were the first who had the right to vote.

It wasn't until the mid-1970s that geographers showed a systematic interest in political geography (156). Part of the reason had to do with the universal franchise that provided a good barometer of public opinion on an inclusive spatial scale. In addition, it wasn't until the mid-1970s that

> a new generation of human geographers had … set out to identify spatial patterns of social deprivation and inequality. They also had begun to develop explanations of how these patterns were produced, reproduced, and ameliorated, and to explore how such patterns might be transcended or otherwise transformed … . ("Political Geography," David R. Reynolds and

151

David B. Knight, 1989. In Gary L. Gaile and Cort J. Willmott [eds.], *Geography in America*, Columbus, OH: Merrill Publishing Company, page 584–585).

The 1970s also saw the growth of electoral geography as a subdiscipline of political geography, looking at electoral geography as an indicator of electoral change and its links to social change.

> Attempts at integration have proceeded along two fronts: 1) efforts to situate political parties and elections within theories of the state, and 2) efforts which have led to the rediscovery of the politics of locality or place as a means of explaining the persistence of regional and local variations in voting in Western democracies (Reynolds and Knight, 1989, page 594).

Certainly by the beginning of the twenty-first century, "most Western democracies have a universal franchise and this general extension of the right to vote has made elections very much more geographically relevant. They are now more truly tests of opinion as a whole rather than measures of particular section interests, even though participation rates are sometimes surprisingly modest, throwing into question the extent to which they are true tests of the overall public mood" (156).

Evaluating the meaning of voting patterns is also affected by what system of voting is used. On the following pages, you will read about three types of voting systems: 1) past-the-post, 2) the single transferrable vote, and 3) the list system. Each one has its advantages and disadvantages, the goal of each of these systems is to provide the fairest way to represent the votes of constituents. Constituents also can be characterized by their demographics; characteristics such as age, gender, religion, ethnicity, and socioeconomic status—and these are constantly changing by region as well due to changes in birth and death rates as well as migration.

> People are increasingly moving much more frequently, both within and between countries [and counties], so that the socioeconomic structure of voter groups may change quite dramatically from one election to the next. Demographic factors, such as birth and death rates and rates of household formation area also constantly changing, and they too will affect what people want from society and the way they vote (157–158).

How do we keep track of all these changes and the locations of these changes? Every ten years the government conducts a census. Then, "constituency boundaries must be drawn in such a way that each includes roughly the same number of people and that, as far as possible, everyone has a similar social mix, a procedure known as districting" (158).

THE SPATIAL ORGANIZATION OF ELECTIONS

By the same token, elections can be manipulated based on how district boundaries are drawn. This is called malapportionment. Historically some parties went to extraordinary lengths to re-draw districts that favored their own constituencies. The illustration shown was first printed in 1821. It indicates the districts that were drawn to favor the candidates of Governor Elbridge Gerry over the Federalists. The shapes of the districts are magnified to highlight the bizarre shapes of the districts to accommodate Governor Gerry. Because the shape closely resembles that of a salamander, it was called a Gerrymander (tacking on the Governor's last name). "Suddenly there was a graphic word to describe the widespread abuse of power through spatial fraud and gerrymandering rapidly became established in the English language across the world" (159).

Figure 10.1. "The Gerry-Mander." Copyright in the Public Domain.

By 1842 Congress passed the Reapportionment Act that required "Congressional Districts be contiguous and compact to prevent perverse and discriminatory boundaries being draw, thereby excluding, for example, certain concentrations of unwanted economic or ethnic groups. The Act was strengthened further by a Supreme Court ruling in 1962, which held that Districts must have fair borders and encompass an appropriate population mix" (159). Then, by 1985, the Supreme Court ruled that "any attempt to manipulate District borders to give advantage to one particular political party was unconstitutional" (159).

All gerrymandering is designed to provide advantage to one particular party at the expense of the other party, and the article clearly lays out what the two most common and blatant practices are (159). Despite the fact there are laws on the books that prohibit gerrymandering, it is very difficult to prove; but as a society we must remain vigilant: "the task is extremely difficult, because bias is all too easy to hide amid constant social change, but the price of failure is high" (158).

ELECTIONS AND SOCIAL CHANGE

If voting districts have been fairly drawn and voter registration provides more people with the opportunity to vote, "elections are good barometers of social change, because they directly involve a greater proportion of the public than any other test of opinion" (160). For most of the history of the US, politics have been divided between the Democrats and Republicans. On one hand, this seems like a simplistic statement to make, but just think about what that means. People usually gravitate toward one party or the other on the basis of deeply-held philosophical differences regarding the role of the state versus power at the local level, and issues such as differences in economic policies, social justice, the environment, and international affairs, to name a few. "Archer and Taylor (1981) made a fascinating analysis of the four-yearly presidential elections over 150 years and identified from the electoral geography a number of key turning points, such as the election of Franklin D. Roosevelt at the height of the economic depression in 1933, following which the underlying cleavages in American society experienced a quantum change as a result of the New Deal programme he inspired" (161). Mapping the results of election issues can provide a clear indicator of how the public is thinking and what it is supporting, or it can be the result of "cynical manipulation" either by gerrymandering or by pork-barreling. This latter term refers to funds that are funneled into districts where constituent support is weak, and in general, "has been shown to be more effective in bolstering the popularity of individual politicians, rather than influencing wider political allegiances" (161).

KEY THEMES AND FURTHER READINGS

In this article we have looked at the "strengths and weaknesses of the main alternative voting systems that are used: a simple majority of votes cast, the single transferable vote, and the list system" (166). Voting systems are important for the stability of democratic societies and "The aim of fully democratic elections should be to ensure that each vote cast counts equally towards the election of representatives, but bias is difficult to eliminate" (166). In this regard, along with voter registration, we need to understand and be aware of any malapportionment or gerrymandering. "Finally, the reader should have some knowledge of the consequences of long-term shifts in voting patterns at the national level" (166).

10. ELECTORAL GEOGRAPHIES

By Mark Blacksell

An election is coming. Universal peace is declared, and the foxes have a sincere interest in prolonging the lives of the poultry.

(George Eliot, *Felix Holt,* 1866, chapter 5)

VOTING, THE WIDENING FRANCHISE, AND THE GROWTH OF ELECTORAL GEOGRAPHY

Elections and the way they are organised are fundamental to the make-up of all democratic societies; they also profoundly affect their social and political geography, in that they provide the means by which people are represented in government. Voting gives people a voice, but the way constituencies at all spatial scales—local, regional, national, and even supra national—are organised is critical in deciding how their voices will be heard and acted upon. As George Eliot noted in her novel *Felix Holt,* elections are the one real opportunity for the people to call to account the executive that normally rules their lives. There are, of course, many other factors which also influence elections, in particular who is eligible to vote, the voting system used, and the frequency with which elections are held, but also the size and shape of constituencies is critical, because quite small demographic shifts can impact radically on the distribution of political power.

It is, therefore, quite surprising how relatively recently electoral geography has established itself as a core element of political geography. Aside from a few isolated research monographs, it was only in the late 1970s that there was any systematic interest shown by geographers in the subject (Taylor and Johnston, 1979), but the upsurge of interest in the UK then sparked not just a great deal of interest in the spatial patterns produced by election results, but also theoretical research on the significance of electoral studies for understanding the underlying dynamics of political geography (Johnston, 1979; Gudgin and Taylor, 1979).

Certainly the lack of attention paid to voting patterns by geographers was not the result of a general lack of interest in the subject. Elections have been pored over in detail by political scientists ever since representative government began to become the norm in the Western world at the end of the eighteenth and beginning of the nineteenth centuries. In the UK this interest dates back to the Reform Act of 1832, which made the first serious attempt to ensure that the franchise in Britain more fairly reflected the distribution of population (Thrasher and Rallings, 2000) (Box 10.1). Not that the first Reform Act itself provided for anything approaching a universal franchise. In common with most democratic societies, the UK has inched towards this goal over a period of nearly two centuries, grudgingly conceding the right to vote to more and more of its people, group by group. Gender and ownership of property were initially the key qualifications. In common with most other countries, the franchise in the UK included only men who owned property, though this was then extended to leaseholders and, subsequently, to most working men. By the end of the nineteenth century, voting was more or less a right for all men over the age of 21, but women were completely disenfranchised. Not until 1918 did women gain the vote and, even then, only those over 30. It was ten years later that voting rights were finally extended to all adults over the age of 21. Since then, the only important change in the franchise has been the reduction in the age limit to 18 in 1970.

At the beginning of the twenty-first century, most Western democracies have a universal franchise and this general extension of the right to vote has made elections very much more geographically relevant. They are now more truly tests of public opinion as a whole, rather than measures of particular sectional interests, even though participation rates are sometimes surprisingly modest, throwing into question the extent to which they are true tests of the overall public mood. In Western Europe, voting is compulsory only in Belgium, Italy, and Luxembourg, though it was compulsory in the Netherlands until 1971. Not surprisingly, these countries have amongst the highest levels of voter participation, consistently running at over 80 percent of the electorate, but there are other countries, such as Iceland and Sweden, where voting is not compulsory and which have similar levels of participation. The missing voters in those countries where voting is compulsory are explained by spoiled ballot papers, as many as 20 percent of the electorate choosing not to cast their vote for any of the candidates on offer. At the other end of the scale, the proportion of the electorate voting in national elections in some countries is often well below 70 percent, the lowest vote in Europe being 45 percent in Switzerland in 1991. Turnout is usually even lower in local elections with turnouts of below 30 percent quite common, and in the elections to the European Parliament the figures have been similarly low.

From a geographical point of view, it also needs to be remembered that the voting system used can have a significant influence on the eventual outcome. That most commonly used is the straightforward one person one vote across a jigsaw of constituencies. Under this first-past-the-post system, those gaining the most votes are duly elected to serve the particular constituency in question. The limitation is that, if there are more than two candidates, then the persons elected will more than likely only have gained a minority of

---

Box 10.1 The Reform Acts

The three Reform Acts of 1832, 1867, and 1884 all extended voting rights to previously disenfranchised citizens. Most controversial was the 1832 Act, which reapportioned representation in Parliament in a way that was fairer to the rapidly expanding industrial cities of the north, and did away with the so-called 'rotten' and 'pocket' boroughs. Old Sarum near Salisbury, for instance, only had seven voters, all controlled by the local squire, yet still sent two members to Parliament. The act not only reapportioned representation in Parliament, so that it more accurately represented the distribution of population, it also extended the franchise to those who were less powerful, socially and economically. The act extended the right to vote to any man owning a household worth £10, thus adding 217,000 to an electorate of 435,000 and giving one man in five the right to vote.

The 1867 Act extended the right to vote still further down the class ladder, adding nearly a million voters, mostly working men, to the electorate and bringing the total number eligible to vote to two million in England and Wales. The 1884 Act, together with the 1885 Redistribution Act, further tripled the electorate and gave the vote to agricultural labourers, by which time voting had to all intents and purposes become a right to all adult men. Women had to wait until the twentieth century to gain similar rights.

---

the votes cast and the wishes of the majority of voters will have been ignored. It also means that no politician can ignore the minutiae of their local constituency affairs, even if they are fully engaged on the national or international stage, and none can take winning their constituency seat for granted.

The single transferable vote is one way of ensuring that voter wishes more nearly match who is eventually elected. Under this system voters rank the candidates and then a process of elimination occurs. At each iteration, the candidate with the least votes is eliminated and the first-choice votes cast for them are redistributed to the voters' second choices. The process ends when one candidate has 50 percent of the votes cast. It is undoubtedly a fairer system, although it too has its disadvantages, notably the fact that voters are encouraged to rank candidates, even though they may know very little about what some of them stand for. It is also a very laborious and slow process to count the votes, but those areas where the single transferable vote is used, such as Northern Ireland, it is a popular system and has succeeded in broadening the political range of candidates elected.

The potential conflict between national and local party loyalties has been tackled in a different way using a list system, whereby the number of candidates elected for a particular party is determined by the proportion of the votes cast for that party. In some instances, such as the Federal Republic of Germany, there are national lists covering the whole country, in others, such as the elections for the European Parliament, there are constituency lists. The problem with the list system is that there is not much direct affinity between the candidates and the voters, who often have little idea who it is who is representing them. The criticism is countered by the argument that there are invariably other, lower tiers of government using the first-past-the-post, or the single transferable vote systems and the candidates elected at these levels can adequately represent individual voters.

Whatever the limitations of elections as measures of public opinion, be it through low levels of participation, or the inherent unfairnesses of the voting systems used, they do provide unparalleled insights into the way societies are changing. People are increasingly moving much more frequently, both within and between countries, so that the socioeconomic structure of voter groups may change quite dramatically from one election to the next. Demographic factors, such as birth and death rates and rates of household formation are also constantly changing, and they too will affect what people want from society and the way they vote. More sinisterly, the manipulation of elections, through where exactly boundaries are drawn and which particular segments of the population are included, or not included, within constituencies can materially influence who is elected.

THE SPATIAL ORGANISATION OF ELECTIONS

Ensuring that elections are fairly and properly managed is one of the most important public duties in a democratic society. All countries with representative forms of government try to ensure that they have in place unambiguous rules for the conduct of elections, as well as the means to enforce them. The task is extremely difficult, because bias is all too easy to hide amid constant social change, but the price of failure is high. Once particular groups or sections of the electorate have been favoured, it is extremely hard to persuade them to relinquish their position and a monopoly of political power and systematic discrimination against those excluded is the result. If not addressed, this can become the source of deep-seated and destabilising social unrest, in extreme cases threatening the stability of the state.

The electoral goal in most countries is to devise and implement a system where every adult of voting age has a single vote of equal weight to all others, following the principle of one person one vote. In addition, constituency boundaries must be drawn in such a way that each includes roughly the same number of people and that, as far as possible, everyone has a similar social mix, a procedure known as districting. Of all countries, the USA has probably legislated most vigorously, though not necessarily most successfully, to achieve proportionality. The number of people eligible to vote per electoral district is regularly reviewed after each census to ensure that none is over or under represented. The US Supreme Court has repeatedly ruled unconstitutional even very small deviations which meant that there was not absolute equality of voters in each district. Most states subscribe in principle to proportionality, but are prepared to tolerate a greater degree of limited deviation in the interests of effective representation. This was the reason given for creating additional constituencies for the 1991 elections in Zambia. In order to ensure that areas with severe communications difficulties were not ignored, a rural bias was engineered and they were allocated a voting strength out of proportion to their population. The process was open and accepted by all sides in the election, but it still meant that some votes were devalued. It goes without saying that the whole process of districting is dependent on the availability of accurate and up-to-date population statistics, something that even countries using the most sophisticated census techniques struggle to achieve (Westminster City Council, 2002). Indeed, in the USA reapportionment used to be undertaken after every Congressional election, but because of arguments about the accuracy of population statistics, it now occurs after the US decennial census.

In the UK the task of ensuring electoral fairness has been the responsibility of the Electoral Commission since 2002, under which there are separate Boundary Committees for England, Northern Ireland, Scotland, and Wales. These committees, previously known as the Local Government Commissions and answerable directly to central government, have extremely wide-ranging powers including a duty to conduct periodic reviews of all constituency boundaries to ensure that demographic changes and population movements do not result in bias and imbalance in the system (Rossiter et al., 1999a). Details of the Electoral Commission's responsibilities are set out in Box 10.2.

Malapportionment, or violation of the norm of equal representation according to population, is an ever-present danger, which those in charge of managing elections must constantly watch for and take steps to eliminate. In the USA, as far back as 1842, the Reapportionment Act required that Congressional Districts be contiguous and compact to prevent perverse and discriminatory boundaries being drawn, thereby excluding, for example, certain concentrations of unwanted economic or ethnic groups. The Act was strengthened further by a Supreme Court ruling in 1962, which held that Districts must have fair borders and encompass an appropriate population mix. A further ruling by the Supreme Court in 1985 deemed that any attempt to manipulate District borders to give advantage to one particular political party was unconstitutional. Despite such actions, however, the risk of malapportionment, intentional or unintentional, remains and the onus should always be on those responsible for managing elections to show that this form of bias is minimised.

There are many ways in which constituency boundaries can be intentionally manipulated for electoral advantage. Such acts are generally known as gerrymandering, after the Governor of the US State of Massachusetts, Elbridge Gerry, who crafted a District that bore a strong resemblance to a salamander for the political advantage of his own party. The ruse was spotted by his opponents, who called it a gerrymander after the perpetrator, a term picked up and publicised by the press. Suddenly there was a graphic word to describe the widespread abuse of power through spatial fraud and gerrymandering rapidly became established in the English language across the world.

All gerrymandering ultimately has the goal of unfairly encompassing an undue proportion of voters from one political party and there are a host of ingenious ways of doing this. The most common and blatant is to draw boundaries in such a way that the opposition is concentrated into a small minority of constituencies, thus reducing, and even eliminating, their chance of ever gaining political power. Social policies and discrimination have been used in the past through ethnic and religious ghettos, a notorious example being the concentration of the Catholic minority in Northern Ireland after the partition of Ireland in 1921 and the subsequent civil war.

A second commonly used stratagem is precisely the reverse strategy, whereby the voting power of the opposition is diluted across as many constituencies as possible, thus preventing them from ever achieving the number of elected representatives that would reflect their true electoral strength. In the UK the Liberal

---

Box 10.2 The Electoral Commission

The Electoral Commission is an independent body set up by the UK Parliament under the terms of the Political Parties, Elections and Referendums Act 2000. Its brief is to increase public confidence and participation in the democratic process within the UK, by modernising the electoral process, promoting public awareness of electoral matters, and regulating political parties.

On 1 April 2002, the Boundary Commission for England, which had formerly been known as the Local Government Commission for England, became a statutory committee of the Electoral Commission. Its main duty is to keep local electoral boundaries under periodic review, to ensure that they reflect as far as possible the distribution of population. There are separate Boundary Commissions for Scotland, Wales, and Northern Ireland. In Scotland, the Boundary Commission is responsible to the Scottish Parliament; in Wales to the Welsh Assembly; and in Northern Ireland to the Northern Ireland Office, though this will change if local government is once again devolved to the province.

Democratic Party and its predecessor the Liberal Party have both campaigned long and hard for some form of proportional representation through a candidate list system to overcome this acknowledged bias. Not surprisingly, the Labour and Conservative Parties, which have monopolised political power since the early part of the twentieth century, have paid little more than lip-service to the Liberal Democrat pleas for greater fairness. The only major concession has been the introduction of a candidate list system in the elections for the European Parliament in 2004.

Both the above techniques of gerrymandering are difficult to prove and hard to eliminate, unlike a third technique, sometimes referred to as the stacked method, whereby small areas that are physically separated are lumped together to form single constituencies favouring the party in power. Invariably, however, attempts to stack votes in this way are so obvious that they rarely succeed.

There have been many attempts to counteract gerrymandering by using computer algorithms to generate constituencies automatically, but success has been very limited. It is not just the shortcomings of the algorithms themselves that pose problems, but also the almost endless scope for challenge by any party that feels it has been disadvantaged. It is a salutary lesson to understand that unless people have confidence in such theoretically unbiased results, the outcome can be just as controversial as more malevolent attempts to draw maps of electoral boundaries.

Finally, reference must be made to the most widespread of all election malpractices, voter registration. Unless voters are registered, it is impossible to conduct fair elections and ensuring that people do register, or are not being prevented from registering, is extremely challenging. Even in the most advanced democratic societies, there is great variation in the proportion of people registered to vote across countries, and in less developed countries it is often even more difficult to ensure the all those eligible are included.

The Westminster City Council Gerrymander

A notorious attempt to gerrymander was perpetrated by a group of senior Conservative Councillors, led by Dame Shirley Porter, on Westminster City Council in central London during the 1980s. Their particular ploy was to use the newly introduced right for council tenants to purchase their houses or apartments to bring more people who were likely to vote Conservative into key marginal wards and thus make it more likely that the ruling party would retain power. The irony of the case was that initially the social policies of the Council had been much praised, especially its 1987 decision to sell 500 homes a year as part of a 'building stable communities' initiative. Only later, under persistent probing by the National Audit Office, did the more sinister political agenda become apparent. The case eventually went to court and Dame Shirley was personally convicted and fined £42 million in surcharges, interest, and costs. She appealed successfully against the conviction in 1999, but this was overturned again by the Law Lords in 2001 and the case was finally settled with a reduced payment of £12 million in 2004. The whole saga illustrates very clearly how insidious gerrymandering can be, and how difficult it is to prove and to bring those responsible to book.

ELECTIONS AND SOCIAL CHANGE

Elections are good barometers of social change, because they directly involve a greater proportion of the public than any other test of opinion. They expose underlying social cleavages and often can provide a clear indication of the ways in which states and regions, at all levels, are changing. Furthermore, the longer established and more mature the democratic process is, the better election data are for uncovering changes of political mood. It is argued that political parties normally go through a three-stage process of development: from cadre parties, largely reserved for wealthy male elites; to mass parties representing particular sectional interests, such as the working class, or the church, or small farmers; to the all-embracing stage, found widely in Western Europe and North America today, where they try to appeal to all sections of society, irrespective of sectional affiliation (Panebianco, 1988). Once political parties have reached this final stage and begun to achieve a universal appeal, election results become a very sensitive measure of shifts in the public mood.

In the USA, two major political parties, the Democrats and the Republicans, have exercised a monopoly of power for most of the past two hundred years and shifts in the balance of power between them across the country are widely seen as reliable indicators of social and political priorities. Archer and Taylor (1981) made a fascinating analysis of the four-yearly presidential elections over 150 years and identified from the electoral geography a number of key turning points, such as the election of Franklin D. Roosevelt at the height of the economic depression in 1933, following which the underlying cleavages in American society experienced a quantum change as a result of the New Deal programme he inspired (Box 10.3).

Shifts such as those identified by Archer and Taylor go beyond the local effects that are evident in some form in all electoral data. Local effects can arise from some kind of genuine regional solidarity, like that traditionally accorded to the Democratic Party in the American South in the south-eastern USA, but they can also be the result of cynical manipulation. Governments always run the risk of being accused of enhancing their electoral fortunes by disproportionately favouring those areas where their support is weak, most frequently by channelling public investment into swing constituencies. The process is known as pork-barrelling and the charge is most frequently levelled at the way Federal spending has been allocated across the USA, though in general it has been shown to be more effective in bolstering the popularity of individual politicians, rather than influencing wider political allegiances.

The Electoral Map of the UK

At the beginning of the twenty-first century, the electoral map of the UK appears to be experiencing the kind of fundamental political shift described above. The Conservative and Labour Parties have dominated the national political landscape for more than half a century, with long periods of Conservative government being occasionally usurped by radical intrusions of Labour rule, notably between 1945 and 1951, and between 1966 and 1970. After 1979, a string of radical and reforming Conservative governments, led by Margaret Thatcher, seemed be decisively breaking this mould. There was widespread speculation that the Labour Party was finished as a national mass party and that its support base had shrunk to the urban and industrial regions of northern Britain. There was talk of a nation dividing and the prospect of growing social tension between a poorer and politically disaffected north of the country chronically lagging behind a prosperous and modern politically right-wing south. Geographers made some significant contributions to the examination of this growing divide through the analysis and mapping of the changes (Johnston et al, 1988a).

A decade later the electoral map had been transformed. The fortunes of the Conservative and Labour Parties had been almost completely reversed and a third party, the Liberal Democrats, which had been insignificant in electoral terms since the early part of the twentieth century, had made significant inroads into particularly the Conservative vote in Scotland and south-west England. In addition, the nationalist parties in Scotland (Scottish Nationalists) and Wales (Plaid Cymru) had both gained significant numbers of

Box 10.3 The New Deal

The New Deal is the name for a raft of government policies developed by President Roosevelt immediately after his election as the US President in 1933 to try to lift the USA out of the Depression. The strategy was basically to initiate a huge programme of public works across the country. A quarter of a million unemployed young men were offered jobs in forestry and flood prevention work, nearly twice as many as were at that time in the US regular army. The Tennessee Valley Authority was set up to revitalise the whole of the river basin of the Tennessee River, one of the rural areas worst affected by the Depression. Legislation was passed by the Congress to ease the burden of debt for farmers and homeowners, thus preventing millions of foreclosures. A huge sum at the time, $500 billion, was granted by the Congress to help states, counties, and municipalities in their duty of care for those who need direct and immediate relief. Finally, the Congress passed legislation allowing those states that wished to the right to sell beer. This resulted in many new jobs being created and a useful new source of tax revenue for the Federal government.

The initiative proved both popular and effective and a second wave of legislation extended further the ability of the Federal government to undertake public works. The Farm Relief Bill enabled huge amounts of public money to be poured into agriculture; legislation was enacted to enable working conditions for industrial workers to be regulated; and the Railroad Bill introduced a degree of central planning into the national railway network.

The New Deal as a whole was viewed by many in the USA as creeping socialism and, for that reason, was treated with great suspicion, but its success in creating a genuine economic revival meant that such fears were never allowed to derail the programme. In any case, the US involvement in the Second World War after 1942 squashed any argument about the rights and wrongs of direct government participation in the productive economy, as manufacturing industry turned increasingly to producing war materials.

seats in their respective regions and were beginning to resemble more closely the well-established regional parties in Northern Ireland.

In the 1997 General Election the Labour Party made sweeping gains—a net increase of 144 seats (53 percent)—right across Great Britain, but particularly in the Midlands and south-east England, and in Scotland and Wales (Figures 10.1 and 10.2). The Conservative Party disappeared as a national electoral force in both Scotland and Wales to be replaced by a combination of Liberal Democrats and Scottish and Welsh nationalists. Even in Northern Ireland the traditionally strong links between the Conservative Party and majority Ulster Unionist Party were severely weakened. Aside from the change of government, therefore, the 1997 election seemed to indicate a real resurgence of the Liberal Democrats as a credible national political force with the prospect of it being able to strengthen its position further in the future from a broad base across the UK. The party gained seats in Scotland and Wales, extended its traditional base in south-west and north-west England, and significantly increased its number of seats in the south and east of England. In Scotland and Wales, the nationalist parties made less spectacular gains, but showed their potential for political influence; while in Northern Ireland multiparty politics became a reality in electoral terms with the fragmentation of the once omnipotent Ulster Unionist Party and the emergence of the nationalist Sinn Fein on the national electoral stage in the UK with a second seat in the Westminster Parliament.

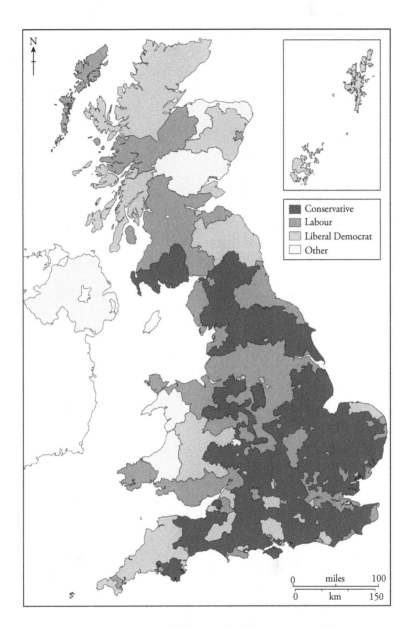

Figure 10.1. Electoral map of the UK after the 1997 General Election.

The General Election in 2001 confirmed the apparently fundamental shift that had occurred in 1997 (Figure 10.3). The Labour and Conservative Parties altered their relative positions hardly at all. The Conservative Party did make some gains, but these were almost completely offset by losses elsewhere, mostly to the Liberal Democrats. The party did make a solitary gain in Scotland, winning back the geographically large but sparsely populated seat of Dumfries and Galloway from the Scottish Nationalists, but effectively it remained what it had become in 1997, an English right-of-centre party. The Liberal Democrats, on the other hand, further consolidated their spectacular gains in 1997. They added 6 seats to the 28 they had gained then, giving the party 52 seats overall, still only a third of the number held by the Conservative

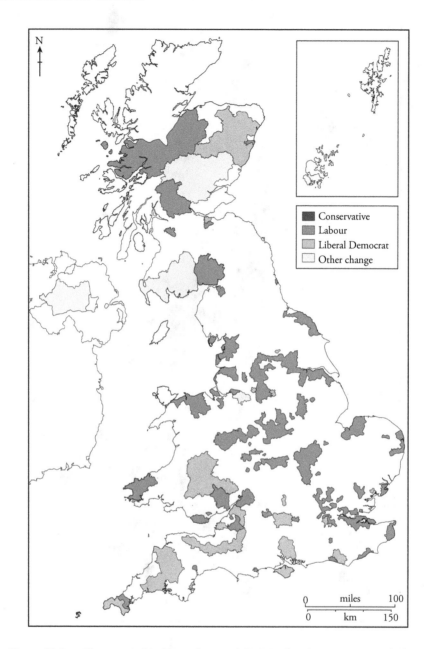

Figure 10.2. Changes to the electoral map of the UK after the 1997 General Election.

Party, but sufficient for the party to be able to play a significant role in the political opposition. The results for the nationalists were much less encouraging. The Scottish Nationalists lost one seat, while Plaid Cymru lost one and gained one.

Meanwhile, in Northern Ireland the Ulster Unionist Party continued to cede ground, losing two seats to Sinn Fein and three to the Democratic Unionist Party, making the political situation in the province even more multiparty, but also isolating it to an even greater extent from the rest of the UK.

Predicting trends in political allegiance is naturally an exercise full of danger, but the changes in the electoral geography of the UK at the turn of the twenty-first century seem to show some fundamental changes in the

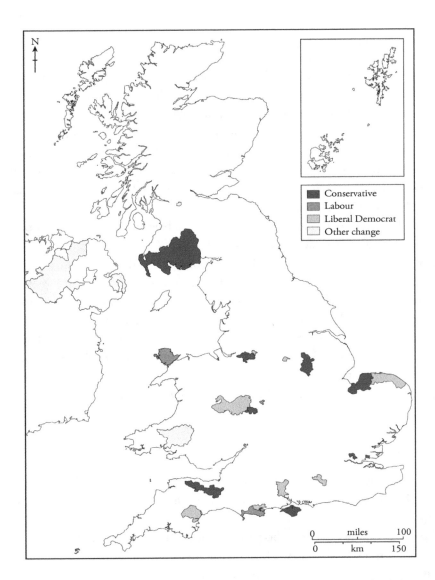

Figure 10.3.   Changes to the electoral map of the UK after the 2001 General Election.

national electoral mood and these changes are clearly illustrated by the cartographic evidence. The Labour Party is now the only political party that can claim to be truly national on the basis of seats won, notwithstanding its complete absence from Northern Ireland, where it has so far chosen not to field candidates. The Conservative Party, which for more than 200 years has taken its pre-eminent position as the national political party in the UK almost for granted, is now barely credible as such. It has shrunk away, not only from Northern Ireland, Scotland, and Wales, but has also largely been replaced in south-west England. The Liberal Democrats, on the other hand, have extended their political foothold all over Great Britain, if not Northern Ireland, and would seem to have a very broad-based launch pad for further growth in their number of parliamentary seats in the future. The outlook for nationalist parties is much less clear. Neither the Scottish Nationalist Party nor Plaid Cymru have really established themselves securely, either on the national stage or in their respective regional assemblies, while in Northern Ireland the divisions between the various nationalist parties remain so deep that participation in any devolved regional government is at present not possible.

KEY THEMES AND FURTHER READING

At the heart of this chapter is the history of democratic elections and the progress made in widening the franchise in different parts of the world since the beginning of the nineteenth century. It is important to understand the strengths and weaknesses of the main alternative voting systems that are used: a simple majority of votes cast, the single transferable vote, and the list system. The aim of fully democratic elections should be to ensure that each vote cast counts equally towards the election of representatives, but bias is difficult to eliminate. Malapportionment, when there is a variation in the number of electors between voting constituencies, is hard to eradicate and the reasons for this need to be clearly appreciated. Similarly, the processes behind the manipulation of constituency boundaries for political advantage, known as gerrymandering, should be understood. Finally, the reader should have some knowledge of the consequences of long-term shifts in voting patterns at the national level.

Two books were instrumental in propelling electoral geography to the centre of the political geography agenda: *Political, Electoral and Spatial Systems* by R. J. Johnston (1979) and *Seats, Votes and the Spatial Organisation of Elections* by G. Gudgin and P. J. Taylor (1979). They are still the best introductions to the subject written by geographers, although there is a huge amount of material written by political scientists. A comprehensive introduction to the facts and figures of British elections is the book edited by Mike Thrasher and Colin Rallings, *British Electoral Facts 1832–1999,* the sixth edition of which was published in 2000. A fascinating study of the changing electoral geography of the UK is to be found in *A Nation Dividing? The Electoral Map of Great Britain 1979–1987* by R. J. Johnston *et al.* (1988b).

STUDY QUESTIONS

1. Among other factors, how does the size and shape of constituencies affect political power?
2. How have a universal franchise and the general extension of the right to vote made elections more geographically relevant?
3. How would you explain the "first-past-the-post" system, and what are its limitations?
4. How does the single transferable vote work and what are its limitations?
5. How is the list system used and what is the problem with this system?
6. How does migration and demographic change affect elections?
7. If elections are not kept fair and equally representative, what is the price of that failure?
8. What is districting?
9. What is malapportionment?
10. What did the 1842 Reapportionment Act require and how was it strengthened in 1962 and 1985?
11. What is gerrymandering?
12. What are the two most common forms of gerrymandering?
13. What is the most widespread of all election malpractices and why?
14. How are elections a good barometer of social change?
15. What is pork-barreling?

Chapter 11 Snapshot
The Politics of Place: Geographic Identities Along the Coffee Supply Chain from Toraja to Tokyo

INTRODUCTION

We've all heard of Swiss cheese, champagne, and Kona coffee, but what we might not be aware of is that in order for these products to have these names, they must come from that part of the world: Swiss cheese is made in Switzerland, champagne is a sparkling wine that only comes from the Champagne region of France, and Kona coffee grows only on the Kona Coast on the Island of Hawaii. These are usually considered to be gourmet foods and we are willing to pay a premium price for them. Regarding coffee, our author, Jeffrey Neilson observes, "There exists a widespread industry belief that coffee grown in a specific geographic region will retain certain quality attributes reflecting the physical and human characteristics of that growing environment" (171). Place names can be used as marketing tools to suggest premium quality, and we will explore this theme in the following article. This chapter explores "the use of geographical identities along a coffee supply chain extending from rural origins in the Toraja region of Sulawesi in eastern Indonesia through to consumption in cosmopolitan Japan" (171).

I included this article because it is such a good example of the power of place and region and the importance of the environment—in this case, not just in terms of the product's origin, but also how the environment is used effectively to control for the purity of the product enabling the company to command premium prices. "Sulawesi coffee is consumed predominantly as a single-origin offering in Japan, where roaster-retailers emphasize regionality to obtain the substantial price premium afforded to this place-informed gourmet product. Geographical specificity and control over the use of the 'Toraja' identity have become critical determinants of economic relationships between supply chain actors" (171).

SUPPLY CHAIN REGULATION THROUGH THE CONSUMPTION OF PLACE

With more and more specialty coffee shops springing up, and long lines at the take-out windows, people appear to be interested in a variety of coffees from Kona to Jamaican, flavors from hazelnut to mocha, and lattes to espressos. "The specialty coffee industry is now the most vibrant and fastest-growing segment of the global coffee market …" (172). Part of that interest is in regionally grown coffees. In some cases, a regional specialty label may mean the depth of roasting or a special blend of coffee beans, but in other cases we can trace the specific geographical origins of single-origin specialty coffee. "The explicit importance of geographical influences in the construction of specialty coffee however, remains polemical. Specialty roasting companies rely heavily on their own marketing image and product branding" (172).

In this article we will look at one particular brand of single-origin coffee and how it is embedded in geographic space and place "where the totality of place-specific socio-cultural, economic and environmental influences interacts with coffee production in a way which significantly affects the dynamics of quality construction" (172). That is, the social and cultural practices and conditions, the economic organization of the growing regions, trading centers, and transportation ports, and the conditions of the weather, soil, elevation, and so on, all interact with coffee production in a way which significantly affects the quality of the coffee produced. This embeddedness is also affected by the vertical integration of the coffee production itself and its supply chain structures; that is, all of the stages in the coffee production process from bean to roasted product and all the places along the way where the quality of the product could be affected. One other way that the coffee production (and therefore the quality of the product) can be affected is by the national and international laws and trademarks that govern such products.

SULAWESI COFFEE PRODUCTION AND EXPORT IDENTITIES

For the highland regions in South Sulawesi, where our story takes place, coffee production is the main source of income. "All exports of *arabica* coffee from Sulawesi in 2002 and 2003 were marked, and subsequently traded internationally, using a geographical place name such as 'Toraja', 'Kalosi', 'Rantepao', 'Sulawesi' or 'Celebes', and all were designated Grade One export quality" (173). However, at the point of roasting the coffee beans, the name of the coffee is typically based on marketing strategies more than geographical origins. "While many industry actors recognize and promote the quality associations of particular growing environments, the authenticity of the use of geographic identities is, for the most part, poorly regulated" (175). South Sulawesi has four major coffee growing regions, each with its distinct language, culture, and agro-ecological systems (see map on p. 174). "The physical characteristics of each growing district differ significantly in terms of topography and altitude, weather patterns and soil types" (175). Once harvested, each region has its own way of processing the beans; however, "of the Sulawesi growing districts, the highest-quality coffee is widely considered by local traders, exporters and international buyers to be grown in the Toraja district" (175).

Before 1905, when the Dutch colonized the area, coffee was traded locally to the port town of Boengie and from there to the main export hub of Makassar. The coffee was known as Boengie coffee and was mainly sold to Europe. Primarily the Duri and Toraja ethnic groups cultivated the coffee. The Duri, who were from Kalosi, had an important role in the trading networks. After the Dutch colonized the region coffee was still exported under the Boengie name. When Indonesia declared independence in 1945, ethnic tensions flared up between the Duri and Toraja ethnic groups that disrupted the coffee networks. Toraja coffee was hardly grown at all because the trade routes were too dangerous. So, the Duri became the primary growers and traders and used both Kalosi and Boengie as market labels for their coffee. These names referred more to a market center than place where the coffee was grown.

Kalosi remains a popular trading name, but by 2002, Toraja has become the most popular name used to identify exports of *arabica* coffee from Makassar. The Kalosi label is used primarily for European markets, Toraja and Kalosi for the US, and Toraja for the Japanese. "These export identities therefore currently reflect consumer market recognition rather than necessarily corresponding to actual coffee origin" (175). Use of these geographical names is, for the most part, poorly regulated … except for the Toraja name. Toraja is an area where specific coffee beans are grown, not a market center. Before Key Coffee, Japan's second-largest coffee company, came to Toraja, the region had fallen into disuse and ruin. The goal of Key Coffee was to bring the Toraja region back to life, creating a "spiritual mystique of Toraja to create a unique, geographically informed product image" (176).

What is it that makes Toraja coffee so distinctive? "The quality associations of Toraja coffee are primarily attributed to higher altitude production, along with prevailing soils, cultural characteristics and to local processing methods" (175). Toraja became a Japanese trade mark in 1977, followed by an Indonesian trade mark for the company logo (a traditional Torajan house) in 1979, and a US trade mark for Toraco Toraja in 2002. What does this trademark do? It "specifically protects against the use of the Toraja name by other roasting companies in Japan, irrespective of the actual coffee origin, whereas the US trade mark includes a disclaimer to such an exclusive right" (176). Japan is the third largest coffee-importing nation behind the US and Germany. Coffee is sold at a higher premium, and Japan routinely buys most of the crop of Hawaiian Kona coffee and Jamaican Blue Mountain coffee "indicating a willingness to absorb the world's rarest and most expensive coffees, and a strong consumer belief in the relationship between quality and the geographical embeddedness of production" (176).

So, how does Key Coffee maintain the purity of Toraja coffee when, theoretically, there are many places along the supply line where other beans could be mixed in and sold? First of all, Key Coffee has an estate plantation located in eastern Toraja 900–1,300 meters high. This plantation supplies 15 percent of the company's export requirements. The remaining 85 percent is sourced through community purchasing operations; that is, beans come from higher-altitude growing villages up to 2,000 meters. Now, it's clear the company can control what is grown on their own plantation, but how do they control for quality and purity when they are buying beans from surrounding areas? The fact that these growing regions and purchasing stations are at a high altitude work to Key Coffee's advantage. Instead of accepting green coffee beans, Key Coffee insists on accepting "only semi-wet parchment coffee [as] … a deliberate attempt to encourage only the supply of locally grown coffee" (178). Due to the climate, coffee beans in a semi-wet stage tends to mold quickly and this would be easily detected during cup tasting. There is a rigorous visual inspection of the beans, a defect count, and cup tasting of each batch of beans before acceptance. "Consequently, the risk of rejection is high for sub-standard coffee, and the inconvenience and costs to local traders of transporting the coffee back to alternative trade networks is substantial" (178). So, although this process isn't fool proof for keeping out non-local coffee "being offered to the company it strongly selects for locally grown beans" (178).

Furthermore, along with offering the highest prices for their coffee, Key Coffee also provides bonuses for defect free coffee, and for those beans with exceptionally good taste, "which the company associates with higher altitude production" (178). These are benefits that go directly to the growers. Key Coffee also opens its purchasing activities in the village of Sapan the day before market day. The hinterland for Sapan village includes some of the highest altitude villages. Again, "local growers and not village traders are encouraged to sell directly to the company …" (178). This highly integrated operation ensures Key Coffee with first pick of the highest quality beans. So, combined with its own plantation production and all of these safeguards related to a strict purchasing program, "the company is therefore able to ensure that virtually all their Sulawesi coffee "is geographically authentic Toraja coffee" (178).

CONCLUSION

So, what are factors of geographical embeddedness? Going back to the beginning of the chapter, embeddedness is where the "totality of place-specific socio-cultural, economic, and environmental influences interacts with the coffee production in a way which significantly affects the dynamics of quality construction at the site of agricultural production" (172) and these factors will vary geographically. When it comes to coffee, however, geographical embeddedness is not always directly related to the geographical identities at the site of origin. That is, once coffee beans are sold to the roasters, it is up to them to name the coffee. One exception to this is Key Coffee's vertical integration of process all along the coffee-supply route for Toraja Coffee.

A Japanese company owning and preserving the purity of Toraja Coffee, an Indonesian product, brings up a set of contradictions regarding geographical identities in the Sulawesi coffee sector. First of all, the entire supply-chain structure surrounding the use of the Toraja identity in the Japanese market is dominated and controlled by a non-local corporate entity, Key Coffee. This includes legal recognition of a trademark supportive industry association (All Japan Coffee Association) that is fundamental to Key Coffee's success. This Japanese company can also maintain market dominance and create scarcity through a legally enforced monopoly while vertical integration of the entire supply chain, from Toraja to Tokyo, ensures economic benefits will be retained within the company.

Coffee producers and exporters in Sulawesi object to the appropriation of a local product with specific geographical identity as foreign property, yet it was key Coffee that ensured the purity, demand, and market of the product. Key Coffee invested a great deal of money to enforce geographical authenticity all along the supply chain, which is the reason for their exclusive trademark.

In many producing countries, including Indonesia, state support for domestic coffee production has been eroded with the increasing penetration of international coffee companies and new forms of industry regulation. "In the specialty coffee sector, the use of geographical identities as a means for quality differentiation is an important component resulting in corresponding changes in supply chain governance" (180).

11. THE POLITICS OF PLACE

Geographical Identities Along the Coffee Supply Chain from Toraja to Tokyo

By Jeffrey Neilson

INTRODUCTION

There exists a widespread industry belief that coffee grown in a specific geographic region will retain certain quality attributes reflecting the physical and human characteristics of that growing environment. As with other selected food and beverage products, such as wines, cheeses and meats, the geographic place name of the producing region, or nearby trading centre, is subsequently applied as a marketing or trade identity by various actors along the commodity chain to indicate the presence of these quality attributes. This chapter explores the use of geographical identities along a coffee supply chain extending from rural origins in the Toraja region of Sulawesi in eastern Indonesia through to consumption in cosmopolitan Japan.[1] The economic importance, appropriation and legal protection of the 'Toraja' identity in the supply chain make this a particularly informative case study. Sulawesi coffee is consumed predominantly as a single-origin offering in Japan, where roaster-retailers emphasize regionality to obtain the substantial price premium afforded to this place-informed gourmet product. Geographical specificity and control over the use of the 'Toraja' identity have become critical determinants of economic relationships between supply chain actors.

SUPPLY CHAIN REGULATION THROUGH THE CONSUMPTION OF PLACE

In the early colonial development of the global coffee industry, geographical identities were an integral element of the descriptive language employed by traders and roasters, who promoted romantic images of the exotic locations where coffee was grown. Decolonization, together with advances in roasting and brewing technology, gradually eroded the importance of regional agricultural associations, as control of product identity shifted to the roasting sector, which was invariably located at the site of consumption. Pendergrast (2001) describes how large-scale roasters completed the transformation of coffee away from a place-differentiated product into one where green beans were used largely as an undifferentiated, commoditized input for industrial processing. The declining use of regional coffee identities coincided with a period of tightly regulated international trade implemented periodically by the International Coffee Organization (ICO) between 1962 and 1989. Rigid control of national outputs through an international quota system during this period seemed to contribute to the standardization of coffee quality associations. More recently, however, a renewed interest in the regional origins of coffee products has emerged in major consuming countries associated with strong growth in the specialty coffee sector.

The specialty coffee industry is now the most vibrant and fastest-growing segment of the global coffee market, although the actual definition of specialty coffee continues to be debated (Specialty Coffee Association of America (SCAA) 1999; ICO *et al.* 2000; International Trade Centre (ITC) 2002; Ponte 2002a; Lewin *et al.* 2004; SCAA 2004). The role of geography in influencing taste profiles and the preservation of geographical identities in the coffee trade were central concerns for Norwegian coffee connoisseur Erna Knutsen, who is widely accredited with coining the term 'specialty coffee' in the 1970s (Holly 2003). The founding members of the Specialty Coffee Association of America (SCAA) similarly agreed to define specialty coffee in 1982 as 'good preparation from unique origin and distinctive taste' (cited in Ponte 2002b: 11). The proliferation and popularity of roaster-retailer chains, offering coffee beans from various regional origins, provide further support for the increased prevalence of geographical specificity within the specialty sector. The explicit importance of geographical influences in the construction of specialty coffee however, remains polemical. Specialty roasting companies rely heavily on their own marketing image and product branding. The widespread use of milk, sugar and other flavourings in espresso bar culture is also often at the expense of an emphasis on agricultural origins. Despite such ambiguities, the use of geographical identities appears to have increased within roasted coffee marketing over the last 15 years.

The quality associations of particular place names are commonly presented as a function of how production is embedded within geographic space. Granovetter's (1985: 482) theory of embeddedness argues that economic behaviour is 'constrained by ongoing social relations'. In this chapter, embeddedness is considered in its geographical context, where the totality of place-specific socio-cultural, economic and environmental influences interacts with coffee production in a way which significantly affects the dynamics of quality construction. The notion of geographical embeddedness is thus used to describe the entanglement of place and quality construction at the site of agricultural production. Importantly, however, the quality associations of particular forms of geographical embeddedness are mediated by, and translated to consumers through, vertically oriented supply chain structures. Through these structures, any inherent value associated with the nature of geographical embeddedness can be manipulated, controlled and reconstructed by non-local, and therefore geographically 'disembedded', actors.

The potential of specialty food products utilizing regional identities to provide an alternative development approach for lagging rural regions has been discussed by Ilbery and Kneafsey (1999) and Ray (2001). Implicit to these analyses is the ability of producers to capture the economic value of quality linked to the geographical embeddedness of production. Indeed, consumer preferences for geographically specific and regional food products are frequently set within the context of emerging regulatory structures associated with the protection of collective intellectual property through appellations systems and Protected Geographical Indications (Moran 1993; Parrot *et al.* 2002; Barham 2003). The implementation of such protection, however, requires substantial financial support from public institutions and highly specific legislative arrangements. In the context of global supply chains, this local support must be further sustained by recognition and a shared understanding of international laws and trade agreements. For the coffee supply chain extending from Sulawesi to Japan, corporate regulation of the use of a regional identity has emerged in the absence of such producer-driven collective protection. This outcome has important implications for market access and the distribution of economic benefits associated with the qualities of geographical embeddedness.

SULAWESI COFFEE PRODUCTION AND EXPORT IDENTITIES

During the period 1991 to 2003, an average 2,500 tonnes of *arabica* coffee were exported annually from the port of Makassar in South Sulawesi, accounting for less than 10 percent of Indonesia's total *arabica* exports.[2] However, for the highland communities where coffee is grown, its production is the principal source of cash income. In Tana Toraja district for example (Figure 14.1) coffee contributes an estimated 20 percent to the gross domestic regional product in an economy otherwise dominated by subsistence rice production (Badan Pusak Statistik (BPS) 2002). Nearly all Sulawesi coffee is sold by exporters to specialized green bean traders in the US, Japan and Europe, who then supply the growing specialty coffee sector in those consuming regions. All exports of *arabica* coffee from Sulawesi in 2002 and 2003 were marked, and subsequently traded internationally, using a geographical place name such as 'Toraja', 'Kalosi', 'Rantepao', 'Sulawesi' or 'Celebes', and all were designated Grade One export quality. These identities feature on the ICO Certificate of Origin, related export documentation, and are commonly printed on individual 60-kilogram bags of coffee. The identity therefore remains the principal means of product differentiation up to the point of roasting. At this point, roasted single-origin coffee is commonly sold under this same geographic identity, or alternatively may assume another identity depending on marketing priorities.

Prior to Dutch colonization of the Toraja highlands in 1905, coffee was traded through indigenous networks west to the port town of Boengie (Figure 14.1), from where it was shipped to the main export hub of Makassar (Bigalke 1981). This coffee was then known as Boengie coffee, and had a particularly good reputation in the European market (Ukers 1935). Smallholder growers belonging to the Duri and Toraja ethnic groups cultivated this coffee, with Duri traders from the town of Kalosi assuming an important role in local trade networks at this time. Even after trade networks were no longer conducted through Boengie port, the Dutch administration recognized the value contained within a place name, and actively attempted to 'protect the good name of Boengie coffee' (Paerels 1949: 106) throughout the colonial period.

Following the Indonesian declaration of independence in 1945, regional instability across South Sulawesi culminated in violent ethno-religious tensions between the Duri and Toraja ethnic groups, disrupting

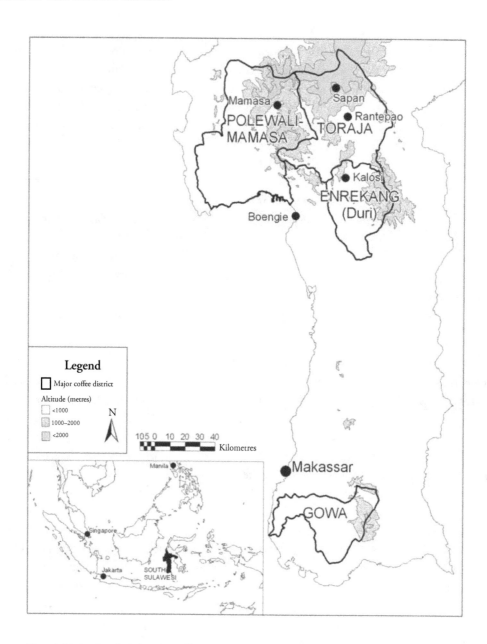

Figure 11.1   South Sulawesi coffee-growing areas.

interregional coffee trade networks. Very little Toraja-grown coffee reached the export market during this period because of the risks associated with transport along the volatile trade routes (Bigalke 1981). Kalosi traders, collecting coffee grown predominantly in the Duri lands of Enrekang, were apparently responsible for the widespread use of Kalosi as a market identity at this time. Interestingly, both the Boengie and Kalosi identities were borrowed from trading hubs and did not refer to a specific growing region.

While Kalosi continues to be a popular trading name today, Table 11.1 indicates that during 2002, Toraja had emerged as the most popular geographical expression used to identify exports of *arabica* coffee from Makassar. The contemporary use of geographical identities, however, demonstrates significant variation dependent on export destination. 'Kalosi' is primarily used for European buyers, while each of the 'Toraja' and 'Kalosi' identifiers are popular for the US market, and the Japanese indicate a clear preference for 'Toraja'. In the Sulawesi coffee supply chains, it is common practice for exporters to apply whichever identity is requested by international buyers. These export identities therefore currently reflect consumer market recognition, rather than necessarily corresponding to actual coffee origin. Moreover, importers have been known to deliberately mislabel Sulawesi coffee as Mandheling, the well-known coffee-growing region in North Sumatra.[3] Mandheling was the third most popular geographical expression used for Makassar exports in 2002 (Table 11.1). While many industry actors recognize and promote the quality associations of particular growing environments, the authenticity of the use of geographic identities is, for the most part, poorly regulated.

Toraja is a growing region and not a trading centre. The increased popularity of Toraja as an export identity therefore appears to represent a heightened international appreciation of the embedded geographies of coffee production in Sulawesi. Toraja is one of the four principal coffee-growing districts in South Sulawesi (Figure 11.1). These four districts are inhabited by distinct ethnic groups, each with a unique language, cultural practices and agro-ecological systems into which coffee production has been inserted. The physical characteristics of each growing district differ significantly in terms of topography and altitude, weather patterns and soil types. On-farm processing of the coffee bean also reflects these divergent geographies, with harvesting, pulping, fermentation and drying methods ranging widely. Of the Sulawesi growing districts, the highest-quality coffee is widely considered by local traders, exporters and international buyers to be grown in the Toraja district. The quality associations of Toraja coffee are primarily attributed to higher altitude production, along with prevailing soils, cultural characteristics[4] and to local processing methods. However, the ability of most international buyers to trace accurately the local origins of Sulawesi coffee is severely limited by the complex nature of existing pre-export trading systems.

Table 11.1   Geographical identities for *arabica* coffee exports from Makassar Port, 2002 (%).

Geographical identity	Export destination				
	Europe	US	Japan	Other Asia	Total Exports
Toraja only	0	23	90	20	41
Kalosi only	64	23	3	11	22
Both Toraja and Kalosi	21	25	6	47	20
Mandheling	9	28	0	21	15
Other	6	1	0	1	2
Total exports (tonnes)	574	1,613	1,194	263	3,644

Source: ICO Certificates of Origin, sighted at Department of Industry and Trade, South Sulawesi.

The Politics of Place

Japan's second largest coffee company, Kimura Coffee (later to become Key Coffee), established a coffee plantation and processing mill in the Toraja region during 1977. According to company pioneers in Toraja, the industry was then in a state of disarray, with little coffee reaching the export market and plantations in a ruined condition of neglect (Key Coffee 2001). Indeed, exports of *arabica* coffee from Makassar had plummeted from a pre-war peak of 1,798 tonnes in 1936 (Paerels 1949) to only 121 tonnes in 1973 (BPS 1974). Early product marketing by Key Coffee was based around a theme of bringing a dying coffee back to life, drawing heavily on cultural images and the spiritual mystique of Toraja to create a unique, geographically informed product image. The company maintains that they began using the Toraja identity when Sulawesi coffee was unanimously referred to internationally as Kalosi, and so claims responsibility for the construction of this particular quality association.

The importance of the Toraja geographical identity to Key Coffee was quickly established when the Sulawesi-based operating company (Toarco Jaya) took its name from an acronym of Toraja Arabica Coffee. Key Coffee registered Toraja as a Japanese trade mark in 1977, followed by an Indonesian trade mark for the company logo (a traditional Torajan house) in 1979, and a US trade mark for Toarco Toraja in 2002 (Dirjen HakI 1979; Industrial Property Database Library (IPDL) 2003; Trademark Electronic Search System (TESS) 2003). The Japanese trade mark specifically protects against the use of the Toraja name by other roasting companies in Japan, irrespective of the actual coffee origin, whereas the US trade mark includes a disclaimer to such an exclusive right. The company has been prepared to take legal action on more than one occasion in Japan to protect their exclusive right (Key Coffee 2001). Correspondingly, a recent request by a rival coffee company to register Toraja Arabica Coffee, with an accompanying map of Sulawesi, as a trade mark in Japan was rejected in 2001 (IPDL 2003).

Despite emerging relatively recently as a major coffee-consuming country, Japan is now the world's third largest importing nation after the US and Germany (ICO 2004). Furthermore, coffee imports to Japan are purchased, on average, at a 10 percent premium above the ICO composite indicator (ICO 1998). Japan also routinely buys most of the crop of Hawaiian Kona and Jamaican Blue Mountain (Pendergrast 2001; Association of Indonesian Coffee Exporters (AEKI) 2002), indicating a willingness to absorb the world's rarest and most expensive coffees, and a strong consumer belief in the relationship between quality and the geographical embeddedness of production.

During much of the 1980s and 1990s, Japan was easily the foremost destination for Sulawesi *arabica* coffee exports. Even though by 1999 the volume of imports to the US had begun to exceed those to Japan, the latter was still the highest value importing country during 2002 (Table 14.2). The average price of imports into Japan was US$2.9 per kilogram, compared with US$1.9 per kilogram for both the European and US markets. Within the Japanese coffee-drinking culture where place names are valuable commodities in themselves, Toraja has emerged with an enviable reputation for quality and routinely demands a premium price.

Local estate owners and Makassar-based exporters in Sulawesi have been understandably frustrated by the restrictions imposed on their ability to benefit from the place-related reputation of Toraja coffee in the lucrative Japanese market. In response to the Toraja trademark held by Key Coffee, the Association of Indonesian Coffee Exporters (AEKI) has prepared applications to register the place names of nine regional coffees across Indonesia as AEKI trade marks, including, somewhat ambiguously, the identity Toraja Kalosi (Kurniasih 2003). Unfortunately, in its current formulation, the AEKI proposal does not offer a mechanism

Table 11.2   Exports of *arabica* coffee from Makassar Port, 2002.

Importing regional country	Volume (tonnes)	Total Value (US$,000)	Average Price ($US/kg)
Japan	1,194	3,496	2.93
Europe	574	1,072	1.87
US	1,612	2,893	1.89
Australasia	264	552	2.10
Total	3,644	8,013	2.25

Source: Deperindag 2002a.

for verifying geographical authenticity or quality of coffee exports, and will not ultimately affect the existing Japanese trademark. Quoted from an article in a Makassar-based newspaper, the Head of the South Sulawesi Branch of AEKI complained in frustration that,

> foreign companies have no right to claim Indonesian coffee products as their own intellectual property, as those coffee names concord with their geographical location within Indonesia. Before those foreign companies registered the Toraja coffee name in America and Japan, we were already popularizing that product.

(Quoted in Fajar 2002)

The Japanese trade mark and the trading implications thereof contrast strongly with other systems of geographic protection, such as those recognized multilaterally as Geographical Indications, under the TRIPS agreement (Trade Related Aspects of Intellectual Property Rights) of the Uruguay Round. Geographical Indications provide communal protection for all producers living in a particular region against the fraudulent abuse of their place name by unqualified producers and traders. In contrast the Japanese Toraja trade mark acts to restrict otherwise geographically legitimate producers from accessing a particular national market.

Geographical Indications have been widely applied by producer associations to protect the market image and authenticity of a variety of mostly gourmet agricultural products, notably wines and cheeses in Europe. Despite the historic association between geographic origin and quality in the global coffee industry, Geographic Indications remain infrequently used in the sector. The location of many coffee-growing regions in the less affluent tropical regions of the South would appear to inhibit such protection due to the substantial costs (heavily subsidized by government institutions in countries such as France) associated with registration and ongoing supervision of Geographical Indications. While Geographic Indications are now being established in the global coffee industry, with countries such as Jamaica, Guatemala and Mexico taking lead roles, industry self-regulation of the use of place names remains dominant.

Toraja to Tokyo Trade Networks

The estate plantation owned and operated by Key Coffee supplied 15 percent of the company's export requirements in 2002 (Hirosan 2002) and is located in eastern Toraja at moderate altitudes between 900 and 1,300 metres. The remaining 85 percent was sourced via community purchasing operations, which are located in the north of Toraja to coincide with access routes to higher-altitude growing villages (up to 2,000 metres).

In itself, the remoteness of the purchasing station functions to encourage the supply of only that coffee grown in its immediate vicinity. The company insistence on accepting only semi-wet parchment coffee is also a deliberate attempt to encourage only the supply of locally grown coffee.[5] The extended storage of semi-wet parchment coffee makes it susceptible to mould formation, which is readily identified during cup-testing. Strict quality control procedures during purchasing include physical inspection, a defect count and rigorous cup-testing of each batch prior to acceptance. Consequently, the risk of rejection is high for sub-standard coffee, and the inconvenience and costs to local traders of transporting the coffee back to alternative trade networks is substantial. Thus, while this purchasing system does not entirely discount the possibility of non-local coffee being offered to the company, it strongly selects for locally grown beans.

In addition to consistently offering the highest (locally available) prices, the company pays significant premiums for defect-free coffee, and for those beans exhibiting particularly desirable cup characteristics (which the company essentially associates with higher altitude production). Nowhere else in Sulawesi are price incentives for quality so immediately transferred to growers, significantly affecting on-farm processing in northern Toraja. Key Coffee has also established a priority purchasing arrangement with Sapan village (Figure 11.1), where the company operates purchasing activities at considerable expense in the village a day prior to the local market. The hinterland for this market village includes the highest-altitude coffee gardens found in Sulawesi. Local growers and not village traders are encouraged to sell directly to the company at this weekly station. Through their own estate production, and implementation of a strict purchasing policy, the company is therefore able to ensure that virtually all their Sulawesi coffee is geographically authentic Toraja coffee. Key Coffee believes in the quality attributes of coffee grown in the villages of northern Toraja and, as a result of their highly integrated operations, is generally able to ensure first pick at this coffee.

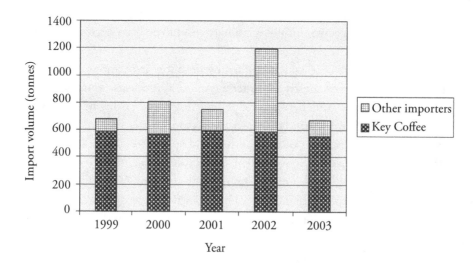

Figure 11.2   Share of Japanese import market held by Key Coffee, 1999–2003.

Key Coffee continues to dominate imports into Japan (Figure 11.2). The company's share, however, was substantially reduced in 2002, when a small importer-roaster imported 414 tonnes of Sulawesi coffee into Japan (Deperindag 2002a). The coffee imported by this company in 2002 was purchased (at an export price significantly below other Japanese buyers) from a single processor-exporter with a mill in the Toraja region, and labelled as Toraja Green coffee. This centrally located mill does not implement the same purchasing system and geographical control as Key Coffee and their coffee originates from the various growing districts of South Sulawesi. More important perhaps than their relative inability to trace the geographical authenticity of their Toraja coffee are the trading restrictions in Japan incurred by Key Coffee's ownership of the Toraja identity. Presumably, this company was unable to benefit from the quality associations of Toraja coffee in Japan, and did not subsequently purchase Sulawesi coffee during the 2003 season.

CONCLUSION: REGULATING THE BENEFITS OF GEOGRAPHICAL EMBEDDEDNESS

There exists a range of physical and cultural environments across sites of coffee production in Sulawesi, such that factors of geographical embeddedness affecting quality construction differ significantly. For the most part, however, quality differentiation according to actual local origins is not consistent with the subsequent geographic identities applied at the site of export. There are currently no local institutions with the political or economic will to ensure the geographical authenticity of the coffee being exported from Makassar under specific geographical identities. Despite these place names remaining principal modes of quality differentiation for importers and roasters in consuming countries, their allocation at the site of export is, to a large extent, arbitrary.

The one exception to this pattern is the vertically integrated structure of Key Coffee supplying the Japanese market. The importance of geographical specificity in the Japanese coffee market has resulted in a high degree of regulation concerning the use of geographical identities. 'Fair Competition Rules, Regulations and Guidelines concerning the Labelling of Regular Coffee and Instant Coffee' are implemented and monitored by the All Japan Coffee Association (AJCA). These also include composition requirements for the use of geographic expressions in blended coffees (Ueshima 2001). The AJCA is also a key actor responsible for the enforcement of Key Coffee's Toraja trade mark (Kito 2002). The enrolment of the AJCA in the protection and valorization of geographical specificity as a means of constructing quality associations has been an important aspect contributing to the appreciation of geographical coffee identities in Japan.

This, then, highlights a set of contradictions with regard to regulating geographical identities in the Sulawesi coffee sector. The current structures surrounding the use of the Toraja identity along the coffee supply chain into the Japanese market are dominated by control and ownership by a non-local corporate entity. Institutional arrangements, which include legal recognition of the geographical expression as exclusive intellectual property and a supportive industry association (AJCA), are fundamental to the ability of Key Coffee to assert this control. This control is further reflected in their ability to maintain market dominance and effectively create scarcity for a particular geographical product through a legally enforced monopoly. Vertical integration of the entire supply chain (to plantation) and tight control of community purchasing operations in northern Toraja ensure that any economic benefits of the geographical associations of quality are retained within the company.

While coffee producers and exporters in Sulawesi reasonably object to the appropriation of a local geographical expression as foreign property, the case of Toraja coffee is complicated by the instrumental role performed by Key Coffee in the initial construction of geographical quality associations within the Japanese market. The company's exclusive rights in Japan are also supported by their Sulawesi-based operations, which take great efforts to enforce geographical authenticity during community purchasing. These factors are emphasized by the company as the *raison d'être* for their exclusive trade mark.

The progressive dismantling of state support for the domestic coffee sector in many producing countries, including Indonesia, corresponds with increasing penetration of international coffee companies and new forms of industry regulation. In the specialty coffee sector, the use of geographical identities as a means for quality differentiation is an important component resulting in corresponding changes in supply chain governance. There are, it would seem, potential economic benefits for producers able to control the quality associations of their geographic embeddedness. However, the case of Toraja coffee in the Japanese market demonstrates that these benefits are not self evident in the popularity and consumer recognition of these associations. Corporate self-regulation of geographical authenticity in other non-Japanese consuming markets is equally problematic, as depicted by the misuse of the Sumatran Mandheling identity for Sulawesi exports to the US, Singapore and Europe. The level of public support required for the collective protection of place names as a Geographical Indication may be untenable in many producing country contexts. Moreover, there continues to be ongoing debate in the WTO about the status of such institutional support as constituting an illegitimate agricultural subsidy.

The increased consumer interest in regional food products suggests that any attempt to understand the multi-faceted reality of agri-food globalization should incorporate the structural trajectories implied by geographic specificity on supply chain structures and trade relationships. This case emphasizes the role of institutional arrangements in determining both the nature of supply chain relationships and the distribution of economic benefits among supply chain actors. Within the coffee supply chain extending from Toraja through to Tokyo, the regulation of geographical specificity has emerged as an important mode of economic ordering. Unlike the re-regulation of agri-food trading systems elsewhere resulting from producer initiatives to protect geographic identities, consumer and near-consumer demands for geographical authenticity are orchestrating the re-regulation evident here. The particular institutional arrangements regulating geographical embeddedness and the use of place names clearly affect the potential for quality-related upgrading by rural producers. Without appropriate institutional support, any values associated with the geographical embeddedness of agricultural production can be effectively controlled and regulated by corporate interests rather than local producers.

NOTES

1. The Toraja region is also known by its official name, Tana Toraja, which refers specifically to the administrative division. For the purposes of this chapter, the two terms are considered synonymous.

2. The export data for Sulawesi (including volume, prices, destinations, international buyers and geographical identities) presented in this chapter was compiled from original export documentation (ICO Certificates of Origin and Export Notification Certificates) sighted by the author at the provincial office of Industry and Trade in Makassar.

3. A highly publicized case of geographical fraud in the coffee industry was the 'Kona Kai Scandal', which apparently 'sent shock waves through the specialty sector' (Pendergrast 2001: 315). In 1996, it was exposed that a California importer was buying cheap Panamanian and Costa Rican beans and rebagging them as Kona. From the evidence in Sulawesi it appears that such practices are more widespread than acknowledged by many industry actors, highlighting the current difficulties in ensuring geographical authenticity in the industry.

4. The Toraja highlands are the foremost tourist attraction in eastern Indonesia due to a unique and complex traditional belief system, ornately carved architecture and a vibrant ceremonial cycle. These characteristics have more recently become a marketing resource in the specialty coffee sector.

5. In northern Toraja, coffee cherries are pulped, fermented and dried for only a few hours by the farmer before being sold to local market traders. In this semi-wet condition, the coffee is purchased by hulling operations. Key Coffee then mechanically dries the coffee prior to hulling, while it is common for other hullers to hull the semi-wet parchment prior to sun-drying the green beans.

References

Association of Indonesian Coffee Exporters (AEKI) (2002) 'Jamaica's Blue Mountain Coffee: the most expensive in the world', *Kopi Indonesia,* 108 (original publication: *Tea & Coffee Trade Journal,* September 2001): 16–18.

Badan Pusat Statistik (BPS) (1974) *Ekspor Menurut Jenis Barang, Negeri Tujuan dan Pelabuhan Ekspor.* Jakarta: Badan Pusat Statistik (National Statistics Agency).

Badan Pusat Statistik (BPS) (2002) *Kontribusi PDRB di Tana Toraja.* Rantepao: Badan Pusat Statisk Kabupaten Tana Toraja (Statistics Agency).

Barham, E. (2003) 'Translating terroir: the global challenge of French AOC labeling', *Journal Of Rural Studies,* 19 (1): 127–38.

Bigalke, T. (1981) A *Social History of Tana Toraja. 1870–1965.* Madison (WS): PhD dissertation, History Department, University of Wisconsin.

Deperindag (2002a) *Pemberitahuan Ekspor Barang (PEB) Export Certificates (raw data).* Makassar: Department of Industry and Trade.

Deperindag (2002b) *Realisasi Ekspor Kopi Sulawesi Selatan tahun 1999 S/D 2001.* Makassar: Department of Industry and Trade, Provincial Office of South Sulawesi.

Dirjen HakI (1979) 'Indonesian Trademark No. 141918 held by PT Toarco Jaya', Jakarta: Directorate General of Intellectual Property Rights, Department of Justice.

Fajar (2002) 'AEKI Daftar Kopi Toraja ke Departemen Kehakiman' [AEKI moves to register Toraja coffee with the Department of Justice], Makassar: Fajar, 5 May (translated by J. Neilson).

Granovetter, M. (1985) 'Economic action and social structure: the problem of embeddedness', *American Journal of Sociology* 91 (3): 481–510.

Hirosan [pseudonym] (2002) Personal communication. Purchasing Manager, PT Toarco Jaya. Rantepao, 16 August.

International Coffee Organization (ICO) (1998) *Importing Members—Japan Country Profile.* London: International Coffee Organisation. Online: www.ico.org.au (accessed 27 January 2004).

International Coffee Organization (ICO) (2004) *Historical Data—Imports of Importing Countries.* London: International Coffee Organisation. Online: www.ico.org.au (accessed 27 January 2004).

International Coffee Organization (ICO), International Trade Centre (ITC) and Common Fund for Commodities (CFC) (2000) *The Gourmet Coffee Project: Adding Value to Green Coffee.* London: ICO, ITC, CFC (UN Conference on Trade and Development (UNCTAD)).

Ilbery, B. and M. Kneafsey (1999) 'Niche markets and regional specificity food products in Europe: towards a research agenda', *Environment and Planning* A, 31: 2207–22.

Industrial Property Digital Library (IPDL) (2003) *Industrial Property Digital Library.* Online: www.ipdl.jpo.go.jp (accessed 19 August 2003).

International Trade Centre (ITC) (2002) 'Chapter three: niche markets, environment and social aspects. Coffee: an exporter's guide', Geneva: ITC/UNCTAD/WTO.

Key Coffee (2001) P*erjalanan Panjang Usaha Kopi di Tana Toraja [The Long Journey of a Coffee Business in Tana Toraja].* Rantepao: Key Coffee Inc (translated by Jeffrey Neilson).

Kito [pseudonym] (2002) Personal communication. Director of Production, PT Toarco Jaya. Rantepao, 19 August.

Kurniasih, T.J. (2003) Personal communication. Intellectual Property Development, AEKI. Jakarta, 4 September.

Lewin, B., Giovannucci, D. and Varangis, P. (2004) *Coffee Markets: New Paradigms in Global Supply & Demand.* Washington (DC): World Bank—Agriculture and Rural Development.

Moran, W. (1993) 'Rural space as intellectual property', *Political Geography,* 12 (3): 263–77.

Paerels, B. (1949) 'Bevolkingskoffiecultuur'. In J.J.V. Hall and C.V.D. Koppel (eds) *De Landbouw in de Indische Archipel.* The Hague: N.V. Uitgeverij W. Van Hoeve: 89–119.

Parrot, N., Wilson, N. and Murdoch, J. (2002) 'Spatializing quality: regional protection and the alternative geography of food', *European Urban and Regional Studies,* 9 (3): 241–61.

Pendergrast, M. (2001) *Uncommon Grounds: The History of Coffee and How it Transformed the World.* New York: Texere.

Ponte, S. (2002a) 'The "latte revolution"? Regulation, markets and consumption in the global coffee chain', *World Development,* 30 (7): 1099–122.

Ponte, S. (2002b) 'Standards, trade and equity: lessons from the specialty coffee industry', *CDR Working Paper,* 02.13. Copenhagen: Centre for Development Research.

Ray, C. (2001) 'Transnational co-operation between rural areas: elements of a political economy of EU Rural Development', *Sociologia Ruralis,* 41 (3): 279–95.

Specialty Coffee Association of America (SCAA) (1999) *Coffee Market Summary.* Long Beach (CA): Specialty Coffee Association of America.

Specialty Coffee Association of America (SCAA) (2004) 'What is specialty coffee?'. Online: www.scaa.org/What_is_specialty_coffee.asp (accessed 5 December 2004).

Trademark Electronic Search System [TESS] (2003) US Patent and Trademarks Office. Online: www.uspto.gov (accessed 19 August 2003).

Ueshima, T. (2001) 'Overview of the coffee market in Japan', *First World Coffee Conference,* 17–19 May. Online: www.ico.org/event/wcc.htm (accessed 27 January 2004).

Ukers, W.H. (1935) *All About Coffee.* New York: The Tea & Coffee Trade Journal Company.

STUDY QUESTIONS

1. What is the main idea of this chapter?
2. Characterize Sulawesi coffee.
3. As of the date of this article, how long had geographical identities been increasing in roasted coffee marketing?
4. How is geographical embeddedness applied to specialty coffee production?
5. Characterize the international marketing of Sulawesi coffee.
6. When did Toraja emerge as the most popular trading name used to identify exports of *arabica* coffee from Makassar?
7. What evidence is there to suggest that the authenticity of the use of geographical identities is, for the most part, poorly regulated?
8. How would you characterize the four principal coffee-growing regions in South Sulawesi?
9. How did Japan first become involved with Toraja coffee?
10. How would you characterize Japan as a coffee-purchasing country?
11. Local estate owners and Makassar-based exporters in Sulawesi have been understandably frustrated by the restrictions imposed on their ability to benefit from the place-related reputation of Toraja coffee in the lucrative Japanese market. What has been the response of the Association of Indonesian Coffee Exporters (AEKI)?
12. What are Geographical Indications?
13. Why do Geographical Indications not apply when it comes to Japans claim to Toraja Coffee?
14. What five conditions virtually assures a quality coffee for Key Coffee Company in Toraja?
15. How would you compare the quality control of other sites of coffee production in Sulawesi to that of the Key Coffee Company?
16. What are some of the contradictions highlighted in this chapter with regard to regulating geographical identities in the Sulawesi coffee sector?

Chapter 12 Snapshot
From Farm to Factory: Village Change in a Rice-growing Region

We've all heard of the western frontier in the US—unexplored, undeveloped land slowly being settled by hardy pioneers. In this article we will be reading about a frontier of a different sort: an industrial development frontier. These are areas of industrial development in mainly rural agricultural areas. What makes this frontier different from the old-fashioned western kind is that this frontier is being settled with investment income and "peopled" by commercial businesses and factories. In addition, these businesses are moving into areas where there are already populations and villages—even strong communities; "the frontier is both a space of habitation by a core population (i.e. village residents) and ... a space of attraction and residence by a population of migrant sojourners from other areas of the country" (192). We are also familiar with the concept of outsourcing, why companies outsource, and how outsourcing affects the sending community's economy. But what happens at the destination of the outsourcing? How does that place change and how does outsourcing figure into the economic development at the local site? These are some of the questions this article will explore.

Ayuthaya Province lies 75 km north of Bangkok, in Thailand (see map, Figure 12.1, page 193). It lies on the Central Plains, historically "the centre of Thailand's export-oriented rice industry" (192). It is also a region that "supports the bulk of Thailand's export-oriented manufacturing enterprises" (192). What makes Ayuthaya Province so interesting to study is that it has "a past history framed in terms of its place at the core of Thailand's 'rice bowl' ... and future prospects seemingly dictated by its position in Thailand's industrialisation project" (192). This study focuses on "two villages in the subdistrict (*tambon*) of Khan Haam, Uthai District, situated around 15 km east of Ayuthaya city": Ban Khan Haam and Ban Khokmayom. In terms of land use, the district is still mostly paddy rice lands but it is also a location of several factories, including Rojana Industrial Park that holds 134 factories employing approximately 43, 410 workers.

Sixty-nine percent of these factories were Japanese-owned, and 16 percent were owned domestically (192). "These factories are engaged in many of the activities that are emblematic of the country's industrialisation drive since the mid-1980s: electronics, auto parts, car assembly, textiles and apparel, footwear, and food and food processing" (192). Some 70 percent of the people working in the park were "non-local, mostly from the poor Northeastern region of Thailand" (194).

Ban Khan Haam and Ban Khokmayom have been strong rice-growing regions for more than a century. Until the 1960s, "only a cart track linked the villages with the main road to Ayuthaya, and during the rainy season, with extensive flooding, the settlements were often only accessible by boat" (194). Almost everyone cultivated rice, fished in the waterways, kept poultry, and grew their own fruits and vegetables; that is, the villages were virtually self-sufficient: "Surpluses of rice were sold to generate a modest cash income" (194). Until the 1960s, economic and social life revolved around agriculture and rice cultivation. But in the 1960s, and "like other agricultural communities in Thailand, agriculture in Tambon Khan Haam has … been squeezed by a range of environmental, economic, and socio-cultural factors such as fluctuating agricultural prices, especially rice prices and declining terms of trade" (194). There was the declining fertility and productivity of the land, poor water management, and continual flooding. Then, in the early 1970s, "a number of textile factories were established in Ayuthaya and a small number of local women took up jobs to supplement their incomes" (196). By the mid-1970s, a laterite (stone) road connected the villages to Ayuthaya, and the gradual but progressive changes to the villages had begun. Farming began to emerge as a generally low-status activity; "the limitations of farming … were becoming evident as households began to find it increasingly difficult to meet their escalating needs from just a single crop of rice, and securing supplementary work during the dry season became increasingly important, even a necessity" (194).

In the 1980s, there were even more "employment opportunities for women as pioneer textile factories in and around Ayuthaya city opened for business" (194). Then, in 1988, Rojana Industrial Park was built, centered in Tambon Khan Haam. "This event caused local (land) prices to soar, from 3,000 to 4,000 baht per rai in the early 1980s, to 60,000 to 70,000 in the mid-1980s, rising to 2 million baht by the end of the decade, and 5–6 million baht/rai today [in 2006]" (194). On the agricultural side of things,

> managing water levels in paddy fields became difficult as drainage channels were blocked and carefully honed systems of water management compromised. Insects became more of a problem for farmers as expanding areas of idle land provided a breeding ground for pests. Local people also highlighted discharges from the surrounding factories contaminating the water and the land (195).

On top of the declining quality of the land and "with the increase in land values due to the factories building in the area, the temptation to sell land, which had remained in the family hands increased" (195). As a result, the land's "potential for agriculture and to meet household needs was in decline" (195). Today, very few people farm. In contrast, as a result of the opening of Rojana Industrial Park, marked structural and livelihood changes began developing in the district (196).

SPATIAL, SECTORAL, AND LIVELIHOOD TURBULENCE ON THE FACTORY FRONTIER

There is a ripple effect in a region as it shifts from one sector of the economy to another, and this is exactly what happened in Tambon Khan Haam. Its past history is agriculture-based and farming-centered, but "its present and likely future are industry- and service-focused and non-farming oriented" (195). This shift has important implications for the core population, migration and circulation patterns, even how the villages become restructured or, as our authors put it, how the villages become "dissociated" (195). The core population has remained stable, but their livelihoods have changed considerably and there are more migrants in the villages who come from other parts of Thailand and owe no allegiance to the villages. Not only has the population grown with the shift from agriculture to industry and services, the population fluctuates more. Another element of change is movement. While the core population does not engage to a great extent in migration it is, nonetheless—and counter-intuitively—highly mobile ... . Instead of walking each day to their fields, villagers and migrants board buses or use personal transportation to work outside of the village.

Up until the 1970s, if we were to look in on these villages, we would see quiet, elongated villages following the rivers, and livelihoods, communities, and spatial activities would all be consistent with an agrarian culture; "the degree of interaction and interdependency with entities beyond the local was distinctly limited, compared with today" (195). Since the 1970s, and especially after the building of Rojana Industrial Park, these villages have seen substantial changes. As we saw above, the population is fluctuating both with new migrants as well as a consistent movement or circulation of people to areas outside the village and back. There are also spatial and landscape changes, especially having to do with industry, that are being driven by outside interests. Village livelihoods are no longer self-contained but are linked to changes in the economy and new village enterprises; in fact, they are dependent on them. "Even village identities have shifted from their prior self-identification as *chao naa*—rice farmers—to something more ambiguous" (196). The authors cite as a specific example of the sectoral shift taking place the difficulty of even getting an accurate count of the population in Ban Khokmayom. The Uthai district census for 2005 lists 378 people. The *tambon* health station indicate there are 1,257 people; and the authors' own survey, that considers the number and size of the dormitories, to be about 3,000. What does this difference in numbers indicate? "This marked discrepancy is due to the fact that the migrants who throng the *hor pak* [dormitories] are not all registered as *de jure* residents of the village, and so do not appear in the official figures" (196). So, in terms of population, what and who actually constitutes the village?

INTERPRETING TURBULENCE ON THE FACTORY FRONTIER

The most significant structural and livelihood changes in the *tambon* were associated with the opening of Rojana Industrial Park in 1988. One of the first "casualties" of the shift to industry was farming; "it had become not just a subsidiary occupation but a relict one undertaken by a few intransigent die-hards" (196). According to our authors, "in the two villages, of the core population aged over 16-years-old, just three individuals out of 508 reported that farming was their main occupation" (196). By the 1990s, this transformation from farm to non-farm was quite advanced (196). If people weren't farming anymore, what were they doing? The skilled, semi-skilled and even casual jobs they would be looking for were "largely located outside the boundaries of the village;" and these jobs occupied over one half of adults in the two villages (196). "Furthermore, the trading, shop-keeping, restaurant and 'private' (mostly dormitory) businesses of around another 10 percent of adults—which are largely situated within the confines of the village—are sustained by the purchasing power of migrants residing in the *tambon* but who work in the industrial estate and other factories in the vicinity" (196).

How have the factories themselves affected the villages? They "not only provide employment for local people, but act as magnets for workers from less prosperous areas of the country" (196). Some of the factories provide places for their workers to live, but most don't, so the villagers of Ban Khokmayom built dormitories (*hor pak*). "In 2006 there were around 30 dormitories within Ban Khokmayom, ranging from small, single-story affairs with just a handful of rooms, to grandiose multi-story structures with 50 to 100 rooms (see Figure 12.1, page 193) … . Many of these have attached toilet facilities and rental rates of 1500 to 2000 baht a month (US$45–65)" (196–197). There are approximately 300 dormitories in the *tambon* and a further 70 in a neighboring *tambon*. The migrants who live in these dormitories share the physical space with the core population, but not the cultural space.

One of the most important markers of wealth in an agricultural economy is land and that also has been greatly affected as the Tambon Khan Haam has been seeing more industry move in. Curiously, in part because of the industry, the quality of the land for agriculture has been declining yet the prices for that land continue to rise. "In total, 39 households, or 29 percent owned land, but must of this was not located in the village, and an even smaller proportion—less than a fifth—was farmed by its owners. It was in the early 1980s … that villagers began to sell land to outsiders, tempted by the simply enormous sums being offered" (198). The land has much less of a role structuring livelihoods in an industrial sector society than in an agricultural one. So, issues of poverty and wealth are no longer tied to the land. "What we identify in this area of Ayuthaya … is a three-fold de-linking of land from its formerly central role: a de-linking of the village from its land resource so that much village land is no longer owned and operated by villagers; a de-linking of livelihoods from land; and a de-linking of inequality and poverty from land" (197).

There is yet another factor of change in the *tambon* as a result of sectoral shift. In most societies there is a generational rite of passage when the young leave their rural home to see the world and earn income. "In time, it is assumed, many will return to farming and, if they have left home, to the village … and it is certainly true that there is a generational pattern to employment in the study villages" (198). But our authors also point to something else going on that has more to do with sectoral transformation than a lifecourse, or generational shift. As a result of the growth of industry and services in Tambon Khan Haam, there has been a shift in employment from farm to non-farm and from unskilled and casual work to semi-skilled and skilled (see Figure 12.3, page 199). "There is a permanent, two-stage change in the complexion of the rural economy and rural livelihoods: first from farm to non-farm (which occurred from the mid-1980s); and the second from unskilled/casual to skilled/semi-skilled (which occurred from the mid-1990s)…" (198). These transformational/livelihood changes will also affect the overall "sustainability of the village and the nature and interplay between production and consumption" (198).

As was stated earlier, before the 1970s, the villages were relatively self-contained and self-sufficient; nearly everything villagers needed they produced themselves. There was very little need to buy anything. However, "from the 1970s and progressively since, the villages have become dependent on external sources and supplies of food, and much else beside. Today villagers buy goods from the local *tambon* market and from mobile markets (*rod kab khab*), which are supplied from Bangkok's wholesale markets, or they travel to supermarkets on the outskirts of Ayuthaya … . There has also been a proliferation of shops in the *tambon*, but these are convenience stores and air-conditioned minimarts selling pre-packed, and often pre-cooked foods, serving the needs of migrant workers and villagers who have disposable income but little disposable time. In addition to food, other aspects of village life have been de-localized such as schooling and entertainment" (198).

Tambon Khan Haam, and especially Ban Khokmayom, has been a destination for migrants from poorer regions of Thailand; first to the rice-growing fields, and now, even more, to the industries and service opportunities that can be found there. It's not just that the villages are dissociating because of the physical presence of industry, but "the settlements themselves are being colonized by migrants from other places who hold no great allegiance to the village. Ironically, while these migrants may be playing a role in dissolving the village as community, they are also, by their presence helping to sustain the village as an economy and as a settlement. The demand for accommodation, not to mention other amenities and services from beauty salons and laundry shops to minimarts and food stalls, sustains the livelihoods of the core population, keeping them in the village even while—some villagers thought—their community was fragmenting" (200). There may be a dissociation of the community, but not the village itself.

CONCLUSION: RE-MAKING THE THAI RURAL ECONOMY AND RURAL LIVELIHOODS

What these authors wanted to emphasize in general: looking at the shift in economy from the rural agrarian sector to the industrial sector has usually necessitated people to leave their rural areas, "denuding the village of its human resource base and leaving it 'bereft' of young people of working age" (202). In the case of Tambon Khan Haam, however, the industry has settled in the rural frontier. They also recognize that the two villages in the study, Ban Kahn Haam and Ban Khokmayom are "atypical in their sheer proximity to the Rojana Industrial Park and, in the case of Ban Khokmayom, in its emergence as a 'dormitory village'" (202).

The authors highlight two main issues. The first issue is that of the broad-level and multi-faceted "dissociation" of the study sites. The authors are as interested in the dissociation *of* the village as *from* the village. That is, they are as interested in how the village is changing from community to settlement as much as they are interested in the migratory shifts from agricultural land to factory park. There are social and cultural meanings that the villagers attach to "their" village, but "there are also framing structures that are economic and material: patterns of land ownership, the presence of *hor pak*, idle land, the shift from water to road transport, polluted waterways, the gates and barred windows that protect villagers and their new-found wealth from the strangers who throng the village, beauty salons and minimarts, motorcycles and, of course, the factories that lie just across the fields" (128). Our authors have meticulously identified these changes that have taken relatively self-sufficient, self-contained rural agrarian communities of space, economy and identity and shown how the development of a rural industrial frontier has fragmented that community "by the intertwined processes of social, economic and spatial change" (202).

The second issue is that of mobility. Our authors have made a clear distinction between migration and daily mobility (circulation) and how it is circulation that characterizes the study sites "as villagers, of all ages but particularly those of working age, move rapidly and frequently across a vital space of economic and social interaction" (202; see Figure 12.4, page 199). They make a point of distinguishing that villages such as Ban Khan Hamm and Ban Khokmayom have been drawn into the process of industrialization that characterizes the extended Bangkok metropolitan region "not as reservoirs of cheap labor, but as sites of industrialisation and metropolitanisation. The village still exists as a physical place but its community has been replaced by a settlement " with a population who owe little allegiance to the land and who have been dependent on work ultimately shaped by forces that lie beyond the area" (203).

12. FROM FARM TO FACTORY

Village Change in a Rice-growing Region

By Jonathan Rigg, Suriya Veeravongs, Piyawadee Rohitarachoon
and Lalida Veeravongs

INTRODUCTION

In Asia, there has been a partial separation of factories from their assumed and traditional urban and peri-urban locations. In Indonesia, Malaysia, Vietnam, the Philippines and—in this instance—Thailand, there are large, export-oriented, often foreign-invested factories in areas that have traditionally been regarded as resolutely 'rural'. The reasons for this are not hard to discern: primarily, cheap land and the availability of low-cost labour. With improving communications and government policies that have promoted the dispersal of industry to poorer (rural) regions, some of the impediments and disincentives for rural industrialisation have also been removed or ameliorated. The result, in Thailand, is that the industrial investment frontier has moved outwards from the metropolitan core (Bangkok), to the wider Central Plains region and Eastern Seaboard, in some instances leap-frogging to even more distant areas in the Northern (Lamphun), Northeastern (Korat) and Southern (Songkhla) regions.[1]

The novelty of the factory frontier extends beyond the driving forces behind the process—the investment decisions of commercial, often foreign firms, supported by national planning agencies. It is novel for two other reasons. First, because it is not physical space being colonised by people, but human (labour) and physical (land) space being colonised by capital. Second, the frontier is both a space of habitation by a core population (i.e. village residents) and, as we will show, a space of attraction and residence by a population of migrant sojourners from other areas of the country. Because of this, we have a series of parallel, but only partially intersecting transformations under way: spatial changes linked to the interplay of farming with non-farming activities and processes; agricultural changes associated with the economic, social (aspirational) and environmental trade-offs between farming and other activities; livelihood changes that arise from the widening opportunities available to both the core, resident population and the in-coming migrant sojourners; and social changes linked to transformations in inter-generational and inter-community relations. Some of these transformations have been explored and elucidated in a separate paper (Rigg *et al.*, 2008); here we wish to focus particularly on the ways in which the village, as a settlement and a community, has been 'deconstructed'.

The Central region of Thailand, including Bangkok and Bangkok's extended metropolitan region, supports the bulk of Thailand's export-oriented manufacturing enterprises. The Central Plains has also historically been the centre of Thailand's export-oriented rice industry. We have in this region, therefore, a rich and complex spatial and economic mosaic of factories and farms. Ayuthaya province, 75 km north of Bangkok by road, was selected as the study site for the manufacturing frontier component of the project because of this duality in the province's character: a past history framed in terms of its place at the core of Thailand's 'rice bowl' (Molle and Thippawal Srijantr, 2003); and future prospects seemingly dictated by its position in Thailand's industrialisation project. Ayuthaya is the site of several industrial parks and estates, and the province was also highlighted as a target province for industrial development in the Sixth National Social and Economic Development Plan (1987–1991). In mid 2005 there were 1425 officially registered factories in the province employing 192,584 workers.[2] This does not include many unregistered—and therefore unrecorded—workers employed in smaller units of production.[3]

THE RESEARCH SITES

The research was undertaken in two villages in the sub-district (*tambon*) of Khan Haam, Uthai District, situated around 15 km east of Ayuthaya city (Figure 12.1 and Table 12.1): Ban Khan Haam and Ban Khokmayom. The district is low-lying and much of the agricultural land well irrigated by the Nakornluang Irrigation Project. Some 87 percent of land in the district is still classified as agricultural, and of this the great bulk is paddy land. The district is also the site of an industrial park and, in this way, has been drawn into Thailand's export-oriented, foreign direct investment-driven, industrialisation drive. Since the mid 1980s there has been a radical reorientation of land-use within Tambon Khan Haam. Large areas of former agricultural land have been turned over to industrial uses, some 1200 rai (192 hectares) in total, with the result that agricultural land in the *tambon* is now a scarce commodity.

The Rojana Industrial Park is centred on Tambon Khan Haam, although its land area extends into neighbouring sub-districts. The park was established in May 1988 and, with successive waves of expansion, now covers an area of 4200 rai (672 ha). In 2005 there were 134 factories operating in the park. The bulk of these—93 or 69 percent—were Japanese-owned, and a further 21 (16 percent) domestically (i.e. Thai) owned. These factories are engaged in many of the activities that are emblematic of the country's industrialisation drive since the mid 1980s: electronics, automobile parts, car assembly, textiles and apparel, footwear, and food and food processing. In 2005 the park employed 43,410 workers. The majority of

Table 12.1   Ban Khan Haam and Ban Khokmayom, background statistics.

		Tambon Khan Haam	Ban Khan Haam (village no. 1)	Ban Khokmayom (village no. 9)
Households (2005)		2603	130	—
Population (2005)		5495	494	162
Primary household	Farming	—	20	38
occupation	Non-farming	—	110	124

Source: Tambon Administrative Organisation Documents

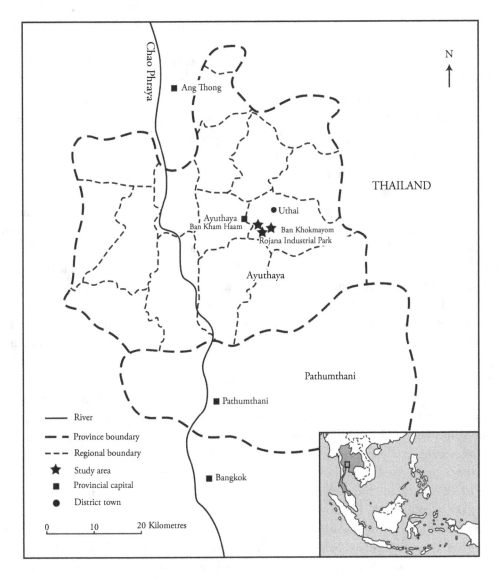

Figure 12.1   Map showing location of study settlements in Central Thailand.

these workers—70 percent according to the park management[4]—were non-local, mostly from the poor Northeastern region of Thailand.

Ban Khan Haam and Ban Khokmayom (Table 12.1) were settled more than a century ago when they were rice-growing communities. Until the 1960s, economic and social life revolved around agriculture and, more particularly, rice cultivation. At that time only a cart track linked the villages with the main road to Ayuthaya, and during the rainy season, with extensive flooding, the settlements were often only accessible by boat. Surpluses of rice were sold to generate a modest cash income, but Ban Khan Haam and Ban Khokmayom were not too far from the subsistence, self-reliant ideal popularised in the work of Chatthip Nartsupha (1986; 1996; 1999).

Since the 1960s, and like other agricultural communities in Thailand, agriculture in Tambon Khan Haam has been squeezed by a range of environmental, economic and socio-cultural factors: fluctuating agricultural prices, especially rice prices; unfavourable input/output ratios; declining terms of trade; poor water management and continuing flooding; the seasonality of work; the declining fertility and productivity of the land; and the emergence of farming as a generally low-status activity. Their location close to an industrial park has provided the inhabitants of the villages, directly (through employment) and indirectly (through the other demands that the factories have generated), with a range of alternative occupations and activities. Ban Khan Haam and Ban Khokmayom were not selected for study just because we were interested in exploring how rural settlements become implicated in Thailand's regional industrialisation strategy, however. We were also intent on investigating how they become magnets for migrants from other places. Ban Khokmayom, particularly, has seen the construction of large-scale dormitories (*hor pak*) for factory workers, in so doing altering the essence of the village community. Ban Khan Haam, by contrast, does not support such dormitories. This is because the settlement is physically (spatially) constrained, limiting the scope for substantial building expansion—although it has, even so, been profoundly influenced by its location at the edge of the industrial park. While the current (and likely future) history of Tambon Khan Haam and the two study villages is in the process of being structured and mapped out by wider national and international policy and investment decisions, the past history of the sub-district and study villages is better illuminated by reference to the area's agricultural and farming roots.

The beginnings of the thorough-going incorporation of the study villages into the mainstream can be linked to the construction of a laterite feeder road, which passed close to the gates of the village monastery, Wat Khokmayom, in the mid 1970s. At that time, rice farming remained the main occupation of villagers and the non-farm jobs that did exist (mainly in construction) were undertaken post harvest, and arranged around the demands of agriculture. The limitations of farming, however, were becoming evident as households began to find it increasingly difficult to meet their escalating needs from just a single crop of rice, and securing supplementary work during the dry season became increasingly important, even a necessity. The 1980s saw the emergence of greater employment opportunities for women as pioneer textile factories in and around Ayuthaya city opened up for business. The 1990s saw these nascent changes—which can be traced back to the 1970s—accelerate and deepen in terms of their impact, influence and ubiquity, propelled in no small way by the opening of the Rojana Industrial Park in 1988.

This event caused land prices to soar, from 3000–4000 baht per rai in the early 1980s, to 60,000–70,000 in the mid 1980s, rising to 2 million baht by the end of the decade, and 5–6 million baht/rai today (2006).[5] As the temptation to sell land which had remained in family hands for a century increased, so its potential for agriculture and to meet household needs was in decline. Managing water levels in paddy fields became difficult as drainage channels were blocked and carefully honed systems of water management compromised. Insects became more of a problem for farmers as expanding areas of idle land provided a breeding ground for pests. Local people also highlighted discharges from surrounding factories contaminating the water and land. Today, farming is the preserve of the very few.[6] Instead villagers work in the industrial park, in the service sector, and as housekeepers, government officers, teachers, and nurses.

In the discussion that follows we shift our locus of discussion between the sub-district (the *tambon*) and the two study villages (Ban Khan Haam and Ban Khokmayom), according to the topic being addressed. The village surveys provide data which are relevant to wider-scale transformations and processes and we use their experiences to reflect on this broader, sub-district, context. On occasion we combine the survey data from both villages to explicate, for example, what we see to be more generic patterns of livelihood change. At other times, however, and particularly when the discussion turns to the place and role of the migrant workers who live in Ban Khokmayom (but not in Ban Khan Haam), we more specifically highlight certain village-focused developments and concerns.

SPATIAL, SECTORAL AND LIVELIHOOD TURBULENCE ON THE FACTORY FRONTIER

Ban Khan Haam and Ban Khokmayom, and Tambon Khan Haam more widely, present a number of practical, methodological and conceptual challenges. These challenges arise from the nature of spatial, sectoral and livelihood change in the villages and the sub-district. To begin with, the past history of the area is agriculture-based and farming-centred. Its present and likely future are industry—and services—focused and non-farming oriented. In terms of practical development interventions, therefore, will the promotion of 'rural' development, in the traditional sense, have any traction and efficacy? Second, the core registered populations of the villages (and particularly Ban Khokmayom) are stable but the *de facto* population is significantly higher and characteristically fluctuating. Methodologically, are we focusing on the social actors that comprise the resident population of the area, or on all those who happen to be residing in the geographical space of Tambon Khan Haam, irrespective of their origins and allegiances? And third, while the core population does not engage to a great extent in migration it is, nonetheless—and counter-intuitively—highly mobile. Conceptually, therefore, how do we think about populations which are, at the same time, becoming less likely to be migrants, but more likely to be mobile?

Until the 1970s, space, economy, society, identity and livelihoods—broadly speaking—mapped onto each other. As a researcher it would have been possible to 'enter' the village and, in so doing, to enter the social as well as the economic universe of the villager. The settlement (the spatial unit), the community (the social entity), the (village) economy, and (household) livelihoods would have been revealed as intersecting and overlapping in intimate and manifold ways.[7] Of course this can be stretched too far. The village was not, in a complete sense, a 'world unto itself' (Elson, 1997: 33), but the degree of interaction and interdependency with entities beyond the locale was distinctly limited, compared with today.

The progressive dissociation of the village in spatial, social, economic and livelihood terms since the 1970s is not just important because of its implications for how we understand the development process and appropriate development interventions, but also because of the implications it has for research methods and our conceptualisation of 'the village study'. Focusing on the latter, it means that the entry point for the traditional village study—namely, 'the village'—is no longer quite so neat and unproblematic. The village is clearly still there, in the rural landscape, but as a container for study it is shot through. The population is in flux; the space economy consists of elements (such as the industrial estate) which are largely rooted and driven extra-locally; village livelihoods are dependent on activities in other spatial and sectoral arenas; even village identities have shifted from their prior self-identification as *chao naa*—rice farmers—to something more ambiguous.

The degree of turbulence is most strikingly illustrated when it comes to pinning down the population of Ban Khomayom. The Uthai district census bureau provides a figure for 2005 of 378. The *tambon* health station, for the same year, has records indicating that the population of the village is 1257. Based on our village survey and the number and size of dormitories in the village, however, we would put the *de facto* population of Ban Khokmayom at around 3000. This marked discrepancy is due to the fact that the migrants who throng the *hor pak* are not registered as *de jure* residents of the village, and so do not appear in the official figures. This presents both a practical, methodological challenge and a more conceptual one: rhetorically, how do we treat this shifting, migrant population when it comes to interpreting village change?

INTERPRETING TURBULENCE ON THE FACTORY FRONTIER

The dissociation of work from the study villages began, as noted above, in the early 1970s when a number of textile factories were established in Ayuthaya and a small number of local women took up jobs to supplement their incomes. These original textile factories have since closed in response to competition from other, lower-wage locations in Asia. Some more adventurous—or more desperate—women migrated temporarily to work in textile factories in Rangsit District, Pathumthani Province, while men left to work on the construction sites of Bangkok. But it was the 1980s that saw really marked structural and livelihood change in the *tambon*, associated with the opening of the Rojana Industrial Park.

The occupations of adults included in the survey clearly reveal how far farming has become not just a subsidiary occupation, but a relict one undertaken by a few intransigent die-hards: in the two villages, of the core population aged over 16 years old, just three individuals out of 508 reported that farming was their main occupation. Moreover, it was clear that this transformation from farm to non-farm was well advanced in the mid 1990s; some 30 individuals reported that farming was their main occupation ten years prior to the survey. Skilled, semi-skilled and unskilled (casual) work, very largely located outside the boundaries of the village, provided the main occupations for over half of adults in the two villages. Given that another fifth to a quarter remained in education, this means that of economically active adults the significant majority build their livelihoods largely beyond the settlement. Furthermore, the trading, shop-keeping, restaurant and 'private' (mostly dormitory) businesses of around another 10 percent of adults—which are largely situated within the confines of the village—are sustained by the purchasing power of migrants residing in the *tambon* but who work in the industrial estate and other factories in the vicinity.

The factories of the Rojana Industrial Park not only provide employment for local people, but also act as magnets for workers from less prosperous areas of the country. While some factories provide on-site accommodation, most do not and the villagers of Ban Khokmayom particularly have exploited the demand for accommodation by building dormitories or *hor pak*.[8] In 2006 there were around 30 dormitories within Ban Khokmayom, ranging from small, single-storey affairs with just a handful of rooms, to grandiose,

Figure 12.2.   Dormitory block in Ban Khokmayom.

multi-storey structures with 50 to 100 rooms (Figure 12.1). Many of these have attached toilet facilities and rental rates of 1500–2000 baht a month (US$45–60). The *tambon* as a whole supports approximately 300 dormitories and Tambon Thanu—the neighbouring *tambon*—a further 70 (interview with Uthai assistant district officer, 5 June 2006).

The migrants who live in the physical space—but not the social space—of Ban Khokmayom are mostly from the Northeast of Thailand. Their clear and driving rationale for coming to Ayuthaya is to find work. This, in itself, is not new. There has long been a flow of migrants from the environmentally marginal and economically impoverished Northeast to the richer Central Plains. Traditionally, however, these migrants worked in the rice fields of the region; now they migrate, and in much larger numbers, to work in the factories of the area. We found no migrant sojourners in Tambom Khan Haam who were employed in the farm sector, although in other areas of the province this is likely to be the case.

Traditionally, in rural village studies, land is the key production resource, the central marker of wealth and, by association, the key indicator—through its lack—of poverty. The centrality accorded to land remains a guiding principle in many studies, as Borras *et al.* (2007: 1) make clear in the introduction to their book on land, poverty and livelihoods: 'in many agrarian settings a significant proportion of the income of the rural poor still comes from farming … [and] hence lack of access to land is strongly related to poverty and inequality'. What we identify in this area of Ayuthaya, however, is a three-fold de-linking of land from its formerly central role: a de-linking of the village from its land resource so that much village land is no longer owned and operated by villagers; a delinking of livelihoods from land; and a delinking of inequality and poverty from land. Across the two villages, of the 133 'core' households surveyed (i.e. excluding migrants to the villages), not one household head reported farming as [its] main occupation, and just three out of 508 aged over 16 years were said to be engaged, primarily, in farming activities. In total, 39 households or 29 percent owned land, but much of this was not located in the village, and an even smaller proportion—less than a fifth—was farmed by its owners. It was in the early 1980s, informants told us, that villagers began to sell land to outsiders, tempted by the simply enormous sums being offered. The two study villages may still be situated in a rural setting (Figure 12.2), but much of the surrounding land is not owned by villagers, and still less is it instrumental in structuring livelihoods and explaining patterns of well-being.

It has been normal to understand the engagement with activities outside farming as linked to life-course transitions. Young people leave home to earn income and see the world as part of a rite of passage into adulthood. In time, it is assumed, many will return to farming and, if they have left home, to the village. It is certainly true that there is a generational pattern to employment in the study villages (Figure 10.2). But, we argue, this is indicative of era-level transformations rather than generational changes, with the non-farm/ farm transition occupying a past transitional stage. Instead, we see working through the population and, we surmise, in quite a permanent manner, a shift from unskilled and casual employment to skilled and semi-skilled. But unlike the 'return to farming' argument, we do not expect there to be a similar 'return to casual work'. This is a permanent, two-stage change in the complexion of the rural economy and rural livelihoods: First, from farm to non-farm (which occurred from the mid 1980s); and second, from unskilled/casual to skilled/ semi-skilled (which occurred from the mid 1990s) (Figure 10.3). The first of these may, to begin with, have reflected generational changes associated with the life-course. The second, though (and, we suspect, increasingly the first) are transformations which will resonate through the generations.

Of course, there is always the possibility that transitions/transformations may be thrown into reverse, particularly when national economic progress is replaced by stagnation or retrogression. This was anticipated, for example, with the onset of the Thai economic crisis of 1997 (Parnwell, 2002; Rigg, 2002). The economic attractiveness of farming can also shift, and the recent (2008) surge in agricultural commodity prices may lead some people to return to farming or to realign the balance of their work between farm and non-farm. Thus the current trend of de-agrarianisation may shade into a degree of re-peasantisation given changing circumstances. Our view, however, is that such a shift 'back' to farming will not occur readily or easily, and only in markedly changed circumstances.

These changes in the complexion of livelihoods and the village economy have a bearing on the sustainability of the village and the nature and interplay between production and consumption. Formerly it was not just production that was centred—spatially—on the village, but so too were patterns of consumption. Through to the 1970s, the village was largely self-sufficient in food. The main source of protein was fish caught in local waterways, most households kept poultry, grew fruit and vegetables in their house compounds and rice, of course, was cultivated by almost everyone. Little was purchased.[9] From the 1970s, and progressively since, the villages have become dependent on external sources and supplies of food, and much else beside. Today, villagers buy goods from the local *tambon* market and from 'mobile markets' (*rod kab khao*), which are supplied from Bangkok's wholesale markets, or they travel to supermarkets on the outskirts of Ayuthaya, such as Big-C, Tesco-Lotus and Carrefour. There has also been a proliferation of shops in the *tambon*, but these are convenience stores and air-conditioned minimarts selling pre-packed, and often pre-cooked foods, serving the needs of migrant workers and villagers who have disposable income but little disposable time. In addition to food, other aspects of village life have been de-localised, such as schooling and entertainment. Better-off villagers send their children to schools in Uthai district or Ayuthaya town,

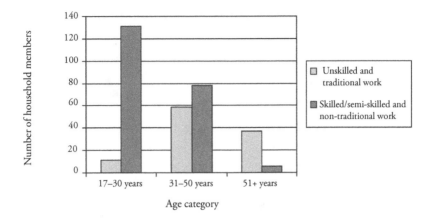

Figure 12.3   Age and occupational status of adult household members: Ban Khan Haam and Ban Khokmayom, 2005.

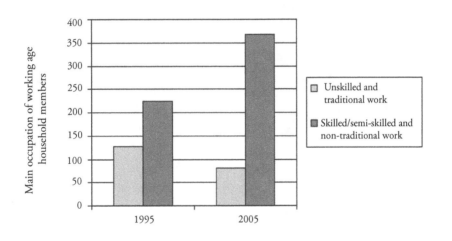

Figure 12.4   Formal/skilled and casual/unskilled occupations among working-age household members: Ban Khan Haam and Ban Khokmayom, 2005.

which are thought to provide a better education than the local school. Privately operated school buses pick children up each morning, depositing them back in the village at the end of the school day.

As noted above, Tambon Khan Haam—and particularly Ban Khokmayom—has become a node of attraction for migrants from other regions of Thailand. It is not, therefore, just that the original settlements are being prised apart by the movement of their core population into activities which are distant geographically and historically from the original community. It is also that the settlements themselves are being colonised by migrants from other places who hold no great allegiance to the village. Ironically, while these migrants may be playing a role in dissolving the village as a community, they are also, by their presence, helping to sustain the village as an economy and as a settlement. The demand for accommodation, not to mention other amenities and services from beauty salons and laundry shops to minimarts and food stalls, sustains the livelihoods of the core population, keeping them in the village even while—some villagers thought—their community was fragmenting.

Perhaps it is for this reason that while we identify a dissociation of the traditional village community, we do not see a dissolution of the village. Indeed the core village, on paper, seems surprisingly resilient. The majority of core villagers (i.e. excluding migrant sojourners) were born in their village of residence or in the neighbouring district: 77 percent and 66 percent in Ban Khan Haam and Ban Khokmayom respectively. In addition, surprisingly few of the surveyed household members—less than a fifth—had engaged in migration involving an absence of three months or longer. These data would, at first sight, indicate that the villages are socially and economically quite 'rooted'. Moreover, this is surprising insofar as Thai society has become increasingly mobile.

On closer inspection, however, the data reveal that mobility is taking on a new guise in the study sites. Rather than long-distance and long-term patterns of movement (i.e. migration), it is quite intense patterns of daily mobility that characterise the villages. Ease of travel coupled with a proliferation of local non-farm employment opportunities have permitted villagers to leave farming, without leaving the village. In the day before the survey, around one half of the 669 household members surveyed had left the village. Of

Table 12.2   Mobility in Ban Khokmayom and Ban Khan Haam.

		Ban Khan Haam	Ban Khokmayom (core villagers)
Household members who have engaged in long term migration (> 3 months' absence) (%)		14	21
Household members who travelled outside the village in the day before the interview (%)		43	58
Purpose of daily mobility (number of household members)	Work, business	79	148
	Social	17	46
	Education	30	52
	Total	126	246
Mode of daily travel (number of household members)	Private (motorbike, car, pick-up)	81	133
	Public or firm-provided transport	31	76
	Other	14	37
	Total	126	246
Household ownership of motorised transport (number of households)	Motorbike	51	72
	Motor vehicle (car, pick-up)	20	79

Source: Author's household survey, 2005.

these daily movements, more than 60 percent were for work or business reasons (Table 12.2). The ease with which people can move relatively long distances, quite quickly, is significant, particularly when compared with the African cases in this volume. Factories in the Rojana Industrial Park provide buses to pick up workers daily up to a radius of 100 km; furthermore, many workers have their own, private means of transport (Table 12.2). Of the households interviewed, over 80 percent owned a motorcycle, and 45 percent a motor vehicle. There is, as one might expect, a correlation between daily mobility and age (Figure 10.4). The members of the cohort aged 0–16 years are primarily leaving the villages for purposes of education; those in the working age cohorts (17–30 years and 31–50 years) depart mainly for work-related reasons; while private errands are concentrated among those villagers aged over 30 years. It is the members of the oldest cohort (51+ years) who are least mobile.

It has been noted elsewhere that development studies and development economics have overlooked the role of mobility in re-working the nature and basis of rural development. As Dercon writes, 'understanding rural poverty changes cannot naively focus only on what happens in the rural sector, or in agriculture … if development has to do with people moving between sectors, then this will often imply spatial movement' (2006: 5 and 6). This experience from Ayuthaya takes the argument one step further in its reconsideration of the bases of rural vitality and development. In Ban Khan Haam and Ban Khokmayom there has, indeed, been a very pronounced shift from farm to non-farm in people's livelihoods. This has been accompanied by marked structural changes in the village economy. There is also a high intensity of mobility. But, at least for the core households in the villages (i.e. excluding migrants), this has not involved leaving the village. The colonisation of rural space by industrial activities, coupled with an efficient transport infrastructure

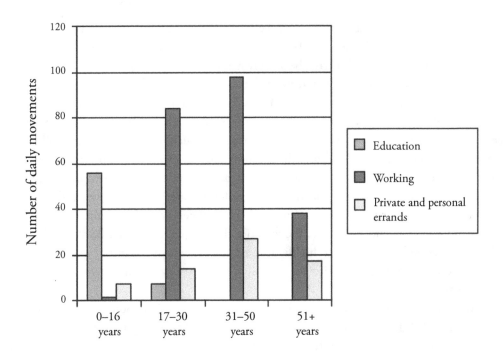

Figure 12.5 Daily mobility and purpose on the day prior to the survey: Ban Khan Haam and Ban Khokmayom, 2005.

and high levels of ownership of private means of transport, has enabled the village economy and rural livelihoods to be fundamentally re-worked without the spatial movements of people that Dercon highlights.

CONCLUSION: RE-MAKING THE THAI RURAL ECONOMY AND RURAL LIVELIHOODS

The implications of structural and spatial changes in the Thai economy for rural livelihoods have been noted elsewhere (see Molle, 2003; Molle and Thippawal Srijantr, 1999; Rigg, 2001, 2006; Rigg and Sakunee Nattapoolwat, 2001). In large part, this work has focused on the way in which people have been attracted (or propelled) out of the village and farming, by opportunities in other spheres and/or by a squeezing of traditional, rural livelihoods. This has necessitated, in many instances, long-term migration, denuding the village of its human resource base and leaving it 'bereft' of young people of working age. Outstanding questions that have not yet been adequately explored include first, whether these trends indicate a permanent transformation in the character of the rural economy and rural livelihoods; and second, how these changes are restructuring the bases of poverty and prosperity in the countryside.

The discussion in this chapter has contributed a slightly different view to the debate over de-agrarianisation in Thailand and, more broadly, in Asia. But before generalising from the experience of Ban Khan Haam and Ban Khokmayom it needs to be emphasised that the villages are atypical in their sheer proximity to the Rojana Industrial Park and, in the case of Ban Khokmayom, in its emergence as a 'dormitory village'. Nonetheless, we highlight as a conclusion two key issues that, we believe, have wider relevance.

To begin with, there is the issue of the broad-level and multi-faceted 'dissociation' of the study sites. Thompson has discussed 'dissociation' with reference to the Malay-peasant complex in his study of Sungai Siputeh (Thompson, 2002, 2003, 2004, 2007). His main concern is to explore dissociation *from* the village of young men (particularly) who have been drawn into the modern economy, creating a degree of separation from their traditional identity and identification as *orang kampung* (people of the village).[10] In the cases of Ban Khan Haam and Ban Khokmayom, we are interested as much in the dissociation *of* the village as in dissociation *from* the village. There is, quite clearly, a relationship between the two insofar as the village is not just a settlement—a place—but a community which is socially and culturally 'made'. That said, while the social and cultural may frame the meanings that villagers attach to 'their' village, there are also framing structures that are economic and material: patterns of land ownership, the presence of *hor pak*, idle land, the shift from water to road transport, polluted waterways, the gates and barred windows that protect villagers and their new-found wealth from the strangers who throng the village, beauty salons and minimarts, motorcycles and, of course, the factories that lie just across the fields. We have sought to describe this multi-faceted dissociation to highlight the degree to which a formerly quite tight association, or nesting, of space, economy and identity has become fragmented by the intertwined processes of social, economic and spatial change.

The second theme that the chapter has explored is that of mobility. As noted above, there is a relative abundance of studies of migration in Thailand.[11] Most of these emphasise migration and the associated spatial and temporal dislocation of people from the village. In this chapter, however, we note the degree to which daily mobilities rather than migration characterise the study sites, as villagers, of all ages but particularly those of working age, move rapidly and frequently across a vital space of economic and social interaction.[12] The

Central Plains region of Thailand, the so-styled 'rice bowl' of the Kingdom, has become functionally part of the extended Bangkok metropolitan region. Villages such as Ban Khan Haam and Ban Khokmayom have been drawn directly into this process, not as reservoirs of cheap labour, but as sites of industrialisation and metropolitanisation. Seductively, the village is still to be seen and studied; it exists as an administrative unit and as a physical entity. But in many other respects the village has become an historical artefact, replaced by a settlement with a population who owe little allegiance to the land and who have become dependent on work ultimately shaped by forces that lie beyond the area.

NOTES

1. For Thai Board of Investment (BoI)-sponsored industrial estates, see http://www.boi.go.th/english/how/industrial_estates.asp.

2. Source: www.industry.go.th/min/intro/province/Ayuthaya/web/factorydata.com.

3. The total population of the province at the end of 2004 was 740,000.

4. Interview with the Rojana Industrial Park officer, 3 November 2005 and the General Manager of the Rojana Industrial Park Company, 16 February 2006.

5. The baht: US$ exchange rate for much of the 1980s and 1990s was 25 baht = US$1. The Thai economic crisis in 1997–98 led to a sharp decline in the value of the baht, bottoming out at 56 baht = US$1 in January 1998. In June 2008 the exchange rate was US$1 = 33 baht.

6. Note that the fieldwork and survey were undertaken before the recent steep increase in the value of rice (and other agricultural commodities).

7. Because of the nature of the landscape in the Central Plain, villages tend to be strung out along waterways rather than nucleated in the way that they are in the Northeastern region and much of the North.

8. We use the word 'dormitory' because these rooms and buildings are generally known as *hor pak*—usually translated as dormitory. However, they are not dormitories in the sense that several people live together in the same room. The rented rooms are for single migrants or couples and newer *hor pak* have attached toilet facilities.

9. Amyot, in his study of village Ayuthaya undertaken in 1969–1970, writes: 'Food consumed in the household is usually that which is found locally such as fish, vegetables from the family garden, and of course rice. Little money is spent on food so that meat and other vegetables not produced by the household are bought only in small quantities' (Amyot, 1976: 80).

10. 'Dissociation, in my view, however, does not signal an end to social and cultural structure or a moment in which "anything goes." Rather, it is a moment in which the prevailing social forces and subjects acting within the constraints of those forces rework the landscape of identity, doing so at points of structural dissociation and indeterminate articulation, such as the points at which Malayness, masculinity, migrancy, and class intersect in Malaysia' (Thompson 2003: 431).

11. See, for example, Esara (2004), Jones and Sirinan Kittisuksathit (2003), Jones and Tieng Pardthaisong (1999), Mills (1997;1999), Rigg (1989), Singhanetra-Renard (1999), Tomosugi (1995).

12. In fact, the villages reveal two forms of movement: the migration of people to the area from other parts of Thailand; and the mobilities that take both these migrants and the core population out of the village on a daily basis.

REFERENCES

Amyot, J. (1976) *Village Ayutthaya: Social and economic conditions of a rural population in Central Thailand*, Bangkok: Chulalongkorn University Social Research Institute.

Borras, S.M. Jr, Akram-Lodhi, A.H. and Kay, C. (2007) 'Agrarian reform and rural development: Historical overview and current issues', in A.H. Akram-Lodhi, S.M. Borras Jr and C. Kay (eds), *Land, poverty and livelihoods in an era of globalization: Perspectives from developing and transition countries*, London: Routledge, pp. 1–40.

Chatthip Nartsupha (1986) 'The village economy in pre-capitalist Thailand', in Seri Phongphit (ed.), *Back to the roots: Village and self-reliance in a Thai context*, Bangkok: Rural Development Documentation Centre.

Chatthip Nartsupha (1996) 'The village economy in pre-capitalist Thailand', in M.C. Hoadley and C. Gunnarsson (eds.), *The village concept in the transformation of rural Southeast Asia, studies from Indonesia, Malaysia and Thailand*, Richmond, Surrey: Curzon.

Chatthip Nartsupha (1999) *The Thai village economy in the past*, Chiang Mai, Thailand: Silkworm Books (transl. Chris Baker and Pasuk Phongpaichit).

Dercon, S. (2006) *Rural poverty: Old challenges in new contexts*, GPRG-WPS-072, Global Poverty Research Group, downloaded from: http://www.gprg.org/pubs/workingpapers/pdfs/gprg-wps-072.pdf, accessed 15 December.

Elson, R.E. (1997) *The end of the peasantry in Southeast Asia: A social and economic history of peasant livelihood, 1800–1990s*, Basingstoke: Macmillan.

Esara P. (2004) '"Women will keep the household": The mediation of work and family by female labor migrants in Bangkok', *Critical Asian Studies*, 36: 199–216.

Jones, H. and Sirinan Kittisuksathit (2003) 'International labour migration and quality of life: Findings from rural Thailand', *International Journal of Population Geography*, 9: 517–30.

Jones, H. and Tieng Pardthaisong (1999) 'The impact of overseas labour migration on rural Thailand: Regional, community and individual dimensions', *Journal of Rural Studies*, 15(1): 35–47.

Mills, M.B. (1997) 'Contesting the margins of modernity: Women, migration, and consumption in Thailand', *American Ethnologist*, 24: 37–61.

Mills, M.B. (1999) *Thai women in the global labor force: Consumed desires, contested selves*, New Brunswick, NJ: Rutgers University Press.

Molle, F. (2003) 'Knowledge in the making: A brief retrospective of village-level studies in the Chao Phraya Delta during the 20th century', in F. Molle and Thippawal Srijantr (eds), *Thailand's Rice Bowl: Perspectives on agricultural and social change in the Chao Phraya Delta*, Studies in Contemporary Thailand 12, Bangkok: White Lotus, pp. 11–35.

Molle, F. and Thippawal Srijantr (eds.) (2003) *Thailand's Rice Bowl: Perspectives on Agricultural and Social Change in the Chao Phraya Delta*, Studies in Contemporary Thailand 12, Bangkok: White Lotus.

Molle, F. and Thippawal Srijantr (1999) *Agrarian change and the land system in the Chao Phraya Delta*, DORAS-DELTA research report no. 6, ORSTOM, Bangkok: Kasetsart University.

Parnwell, M.J.G. (2002) 'Coping with crisis and migration "reversal" in Thailand', in P.P. Masina (ed.), *Rethinking development in East Asia: From illusory miracle to economic crisis*, Copenhagen: NIAS, pp. 261–82.

Rigg, J. (1989) *International contract labor migration and the village economy: The case of Tambon Don Han, Northeastern Thailand*, papers of the East-West Population Institute, East-West Center, Hawaii, No. 112 (July).

Rigg, J. (2001) *More than the soil: Rural change in Southeast Asia*, Harlow, Essex: Prentice Hall.

Rigg, J. (2002) 'Rural areas, rural people and the Asian crisis: Ordinary people in a globalising world', in P.P. Masina (ed.), *Rethinking development in East Asia: From illusory miracle to economic crisis,* Copenhagen: NIAS, pp. 241–60.

Rigg, J. (2006) 'Land, farming, livelihoods and poverty: Rethinking the links in the Rural South', *World Development,* 34(1): 180–202.

Rigg, J. and Sakunee Nattapoolwat (2001) 'Embracing the global in Thailand: Activism and pragmatism in an era of de-agrarianisation', *World Development,* 29(6): 945–60.

Rigg, J., Suriya Veeravongs, Lalida Veeravongs and Piyawadee Rohitarachoon (2008) 'Re-configuring rural spaces and re-making rural lives in Central Thailand', *Journal of Southeast Asian Studies,* 39(3): 355–81.

Singhanetra-Renard, A. (1999) 'Population mobility and the transformation of the village community in Northern Thailand', *Asia Pacific Viewpoint,* 40(1): 69–87.

Thompson, E.C. (2002) 'Migrant subjectivities and narratives of the *kampung* in Malaysia', *Sojourn,* 17(1): 52–75.

Thompson, E.C. (2003) 'Malay male migrants: Negotiating contested identities in Malaysia', *American Ethnologist,* 30(3): 418–38.

Thompson, E.C. (2004) 'Rural villages and socially urban spaces in Malaysia', *Urban Studies,* 41(12): 2357–76.

Thompson, E.C. (2007) *Unsettling absences: Urbanism in rural Malaysia,* Singapore: NUS Press.

Tomosugi, T. (1995) *Changing features of a rice-growing village in Central Thailand: A fixed-point study from 1967 to 1993,* Tokyo: Centre for East Asian Cultural Studies.

STUDY QUESTIONS

1. How has the spatial pattern of the industrial investment frontier changed in Thailand and what are some of the overarching reasons?
2. In what ways is this novel factory frontier redefining rural space?
3. What is the main focus of this chapter?
4. Identify the following sites in the research area:
   Uthai:
   Tambon Khan Haam:
   Ayuthaya:
   Ban Kahn Haam and Ban Khokmayom:
5. How would you describe the radical reorientation of land use in the Tambon Khan Haam since the 1980s?
6. Where is the Rojana Industrial Park located and how many factories can be found there?
7. How many people are employed at the Rojana Industrial Park and where do they come from?
8. How would you characterize Ban Khan Haam and Ban Khokmayom up to the 1960s?
9. What has happened to agriculture in these two villages since the 1960s?
10. Why were Ban Khan Haam and Ban Khokmayom selected for this study?
11. What is one of the main distinctions between Ban Khokmayom and Ban Khan Haam?
12. Why did farming start to become too limited as a sole economic activity and what happened in the 1980s and 1990s?
13. With the building of the Rojana Industrial Park, what happened to land prices and environmental conditions?

14. The progressive dissociation of the village in spatial, social, economic, and livelihood terms since the 1970s means there have been many changes in these areas transforming the traditional village. What are some of those changes listed?

15. Skilled, semi-skilled, and unskilled (casual) work, very largely located outside the boundaries of the village, provided the main occupations for one half of adults in the two villages. What does this mean for the majority of all adults who are building their livelihoods in the area?

16. When did villagers start selling their land and why?

17. Through to the 1970s, the village was self-sufficient in food and little was purchased. What have been the purchasing problems since the 1970s?

18. The researchers stated that they identify a dissociation (separated from) of the traditional village community, they do not see a dissolution (break up) of the village. What do they mean by this and what is ironic about this?

19. Why do the researchers say that mobility is taking on a new guise?

20. What are the two key issues emphasized in this chapter?

Chapter 13 Snapshot
Firm Linkages, Innovation and the Evolution of Urban Systems

I chose this article to extend our understanding of urban systems beyond the Christaller model. The more globalized the world becomes, the more everything else around us changes—sometimes in dramatic ways and sometimes in ways that are slow and subtle, but no less powerful. One of the characteristics of globalization has to do with the power of communication channels. Before the advent of electronic media, the only way to communicate with someone at a distance was either to travel there or physically send a written message by relatively slow transportation means. This greatly limited the interaction capability of cities and towns to those that were in relatively close proximity. The towns that grew were most often on a transportation line—a river, a major road, or later, the railroad. Travel distance was an important element in a city's size and relative place in the hierarchy of a network of cities. This is one of the dynamics fundamental to the Christaller model. These networks most typically "link neighbouring towns and cities located on the same regional or national territory" (215). Increasingly today, however, in contrast to the Christaller model of embedded hierarchies, "cities also have relationships with more distant competitors, especially in specialised networks which is more and more the case in the current context of an increasingly global economy …" (215). As a result of digital communication and overnight travel just about anywhere, "the multiple links connecting towns and cities can go anywhere" (215). Cities thrive on interaction with other cities and their evolution and growth are "influenced or limited by the towns and cities in the same interaction networks" (215). The structure of these urban systems is not limited to physical proximity alone, but is shaped by recurrent interaction patterns (215). Unlike the Christaller model that uses distance (range of a good, threshold) as a prime factor in developing its hierarchy, the paper by Rozenblat and Pumain focus on the "gradual emergence of an urban system on the scale of Europe through the interaction created by firm [business] linkages" (216). The "firm linkages" model put forward in this article suggests that size of population, gross product, or even influence "can be defined by the relative position of a city in interaction networks (centrality, betweenness) as well as by the urban attributes representing the cumulative effects of that position over time" (216). The current article presents the results of a survey illustrating the gradual emergence of an urban system on the scale of Europe through the interactions created by firm linkages. A subsidiary owned by a multinational firm in a foreign country is interpreted as a direct interaction with the city where the subsidiary is owned. The authors examine the position of cities in these ownership networks, which provides insights about the main factor in a city's capacity to participate in the formation of a system of cities on the European scale (216).

CITIES AND THEIR NETWORKS IN EUROPE

The ways in which cities become linked throughout Europe increases European integration. Linkage implies networking and expansion of interaction; in fact, "urban development can no longer be understood … without considering the networks and systems to which cities belong" (216). When we speak of global cities, we are talking about cities that have such transnational connections that they can actually challenge states. Global cities continue to raise "new theoretical questions about the role of cities in the globalisation of the economy …" to the effect that "the changing status of cities and regions in a context of weakening nation-states" challenges the very governance of nation-states. We find that increasingly these global cities actually negotiate "directly with the actors involved in building global networks" (216). Your authors, Rozenblat and Pumain, point to the airline industry as an example. It is the airline companies themselves along with airports that negotiate directly with cities they will use and how the networks will develop that connect cities. The airline industry is a good example because it depends on efficient networking. "In more and more situations, the economic competitiveness of places is now assessed from the perspective of networks" and this is true for urban development itself as well; it can "no longer be understood (and perhaps never was) without considering the networks and systems to which cities belong" (216).

One of the traditional ways to evaluate the status of a global city is by "a scale of urban attributes" (216) such as population, gross product, number of multinational companies, and other economic activities. This will enable us to compare cities and even rank them in a hierarchy from those with strongest global city characteristics to weakest. Table 13.1 shows a comparison of 180 European cities in the European Union, "using a set of 15 synthetic indicators of their global weight or influence" (216). This, however, doesn't tell us anything about the linkages *between* cities. So, a second way to evaluate global cities has to do with "how they are connected by a subset of links or flows in one or several networks" (216). Our authors classified cities "according to their global influence" (217) and devised "four different principles of spatial ordering and distribution of international functions …" (217) two of which specifically have to do with a city's hierarchical networking and its regional cross border integration. The other two principles relate to national integration and selective specialisation (217). One way to assess the linkage between cities is to note the number of multinational headquarters located there. On one hand, this is an attribute of the city (node) itself, but it also suggests linkages (networks) to other cities in other countries. The map in Figure 13.1 represents the distribution of multinational firm headquarters in Europe. This map reveals that "besides the dominance of London and Paris, many headquarters are still located in old industrial cities of the Ruhr, and they include new activities such as banking, insurance, and new technologies" (218). Banking is a significant attribute for evaluating a city's level of networking and integration because "banking networks are now multinational and use the upper part of the national urban systems for locating their branches" (see Figure 13.2, 219). Major stock exchanges also indicate linkage and flow between cities as much as their presence can be considered an attribute of a specific city: "The major stock exchanges in Europe are located in only four cities: London, Paris, Frankfurt, and Luxembourg. They concentrate 80 percent of European financial flows…" (218)

Transnational flows certainly rely on telecommunications for electronic transfers of funds and information. Does this mean that in the 21st century digital communication has made the strategy of spatial location irrelevant? Is the Christaller model no longer valid? Our authors find that "physical accessibility still contributes to the development of every international function" (218). The map in Figure 13.3 measures accessibility for each of the 180 European cities they compared based on the "number of cities that can be reached by plane or train in a one-day return trip. Despite the hierarchical ranking produced by the airline connections of large capitals, many places located in border regions are also highly accessible, thanks to the high density of the neighbouring cities. This is the case in the Rhine Valley in Germany (especially Düsseldorf), in northern Italy with Bologna, and in France with Lyons" (218). So the concept of proximity, that underlies the Christaller model, is still important; however, instead of evaluating city size, range of a good, and threshold, "[o]ther significant correlations are found with regional urban density and proximity to international borders. With an equal population size, the number of cities that are accessible from a European city is fairly highly correlated with the number of international banks located in that city … the number of conferences held there … and, to a lesser extent, the number of headquarters, … tourists, … and international fairs" (219). Based on our authors' survey of 180 European cities, then, "there is some evidence that regional and long-range accessibility together with urban hierarchy, national divisions and economic specialisation are the basic structures influencing the integration process of cities in Europe. Their effects are combined differently depending on the nature of each function and the city's location in the European urban system, since the international division of labour creates some specialisation in each city and corresponding specialised inter-urban connections" (219).

An Example of the Inter-urban Connection Process

Our authors were curious about how inter-urban connections or linkage can be created by the locational decisions multinational firms make when selecting a European city site. "The spatial strategies of firms aim to select locations that supply many kinds of local resources (natural and human resources, knowledge, infrastructure and institutions) to serve their purposes" (220). Multinational firms will locate in places that best suit their purposes and give them the best competitive advantage. "There is thus an interaction between private global strategies and local attractiveness" (220). The ways that multinational firms choose locations to benefit the building or strengthening their overall network and integration could be called "'network economies' by analogy with 'agglomeration economies'" (220).

Source Material: Two Surveys of Foreign Firms' Networks in Europe

Rozenblat and Pumain conducted two additional surveys of multinational firms and their subsidiaries in Europe to get at firm ownership linkages and locations. The surveys were conducted in 1990 and 1996 gathering "information on the 300 largest European firms (i.e. headquartered in Europe), about the exact location of all the entities they owned in other European countries, their size (turnover and number of employees), their sector of activity and their function in the firm" (220). A subsidiary is a company owned by another company, and our authors "collected a sample of approximately 3,000 subsidiaries in 1990 (western Europe) and another sample of more than 4,000 subsidiaries in 1996 (western and central Europe)" (221). Looking at these ownership linkages has seldom been done, but they are "a marker of the decision-making and power channels between firms" (221). Rozenblat and Pumain have characterized this subsidiary ownership to be based in part "on the degree of centralisation of the decision-making process" (220) that also depends on their functions within the overall company. For example, <u>headquarters</u> are more concerned with strategic functions than administrative ones. They focus more on "strategic policy, common principles, oversight and benchmarking tools" (221). These are becoming more and more centralized along with <u>purchasing</u> "in order to take advantage of economies of scale" (221). <u>Production</u> on the other hand, is more regionally based, taking advantage of specific places or regions that contribute best to the product, or use of geographic location to best "capitalise on the specific resources of a region" (221). The project structure regarding <u>research and development</u> "fosters association between researchers, engineers, and marketing specialists, without necessarily bringing them spatially closer" and "the <u>marketing</u> function seems to be the link between all the organisational scales, because it is present at all levels" (222). With so many levels of firm ownership identified, which one should be used to identify the presence of a firm or its subsidiary in a particular city? The commonality among all five of these levels of firm ownership is their legal structure, so our authors count all five to "describe the economic linkages between cities in the globalisation process" and illustrate some examples of firm networks through ownership linkages in Figure 13.5. "The location of the headquarters of three large firms is represented by a triangle (and) the links between cities are legal ownership relationships (subsidiaries at least 50 percent owned)…" (222). On studying Figure 13.5, we can see that "one headquarters can own several subsidiaries which in turn can own several sub-subsidiaries and so on;" (222) that is, firm ownership can, in some cases be very indirect, relatively independent, with decision-making occurring at all levels (222). Thus, outside of the multinational company's headquarters, there can be several levels of subsidiaries and sub-subsidiaries creating "three 'types' of intermediate cities": bridgehead, outpost, and turntable cities as described in Figure 13.7 (225). Rozenblat and Pumain use a stream analogy to describe the relationship of subsidiary and sub-subsidiary firms to the headquarters as well as distinguishing whether their locations are in domestic or foreign territories:

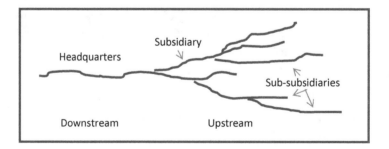

<u>The bridgehead city</u> has one or several subsidiaries of a firm *in a foreign country* which, in turn have one or more subsidiaries *in the same country.* The bridgehead city "is used as an entry point for foreign investment

… and connected to foreign cities by links of subordination (e.g. firm control) and downstream it dominates other cities in its own territory through linkages of control" (224). Examples of these intermediate cities such as the primate cities of London, Paris, Vienna, Milan, Madrid, Barcelona and Brussels, "act as entry points for foreign investment" and are the largest cities in each country. "From these central cities foreign countries thus radiate to other cities in the same country" (224). The bridgehead city usually reinforces national or regional urban hierarchies because they magnify the central role of these cities. This is essential in the early stage of capital diffusion (224). "These cities provide companies with the necessary information and knowledge about a whole national territory. These cities are also selected for their accessibility in terms of transport, institutional contacts, etc. This process reinforces the need for central administative offices and infrastructure in these cities, which in turn enhances the attractiveness of the cities" (226).

A second type of intermediate city is the outpost city. Here the authors "measured the number of *domestic subsidiaries controlling sub-subsidiary companies abroad.*" Again Rozenblat and Pumain use the stream analogy to indicate the outpost city's place in the urban hierarchy of firm linkages: "Upstream it is connected to a city on its own territory where the headquarters of the group are located, and downstream it is directly connected to foreign cities in which it controls subsidiaries. These outpost cities act as a springboard towards foreign countries, as is the case for Paris, London, and Vienna" (226, italics added). Finally, there are multinational 'turntable' cities. These are cities where "a number of *foreign subsidiaries own sub-subsidiaries abroad*" (226, italics added). A good example of a multinational turntable city is Amsterdam. "The function of these intermediate subdsidiaries is primarily fianncial. They also take advantage of Amsterdam's international functions, which are more developed in the sectors of finance and air transport, which are the activities most strongly related to the attractiveness for the location of registered offices" (227). In all cases, multinational corporations that have such firm linkages, bridgehead, outpost, and multinational turntable, must pay attention to the rules and regulations in those countries in which they have subsidiaries or sub-subsidiaries. Nationality matters.

Centrality and hierarchical innovation diffusion as characteristics of inter-city linkages and their evolution

Centrality also matters in relation to accessibility. "On the basis of the relationship of control between headquarters and their subsidiaries, one can define relative measures of centrality among cities. In geography the center always represents a place that dominates relationships based on unequal exchange … . Centers and peripheries are thus distributed among the nodes of a network … representing the geographical positions of the headquarters of the group relative to their foreign subsidiaries" (228). Between 1990 and 1996, the dates of the study conducted by the authors, the position of most central cities have been strengthened regarding their networks of control: "this is the case for the London-Paris-Brussels triangle, as well as for German, Dutch and Swiss cities in the centre of Europe" (228). In fact, these cities "can be considered to form a 'European urban system' representing the major centres connected through European economic integration. The most central cities are above all those for which the ratio of the number of headquarters to the number of foreign subsidiaries is highest" (228).

The very process of European investment in foreign markets in this way "can be seen as a special case of the hierarchical diffusion of an innvation in a multinational urban system … and is one of the organisational innovations of the last third of the twentieth century" (229). There is a strategy to this investment. First, firms must enlarge their own market by locating in territories outside their own country. Second they need to pay attention to local demand in diversifying their product or need for labor. Third, they need to be alert to ways they can make use of comparative advantage in their new location. So, what criteria do such firms use in order to select a location in the first place? "First they select locations that offer good connections in a whole country and that minimise the risks associated with the investment . . . . From a city's perspective, that innovation requires a minimum level of international functions in order to provide a favourable business environment and suitable living conditions for foreign firms' employees" (229).

> Different sectors are at different stages of the diffusion process of globalisation. The most advanced sectors in this process have a higher number of foreign subsidiaries. At the dates of both surveys, chemicals, electrical and electronics sectors account for more than half of the sample of foreign subsidiaries. These activities are also among the most concentrated in the large cities. Subsidiaries in the construction sector and financial services are the most concentrated in cities in 1990. The concentration of business services subsidies in the largest cities increased between 1990 and 1996, whereas most other types of activity seem to have diffused to smaller cities. Some urban specialisations appear in the subsidiaries hosted, very often reinforcing existing local specialties: with equal activity and city size Amsterdam and Zurich are specialized in finance activities and business services (229).

Paradoxically, the cities that accommodate the most subsidiaries are less strong when it comes to specializations. This is because they "have a more diverse range of activities: their markets (consumer and labour, infrastructure and hosting capacity) increase their attractiveness for all types of activity from abroad" (229). There are other effects that affect the quality and depth of innovation diffusion of foreign subsidiaries. The size of the cities are affected by their nationality, and "the level of functions not only reflects the size that cities have acquired over a long period, mainly in line with the development of the national urban system to which they belong… . a country's openness also determines its cities' average capacity to host foreign multinational corporations" (229). Multinational corporations that seek to diffuse must pay attention both to the geography of a country's urban structures as well as national structural characteristics. "It is, therefore, important to keep in mind the spatial pattern of European cities" (231).

INNOVATION AND EVOLUTIONARY THEORY OF URBAN SYSTEMS

So, how can we generalize some of what we have learned from Rozenblat and Pumain's studies? What have we come to understand about the macro level of a system of cities on the scale of Europe? First of all, that cities are integrated through a multitude of networks composed of "exchanges between people, goods, and information that circulate continuously from one city to another" (231). On one hand there are some principles of urban development that are similar to all countries regardless of their period in history. There is a "principle of hierarchical organisation, including important scaling properties for attributes such as size, spacing, and level of socio-economic activities of towns and cities. These features were previously formalised by central place theory" (231). Christaller's model is still valid and "hierarchical structure and spacing regularities are still relevant" (232). Like Christaller's model, the hierarchical structure of urban systems at the scale of Europe "is produced by the multiple interactions occurring between individual towns and cities. Urban hierarchy and functional diversity are emergent properties stemming from a co-evolution process of towns and cities which are cooperating and competing for access to socio-economic innovations, by attempting to secure better relative positions in spatial and social networks" (233).

CONCLUSION

These studies also have addressed some areas of weakness with Christaller's model, where some "geographers have criticised that theory because it is static and based upon a restricted set of urban activities (mainly services to residents) which does not consider specialisations in non-central functions (for instance industry and tourism)" (232). Rozenblat and Pumain have superimposed two processes "on the classical hierarchical diffusion process" (235). First they reinforce the importance of specialisation in multinational activities for cities already engaged in international business, especially financial business (as in the case for Brussels, Luxembourg and Zurich) …" (235). They also emphasize the importance of "national borders, which guide the location of foreign firms towards national capitals regardless of their relative size within the European urban system and towards cities located close to international borders (which also gives an advantage to cities in the smallest countries, which are on the whole more 'open' to external exchanges than the largest countries)" (235). Rozenblat and Pumain believe that the European system has the potential to be reshaped by these two processes and that much more work on this topic needs to be done.

13. FIRM LINKAGES, INNOVATION AND THE EVOLUTION OF URBAN SYSTEMS

By Celine Rozenblat and Denise Pumain

INTRODUCTION

Because a city cannot be conceived of as an isolated system but is always part of a *system of cities* (Berry 1964), interaction between cities is an essential component of the dynamics of urban systems. Each town or city is a persistent and relatively autonomous entity whose evolution is influenced or limited by the towns and cities in the same interaction networks (Pred 1977). It has been demonstrated that competition between towns and cities for resources and growth is the main driving force in the dynamics of systems of cities, which also explains the pervasiveness of their structure (Pumain 2000). Most systems of cities link neighbouring towns and cities located on the same regional or national territory. But cities also have relationships with more distant competitors, especially in specialised networks, which is more and more the case in the current context of an increasingly global economy. Therefore, the hierarchical organisation of cities in systems of cities is no longer an inclusive one (if ever it was, as a too strict acceptation of the Christallerian model of embedded hierarchical levels would suggest), since the multiple links connecting towns and cities can go anywhere. However, many of the relationships between urban actors are recurrent or use the same communication channels. Recurrent interaction patterns shape the structure of urban systems. This structure is universally characterised by strong hierarchical differentiation (Pumain 2006). Several orders of magnitude separate the importance of towns and cities, in terms of population, gross product or influence. This importance can be defined by the relative position of a given city in interaction networks (centrality, betweenness), as well as by the urban attributes representing the cumulative effects of that position over time. Interaction flows in turn reflect (or are induced by) this structure of the urban system, since they are generated by the attributes of one city rather than another.

We therefore share P.J. Taylor's (2001) view that there is a need for more studies about networks of cities, particularly studies that draw on databases of inter-urban flows. This paper presents the results of a survey illustrating the gradual emergence of an urban system on the scale of Europe, through the interactions created by firm linkages. A subsidiary owned by a multinational firm in a foreign country is interpreted as a directed interaction between the city where the headquarters are located and the city where the subsidiary is owned (after the foreign subsidiary is set up or acquired). We examine the position of cities in these ownership networks, which provides insights about the main factors in a city's capacity to participate in the formation of a system of cities on the European scale.

CITIES AND THEIR NETWORKS IN EUROPE

The integration of European society and territory is achieved mainly through the development of new linkages between cities, especially the largest. But, even if the familiar process of hierarchical diffusion of innovation in urban systems (Pred 1977) is at work here, these linkages cannot be considered in principle as being limited to only a few cities or capitals. National urban systems as a whole are or will be involved in the expansion of interactions between territories at the international level. However, after a wave of comparative studies of large sets of European towns and cities in the 1980s and 1990s (Brunet 1989; Conti and Spriano 1990; Pumain and Saint-Julien 1996; Cattan *et al.* 1999), there has been a shift in research towards monographs addressing a small number of global cities (Sassen 1991; Hall 1995).

Global cities raised new theoretical questions about the role of cities in the globalisation of the economy (Friedmann 1986). Meanwhile, the changing status of cities and regions in a context of weakening nation-states was everywhere challenging the forms of their governance (Scott 2001). On account of regional decentralisation and increasingly independent urban management, 'city-regions' began negotiating directly with the actors involved in building global networks. For instance, the deregulation of the airline industry in 1993 gave a stronger role to airlines, airports and their strategic agreements in the organisation of the air transport networks connecting cities (Storper 1997; Graham 1998). Urban development can no longer be understood (and perhaps never was) without considering the networks and systems to which cities belong. In more and more situations, the economic competitiveness of places is now assessed from the perspective of networks. For example, the European Commission recommends a policy for developing polycentric urban systems to improve the capacity of the European space to be equitable and redistribute key activities (European Communities 2001; ESPON 2003). On another scale, urban managers frequently request assessments of the position and influence of their city in the European urban system, but there is a dearth of comparable urban data.

Relative positions in multinational networks can be defined according to two kinds of complementary information. To describe the power of nodal cities, their importance can be compared using a scale of urban attributes, or by measuring how they are connected by a subset of links or flows in one or several networks. These two methods of measurement are not opposite in significance, since both types of data can be represented either as attributes of the node, or by the intensity of some linkages (there is always a dual representation in networks). Even when the analysis is strictly limited to the relative position of the nodes in terms of their accessibility within a network, this structural analysis can give rise to different rankings of the nodes: a recent study of the worldwide air transport network (Guimera *et al.* 2005) demonstrated that the most connected cities (the nodes with the highest score or number of incident connections) are not necessarily the most central in the network (that is, cities through which most shortest paths go). Apart from physical networks, most studies of the global power of cities, in terms of the importance of their international activities or their actual or estimated linkages, give figures relating to economic activities or multinational firms (Cohen 1981; Rozenblat and Pumain 1993; Taylor and Walker 2001). Another recent study conducted for the public management board of the City of Marseilles, Euromediterranee, and Datar (the territorial development and regional action division of France's ministry of regional development), compared 180 European cities (urban areas with a population of at least 200,000 in 2000) in the European Union, Norway and Switzerland using a set of 15 synthetic indicators of their global weight or influence (Table 13.1) (Rozenblat and Cicille 2003).

The classification of cities according to their global influence revealed four different principles of spatial ordering and distribution of international functions (Rozenblat and Pumain 2004), satisfactorily validating the theoretical approach previously suggested by Cattan *et al.* (1999) and put forward in ESPON (2003):

1. principle of hierarchical networking;
2. principle of national integration;
3. principle of selective specialisation;
4. principle of regional cross-border integration.

Table 13.1—Fifteen indicators of global influence

Indicators	Source
Population of urban agglomerations 2000	*National censuses*
Population change (1950–1990)	*Geopolis, 1993*
Harbour traffic 1999	*Journal de la marine marchande, ESPO*
Airline passengers 2001	*Airports Council International*
Airline and railway accessibility 2002	*Amadeus Global Travel Distribution*
Headquarters of large European firms	*Forbes, 2002*
Stock exchanges	*The Bankers Almanac 2002 (Reed BI)*
Tourist overnight stays 2001	*National censuses and tourist sites*
Fairs and exhibitions 2002–2003	*Paris Chamber of Commerce*
International conferences 1993–2000	*Union des Associations*
Museums 2002	*Internationales International Council of Museums (ICOM)*
Cultural sites and events	*Michelin 2001*
Students 2001	*National or regional institutes*
Scientific publications	*Institute for Scientific Information (ISI) 2000*
Research networks	*CORDIS, 2002*

Source: Rozenblat and Cicille (2003).

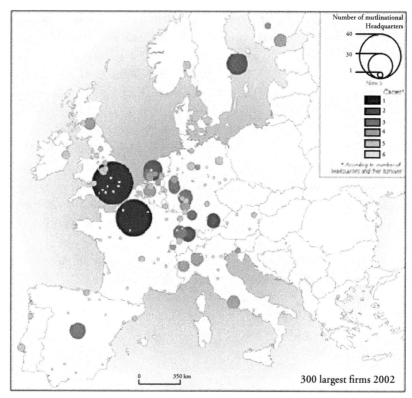

Figure 13.1   Headquarters in European cities.

Particularly in the case of network functions, the combination of these principles creates complex effects, exhibiting at the same time high concentrations in a few cities and a wide variety of urban configurations.

For example, the map representing the distribution of multinational firms' headquarters (Figure 13.1) reveals that, besides the dominance of London and Paris, many headquarters are still located in old industrial cities of the Ruhr, and they include new activities such as banking, insurance and new technologies. In the case of banking, concentration, which occurred earlier than in other sectors, increased the size of financial groups while reducing the number of banks. Banking networks are now multinational and use the upper part of the national urban systems for locating their branches (Figure 13.2). The major stock exchanges in Europe are located in only four cities: London, Paris, Frankfurt and Luxembourg. They concentrate 80 percent of European financial flows (Pagetti 1998). German cities are organised into a polycentric system of eight cities with stock exchanges. Other locations of European stock exchanges linked to Euronext include Lisbon, Porto, Valencia and Bilbao.

Even if the networks of economic activities are largely coordinated through telecommunication systems, physical accessibility still contributes to the development of every international function. As an illustration, we provide an accessibility map,which measures for each of the 180 European cities the number of cities that can be reached by plane or train in a one-day return trip (Figure 13.3). Despite the hierarchical ranking produced by the airline connections of large capitals, many places located in border regions are also highly accessible, thanks to the high density of neighbouring cities. This is the case in the Rhine Valley in Germany (especially Dusseldorf), in northern Italy with Bologna, and in France with Lyons. Accessibility is theoretically related

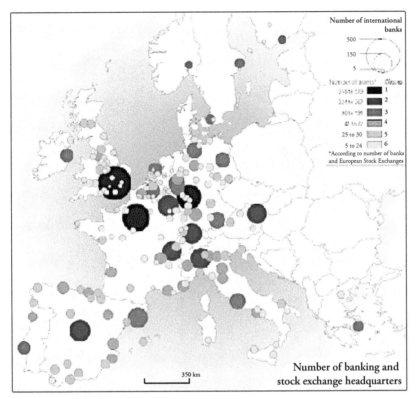

Figure 13.2   Stock Exchanges in European cities.

to the centrality of cities within all urban systems, because their potential for trade depends on their position. Hence good international accessibility is favourable to the development of international functions. We observed that our indicator is only partly related to a city's size. Other significant correlations are found with regional urban density and proximity to international borders. With an equal population size, the number of cities that are accessible from a European city is fairly highly correlated with the number of international banks located in that city (R = 0.76), the number of conferences held there (R = 0.7) and, to a lesser extent, the number of headquarters (R = 0.49), tourists (0.43) and international fairs (0.41).

According to that study (Rozenblat and Pumain 1993, 2004), there is some evidence that regional and long-range accessibility, together with urban hierarchy, national divisions and economic specialisation, are the basic structures influencing the integration process of cities in Europe. Their effects are combined differently depending on the nature of each function and the city's location in the European urban system, since the international division of labour creates some specialisation in each city and corresponding specialised inter-urban connections.

AN EXAMPLE OF THE INTER-URBAN CONNECTION PROCESS

We shall examine here how a specific kind of inter-urban connection is created through the location process of multinational firms in European cities. The spatial strategies of firms aim to select locations that supply many kinds of local resources (natural and human resources, knowledge, infrastructure and institutions) to

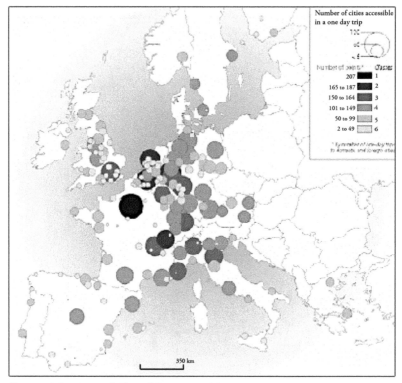

Figure 13.3   Accessibility of European cities.

serve their purposes. The multiple locations of a multinational firm reflect complementary choices and may create networks linking different cities. Each city where a firm is located contributes to the competitiveness of that firm's economic network . There is thus an interaction between private global strategies and local attractiveness. The wealth and resources of each territory combine with global economic and political actors' behaviour to form a complex system (Dicken and Malmberg 2001). The associated advantages probably constitute a new kind of external economies, which can be called 'network economies' by analogy with 'agglomeration economies'. In order to understand the interdependencies created between urban developments (Storper 1997) through this process, we have decided to observe directly some effective linkages created by multinational firms between European cities.

Source material: two surveys of foreign firms' networks in Europe

We conducted two surveys (1990 and 1996) of foreign subsidiaries of multinational firms in Europe (Rozenblat 1992; Rozenblat and Pumain 1993; Rozenblat 1997). We collected information on the 300 largest European firms (i.e. headquartered in Europe), about the exact location of all the entities they owned in other European countries, their size (turnover and number of employees), their sector of activity and their function in the firm. The questionnaire, which was sent by post, asked each subsidiary the date it was set up or acquired, its activity and functional role in the group and various size-related criteria for the purposes of comparison. Although most companies simply sent back their annual reports, without answering our

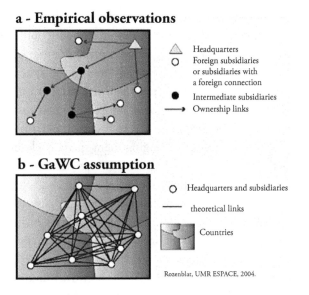

Figure 13.4   Firm linkages.

questions precisely, we extracted information from the annual reports and requested additional information by letter or telephone where required.

We thus obtained homogeneous and usable information about thousands of subsidiaries, including their addresses, functions, activities and ownership links with subsubsidiaries. From one-third of the companies at each date (approximately 100 of the largest 300 groups) we collected a sample of approximately 3,000 subsidiaries in 1990 (western Europe) and another sample of more than 4,000 in 1996 (western and central Europe). Based on the links of secondary ownership describing up to five successive levels of branching, we established the architecture of the ownership linkages connecting them.

Firm ownership linkages have rarely been used to describe the structure of city networks, although they are highly significant. The architecture of ownership linkages is a marker of the decision-making and power channels between firms. Financial ownership controls the strategic orientation of the subsidiaries. However, not all firms are organised in the same way. There are differences in the structure of holdings depending on the degree of centralisation of the decision-making process. For example, in 64 percent of the 81 cases analysed by Francfort *et al.* (1995), the company organisation is highly centralised. In concrete terms, this involves a 'system of control' operated either by means of 'contracts' for subsequent control of results (60 percent of the cases) or by 'standards, means or objectives' for prior planning of actions (40 percent) (Mintzberg 1994; Francfort *et al.* 1995). The architecture of ownership linkages thus reflects the hierarchical decision-making process in a majority of groups of companies. According to many specialists, these features are even more important in the case of multinational corporations (Veltz 1998; Zimmermann 1995; Michalet 1997; Mucchielli 1998; Bouinot 2004).

The circulation of decision-making between the many entities of a multinational firm also varies depending on their functions. Headquarters perform fewer and fewer administrative functions to concentrate on strategic functions. These strategic functions, including strategic policy, common principles, oversight and benchmarking tools, are becoming more and more centralised. At the same time, purchasing is increasingly centralised to generate economies of scale. But 'it is rare that production is formally organised on a world level' (Veltz 1998). Production is generally organised into product or geographical divisions, for which the continent appears to be the most relevant scale. Between units on the same continent, coordination is closer and a decision to concentrate on some sites can put them in competition with each other. The marketing function seems to be the link between all the organisational scales, because it is present at all levels. In the case of research and development, the project structure fosters association between researchers, engineers and marketing specialists, without necessarily bringing them spatially closer (Zarifian 1993).

This description of operations within multinational groups demonstrates the decisive role of the legal structure of firms in their concrete organisation. We therefore decided to use the legal structure to describe the economic linkages between cities in the globalisation process (Figure 13.4). Instead of using the GaWC method, which implies that cities are connected to all the other cities where a subsidiary of the same group is located (Figure 13.4b), we use the network of firm ownership in the strict sense to determine which cities are actually connected by ownership linkages (Figure 13.4a). Contrary to the GaWC's research, we do not create more information than we have in our data. The networks linking cities through the location of multinational firms that we show thus represent the minimum but actual inter-firm networks, whereas the GaWC maps show the maximum possible networks.

Examples of firm networks through ownership linkages

In Figure 13.5, the location of the headquarters of three large firms is represented by a triangle. The links between cities are legal ownership relationships (subsidiaries at least 50 percent owned) either between the headquarters and subsidiaries located in a foreign city (the size of the circle representing the city is proportional to the number of branches) or between a national subsidiary and its sub-subsidiary located in a foreign city. These three examples of firm networks demonstrate that firm ownership linkages between cities in different countries are sometimes very indirect, highlighting the role of intermediate subsidiary companies in the globalisation process. One headquarters can own several subsidiaries, which in turn own several sub-subsidiaries, and so on. A firm's foreign subsidiaries are not necessarily owned or directly controlled by its European headquarters, but by intermediate headquarters. This legal organisation may reflect a decentralised management organisation, based on a regional and/or sector division of labour or markets. Several decision-making levels (continental, national, by branch or product) can remain relatively independent from each other (as shown by Veltz 1998; Crozet et al. 2004).

This representation of the effective linkages between firms considerably improves on the description that is generally made of the globalisation process using data on foreign direct investment (FDI) (Michalet 1999; Mucchielli 1998). FDI is calculated by national statistics offices from capital flows across international boundaries. These figures do not take into account possible multiple locations of investment within a foreign country. Also, because they do not identify the national origin of headquarters, they do not show the globalisation networks created by firm ownership linkages. FDI data thus produce a fragmented image of the globalisation of companies, failing to show their overall strategies. This image is not without interest, in particular for representing spatial interactions between countries, but is only a partial view of complex multinational economic networks.

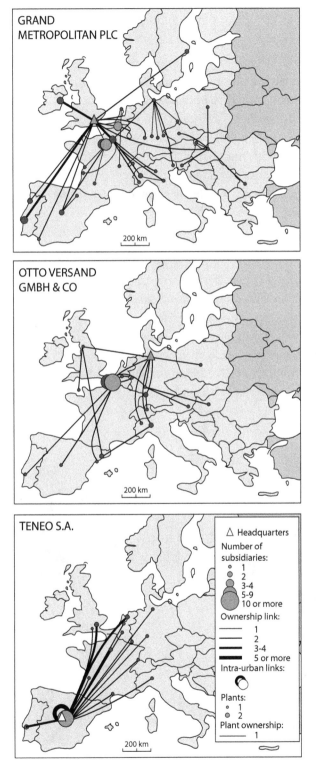

Figure 13.5   Three examples of multinational firms'
ownership networks in 1996.

Types of intermediate cities as a distinctive characteristic of city networks according to firm ownership linkages

Using 100 firm networks, we calculate the links connecting two cities *i* and *j* according to the number of times that a firm located in city *i* owns a subsidiary in city *j* (Figure 13.6). One link of legal ownership represents one link between city *i* where the headquarters of firm *K (A, B* or *C* on Figure 13.6) is located and city *j* where the subsidiary of firm *K* is located. To construct the graph of connections between cities through firm ownership linkages, we look at the orientation of the links. In order to describe the basic networks connecting cities through multinational firm ownership linkages, a first qualitative distinction can be made according to the relative position of cities where subsidiaries are located. A comparison of the nationalities of the three cities—the city of the intermediate subsidiary, the city of its headquarters, the city of its sub-subsidiary companies—shows up three 'types' of 'intermediate' city (Figure 8.7):

> A: 'Bridgehead' cities. These cities host one or several subsidiaries of a firm in a foreign country; they in turn have one or more subsidiaries in the same country. The bridgehead city is used as an entry point for foreign investment: upstream it is connected to foreign cities by links of subordination (e.g. firm control), and downstream it dominates other cities in its own territory through linkages of economic control. When companies are organised by region, these intermediate headquarters generally control the subsidiaries in the country of investment. Most of these intermediate cities that act as entry points for foreign investment are the largest cities in each country, especially those where the urban system is dominated by primate cities, such as London, Paris, Vienna, Milan, Madrid, Barcelona and Brussels. From these central cities, foreign companies thus radiate to other cities in the same country.

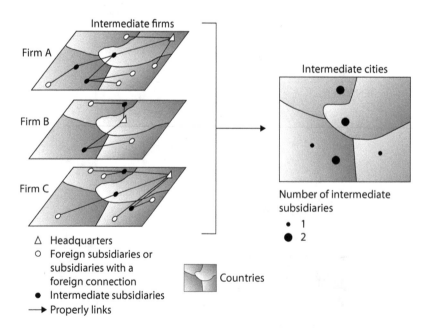

Figure 13.6   From firm linkages to urban networks.

A- Bridgehead Cities

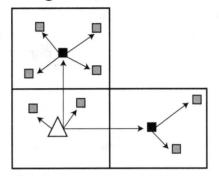

B- Outpost Cities

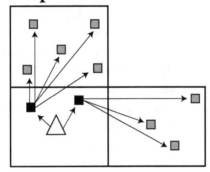

C- Turntable Cities

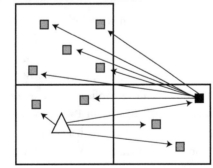

△ Headquarters
■ subsidiary
■ intermediate subsidiary
National borders

Figure 13.7   Intermediate cities in international firm ownership linkages.

However, this type of nodal function has different spatial configurations. For example, Madrid and Barcelona perform this role with the same intensity, but not with the same territorial extension: Madrid controls sub-subsidiary branches of foreign companies all over Spain, whereas Barcelona's range is limited to Catalonia. From this point of view, London is similar to Barcelona: more than half of the foreign sub-subsidiary companies that it controls are located in its own urban area. In general, the bridgehead function reinforces national or regional urban hierarchies by magnifying the central role of some cities, which are essential in the early stages of capital diffusion. These cities provide companies with the necessary information and knowledge about a whole national territory. These cities are also selected for their accessibility in terms of transport, institutional contacts etc. This process reinforces the need for central administrative offices and infrastructure in these cities, which in turn enhances the attractiveness of the cities.

B: 'Outpost' cities. For each city we measured the number of domestic subsidiaries controlling sub-subsidiary companies abroad. The city is used here as a node for foreign direct investment: upstream it is connected to a city on its own territory where the headquarters of the group are located, and downstream it is directly connected to foreign cities in which it controls subsidiaries. These outpost cities act as springboards towards foreign countries, as is the case for Paris, London and Vienna. In other cases, this situation results from the vertical or horizontal integration of companies whose various headquarters have remained fairly independent. Veba, a company present in both our surveys, is typical of this form of organisation. The company is the result of an industrial merger of petrochemical firms (Huls AG, Raab Karcher and Veba Oel headquartered in Essen, and Stinnes Interoil headquartered in Hamburg), energy companies (Preussenelektrika in Hanover), storage firms (in Essen and Lubeck) and wholesale firms (in Essen and Kaiserslautern). Veba's foreign subsidiaries are controlled from the total subset of these cities. It is well known that similar mergers or acquisitions of companies have occurred since the 1990s, with the same intensity in all countries. Conversely, not all urban systems offer companies the same opportunities for maintaining headquarters simultaneously in several places. Whereas German cities (Essen, Stuttgart, Koln-Bonn and to a lesser degree Frankfurt) and some British cities (such as Birmingham) and Austrian cities (such as Linz) can perform the function of headquarters for foreign subsidiary companies, this is less common in French cities other than Paris. In the territory of France, a study of inter-urban command by the headquarters of multi-entity firms confirms, on another level of company organisation, the strong polarisation of companies' national capacity in Paris (Rozenblat 1998). Other French cities may act as small, secondary centres, because they host the headquarters of large national companies. This is the case, for example, of Clermont-Ferrand (Michelin), Lyons (Renault Trucks), Saint-Etienne (Casino) and Strasbourg (Aventis, Kronenbourg). In recent years, headquarters located in French regional capitals have tended to lose strategic power. Indeed, in the past decade, most strategic functions have moved to the capital, whereas an increasing number of entities dedicated to other functions (mainly production) have moved out of Paris (Jourdan 2004).

C: Multinational 'turntable' cities. For each city we counted the number of foreign subsidiaries that own sub-subsidiary companies abroad. Amsterdam seems to play a specific role as an international node for almost half the groups in our sample (in both 1990 and 1996). Many European groups locate foreign subsidiaries in Amsterdam, and these subsidiaries develop sub-subsidiaries abroad. The function of these intermediate subsidiaries is primarily financial. They benefit from the advantageous tax treatment offered by the Netherlands for both foreign subsidiary companies and companies that own other subsidiaries abroad (Mignolet and Pierre 1998). They also take advantage of Amsterdam's international functions, which are more developed than one might assume from its population size (under 2 million, Rozenblat and Cicille 2003). The international functions of Amsterdam are particularly developed in the sectors of finance and air transport, which are the activities most strongly related to attractiveness for the location of registered offices. The city of Luxembourg also plays a similar role, but with less intensity (12 groups from the sample in 1990 and eight in 1996).

In the hierarchical legal organisation of the companies, the intermediate subsidiaries enable cities to maintain positions of both control and dependence at once. Indeed, the cities accommodate the two positions simultaneously because the same subsidiary is at once under the domination of its head office and dominant over its sub-subsidiaries. Crozier and Friedberg (1977) have stressed the essential role of nodes in any organisation. These nodes have a dual function (Crozier and Friedberg 1977:164). On the one hand, for the organisation, they constitute a 'segment of environment', a source of information on the organisation's ability to adapt to the environment (past history, institutions, resources, culture etc.) and thus can be considered as 'reducers of uncertainty'. In addition, for the environment, they represent 'the organisation and its interests'. They form part of 'a permanent process of exchange through which an organisation opens, so to speak selectively, into the broader system in which it takes part, and by which it integrates more or less permanent parts in its own system of action for thus being able to adapt it to its own requirements' (1977:179). For this reason, a group's intermediate subsidiaries are the interfaces between the group and the economic environment and territory. One aim of our approach is to understand the role played by these intermediate subsidiaries between territories, given that their nodal position depends on the 'degree of monopoly available to each partner vis-a-vis the other in both space and time' (Crozier and Friedberg 1977:172). The positions of the intermediate subsidiaries (and the nodal cities that host them) depend on the nationalities of their headquarters and of their sub-subsidiary companies.

Centrality and hierarchical innovation diffusion as characteristics of inter-city linkages and their evolution

The combination of all firms' networks according to their location in cities can give rise to a more general network representing the position of cities within linkages of firm ownership. Because the ownership linkages are oriented, the network is also an oriented graph where the arcs connect a subsidiary-sending city to a subsidiary-receiving city. According to the analysis outlined above, the arcs follow the decision-making path and thus reflect a city's position in the process of European economic integration. In our approach, foreign subsidiaries are considered as being under the direct control of the decisions taken by their headquarters, which can centralise the design of new products, the organisation of production, decisions about training, and industrial and financial strategies. Through a common policy, the headquarters control all the activities of the group's entities and subsidiaries (Dicken 1992). By putting all the foreign subsidiaries under the direct control of the European headquarters, centralisation of decisions within the firm is taken to the extreme. Domestic companies taking part in the globalisation process are not taken into account. This representation is only a partial reflection of the actual operation of groups, since practices may vary from one group to another, and even within the same group, depending on the sector of activity. This step nevertheless makes it possible to map out a system of control-dependence between the cities hosting the headquarters and the cities where the groups' foreign subsidiaries are located. This approach has been used previously by Alan Pred for the United States (1973, 1977), and by Paul Le Fillatre (1964) for France (headquarters-entity links were identified from the first annual survey of firms by INSEE), in order to represent the spatial configuration of economic control between cities.

On the basis of the relationships of control between headquarters and their subsidiaries, one can define relative measures of centrality among cities. In geography, the centre always represents a place that dominates relationships based on unequal exchanges. The exchanges generated by the relationships of subsidiary ownership are indeed asymmetrical, since they include interactions of dependence that arise from strategic decision-making, financial transfers and sometimes human transfers or trade in goods. Centres and peripheries are thus distributed among the nodes of a network shown in the oriented graph representing the geographical positions of the headquarters of the groups relative to their foreign subsidiaries.

We plotted the graph of inter-city linkages F_{ij} through foreign firms' property by using the following equation:

$$F_{ij} = \sum k PL_{kij}$$

where PL_{kij} represents the ownership link between the headquarters located in city i and the subsidiary located in city j (in another country) for the firm k.

The position of each city on the graph of the relationships of control or dependence defines its degree of centrality. Interpreting the cumulated linkages in terms of 'power over' and 'power to' command other cities, means a capacity or a medium (Friedmann 1978; Allen 1997; Taylor *et al.* 2002). The transfer of companies' power to their space of reception is part of the process through which a centre reproduces the conditions of its centrality and a periphery reproduces the conditions of its peripherality. However, the dynamics of cities, considered on the scale of urban systems, are clearly a different process from the centralisation that describes the concentration of power at the level of the internal organisation of institutions, whether economic or associative (as opposed to decentralisation). Furthermore, the location of the centre depends on the geographical scale that is considered, a fact that is usually overlooked in traditional approaches (Myrdal 1957; Hirschmann 1958; Amin 1973; Wallerstein 1980; Reynaud 1981). Depending on the geographical scale under consideration, the centres and peripheries may change role, since a central position in one network can become peripheral in a network on a higher scale.

Within a relatively short period of time, between 1990 and 1996, this system of enterprise control between cities has reinforced urban interdependency on an increasingly vast territory, while remaining highly selective (Figure 13.8). By a process of hierarchical innovation diffusion, the most central cities have strengthened their positions in the networks of control: this is the case for the London-Paris-Brussels triangle, as well as for German, Dutch and Swiss cities in the centre of Europe. On the geographical periphery, cities such as Lisbon, Stock-holm and Budapest have joined the network. Thus, the system of European cities strongly integrated by multinational corporations is reinforced and made more compact. Interactions between these cities are increasing, with a growing number of ownership linkages. They can be considered to form a 'European urban system' representing the major centres connected through European economic integration. The most central cities are above all those for which the ratio of the number of headquarters to the number of foreign subsidiaries is highest (Figure 13.8). From this point of view, London is the main centre in the network of company control. However, Paris is connected to the highest number of cities and therefore has the highest betweenness centrality. In 1990, Brussels, Milan and Madrid formed a first peripheral crown, which was confirmed in 1996. New linkages of economic control have arisen since 1990 in the vicinity of Vienna and from Brussels to Milan. These 'transversal' links, which are developed across the levels in the size hierarchy, are more common in 1996, in the vicinity of Dusseldorf, Essen, The Hague and Zurich. These cities form secondary centres of control by multinational corporations.

The most satisfying interpretation of these observations is that investment in foreign markets by European firms can be seen as a special case of the hierarchical diffusion of an innovation in a multinational urban system. The process of foreign investment, leading to the international expansion of firms, is one of the organisational innovations of the last third of the twentieth century (Dunning 1977, 1992). The strategy of firms is first to enlarge their own market by taking positions on territories outside their country of origin (Dicken 1992), second to diversify their production to adapt it to local demand (Krugman 1988), and third to make use of some comparative advantage that the new locations can offer, within the framework of 'flexible capitalism' (Porter 1996, Storper 1997). First they select locations that offer good connections in a whole country and that minimise the risks associated with their investment. Most European capitals and large economic metropolises now meet these conditions. From a city's perspective, that innovation requires a minimum level of international functions in order to provide a favourable business environment and suitable living conditions for foreign firms' employees. Since more than half of European companies' headquarters are concentrated in London and Paris, it is not surprising that these two leading cities, far ahead of any other in size, form the core of the diffusion process. The first tiers of cities reached at a second stage by the 'innovation' process are of two kinds: cities that belong to the core of urban Europe and specialise in international activities, such as Brussels and Luxemburg, and major cities or capitals of the main countries, such as Milan and Madrid. Although the diffusion process follows a classical hierarchical pattern in what could be considered to be an emerging European system of cities, it remains hindered by national boundaries and cities' former functional specialisations.

Different sectors are at different stages of the diffusion process of globalisation. The most advanced sectors in this process have a higher number of foreign subsidiaries (Mucchielli 1998). At the dates of both surveys, chemicals, electrical and electronics sectors account for more than half of the sample of foreign subsidiaries. These activities are also among the most concentrated in the large cities. They tend to spray out of the large cities like all businesses involved in the manufacture of staple consumer goods. This trend is also observed for some chemicals subsidiaries that process farm goods (such as those of Ciba-Geigy), which are naturally located outside urban environments (Rozenblat 1992). Subsidiaries in the construction sector and financial services were the most concentrated in large cities in 1990. The concentration of business services subsidiaries in the largest cities increased between 1990 and 1996, whereas most other types of activity seem to have diffused to smaller cities (Rozenblat 1997). Some urban specialisations appear in the subsidiaries hosted, very often reinforcing existing local specialties: with equal activity and city size, Amsterdam and Zurich are specialised in financial activities and business services. But these specialisations are not very strong and the higher a city is in the urban hierarchy, the less strong its specialisations (Pumain and Saint-Julien 1989; Rozenblat 1992). Thus, the largest cities, which accommodate more subsidiaries, have a more diverse range of activities: their markets (consumer and labour), infrastructure and hosting capacity increase their attractiveness for all types of activity from abroad.

In addition to urban effects, there is a strong national effect that results in significantly different rates of penetration of foreign subsidiaries in different countries. The global impact of the size of cities takes different values depending on their nationality (Rozenblat and Pumain 1993). For instance, with equal population, a

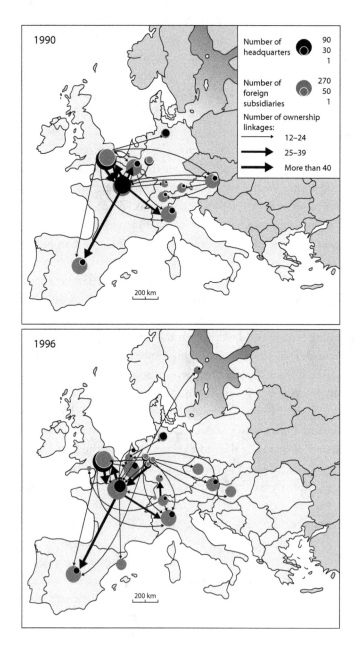

Figure 13.8   Centres in economic networks: main linkages through subsidiary ownership.

Dutch city will tend to attract more foreign subsidiaries than a French city. This can be checked statistically using variance analysis (taking into account the nationality of the cities) combined with regression (taking into account their population). One thus obtains a strong statistical explanation for the number of foreign subsidiaries in a city (R^2 = 94°%). This demonstrates that national effects remain highly significant in the diffusion process (approximately 30 percent of the variance, with city size alone accounting for 64 percent). The level of functions not only reflects the size that cities have acquired over a long period, mainly in line with the development of the national urban system to which they belong. A country's openness also determines its cities' average capacity to host foreign multinational corporations. According to Mucchielli and Puech (2003), the varying attractiveness of European countries for foreign companies can be attributed mainly to differences in payroll costs. Other authors stress the tax burden (Mignolet and Pierre 1998).

The two geographical levels, urban and national, thus combine to determine location choices in a multi-level approach, also according to regional data analysed by Mucchielli and Puech (2003). Cities' population size and national structural characteristics are still essential for understanding the current development of territories. It is therefore important to keep in mind the spatial pattern of European cities. The hierarchy of cities and their spacing remain two major factors in their integration into global networks. Networks where large cities are regularly spaced, as is the case in eastern Europe, could induce a broad diffusion of global networks in the urban system. However, foreign investment in those countries is riskier than elsewhere in Europe (Michalet 1999). The evolution of the relative concentration of headquarters and subsidiaries, compared with the concentration of urban size, seems to depend on how long the process of multinational integration of cities has been operating in each country. The urban hierarchy can thus be interpreted as a kind of attractor, exerting a feedback effect from the macro geographical system to the behaviour of urban actors. Over the long term, the various hierarchies of the same territory fit together and mutually reinforce each other. The urban hierarchy itself can also undergo transformations due to the concentration of the other functions. These characteristics can be interpreted within the framework of a more comprehensive evolutionary theory of urban systems.

INNOVATION AND EVOLUTIONARY THEORY OF URBAN SYSTEMS

Many uncertainties still hamper our ability to forecast the future of urbanisation. With the advent of new technologies and the political reorganisation of territories, geographers observing globalisation processes are puzzled by the possible next trends in urban concentration, dispersion and relative growth. By applying ideas and models developed by a new field of investigation known as complexity theory, we could learn more about the universe of possible evolution stemming from observed urban dynamics, and perhaps discover some abstract hidden processes that may better explain the similarities appearing in urban structures and evolution, despite the overwhelming diversity of physical, economic, political, social and cultural forms that urban systems take around the world. The concept of urban system is actually a good example of a complex system (Pumain 1998). Urban systems produce self-organised multilevel structures that are evolving via dynamic social processes where non-linearity, discontinuity and irreversibility, as well as permanent adaptation through cooperation and competition, are general rules.

What are the emergent properties of urban systems and how are they produced? We shall focus here on structural features that characterise the macro level of a system of cities, and that emerge from the interactions between towns and cities at the meso level. In this case, interactions occur through multiple exchanges of people, goods and information that circulate continuously from one city to another through a multitude of networks (Allen *et al.* 1999; Massey *et al.* 1999). Since it is hardly possible to represent all of them in a model, we have selected those that are considered responsible for the emergence and maintenance of structural features at the upper level, and chosen to represent them in an abstract way.

The main structural features of urban systems are defined according to the principles that organise their internal diversity, regardless of the period or country in which the system is observed. Such general features are well known. First there is a principle of hierarchical organisation, including important scaling properties for attributes such as size, spacing and level of socio-economic activities of towns and cities. These features were previously formalised by central place theory. Geographers have criticised that theory because it is static and based upon a restricted set of urban activities (mainly services to residents), which does not consider specialisations in non-central functions (for instance industry and tourism). Therefore, a more general framework is needed.

However, this does not mean that all the observations explained statically by central place theory are no longer valid. Hierarchical structure and spacing regularities are still relevant, as shown for instance by the map in Figure 13.9, representing the location and size of towns and cities (urban agglomerations with populations of more than 10,000 defined in a comparable manner) in countries of western and eastern Europe. A simple analysis of this map by the cartographic filtering method illustrates the evidence of the

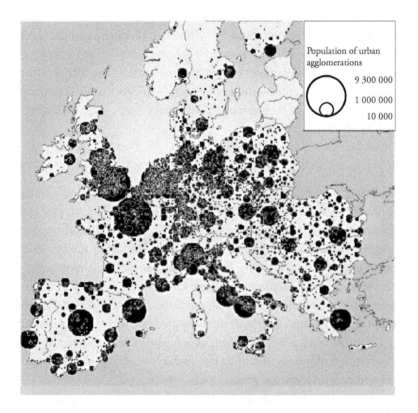

Figure 13.9   Population of European cities.

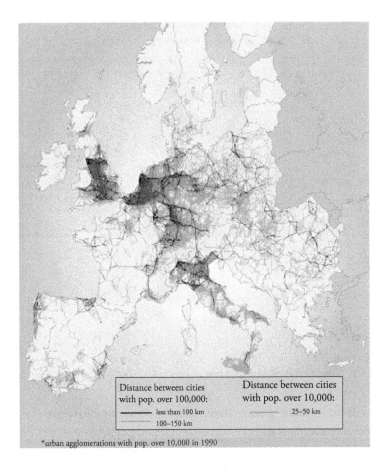

Distance between cities
with pop. over 100,000:
———— less than 100 km
———— 100–150 km

Distance between cities
with pop. over 10,000:
———— 25–50 km

*urban agglomerations with pop. over 10,000 in 1990

Figure 13.10   Patterns of urban systems in Europe.

hierarchical and spatial organisation of urban systems, according to research by Celine Rozenblat (1995). In Figure 13.10, the agglomerations in Figure 13.9 were initially connected by a straight line when the distance between them was less than 25 km. The resulting pattern clearly shows three main types of urban system in Europe: a central part with much higher densities, a more contrasting western part (mainly France and Spain) and an eastern part with highly regular spacing. Combined with size, these three types would fit into the typology established by Etienne Juillard ('Rhenish', 'Parisian' and 'peripheral' urban networks, Juillard and Nonn 1976). But the point here is that the general pattern is maintained if the minimum distance is raised to 50 km, or the minimal population size to 100,000 (with separating distances of 100 and 150 km). This result confirms the high consistency of the hierarchical and spatial organisation of urban systems.

The hierarchical organisation is an emergent property that characterises the level of observation of systems of towns and cities. It is produced by the multiple interactions occurring between individual towns and cities. The facts that a town or city keeps its size to a given proportion of other cities' sizes, that the spacing between cities is more or less regular and that over long periods of time there is a fairly consistent persistence of the hierarchical order cannot be inferred from the nature and function of a single city. One has to search for processes that can explain this emergent property at the level of the urban system according to the *rules of interactions* occurring at the level of individual cities.

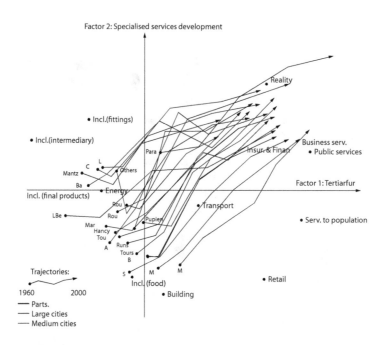

Figure 13.11   Trajectories of French cities in economic space (source: Paulus 2004)

This has been interpreted in many models by simulating the competitive growth process, which represents both the dynamics of each town and the resulting statistical aggregate in the form of the distribution of city sizes (Robson 1973; Pumain 1982; Guerin-Pace 1993). However, the demonstration in these models is statistical and non-spatial. We have formalised the complex dynamics of spatial interactions in the growth process, including reversal of influence over time according to the definition of neighbouring places by a simple modular model (Page *et al.* 2001). The relationships between cities' mass and spacing, and the evolution of these relationships over time, have been studied by Anne Bretagnolle (1999), who showed how urban interactions regulate the relative size of the elements in an urban system, depending on the speed and intensity of spatial interactions. The hierarchisation is generated from the bottom by the short-circuiting of smaller intermediate centres linked to the process of space-time convergence, and from the top by the various processes of hierarchical diffusion of innovations in the urban system (Bretagnolle *et al.* 2002).

A link is then established with the second main structural property of urban systems, which is their qualitative socio-economic diversity, as expressed in typologies of the functional specialisation of towns and cities, which generally lasts without major changes for several decades. These slow dynamics of relative change in the inter-urban division of labour are produced through small deviations in a general process of diffusion of socioeconomic changes, which is much more rapid (Paulus 2004). According to that extremely incremental process of interactive adjustments, all cities change in more or less the same direction and intensity in the space of activities phase, as illustrated by a correspondence analysis for French cities for the period 1962–90 in Figure 13.11. This result introduces a way for generalising central place theory in the broader framework of an evolutionary theory of urban systems (Pumain 2000). Urban hierarchy and functional diversity are emergent properties stemming from a co-evolution process of towns and cities, which are cooperating and competing for access to socio-economic innovations, by attempting to secure better relative positions in spatial and social networks.

CONCLUSION

The observations we make about the location of multinational firms in Europe and their ownership linkages among cities, at two dates, 1990 and 1996, are a good example of urban co-evolution, even as these new connections contribute to the creation of a still emerging 'European system of cities'. The former hierarchical structure of the urban system has a strong regulation (or feedback) effect: the main capitals, London and Paris, are at the core of the process, whereas almost none of the smallest towns (population under 200,000) are involved in the diffusion process as yet. But two distinct processes are superimposed on the classical hierarchical diffusion process: one is a reinforcement of specialisation in multinational activities for cities already engaged in international business, especially financial business (as is the case for Brussels, Luxemburg and Zurich); the other, even more effective, process is linked to the existence of national borders, which guide the location of foreign firms towards national capitals, regardless of their relative size within the European urban system, and towards cities located close to international borders (which also gives an advantage to cities in the smallest countries, which are on the whole more 'open' to external exchanges than the largest countries).

These two processes have the potential to reshape the European urban system, but to what extent? Two points in time are not enough to identify the possible consequences of these trends. A third survey, currently in progress, could bring clearer answers.

REFERENCES

Allen, J. (1997) 'Economies of power and space', in R.Lee and J.Wills (eds) *Geographies of Economies,* London: Arnold, pp. 59–70.

Allen, J., Massey, D. and Pryke, M. (1999) *Unsettling Cities,* London: Routledge.

Amin, S. (1973) *Le Developpement inegal: essai sur les formations sociales du capitalisme peripherique*, Paris: Editions de minuit.

Berry, B.J.L. (1964) 'Cities as systems within systems of cities', *Papers of the Regional Science Association,* 13:147–63.

Bouinot, J. (2004) 'Des evolutions dans les comportements spatiaux des entreprises en 2003?', *Cybergeo,* http://www.cybergeo.presse.fr/.

Bretagnolle, A. (1999) *Espace-temps et systeme de villes: effets de l'augmentation de la vitesse de circulation sur l'espacement et l'etalement des villes*, doctoral thesis, Universite Paris I.

Bretagnolle, A., Paulus, F. and Pumain, D. (2002) 'Time and space scales for measuring urban growth', *Cybergeo,* 219.

Brunet, R. (1989) *Les Villes europeennes,* Paris: Datar-La documentation Franfaise.

Cattan, N., Pumain, D., Rozenblat, C. and Saint-Julien, T. (1999) *Le systeme des villes europeennes,* 2nd edition, Paris: Anthropos.

Cohen, R.B. (1981) 'The new international division of labor, multinational corporations and urban hierarchy', in M.Dear and A.J.Scott (eds) *Urbanization and Urban Planning in Capitalist Society,* New York: Methuen, pp. 287–315.

Conti, S. and Spriano, G. (1990) *Effetto Citta,* Turin: Fondazione Agnelli.

Crozet, M., Mayer, T. and Muchielli, J.L. (2004) 'How do firms agglomerate? A study of FDI in France', *Regional Science and Urban Economics,* 34:27–54.

Crozier, M. and Friedberg, E. (1977) *L 'Acteur et le systeme,* Paris: Editions Du Seuil.

Dicken, P. (1992) *Global Shift: The Internalization of Economic Activity,* 2nd edition, New York: Guilford Press.

Dicken, P. and Malmberg, A. (2001) 'Firms in territories: a relational perspective', *Economic Geography,* 77:345–63.

Dunning, J.H. (1977) 'Trade, location of economic activity and the MNE: in search of an eclectic approach', in B.Ohlin, P.O.Hesselborn and P.M.Wijkman (eds) *International Allocation of Economic Activity,* London: Macmillan.

Dunning, J.H. (1992) *Multinational Enterprises and the Global Economy,* Wokingham: Addison Wesley.

European Communities (2001) *Unite de l'Europe, solidarite despeuples, diversite des territoires,* deuxieme rapport sur la cohesion economique et sociale, Luxembourg: Office des publications officielles des communautes europeennes.

ESPON (2003) 'The role, specific situation and potentials of urban areas as nodes in a polycentric development', *ESPON Project 1.1.1,* Third interim report, August, http://www.espon.lu/online/documentation/projects/thematic/index.html.

Francfort, I., Osty, F., Sainsaulieu, R. and Uhalde, M. (1995) *Les Mondes sociaux de l'entreprise,* Paris: Desclee de Brouwer.

Friedmann, J. (1978) 'The spatial organization of power in the development of urban systems', in L.S.Bourne and J.W.Simmons (eds) *Systems of Cities,* Oxford: Oxford University Press, pp. 328–40.

Friedmann, J. (1986) 'The world city hypothesis', *Development and Change,* 17:69-84; also in P.Knox and P.J.Taylor (eds) (1995) *World Cities in a World System,* Cambridge: Cambridge University Press, pp. 317–31.

Graham, B. (1998) 'Liberalization, regional economic development and the geography of demand for air transport in the European Union', *Journal of Transport Geography,* 6: 87–104.

Guerin-Pace, F. (1993) *Deux siecles de croissance urbaine: la population des villes frangaises de 1831 a 1990,* Paris: Anthropos.

Guimera, R., Mossa, S., Tutschi, A. and Amaral, A.N. (2005) 'The worldwide air transportation network: anomalous centrality, community structure, and cities' global roles', *Proceedings of the National Academy of the Sciences of the United States of America,* 102 (22):7794–99.

Hall, P. (1995) 'Toward a general urban theory', in P.Hall, P.Newton, J.Brotchie, M.Batty and E.Blakely (eds) *Cities in Competition: Productive and Sustainable Cities for the 21st Century,* London: Longman, pp. 3–31.

Hirschmann, A. (1958) *The Strategy of Economic Development,* New Haven, CT: Yale University Press.

Jourdan, N. (2004) *Les Transferts interregionaux d'etablissements—Forte progression entre 1996 et 2001.* Insee Premiere 949 (February).

Juillard, E. and Nonn, H. (1976), *Espaces et regions en Europe occidentale,* Action Thematique Programmee 10, Paris: CNRS.

Krugman, P. (1988) *Strategic Trade Policy and the New International Economics,* Cambridge, MA: MIT Press.

Le Fillatre, P. (1964) 'La puissance economique des grandes agglomerations frangaises deduite de 1'etude de la localisation des sieges et des succursales d'entreprises a etablissements multiples', *Etudes et conjoncture,* 19(1):1–40.

Massey, D., Allen, J. and Pile S. (eds) (1999) *City Worlds,* London: Routledge.

Michalet, C.A. (1997) 'Strategies of multinationals and competition for foreign direct investment', Foreign Investment Advisory Service, occasional paper 10.

Michalet, C.A. (1999) *La Seduction des nations ou comment attirer les investissements,* Paris: Economica.

Mignolet, M. and Pierre, I. (1998) 'Fiscalite et distribution des unites au sein de multinationales: l'exemple des groupes belges', *Revue d'Economie Regionale et Urbaine,* 2: 251–80.

Mintzberg, H. (1994) *The Rise and Fall of Strategic Planning*, New York: Prentice Hall.

Muchielli, J.-L. (1998) *Multinationales et mondialisation*, Paris: Seuil.

Muchielli, J.-L. and Puech, F. (2003) 'Internationalisation et localisation des firmes
multinationales: l'exemple des entreprises frangaises en Europe', *Economie et Statistiques*, 363-365:129–44.

Myrdal, G. (1957) *Rich Lands and Poor*, New York: Harper and Row.

Page, M., Parisel, C., Pumain, D. and Sanders, L. (2001) 'Knowledge-based simulation of settlement systems', *Computers, Environment and Urban Systems*, 25:167–93.

Pagetti, F. (1998) 'La rete bancaria nel sistema urbano europeo', in P.Bonavero and E.Dansero (eds) *L'Europa delle regioni e dele reti, i nuovi modelli di organizzazione territoriale nello spazio unificato europen*, Turin: UTET Libreria, pp. 361–71.

Paulus, F. (2004) *Coevolution dans les systemes de villes : croissance et specialisation des aires urbaines frangaises de 1950 a 2000*, doctoral thesis, Universite Paris I.

Porter, M. (1996) 'Competitive advantage, agglomeration economies and regional policy', *International Regional Science Review*, 19:85–90.

Pred, A. (1973) 'Systems of cities and information flows', *Lund Studies in Geography*, Series B, 38.

Pred, A. (1977) *City-systems in Advanced Economies*, London: Hutchinson University Library.

Pumain, D. (1982) *La Dynamique des villes*, Paris: Economica.

Pumain, D. (1998) 'Les modeles d'auto-organisation et le changement urbain', *Cahiers de Geographie de Quebec*, 117:349–66.

Pumain, D. (2000) 'Settlement systems in the evolution', *GeografiskaAnnaler*, 82B (2): 73–87.

Pumain, D. (ed.) (2006) *Hierarchy in Natural and Social Sciences*, Dordrecht: Springer.

Pumain, D. and Saint-Julien, T. (1989) *Atlas des villes de France*, Paris: La Documentation Franfaise.

Pumain, D. and Saint-Julien, T. (eds) (1996) *Urban Networks in Europe*, Paris: John Libbey-INED, Congresses and Colloquia, 15.

Reynaud, A. (1981) *Societe, espace et justice*, Paris: PUF.

Robson, B. (1973) *Urban Growth, an Approach*, London: Methuen.

Rozenblat, C. (1992) *Les Reseaux des entreprises multinationales dans le reseau des villes europeennes*, doctoral thesis, Universite Paris I.

Rozenblat, C. (1995) 'Tissu d'un semis de villes europeennes',*Mappemonde*, 4:22–7.

Rozenblat, C. (1997) 'L'efficacite des reseaux de villes pour le developpement et la diffusion des entreprises multinationales en Europe (1990-1996)', *Flux*, 27/28:41–58.

Rozenblat, C. (1998) 'Commandement et dependance', in T.Saint-Julien (ed.), *Atlas de France: l'industrie*, Reclus-La Documentation Franfaise, 9:74–8.

Rozenblat, C. and Cicille, P. (2003) *Les Villes europeennes: analyse comparative*, Paris: Datar—La Documentation franfaise.

Rozenblat, C. and Pumain, D. (1993) 'The location of multinational firms in the European urban system', *Urban Studies*, 10:1691–1709.

Rozenblat, C. and Pumain, D. (2004) 'Articulated modes of integration: the structure of European urban system', in M.Pacione (ed.). *Changing Cities: International Perspectives*, Glasgow: Strathclyde University Publishing, pp. 91–105.

Sassen, S. (1991) *The Global City: New York, London, Tokyo*, Princeton, NJ: Princeton University Press.

Scott, A. (2001) *Global City-Regions: Trends, Theory, Policy*, Oxford: Oxford University Press.

Storper, M. (1997) *Regional World: Territorial Development in a Global Economy*, New York: Guilford Press.

Taylor, P.J. (2001) 'Specification of the world city network', *Geographical Analysis*, 33(2): 181–94.

Taylor, P.J. and Walker D.R. (2001) 'World cities: a first multivariate analysis of their service complexes', *Urban Studies*, 38:23–47

Taylor, P.J., Walker D.R.F, Catalano, G. and Hoyler, M. (2002) 'Diversity and power in the world city network', *Cities*, 19 (4):231–41.

Veltz, P. (1998) 'Globalisation et territorialisation des groupes industriels: rapport de synthese', Paris: Datar—La Documentation Franfaise.

Wallerstein, I. (1980) *Le Systeme-monde du XVe siecle a nos jours*, Paris: Flammarion.

Zarifian, P. (1993) *Quels nouveaux modeles d'organisationpour l'industrie europeenne?* L'emergence de la firme coopera-trice, L'Harmattan.

Zimmermann, J.B. (1995) *L'Ancrage territorial des activites industrielles et technologiques*, Paris: Commissariat General du Plan.

STUDY QUESTIONS

1. In what important ways does the "firm linkages" model contrast with the strict Christaller hierarchical model?
2. Several orders of magnitude separate the importance of towns and cities in this model, in terms of population, gross production, or influence. By what is the importance of a city defined?
3. On what scale is this urban system placed?
4. By what is the integration of European society and territory achieved?
5. How would you characterize the changing status of city-regions compared to nation-states in this model?
6. What role do networks and systems play in urban development?
7. What are the basic structures influencing the integration process of cities in Europe?
8. What are some of the spatial strategies behind multinational firms choosing multiple locations?
9. How would you characterize the new kind of external economics?
10. How would you characterize the scale of decision-making and functions of headquarters, purchasing, and production in this new "firm linkages" model?
11. What are bridgehead cities and how would you characterize them?
12. What are outpost cities?
13. What are the main characteristics of multinational "turntable" cities? Give an example of a turntable city.
14. How would you characterize "centrality" in this "firm linkages" model?
15. How does hierarchical innovation diffusion figure into the characteristics of inter-city linkages? Give examples.
16. What is one of the organizational innovations of the last third of the 20th century?
17. From a city's perspective, what does this innovation require?
18. What kind of foreign subsidiaries do we find in the most advanced sectors of this process of diffusion?
19. Why is it that the higher a city is in this urban hierarchy, the less strong its specialization?
20. Which two distinct processes are superimposed on the classical hierarchical diffusion process?

Chapter 14 Snapshot
Senegalese Émigrés: New Information & Communication Technologies

I chose this article to highlight some of the ways migrants, in their host countries, stay in touch with their families with some surprising results. How is it that a single cell phone can change the roles of women and young people and bring an entire village out of isolation? We will see that there are strong links between technological innovation and social change, and ways new information and communication technologies (NICTs) alter perception of space and time. We will consider the match between technology and oral languages and ways émigrés can be more helpful to their families and villages by staying out of the country. We will see the impact of television on village life and how accessibility to NICTs affects family finances, local economics, and forges new business relationships—and even social restructuring. We will find that cell phones transform private space to public space (instead of the other way around) for the entire village. We will explore what it means to see globalization from the bottom up instead of from the top down. This study focuses on the country of Senegal in West Africa. Here we are going to look at specific regions of Louga and Kébémer (see map) and the impact of their appropriation of NICTs.

ÉMIGRÉS ADOPT NICTS & STRENGTHEN "LONG DISTANCE RELATIONS"

As soon as émigrés find work and a place to live, the first thing they want to do is connect with their families back home. They can certainly send letters or pass word along with friends who are traveling back home (and this has been a traditional form of communication), but the most popular way to connect with family is by telephone. Unfortunately, not everyone—or even most people in an émigré's village has access to a telephone, so in order to communicate by phone, often the émigré has to provide the phone for his family and actually pay to have a land line connected to his family's house. Or, he purchases a cell phone that he leaves with his family when he visits them. "The telephone expands the circle of interpersonal relations beyond national borders, eliminates the time delay in communications, and makes communication a dynamic and interactive process" (247). It is easy to see the impact émigrés have had on the development of telephone diffusion in regions such as Louga and Kébémer: "The change in the number of landline telephone connections was particularly rapid in the region of Louga where the number of subscribers tripled in less than seven years, growing from 1,821 to 5,963" (247). Much of this growth can be attributed to "émigrés building houses and equipping them with telephones, thereby providing telephone access for the family as a whole" (247). We see a similar pattern in Kébémer. "It is as if the telephone were a means of extending the home space in the new country—and this among people for whom the family structure is 'traditionally' based on oral communication" (247).

The telephone is particularly suited as a communication choice (compared to, say, the Internet) because Senegal is a country where several of its 38 languages are oral only—that is, these languages have no written component. French is the official language and is only spoken by those who are educated, but the telephone can be used by those especially in rural areas, where formal education is less well-developed than in urban areas. Telephones can be used equally by the educated and non-educated, the rural as well as the urban resident. "The cellular telephone, which developed rapidly in Senegal, represents a response to the mobility of Senegalese people and was rapidly integrated in a social milieu characterized by orality and illiteracy" (247). However, cell phones are extremely expensive in Senegal, too expensive most especially in rural areas. According to a survey of 100 people contacted by the author, "97% received [cell phones] free from a relative, with 95% of the donors being émigrés who left telephones behind at the end of vacations in Senegal" (248).

Many times, as is demonstrated in the case studies presented, the phone provided by the émigré is the village's sole connection to the outside world. In the village of Gade Kébé, in the region of Louga, "[a]ll of the inhabitants adopted this single instrument of communication, which linked the village to the world beyond" (248). One of the more practical barriers émigrés face when attempting to build a communication link to their families is that many areas of Senegal don't have electricity. So, even the use of cell phones have their limitations even if they do have phone service available. They must have some way to recharge the batteries. In the village of Dawakh, Sarakh Séne had the only cell phone, provided to him by his brother. He had two cell phone batteries, which he would recharge each week at the local market; as well as an automobile charger for the cell phone. Someone in the village had a car. Sarakh didn't just use the phone for himself:

> Through his intermediation the NGO [non-governmental organization] operating in the village would inform the population of upcoming meetings and activities. Thus, he served as the interface between the village and its members located abroad, or with those living in Touba and Dakar [larger urban centers in Senegal; Dakar is the capital]. As a result, he was propelled to the head of organisations of young people in the village—youth groups, the literacy committee, etc. (249).

In both case studies, the telephone was provided by a relative so he could maintain connection to his family while he was away, but it provided so much more to the family member, allowing him or her to take on a leadership position in the village. "New leaders are emerging in spite of sectarian or traditional affili-ations, whose role is linked primarily to mediating between people and the outside world—a role that has allowed them to externalize capacities for sharing, communicating and negotiating" (249). This important new role in the village isn't limited to men either, or to the elders of the village. One woman in Gade Kébé has taken on a similar role to that of Sarakh Séne in Dawakh:

This woman demonstrated, in the handling of her portable telephone, the ability to interface between the village and the outside world—showing mediating qualities such as confidentiality, availability, altruism and solidarity. By projecting her capabilities in the collective awareness, she systematically positioned herself as a leader, despite her youth and gender, gaining responsibility for directing other activities in the village and thus playing a role in social mediation (249).

Televisions and camcorders are also being used in innovative ways in rural Senegal. In some places, like Gade Kébé, television sets are powered by car batteries, and in other villages, such as M'Benguné, they are solar powered. Few homes have television sets so television viewing is for the whole village. "According to the adults in the village, television is primarily for young people and women," the women being responsible for turning the television on (250). But the impact of television-viewing has important cultural implications: "television changes the modalities and timing of village night life .... Certain traditional activities (cultural gatherings, song, funeral gatherings) are increasingly forgotten" (250). While the television can be culturally divisive, the camcorder links émigrés to their home villages in some surprising ways. Émigrés purchase camcorders for their families, too, so that important family and village events can be recorded. "In the suburbs of Dakar and in the villages in the country's interior, centers specialising in the reporting of family ceremonies—using sophisticated cameras and post-production techniques that add sub-titles—are springing up" (251). But that's not all. Video cassettes sent to émigrés allow them to stay current with local television shows, family events, and they can also serve as audio-visual *matchmakers*.

Video cassettes expand the field for encounters and reinforce exogamous relations for people who often have a limited circle of acquaintances in the host country ... and whose vacations in their country of origin are often too brief for encounters outside the circle of family and/or neighbourhood acquaintances ... (251).

In fact, the camcorder has altered "marriage strategies and traditional procedures for finding partners, with physical aesthetics taking on a more determining role than kinship links" (251).

Finally, the radio has had a technological facelift (thanks to digital receivers) and, by being linked to cell phones in the host country, are providing émigrés with a new venue for real-time discussions and interactions with the home country. "With the telephone, radio is no longer merely an instrument for providing information, but is also a tool for communication, i.e. for establishing an interactive and dynamic process of information exchange and communication" (252). Émigrés in Italy or elsewhere can listen to call-in radio talk shows broadcast from Senegal, and they can participate real-time using their cell phones. In this way, "émigrés have begun to create venues for dialog and create Senegalese 'islands' within their adopted country. With this real-time interactivity, émigrés are participating directly in broadcasts" (252).

Whereas radio, television, camcorder, and phones have been instrumental in changing lives and connecting rural villages to the outside world, what about the Internet? As of the publishing date of the article, 2004, "access to the internet in rural Senegal is still limited" (252). There are a couple of other challenges to Internet use in rural Senegal not present with the other forms of NICTs already discussed. First, "while most émigrés are from rural regions and are either illiterate or have very little education, the Internet is viewed as a tool for intellectuals, an essentially urban Dakar phenomenon" (252). The NICTs the émigrés have appropriated are easily used by people who are either illiterate or who only speak oral languages. There is also a lack of Internet hosts and, therefore, a lack of connectivity in much of Senegal outside of Dakar. However, within host countries, where the Internet is firmly established, émigrés can use it for listening to the radio or reading newspapers online. In addition, "émigrés' familiarity with the Internet can be a determining factor in the creation of virtual communities in the host countries" (141). In fact, "the Internet is a means for gaining exposure and of rebuilding solidarity. Nonetheless, the Internet in Senegal represents more a political resource … (253).

TOWARD THE GLOBALIZATION OF FUNDS

A large portion of the money émigrés make in the host country is sent home to the families in the villages (remittances). NICTs also play an important role here. They provide many more ways, both formal and informal, that this money can be transferred. "Beyond their contribution to the country's balance of payments, financial flows sent by migrants raise the standard of living of households and contribute to the emergence of an entrepreneurial sector and to the development of rapid transnational circulation of capital" (141). Besides being able to wire money home by Money Gram and Western Union, "telephone, fax and telematics transfers have led to new non-physical means of financial circulation and a diversification of mechanisms for conveying money, émigrés are able to make major amounts of money available to recipients through a simple phone call" (253). For example, the émigré can call merchants in his home village and request that his family's needs be taken care of. Arrangements are then made for the émigré to repay the merchants on his next visit home.

> This type of transfer, which presupposes frequent and regular returns to Senegal on the part of the émigré, as well as his having established himself in the business community, makes it possible for the émigrés to control the family budget … . With such a procedure, no transfer of money is made to Senegal … . Émigrés, in coordination with merchants, have developed a complex system of advancing and clearing funds, and of social control, supported by the telephone (254).

Another method of funds transfer is to use the Kara International Exchange set up by a Senegalese émigré and now widely used. It requires at least two offices: one in the host country and one in the home country, in this case, Dakar. The émigré goes to the Kara office in the host country with an amount of money he wants to send home. He provides the office with the recipient's (correspondent's) information, turns over the cash, pays the commission fee, and receives a receipt. The Kara office in the host country then faxes this information to the Kara office in Dakar to make the money available to the correspondent. It is the responsibility of the émigré who is sending the funds to notify their correspondent of the transfer. It is not necessary for the émigré or correspondent to be able to read or write to make this transfer. However, you might ask, without the physical transfer of funds, how does the Kara office in the home country have the money to pay out to the émigré's correspondent? There is yet another type of exchange that goes from the host country to the home country that provides the Kara office in the home country with the funds.

Merchants who are traveling from Senegal to the host country for business also use the Kara International Exchange. To avoid carrying large sums of money when they travel, they deposit their money in the Kara office in Dakar (like a bank), and take out the same amount when they arrive at the Kara office in the host country. That money has been deposited by several émigrés using the Kara office to "send" money home and the émigré's correspondent actually picks up money in Dakar that had been deposited by the merchants. Hence, the exchange between the émigrés and merchants, who have no relationship with each other except through the Kara Exchange that operates in similar ways as a bank, "with a system of tacit compensation, wihtout physically transferring money" (256). The basis of these transfers by Senegalese émigrés is the networking and support of the family in the home village, but these are made possible only by the use of NICTs. "Transfers have contributed, by relying on NICTs, to a new globalization of finance and commerce … . Above all, however, these agents have been able to find sources of financing and other forms of backing outside of banks and the State" (257).

NICTs & SOCIAL RESTRUCTURING WITHIN THE MIGRATORY SYSTEM

Throughout this article we have seen several examples of social restructuring as a result of émigrés appropriating NICTs. First have been the opportunities for social management. Émigrés, through the use of NICTs, have "access to a mechanism for real-time family decision-making. NICTs are breaking down barriers and challenging assumptions regarding temporal and spatial frameworks" (257). We have also seen the increase of social changes and the rebalancing of roles "guaranteeing vulnerable social segments of the population access to information and to decision making" (257). Third, we have seen how NICTs "make it possible for émigrés to control domestic space. Managing such a sphere involves the power of financial resources, and makes it possible to direct spending, give orders, deal with conflicts—all matters that the migrant can now do by telephone on almost a daily basis. "What is presently occuring is a globalisation of family management" (258).

NICTs & INFORMAL GLOBALISATION

One thing NICTs have brought to relationships with their use is the sense of "real time" happening between two places at the same time. The notion of "here" and "elsewhere" is not so different because of the "simultaneity and everyday nature of exchanges between émigrés and their places of origin" (259). Up to now, people who were closer to each other in physical space (proximity) could exert more social control than those who were further away. However, NICTs enable a 'virtual' proximity to develop "that relies on oral communication and financial relationships" (259). NICTs have also changed the balance of power within the villages themselves. For example, *griots* are traditional oral historians, story-tellers, and "disseminators of domestic information on family ceremonies and village gatherings" (259). Today, however they are "receiving competition from those who possess the local NICT devices. There is a hoarding phenomenon that occurs and that contributes to widening the gap between those who have acquired these technologies and those who have not" (259).

"Social networks are energised by technical networks" (259) and access to NCITs is more important than physical proximity in strengthening social connectedness. When émigres are in a number of host countries, their connection to the village can "strengthen the role of local powers at play within the village. Thus, the village reaches beyond physical limitations. We are witnessing the establishment of direct links between local and global networks, staking out a new form of globalisation" (260). Conversely, where there are several émigrés living in the same town abroad, the boundaries of the village, such as M'Benguné, seem to stretch or, rather, the village becomes "part of a complex system of multiple residences (village, nearby town, places abroad, Touba) interconnected by NICTs. In the village and the outside world, bonds dominate distance, time dominates space. The world abroad is a limiting concept because émigrés consider their nationals to be full members of the community, whom they are obligated to keep informed of the life of ther village down to the most trivial details" (260). Our author asks, "is not this creation of transnational spaces outside the limits of national borders a type of globalisation from the bottom up, one that is being advanced more rapidly by communities more than by states? It constitutes globalisation that is occurring bit by bit, through a process of hybridisation one step at a time, through open, flexible social networks …" (260).

NITCs are shifting and strengthening social networks; they are enabling émigrés to become "intermediaries for the collection of resources" (260) and enabling them to "bypass the national level [the state] with its bureaucratic constraints or its deficiencies in terms of mobilising financial resources suited to the needs of the people …" (260). The roles of women and young people have been strengthened, the circle of social relations have been expanded, and the space between distant places is collapsing in a new form of globalisation from the bottom up. Our author concludes:

> Those in possession of information differentiate themselves from and oppose the classical elites, to whom this role traditionally belonged. This fragmentation between the modern and the traditional leads to: the multiplicity of decision-making poles within the rural setting; the diversification and break-down of sources of leadership; and the tentative beginning of a process of democratising social functions (261).

Map 14.1   Map of Senegal. Copyright in the Public Domain.

14. SENEGALESE ÉMIGRÉS

New Information & Communication Technologies

By Serigne Mansour Tall

Emigration from Senegal increased rapidly between 1980 and 1990, and its economic and social implications grew in significance. These migratory flows diversified in terms of their departure points and destinations, making complex the challenge of preserving relationships with families at home. As Senegalese emigrated to countries with fewer links to Senegal, the need to find ways of maintaining long-distance relationships became more urgent.

How do the émigrés appropriate New Information and Communications Technologies (NICT)? How do the new technologies provide for financial transfers without the physical movement of funds? What role do the émigrés play in the penetration of new technologies in certain disadvantaged sectors? What are the economic and social implications of this advance of NICTs? Tall shows that the types of use made of the new technologies follow from a complex process of appropriation that can make a highly personal tool such as the cellular telephone into a collective instrument to bring a village out of its isolation and connect it with the world.

Serigne Mansour Tall; trans. Paul Keller, "Senegalese Émigrés: New Information & Communication Technnologies," *Review of African Political Economy*, vol. 31, no. 99, pp. 31–48. Copyright © 2004 by Serigne Mansour Tall. Reprinted with permission.

Tall concludes that the emergence of the new technologies and their appropriation by émigrés creates new social configurations both in the new home and in the community of origin, and contributes to the emergence of new spatial understandings.

New information and communication technologies (NICTs) are the modern tools (cable, satellite, the Internet, telematic applications) that facilitate the circulation of ideas and bring together data and people. This study attempts to shed light on the role of NICTs in the 'long-distance relations' between émigrés and their families in their country of origin. The ways in which these technologies are used and appropriated by émigrés are complex. In the specific context of this study, dealing with the places of origin of émigrés who have long lacked connection with the modern communications network, the phrase 'new technologies' may be disconcerting to the reader. Indeed, the landline telephone may be old and commonplace in Dakar, while it is just becoming known in M'Benguène, the village in the department of Kébémer that has just emerged from technological isolation, thanks to investments from its national émigrés in Italy. Thus, as Mucchielli (1998:9) observes, 'the analysis of contexts and, consequently, of approaches at work in the communications realm, is therefore fundamental.' Our field research was set in the central-west region of Senegal. The onset of chronic drought at the beginning of the 1970s seriously endangered peanut production, which represented the primary agricultural industry, and led to the mass departure of its inhabitants to Italy in the mid-1980s. This study analyses the appropriation of NICTs by the émigrés and the rationales it engenders, which, according to Mucchielli (1998:10), are 'organisational rationales of power and knowledge and of hierarchical power, a cultural rationale of propriety, a cultural rationale of *savoir-faire*, psychosocial rationales of fear of the loss of prestige or control …' As with any innovation, NICTs bring into question age-old beliefs and knowledge, long-established positions and well-established local structures.

How, then, do émigrés appropriate NICTs? What is the role of NICTs in eliminating the physical element in the financial transfers of émigrés and promoting the circulation of private capital? What is the role of migrants in the penetration of these technologies in villages that are, *a priori*, isolated? What are the social and economic implications of accessibility to NICTs? This study attempts to gain an understanding of how Senegalese émigrés and their families who remain behind are served by these new communications tools and how, in turn, these tools influence their lifestyles. Thus, the study is built around a consideration of this dialectic of passive and receptive use of NICTs, and their dynamic and active appropriation. By relying on the opportunities offered by NICTs, émigrés, thanks to their money and *savoir-faire*, are attempting to instill a new dynamic in their relations with families who remain in their country of origin. Thus, this study is focused squarely on the link between technological innovation and social changes, under the influence of one key actor: the émigrés.

The methodology combined a macro approach (an inventory of local and national statistics on teledensity) and a micro approach (a qualitative analysis of changes brought about by NICTs at the local level). Collection of statistical data on telecommunications companies made it possible to construct a quantitative foundation on the rapid changes that the telephone has undergone in Senegal. It also made it possible to provide a status report on the telephone: number of subscribers and connections, changes in the nature and number of calls, the origin and destination of calls, etc. Qualitative surveys (focus groups, semi-structured interviews [SSI]), interviews, structured surveys and participatory surveys were conducted. The study of long-distance relations between émigrés and their families in the homeland was carried out using a combination of qualitative and statistical data collection on the role of NICTs in the financial transfers of Senegalese émigréss through specialised entities. The analysis of certain reference sites visited frequently by émigrés rounded out this research. These sites represent extensions of Senegalese media in the host country.

ÉMIGRÉS ADOPT NICTs & STRENGTHEN 'LONG-DISTANCE RELATIONS'

As soon as émigrés manage to find work in the host country, they re-establish ties with their families back home. For this, the telephone is the most frequently used tool. Often, émigrés take collective responsibility for the charges of providing electricity and telephone service in their villages. They ensure access to a telephone line and pay the bills their families receive. Émigrés also bring back, during their vacations in their home country, various electronic products (cellular telephones, televisions and radios, camcorders), which help equip their homes with improved technology. They appropriate new communications tools by bringing them into their own environment. They use NICTs in a manner at odds with the nature of the technologies, i.e., they adapt them to their personal needs, which often are different from the original intended use of the technology. In practice, the ways in which NICTs are used flow from a complex process of appropriation, making an instrument—even one as personal as the cellular telephone—a communal instrument through which villages gain access to the wider world. The social function still remains the dominant factor in the process by which émigrés appropriate these technologies. The telephone expands the circle of interpersonal relations beyond national borders, eliminates the time delay in communications, and makes communication a dynamic and interactive process.

FIXED & CELLULAR TELEPHONES & THE EXPONENTIAL INCREASE IN TELEDENSITY

Between its creation as a national telecommunications monopoly in 1985 and the year 2001, the number of fixed lines operated by SONATEL (the national telecommunications company) grew by nearly 20% annually. This growth is particularly informative at the local level. The change in the number of landline telephone connections was particularly rapid in the region of Louga where the number of subscribers tripled in less than seven years, growing from 1,821 to 5,963. This was the result of émigrés building houses and equipping them with telephones, thereby providing telephone access for the family as a whole. Thus, the first investment of migrants is the telephone used to maintain relations with the family in their home country. This growth is all the more paradoxical for the fact that the regional economy has experienced structural difficulties related to the dependence of the local economy on peanut cultivation, which has been strongly affected by drought. The situation is similar in Kébémer where the number of fixed-telephone subscribers tripled between 1991 and 2001. SONATEL officials estimate that émigrés account for nearly 400 telephone lines (or half of the subscriptions) in Kébémer. It is as if the telephone were a means of extending the home space in the new country—and this among people for whom the family structure is 'traditionally' based on oral communication.

The cellular telephone, which developed rapidly in Senegal, represents a response to the mobility of Senegalese people and was rapidly integrated in a social milieu characterised by orality and illiteracy. By

2001 SONATEL had more than 200,000 mobile subscribers, while SENTEL (the number two provider of mobile telephone service) had nearly 50,000. Given that the price of the cellular telephone is still prohibitive for the vast majority of Senegalese, its rapid development may seem paradoxical. However, according to our survey of 100 persons with cellular telephones in rural settings, 97% received them free from a relative, with 95% of the donors being émigrés who left telephones behind at the end of vacations in Senegal. An analysis of the appropriation of the cellular telephone in two villages studied shows the complexity of its use by the population. These two villages, without fixed-telephone service, suffered from under-supply, despite their proximity to the city of Kébémer. The two individuals with cell phones (Khady Diagne and Sarakh Séne) were young people who, as of March 2000, possessed the only cellular telephones in their villages.

'ALIZÉ KHADY DIAGNÉ': THE UMBILICAL CORD LINKING GADE KÉBÉ WITH THE REST OF THE WORLD

Khady Diagné is a married émigré of approximately 30 years of age from the village of Gade Kébé in the Louga region. This village of just under 150 inhabitants, two kilometers from Kébémer (the administrative center of the department), has no landline telephone. In order to communicate with his wife, the husband, who emigrated to Italy, left her a portable telephone that he used during his last vacation back in Senegal. This represents the sole material link between the village and the outside world. This personal tool—the portable telephone of Khady Diagné—is known in the village by SONATEL's commercial name, 'Alizé Khady Diagné'. All of the inhabitants of this village adopted this single instrument of communication, which linked the village to the world beyond. The 'Alizé de Khady Diagné' fulfilled, among others, the following functions:

- as a reception point for domestic calls for all of the villagers. The Khady Diagné number functioned, in reality, as the common number for the community. Often, the owner of the telephone would give it to a child, who would then be responsible for taking it to the intended recipient of a call;
- as an instrument for disseminating information on family ceremonies. News of people living in the village (family events, death notices, administrative meetings) are communicated to Khady Diagné, who is responsible for calling the people involved;
- as a point of contact for village girls who work as domestics in the nearby city and need to communicate with their employers;
- as the intermediary for street merchants (known as *banas banas* merchants), who need to contact their clients and correspondents, or who need to know the status of the markets.

This example gives an idea of the transformative capacities of a personal communications tool, such as the cellular telephone, which can become a community instrument for relaying messages between the village and the outside world. An entire system of solidarity and a complete social structure are at the heart of this appropriation. Here, the cellular telephone, a personal tool *par excellence,* is shared among several people. Just as telecenters democratised access to the telephone by allowing all those with money to correspond with each other, the cellular telephone made it possible to extend the telephone to the most remote villages, which are not likely to benefit from programmes to extend service in the foreseeable future.

The development of this type of telephone is facilitated by the relative speed of connection (compared to installing fixed telephone lines), the fact that subscribers, by using prepaid 'Diamono' cards, have no need to pay a bill, and the flexibility of use. There are, however, certain obstacles to its adoption: the cost of the phone, the fact that cellular networks are not present in all places, the high rates charged for cellular calls vs. fixed-telephone calls, phone theft, and the need to recharge the batteries in locations where electricity may not be available.

THE CELL PHONES OF SARAKH SÈNE IN DAWAKH

In the village of Dawakh Gadiaga, where approximately 100 people live in ten households a short distance east of the city of Kébémer, the only cell phone, as of March 2000, belonged to Sarakh Sène, a 30-year-old man. The phone was offered to him by his brother who emigrated to South Africa and who was experiencing enormous problems contacting his family back in his native village. He provided the telephone for the village, where there was not yet any landline telephone service. Sarakh located, within the village, the area where access to the network would be best (near the standpipe and the mosque). Since the village had no electricity, Sarakh equipped his phone with two batteries. However, because of the frequency and length of calls from abroad, the battery's charge quickly became exhausted. Thus, every Monday, at Kébémer's weekly market, Sarakh would recharge his two phone batteries. He also had an automobile charger for the cell phone batteries and took advantage of the presence of a vehicle in the village (that of an NGO or of an individual) to recharge the batteries. The communal involvement in operating the cell phone allowed Sarakh to play a role in mediating between the village and the outside world. Through his intermediation, the NGO operating in the village would inform the population of upcoming meetings and activities. Thus, he served as the interface between the village and its members located abroad, or with those living in Touba and Dakar. As a result, he was propelled to the head of organisations of young people in the village—youth groups, the literacy committee, etc.

Based on these two examples, typical of other villages in central-west Senegal that have experienced strong emigration, one can see that the cellular telephone is producing new relationships and, at the same time, assuring cell phone owners a new social role. The fixed and cellular telephone contributed to the emergence of new venues for coordinating local development activities in the rural setting. How, then, are families affected by these new networks? New leaders are emerging, in spite of sectarian or traditional affiliations, whose role is linked primarily to mediating between the people and the outside world—a role that has allowed them to externalise capacities for sharing, communicating and negotiating. Places where telephones are located have become unprecedented opportunities for innovation, allowing one woman to become the primary point of attraction within the village of Gade Kébé. This woman demonstrated, in the handling of her portable telephone, the ability to interface between the village and the outside world—showing mediating qualities such as confidentiality, availability, altruism and solidarity. By projecting her capacities in the collective awareness, she systematically positioned herself as a leader, despite her youth and gender, gaining responsibility for directing other activities in the village and thus playing a role in social mediation.

In the rural environment, according to the results of our survey, people invoke the lack of telephone lines (38%), mobility (60%) and the desire to stand out (2%) as reasons for choosing the cellular telephone—a highly dynamic new technology. The telephone companies are offering new options and are lowering connection and communication costs, expanding network service as a result of both competition and technological advances. The cellular telephone is replacing fixed telephony in regions not yet served by the landline telephone and supplements the fixed telephone in well-off households, while increasingly competing with the fixed telephone among some poor families, who either give up their fixed phones or restrict themselves to using phones restricted to outgoing calls.

TELEVISION & CAMCORDER: IN TUNE WITH THE SOCIAL LIFE

Television is a new communications tool in rural Senegal. The camcorder makes it possible to live in the adopted country without being completely cut off from social life in the country of origin. Festivals, family ceremonies and major television events are experienced by international migrants thanks to the video cassette. The success of audiovisual media is linked to their easy use in the community and the simplicity of the information (image and sound), which is easy to decode by all. Everything happens as if the traditional evenings that punctuate the cultural life of the villages were passing before one on the small screen.

THE PRESENCE OF TELEVISION IN THE VILLAGES

While televisions are common, the development of television in the villages is slowed somewhat by the absence of electricity and by poor reception. Émigrés are increasingly providing their families with television sets that operate on solar energy, as is true in the village of M'Benguène. In other villages that lack electricity (direct current or solar), such as Gade Kébé, television sets are powered by automobile batteries. In general, only a few homes are equipped with television sets and television viewing is done collectively. The women are responsible for turning on the television sets. Television is watched selectively—first, to preserve the solar batteries, and second, because a degree of organisation is needed to take the television set out to the courtyard, plug it in, and provide mats and chairs for the viewers. With only programmes on the national channel available, programmes are watched parsimoniously. The programmes chosen in M'Benguène, for example, are the Tuesday dramas in Wolof, the Thursday evening Islamic broadcasts, the Friday television series, and Saturday programmes of local music or traditional songs.

According to the adults in the village, television is primarily for young people and women. The penetration of a modern communications tool in a traditional arena governed by long-standing control mechanisms has an undeniable cultural impact. Television changes the modalities and timing of village night life. The return of émigrés coincides with festive night-time events during which videocassettes and music are enjoyed late into the night. Certain traditional activities (cultural gatherings, songs, funeral gatherings) are increasingly forgotten. And while the content of television programmes gives the village exposure to the outside world, it does little to replace the role of traditional games and evening gatherings in the education of the young people. At the same time, the camcorder allows migrants to produce material consistent with their needs and makes it possible for them to participate in the social life of their villages.

THE CAMCORDER: MAKING UP FOR THE LACK OF IMAGES

The camcorder is a communications tool *par excellence*, making up for the lack of images shared between émigrés and their families. It provides images that neither the telephone, e-mail nor letter writing offers. Innumerable émigrés have come to know their future spouses through cassettes viewed collectively in Brescia or Brooklyn. Video cassettes of family ceremonies in Senegal function as audio-visual matchmakers. A break is occurring in the marriage strategies and traditional procedures for finding partners, with physical aesthetics taking on a more determining role them kinship links. These audiovisual encounters are followed and supplemented by the telephone. This phenomenon is gaining currency with the proliferation of portable telephones, which provide the opportunity for intimate conversation. Video cassettes expand the field for encounters and reinforce exogamous relationships for people who often have a limited circle of acquaintances in the host country—acquaintances made through the daily routine of commuting and work—and whose vacations in their country of origin are often too brief for encounters outside the circle of family and/or neighborhood acquaintances. Émigrés who are unrelated often watch videos in groups in the host country. Sectarian links, professional relationships or mere opportunity may bring together émigrés in the same apartment. The video promotes an extension of the types of relationships and expands the circle of acquaintance.

Some migrants buy camcorders for their families so that all important events can be filmed: religious events, family ceremonies, etc. The video is more a communications tool than an instrument for storing information. In the adopted country, the video is a tool for connecting the émigrés with the family milieu. Thus, one can hardly imagine a marriage of an émigré, even in remote villages, that is not filmed. It is reported that an émigré whose marriage cassette was damaged before he had a chance to see it financed a new ceremony so that he could have his own cassette. In the suburbs of Dakar and in the villages in the country's interior, centers specialising in the reporting of family ceremonies—using sophisticated cameras and post-production techniques that add sub-titles—are springing up. Thus, the video serves as a sort of live iconographic memento.

In the host country, video cassettes make it possible to keep abreast of local television programmes. Indeed, major broadcasts are transported the next day on the first flight bound for Italy or the United States. Major television events in Senegal (wrestling matches, political debates, broadcasts of traditional events, excerpts and Tuesday dramas in Wolof) are sometimes seen on video cassette by émigrés with only a slight delay. Cassettes are sold on New York City's 116th Street for $10, at the Lyon train station for 100 French francs, and in Brescia two days later. Folkloric troupes specialising in the production of made-for-television movies on video sell their products abroad to émigrés, who often see cassettes that are not sold to national television until long after they have been disseminated abroad. For émigrés, videos function much like local television, personalising and harnessing the television image which, until then, had been a monopoly of the powerful.

RADIO: AN OLD TECHNOLOGY WITH NEW ADVANCES

Radio has existed in Senegal since the time of communal receivers. However, with the arrival of FM in the villages at the beginning of the 1990s, radio experienced a renewed life. By same token, émigrés in Italy listening to radio stations broadcasting from Senegal (thanks to digital receivers) is certainly a new phenomenon. FM radio and inter-activity brought about by the telephone provide a new venue for dialogue between listeners. People feel a sense of solidarity from these radio stations and have the sense that they are participating in the broadcasts. All in all, the marriage of the telephone and the radio provides a link between mass information and interpersonal information, constituting a new space for sociability adopted by those excluded from the normal circulation of ideas in order to make themselves heard.

The *WorldSpace* system, founded in 1990, allows for live reception of satellite audio programmes from portable radios. Three geostationary satellites, put into orbit at 35,000 km above the equator, provide reception of programmes with high-quality sound and ease of use. 'Afristar' was launched into orbit in 1998, 'Asiastar' in 2000, and 'Ameristar' in 2001. Digital receivers cost 120,000 CFA francs in 2001. With *WorldSpace*, émigrés are able to listen, live by satellite, to local FM radio stations *(Wal Fadjri,* Sud FM, 7FM, Radio Senegal International) from their adopted country *(Wal Fadjri,* 27 June 2000). Announcements and news releases on deaths, political debates, along with local information, are heard live by émigrés who, using the telephone, participate in an exchange of opinions. With the development of the *WorldSpace* digital receiver, émigrés are able to systematically participate, by telephone, in FM radio broadcasts. With the telephone, radio is no longer merely an instrument for providing information, but is also a tool for communication, i.e., for establishing an interactive and dynamic process of information exchange and communication. Émigrés have begun to create venues for dialogue in their host countries in order to pre-serve identity and create Senegalese 'islands' within their adopted country. With this real-time interactivity, émigrés are participating directly in broadcasts. Indeed, long before the development of *WorldSpace,* émigrés had attempted to secure radio air time in their host countries.

ILLUSIONS & GLIMMERS OF INTERNET PENETRATION IN ÉMIGRÉ COMMUNITIES

Access to the Internet in rural Senegal is still limited. Although émigrés have been instrumental in securing telephone connections for their families at home, they are only vaguely familiar with the Internet and have been unable to facilitate access to the Internet in the same way. While most émigrés are from rural regions and are either illiterate or have very little education, the Internet is viewed as a tool for intellectuals, an es-sentially urban Dakar phenomenon. Connection to the Internet was not yet available in the region studied. However, the ease with which émigrés can access the Internet in their host country suggests that this tool will come to be used extensively by émigrés. Those with access to the Internet in the United States, where *WorldSpace* is not yet available, spend long hours online reading newspapers and listening to radio stations. It seems that émigrés are using the Internet when they lack access to audiovisual media. The Internet is therefore used in place of radio and television. And while a certain category of émigrés has taken to using e-mail to exchange personal messages, Internet communication between émigrés and their families is limited by the lack of connectivity in Senegal, even though there are some initial signs of improved penetration by the world wide web. Nonetheless, the benchmark site, Homeview, as well as Webtv, are viewed as having real potential.

The appropriation of NICTs by émigrés is facilitated by the high degree of compatibility with systems of oral communication. Émigrés make their own use of NICTs. The adoption of similar technological innovations is a function of the skill of the users. While no real skill is required for the telephone, the same is not true of the fax, since the sending of documents involves knowing how to read. Senegal has entered the information society or, more precisely, the network society. This is true, at times, even for remote villages or NGOs, with émigrés providing their families with access to NICTs to maintain regular contact despite geographic separation. Old communications tools, such as the radio, rely on new advances that facilitate their accessibility as well as their connection with other information technologies. Radio offers an opportunity for freedom and for citizen participation, while the Internet generates social links and provides an opportunity for those escaping territorial control. This makes it possible to leap political borders and ensure continuing émigrés contact with their home countries. Similarly, émigrés familiarity with the Internet can be a determining factor in the creation of virtual communities in host countries. People appropriate NICTs according to their own logic, by integrating them into their lived experiences and internalising them. This contributes to changing their organisational methods, as well as expanding their relationship with the outside world. Thus for the Mouride diaspora, as Guèye shows elsewhere in this Issue, the Internet is a means for gaining exposure and of rebuilding solidarity. Nonetheless, the Internet in Senegal represents more a potential resource: many villages live essentially from financial resources sent by those who have emigrated, and with the development of NICTs, funds sent from abroad arrive more quickly.

Toward the Globalisation of Capital

The desire to earn money is at the core of migration. A large portion of the money accumulated is sent to the country of origin. The residence status of the émigrés in the adopted country plays a role in the frequency of transfers, with illegal or unofficial immigrants making frequent and major transfers of money in order to prepare for the extreme eventuality of expulsion. Work status in the adopted country determines the transfers, with merchants who have easier access to informal channels sending money back more often than other migrants. Certain family events increase the transfers by émigrés: the birth of a child, the marriage of someone close to them, illness among family members, etc. The start of the school year, religious festivals and holidays (the Touba Magal, Maouloud, the end of Ramadan, Tabaski) are times of increased transfers. This variation in the pace of transfers contributes to an increase in types of transfers. The impact of NICTs in financial transfers translates into an increase in the methods for moving funds and in the amount of money moving between host country and homeland. Beyond their contribution to the country's balance of payments, financial flows sent by migrants raise the standard of living of households and contribute to the emergence of an entrepreneurial sector and to the development of rapid, transnational circulation of capital.

Since the beginning of the 1980s, the classic transfers (money orders, postal orders) have been used less and less by Senegalese émigrés, given the relatively long delivery times and delays in payment associated with these methods. Since the 1990s, new methods of transferring funds have been instituted to mitigate these constraints. These new methods, based on the use of NICTs, include new and much faster formal methods of transfer, such as Money Gram and Western Union. They also involve less formal methods, which help support social networks and inject major amounts of money directly into household budgets and local investments. Telephone, fax and telematic transfers have led to new, non-physical means of financial circulation and a diversification of mechanisms for conveying money, émigrés are able to make major amounts of money available to recipients through a simple phone call. Rudimentary at the start, these systems of transfer are being modernised as a result of NICTs and are becoming true financial products which, through an ongoing process of improvement, may give rise to new instruments adapted to the financial habits of émigrés and merchants.

'VIRTUAL' TRANSFER OF FUNDS

Commercial networks and migrant networks are juxtaposed. To merchants, the collection of money from émigrés provides very short-term loans, which are invested in the purchase of handbags and shoes in Italy, electronic equipment and cosmetics in New York, and articles of clothing in France. Merchants acting as couriers can earn significant sums by dabbling in variations in exchange rates before delivering the money to the recipients. Independent of these earnings, the merchant increases his capacity for supply and can rapidly repay the amounts collected, particularly since he is acting as both a wholesaler and retailer. Thus, the amounts entrusted to him are a sort of loan that he uses to stock merchandise, and which he repays upon his return after having sold his products. For this type of transfer, the telephone is merely an instrument for control or to inform the recipient. However, with the increasingly widespread links between merchants and émigrés, this technology is key to the transfer process. A telephone call is sufficient to make specified amounts of money available to correspondents. With the development of NICTs, the émigré can put himself in the more favorable position of creditor by requesting by phone that the expenses of his family be taken care of, while not repaying the merchant until his next visit to the adopted country. In such a case, it is the merchant who provides a bridge loan for the émigré's expenses.

Funds are made available based on the financial viability of the merchant. At the instruction of migrants who have already paid them an amount of money in the adopted country, merchants request their correspondents in Dakar, by phone, to pay out to the party specified by the émigrés, the corresponding amount of money. The withdrawal of the money is carried out in Dakar shops: souks in Sandaga, stores that sell spare parts, telecentres, etc. Locations for making withdrawals are proliferating in certain settlements in the country's interior—primarily in Touba (see also Guèye, this volume)—with accounts settled upon returning to the country. However, adjustments in expenses and money entrusted to the merchant are made periodically via the telephone; thus, the telephone functions as an accounting instrument.

Migrants make transfers without actual movement of financial flows. This system consists of orders for expenses, made by telephone. The émigré, from his adopted country, requests a merchant to provide his family with food products. The accounting is made upon the return of the migrant, who honors all expenses incurred during his absence. This type of transfer, which presupposes frequent and regular returns to Senegal on the part of the émigré, as well as his having established himself in the business community, makes it possible for the émigrés to control the family budget. The émigré pays a merchant in New York, who takes responsibility for providing, through an intermediary in Dakar, the products needed to sustain the family. With such a procedure, no transfer of money is made to Senegal. One example of a migrant with access to this type of transaction is Mr. Ndiaye, who lives in Italy and established himself in the business community, prior to his departure, in his uncle's food-import business. Financed and assisted by his uncle, he left for Italy at the age of 18. He built a house in the Parcelles Assainies section and stays in Senegal from November to March every year. The only breadwinner in his household, which consists of his wife, her mother and three brothers and sisters, he paradoxically makes no financial transfers. It is in one of the wholesale shops of his uncle, managed by one of his cousins, that the migrant's wife obtains everything she needs during the absence of her husband; the latter brings back cars for sale, and uses the proceeds to settle the debts and expenses incurred by his wife. He benefits doubly from the sale of the automobiles, since this also allows him to defray the cost of their shipment.

The migrant can also leave significant amounts of money with the merchant for the subsistence needs of his family. The merchant becomes the *de facto* manager of the émigrés' assets. The money, as hard currency, is enhanced even more by émigrés making very short-term investments, primarily in vehicles, spare parts, or secondhand electronic equipment, rather than using the funds for a direct transfer. Moreover, a rapid increase in this type of commerce can be seen, financed by the transfers of émigrés who control these sectors and are able to obtain these articles in the adopted country.

The creation, by émigrés and merchants, of original instruments for transferring funds is governed by an organisational approach that entirely avoids the constraints and administrative complications of official transfers. Émigrés, in coordination with merchants, have developed a complex system of advancing and clearing funds, and of social control, supported by the telephone.

KARA INTERNATIONAL EXCHANGE: THE INFORMAL TRANSFER OF FUNDS

One highly developed, and now much imitated example of this is the Kara International Exchange. This was initiated in 1991 by a Senegalese émigrés, who was working as an assistant at a wholesale merchant on New York's Broadway, much of whose business was with foreign clients and involved negotiating preferential exchange rates with local banks. This gave him ideas for new methods of assisting émigrés to repatriate their money. His family, his extensive network of merchant contacts both in New York and in Dakar, where he had previously worked in the Sandaga market, and the Mouride Brotherhood, in which he was an active member, helped to create the social and commercial bonds and the trust which would enable his ideas to work.

The migrant who wishes to transfer money using Kara goes to the modest Broadway apartment that serves as its office, warehouse and counter. Migrants do not have to fill out forms or sign documents, and they need not identify themselves. It is sufficient for them to indicate the amount to be sent. After receiving the funds, the Kara New York employee enters on the computer—his only work tool—the references provided by the client. On the printout given to the client are the complete names and addresses of the sender, the recipient, the amount sent, in short, the various items of information given by the migrant. The date of the transaction and the amount sent are also given on the receipt, which can serve as verification, in the exceptional event of a claim, for the client in New York. For the Kara Dakar correspondent, it can also be a means of identifying the recipient.

After the turning over of the money to be transferred and payment of the relevant commission, the Kara New York office requests, by fax, that the Dakar agency remit the amount deposited by the migrant to his correspondent. The recipient of the transfer is informed by the migrant at his own expense. This is a strategy for limiting the costs of operation by Kara New York, which recently installed a telecentre in its Broadway offices to reduce the transfer time.

The speed and simplicity of the transfer transaction are the main reasons migrants give for choosing this institution. They need not be able to read or write in order to make a transfer. Most of the clients are merchants. The security of the transfers by fax is guaranteed by the social relationship between Kara and the merchants. The payment orders requested of the Dakar agency, and made by fax, carry the number of the sending fax. The authenticity of the fax is recognised by a secret encoding system for the writing of payment orders in numeric form. The payment orders are handled only by Kara. The sender, at most, is given a receipt, while the recipient receives notice to go and withdraw a particular sum of money *and simply has to identify him- or herself.* Any doubt Kara has about the authenticity of the fax is verified by a telephone call to the Kara New York office. Transfer times are short. Generally, a transfer made by a migrant in New York before 10 a.m. local time can be received by the migrant's correspondent around 3 p.m, local time. Were it not for the time difference (Sandaga is bustling at noon while New York is just beginning to stir), the transfer would be nearly instantaneous.

The compensation between Kara New York and the Dakar correspondent is made using the money deposited by merchants who are preparing to go to New York. In order to avoid carrying large sums of money and having trouble with Senegalese customs, these merchants deposit their money with the Dakar correspondent at Kara Sandaga, who uses it to pay the recipients amounts 'sent' by migrants from New York. Kara acts as a bank with a system of tacit compensation, without physically transferring money.

NICTs provide formal transfers with security and speed, the essential factors that make them profitable. By relying on the postal network, formal transfers have increased the accessibility of regions served extensively by the postal service. NICTs improve the productivity, speed, security and flexibility of informal transfers, while making use of oral communication. This is the basis of the trust and the concept on which the system of transfer relies. A simple telephone message can make available to correspondents thousands of miles away, in real time, major sums of money. As Bougnoux (1998:110) states, 'there is an overlap between financial agents and those handling information.' Castells (1998:8) also observes, quite correctly, that 'the possibility of communicating, without time delays, with any point on the globe promotes the rapid movement of capital'. NICTs are also a means of monitoring transfers and economic investments. Correspondents can keep accounts, émigrés can monitor the fulfillment of obligations and of set time frames. This is what Castells (1999:430) calls 'communities of resistance that defend their space, their places, against an unfamiliar dynamic: the characteristic flows that determine social dominance in the information age'.

Conversely, NICTs also lead to increasingly individualised financial relationships between the international migrant and his village. We are witnessing an end to group transfers carried out by a person delegated by émigrés living in the same area. This is provoking an unraveling of community-based investments in the areas of origin, and the redirecting of expatriate investment toward the cities. The bonds of common identity based on common village origin are being blurred by greater accessibility to NICTs. The impossibility of maintaining frequent relationships with one's village of origin led migrants to set up, in their adopted countries, 'miniature villages' where news from their homeland is collected, along with collective strategies for transferring financial resources and making investments in the village. As a result, NICTs have produced social restructuring in the places of origin.

> NICTs and interdependence between local economies and the economies of destination countries: 'when Lombardy (northern Italy) sneezes, Ndiambour (central-northern Senegal) catches cold'.

With the tendency among migrants to make regular return visits to Senegal once they are established in their host countries, we are witnessing the emergence of business partnerships involving residents of both Senegal and the host countries of Senegalese émigrés. The latter are setting up 'bipolar' enterprises with one foot in Italy, say, and the other in Dakar or Touba. These hybrid enterprises are established on the basis of family networks, but are underpinned by high-quality communications technologies and relationships built on *ad hoc*, opportunistic arrangements. This reconfiguration of systems of connection between social entities and technological instruments is not in any way contradictory to those elements that serve as protectors of identity—the sect, the family, etc. Thus, a consolidation of partnerships is occurring between émigrés and economic agents in their host countries, through a merging of social networks and commercial networks, all due to NICTs. Émigrés are building a 'bipolar' form of commerce using these resources, encompassing a vast network of financial flows.

> The émigré entrepreneurial sector is based on partnership and, thus, on negotiation and dialogue. NICTs facilitate oral modes of forming contracts in the informal sector, where writing is more for legal/contractual purposes than as a form of communication.

Transfers have contributed, by relying on NICTs, to a new globalisation of finance for commerce. A survey of some 13 enterprises selling automobile parts and motorcycles, purchased primarily in Italy, revealed that the use of the telephone and fax is essential in handling their activities; these technologies have opened up new markets and better control of local markets. Above all, however, these agents have been able to find sources of financing and other forms of backing outside of banks and the State. In the automobile-parts sector—a preferred area of investment for émigrés—NICTs have facilitated the establishment of partnerships with Italian automobile scrap yards for vehicles no longer in use in Europe. Merchants fax lists of parts to be loaded in their containers, accompanied by requests that bills of lading or shipping invoices for the containers are sent in a timely manner, so that they can initiate customs clearance and transit, and thus reduce warehousing charges at the port in Dakar. This form of entrepreneurship, involving the straddling of two countries, requires an intensification of exchanges of information, leading to a strengthening of interpersonal relationships and confirming Castells' view (1998:21) that '[e]conomies everywhere are becoming interdependent and thus are introducing a new form of relationship between the economy, the State and society, in a flexible system.'

NICTs & Social Restructuring within the Migratory System

NICTs foster the creation of long-distance interpersonal relationships and are part of a new process of exchange. Opportunities for social management are appearing, even for émigrés staying in their adopted country. They have access to a mechanism for real-time family decision-making. NICTs are breaking down barriers and challenging assumptions regarding temporal and spatial frameworks.

Family institutions and social organisations are a couple of examples that are useful in examining the impact of NICTs on individuals and society. These technologies are accelerating the process of social change. Their accessibility, even for groups which, until now, have participated little in decision-making mechanisms, provide new power. Relationships of dependence become relationships of exchange. There is a renewal of local awareness and a strengthening of the feeling of belonging. This rebalancing of roles guarantees vulnerable social segments of the population access to information and to decision making. These groups have a firmer grasp of the use of the telephone than do older people. This creates a reversal of roles, given the fact that the technology is dependent on resources from migrants. NICTs promote a new form of social mobilisation of nationals from a region beyond national borders. Linking local challenges to the broader world context is another means of joining the global community. Places of communication are becoming new places for social negotiation. With NICTs, a transformation of private spaces to public spaces is occurring. In the public squares of popular neighborhoods and in certain villages, where bedrooms are used as offices or as living rooms, the placement of the telephone can elicit or revive numerous conflicts. In Wolof households, management of common family assets is, theoretically, the domain of the 'senior' wife. However, some young émigrés have a tendency to install telephones in their wives' rooms, thereby by-passing the management role of their mothers or aunts. The émigré, knowing that, during his stay, he is the person most frequently called, is instinctively inclined to install the telephone in his wife's room. However, this poses problems of accessibility for male adults and for elderly individuals.

Now, these groups [of] NICTs are making it possible for traditionally excluded rural groups such as women and young people to have a voice and even participate in decision-making. However, unequal access to NICTs could lead to instability in society. The sharing and collective use of existing lines [are] producing dependent relationships. As early émigrés, who were from some of the most disadvantaged families and groups, were the first to provide their families with telephones, this has enhanced their status in society. They can no longer be excluded from the opportunities to access information and the arena of decision-making. Furthermore, by entrusting the management of the telephone and of the cellular telephone to their sisters and wives, émigrés contribute to the latter's empowerment, and give them an entree into the public sphere. Given that they spend more time at home than men do, they are more likely to receive incoming telephone calls and become, in this way, repositories of information. They are also active in administering local associations, thereby enhancing their powers of influence even further. NICTs help to consolidate their place as agents of social change and give them a sense of political awareness. Group strategies solidify inter-personal links and lead to a reordering of women's relations with other groups. However, this poses problems, for it challenges traditional conceptions of the balance of power between the sexes, and presages a renegotiation of gender roles, both within the family and in the wider society. This has led to interpersonal and inter-group conflicts.

NICTs make it possible for émigrés to control domestic space. Managing such a sphere involves the power of financial resources, and makes it possible to direct spending, give orders, deal with conflicts—all matters that the migrant can now do by telephone on an almost daily basis. What is presently occurring is a globalisation of family management. The social connection is no longer a set of innate or established statutory relationships, but rather the result of social interactions constructed in the complex mesh of a multitude of networks, including those linked to NICTs, driven by interested players bringing to bear an approach involving negotiation and exchange, rather than one of exclusion and hoarding. New technologies facilitate the reestablishing of communal links. The use of the telephone in the rural setting shows the true complexity of how the telephone is handled, in relation to previous modes of organising and managing information.

Traditionally, the local dissemination of information is governed by rules rooted in the local structure. Sensitive news is transmitted to the village chief, who makes a determination as to the appropriateness of disseminating it more widely, and as to those to be informed. Felicitous news, such as family ceremonies, falls under the responsibility of the *griot* (or village elder) who, depending on the target audience, presents the news in an agreeable and lively manner. This is also a matter of reestablishing age-old links. Private news is delivered word for word to the recipient by a messenger. Increasingly individualised access to the telephone will make it difficult to perpetuate these strategies for organising and controlling information locally. Are things moving toward conflict or toward better relationships between actors? Are we not witnessing new forms of inequality between those with access to NICTs and those excluded from such access? In post-colonial Africa, cities are made up of different diasporas and of different flows of migrants, linked to the globalised flow of capital and information.

NICTs & Informal Globalisation

International migrations are driven by complex spatial/geographic factors. NICTs function as a domestic challenge and an instrument of globalisation of family relationships. Inter-personal exchange and communication on the family-unit level are based on the neighborhood or on geographic proximity. In this regard, there are exchanges of money and goods. With NICTs, the exchanges go beyond the material realm, encompassing ideas and involving an increasingly distant outside world. The dialectic of the 'here' and the 'elsewhere' is called into question by the simultaneity and everyday nature of exchanges between émigrés and their places of origin. What is occurring is a globalisation of the domestic realm from the bottom up. Proximity—until now a means of exerting social control—has been superceded by a 'virtual' proximity that relies on oral communication and financial relationships. In certain villages in the Louga region, the Italian cities of Florence, Pescara and Rimini are more widely known (even by the elderly) than cities in Senegal.

NICTs shorten the distances and strengthen the significance of urban spaces within the rural environment. Migrants straddle the local and the global, mobility and identity, the altruistic and the profitable. These technologies foster a reinvention of the social bond. The traditional methods of relaying information are being short-circuited by new mechanisms such as the rural telephone and the cell phone. *Griots*, disseminators of domestic information on family ceremonies and village gatherings, are receiving competition from those who possess the local NICT devices. There is a hoarding phenomenon that occurs and that contributes to widening the gap between those who have acquired these technologies and those who have not. With NICTs, the social link no longer depends on spatial proximity—producing in turn a breakdown of space-based identity, a strengthening of bonds of other kinds and a shrinking of distance. These technologies facilitate the dissemination and segmentation of information and expand the number of depositories. Until recently, ceremonial information was overseen by the *griots*, who took charge of it and disseminated it through their own channels; this type of information is now disseminated via the telephone. In villages where information comes by means of telephone wires, through an intermediary in possession of a telephone, the *griot* usually takes responsibility for redistributing it in the squares. This role, which has disappeared in the city, is still intact in the village, where teledensity is still low. Thus, social status and age-old roles are changing and being questioned, while new networks are being promoted by NICTs, which have become the key to the emergence of a new model for information sharing. Those with the necessary tools for disseminating information become the depositories of information.

With the advent of the GSM, SONATEL is developing cellular service in rural areas where the landline telephone network does not yet exist. In June 2000, only 646 villages out of a total of 16,000 in Senegal were equipped with telecentres. The cellular telephone can open up rural towns not yet served by the landline telephone network to the outside world. NICTs are being developed in regions where there is strong demand for access to information and in which there is competition between social and family environments, on the one hand, and modern, outside influences on the other. New technologies are breaking down spatial barriers. However, one cannot yet speak of openness to the outside world, given the condition of the roads and the obsolescence of the rural transportation system. The unit cost of linking subscribers to the telephone network is ten times more expensive in rural than in urban areas. For commercial reasons, SONATEL is not making investments of this type unless it is certain that they will be profitable. Installation of the telephone in isolated regions is dependent on the existence of a certain number of pending requests. In this respect, the financial well-being of émigrés creates an increasing number of connection requests, thus making investment by the telephone companies feasible.

NICTs promote the resurgence of local powers, due to the consolidation of individual initiatives. Relationships among villagers scattered throughout the world strengthen the role of local powers at play within the village. Thus, the village reaches beyond physical limitations. We are witnessing the establishment of direct links between local and global networks, staking out a new form of globalisation. One can see the forming of relationships with increasingly distant environments as a result of NICTs.

In regions with strong emigration, one sees the paradox of a village in which the strongest links are to Italy, where the largest proportion of its departed offspring live. Thus, there is an expansion of the village's opportunities for exchange and a questioning of the classic foundations of relationships. The social and economic life of the village unit has been broken into several interconnected pieces by NICTs. Social networks are energised by technical networks. Distance is no longer a constraint in itself, and access to communications networks makes it possible to integrate social networks. This is all the more relevant when émigrés living in the same village tend to emigrate to the same city abroad. The village of M'Benguène is not a distinct entity, but rather part of a complex system of multiple residences (village, nearby town, places abroad, Touba) interconnected by NICTs. In the village and the outside world, bonds dominate distance, time dominates space. The world abroad is a limiting concept, because émigrés consider their nationals to be full members of the community, whom they are obligated to keep informed of the life of the village, down to the most trivial details. Since they often cannot attend village ceremonies, émigrés participate in them by underwriting the associated financial costs. Absence, they say, means being present but unable to do anything.

Analysing the types of telephone relationships between the village of M'Benguène and the outside world is a complex task. The importance of phone connections between the village and the outside world lies in social, administrative and economic factors. Prior to the existence of the telephone, relationships were limited and depended on people physically moving from one place to another. With NICTs, the roles of mediating with the outside world are reversed. Financial relationships are geared exclusively to Italy or to nearby villages, with the social dynamic based on kinship. In contrast, relations with Touba encompass the full range of religious and economic relationships. Only the village of Diawar and the city of Kébémer are geographically close to the village. The perception of relationships for the villagers is based more on the ease of relations than on geographic proximity. We are witnessing an opening up of the village to greater opportunities for accumulation. Émigré's, then, are intermediaries for the collection of resources. Is not this creation of transnational spaces outside the limits of national borders a type of globalisation from the bottom up, one that is being advanced more rapidly by communities more than by states? It constitutes globalisation that is occurring bit by bit, through a process of hybridisation, one step at a time, through open, flexible social networks. New types of relationships are being established, new exchanges of information with increasingly distant places are taking place, along with financial transactions beyond borders and without the intervention of the State. NICTs allow émigrés to bypass the national level with its bureaucratic constraints or its deficiencies in terms of mobilising financial resources suited to the needs of the people. Those entities that seek to embody a collective identity (family, sect, merchant) appropriate NICTs to escape the control of the State. The installation of the telephone in the rural environment of Louga is changing the rules for handling information and the local mechanisms for communication. There is a strengthening of the role of young people and women, expansion of the circle of social relationships, implementation of links with distant places, a range of interests arising out of the use of the telephone by different actors.

The impact of NICTs on family relationships and on power structures is all the more complex given the fact that all those involved have an interest in it. Those in possession of information differentiate themselves from and oppose the classical elites, to whom this role traditionally belonged. This fragmentation between the modern and the traditional leads to: the multiplicity of decision-making poles within the rural setting; the diversification and break-down of sources of leadership; and the tentative beginning of a process of democratising social functions.

STUDY QUESTIONS

1. What is the purpose of this study?
2. What is one of the first things émigrés do once they have found work in the host country and have re-established ties with their families back home?
3. Why is the growth of telephone lines in Louga and Kébemér considered paradoxical?
4. What did this increase in phone lines do for the people of Louga and Kébemér, and why was this especially appropriate?
5. Why is the cell phone in the rural village of Gade Kébé called Khady Diagné?
6. What four functions did this telephone serve in the village?
7. In what way or ways is the cell phone transformative in the rural village?
8. What are some of the obstacles for rural villages adopting cell phone technology?
9. How did the social role of Saralch Sene change after his brother, who lived in South Africa, gave him a cell phone?
10. How are people's roles and places affected by these new networks?
11. What have been the pros and cons of the impact of television on village night life?
12. How is the camcorder being used to develop personal relationships, and what has changed from the more traditional procedures?
13. What new "spaces" have opened up for émigrés with the combination of FM radio and telephone?
14. What are émigrés able to do with the development of the World Space digital receiver, and what venues are they creating?
15. What is the status of the Internet in rural Senegal?
16. What has been the impact of NICTs in financial transfer?

17. What are two ways migrants make transfers without actual movement of financial flows?
18. Describe "bipolar" enterprises that connect Italy and Senegal.
19. NICTs foster the creation of long-distance interpersonal relationships and are part of a new process of exchange. How does access to NICTs accelerate the process of social change; that is, what are some of the positive social effects on village life?
20. How do NICTs empower women and what is a drawback?

CPSIA information can be obtained
at www.ICGtesting.com
Printed in the USA
BVHW051920310820
587711BV00008B/680